To Curtis (Treis) I. Crenshaw, III

Every father wants a son; God has granted me one. Naturally, he has my name. My constant prayer for him is that he will stay in the truth of God's Word, not be side-tracked into some false gospel, and that we shall spend eternity together in heaven. He is a joy to my heart.

Man as God:

The Word of Faith Movement

An Evangelical analysis of the beliefs with the Christian alternative also presented

by Curtis I. Crenshaw

Man as God: The Word of Faith Movement

© *Footstool Publications 1994*
PO Box 341606
Memphis, TN 38184

(Second printing, November, 1994 with minor changes in chapters 3, 8, 9, 12, and Appendix 2, and a Bibliography was added.)

ISBN: 1-877818-11-9

Table of Contents[1]

Man as God: The Word of Faith Movement

Foreword
Acknowledgements
Introduction 1
Ch. 1: What Do They Believe? (Assumptions) 11
    Pantheism 12
    Dualism 13
    Knowledge is Salvation 14
    Direct Revelation from Within 18
    Man is Sovereign 19
    Universe Governed by Spiritual Law 21
    Faith Determines All 23
    Healing Is Available for All 24
    Elitism 24
    Individualism 25
    Syncretism 26
    Narcissism 26
    Salvation 26
    Pragmatism 27
    No Old Testament 28
Ch. 2: Where Did They Come From? (Nothing New) 31
    Montanism 34
        Prominence of Women 34
        Required Recognition 35
        End of the World 36
        Miracles Are Normative 37
        Directly Called by God 37
        Anti-Trinity 38
    Anabaptists 39
    Colonial Period 40
    Edward Irving 45

---

[1] One may read these chapters to understand the essence of the Word of Faith movement and the refutation: 1, 3, 6, 8, 9, 12, 13. Important parts of chapters in the table of contents are in italics.

John Alexander Dowie 51
Twentieth Century 52
- Smith Wigglesworth 52
- E. W. Kenyon 53
- Oral Roberts 58
- Others 61

Ch. 3: What Governs the Universe? (Metaphysical Law) 67
What Is Spiritual Law? 67
How Do These "Laws" Work? 69
- Knowledge 69
- "Faith" is a spiritual force 71
- Visualization 74

Who Is Subject to Spiritual Law? 78

Ch. 4: Are Miracles Normal? 81
Miracles in the Early Church 82
Assumptions 85
Definition of a Miracle 87
Purpose of Miracles 89
Jesus' Miracles Versus Today's Miracles 97

Ch. 5: Natural Healing (Doctors, and Medicine) 103
Common Grace & Medicine 104
Extremes 108
Balance: James 5:14-16 109
Bible & Medicine 113
Does God Want You Healthy? 115
- Paul's Thorn 121

Ch. 6: Supernatural Healing (the Atonement) 129
Healing & the Atonement..129
- *Essence of the Atonement* *129*
- Isaiah 53:9 & Two Deaths 133
- Matthew 8:17 135
- 1 Peter 2:24 139
- Objections to Orthodox View 142

Must We Have Faith to be Healed? 146
Health Problems Healers Avoid 149
How Did the Lord Heal? 151
- Gradual Healings? 151

Making the Exception the Rule 152
The Modern "Rules" for Healing 154

Ch. 7: Does God Want Us Rich? (Wealth & Faith) 159
Profligate Prosperity Preachers 161
Who in Scripture Did Not Have Money? 169
Does God Want You Wealthy? 170
- 3 John 2 170

Table of Contents

— 2 Corinthians 9:6 173
— Luke 6:38 173
— Deuteronomy 8:18 173
— Psalm 118:25 174
— Philippians 4:19 174

Ch. 8: Verbally Directing Reality (Man as God) 177

What Is Positive Confession? 177
— What Do They Mean by Positive Confession? 181
— How Does Positive Confession Work? 182
— Do We Create Our Own Realities? 187

Does God Answer All Prayer? 188
— Have We Asked Properly? 190
— The Prayer of Agreement 190

Passages Used for Positive Confession 191
— Joshua 1:8 191
— Mark 11:22-24 191
— Deuteronomy 28:1 193
— Hebrews 1:3 195
— Romans 4:17 196
— Hebrews 1:14 196
— Proverbs 6:2 198
— Matthew 18:18 198
— Balance 198

Can We Do What God Does? 199
— Are We God-Like? 199
— Is God Human? 204

Negative Confessions in the Bible 206

Ch. 9: Is the Bible Enough? (Sufficiency of Scripture) ... 211

Mysticism & the Bible 212
Infallibility Inescapable 214
Bible Is, Contains, or Becomes God's Word? 216
Who Can Understand the Bible? 219
Is the Bible Enough? 222
— Sufficiency of Scripture 222
— New Charismatics Deny Scripture's Sufficiency..228
— New Charismatics & the New "Prophets" 229
— New Charismatics & the New "Prophecy" 232

Holy Spirit & the Written Word 235
— New Charismatics & Guidance of the Spirit 238
— How to Have Guidance 245

Restoration Movement 250
— Unity versus doctrine 252

Ch. 10: What is God Like? (Sovereign) 255

If God Were Not Sovereign 257
God Has Dominion Now 260
— God's Dominion & Creation 263
— God's Dominion & the Nations 264

— God's Dominion & Evil 265
Who Is Lord of the Earth? 268
Does God Have Needs? 276
Is God Accountable to Man? 278
Who Is Lord of Natural Disasters? 280
Who Controls Our Trials? 281
    — God Controls Our Trials 282
    — Job 284
    — Romans 8:28 287
    — Hebrews 12:5-16 288
    — God's Providence Versus Metaphysical Laws 289

Ch. 11: Can We Make It Alone? (The Church) 293
Is There Salvation Outside the Church? 295
Call to the Ministry & Purity of Church 295
Worship of God 297
Word & Sacraments 297
Accountability 300
"No Man Is an Island" 301

Ch. 12: Another Jesus? (Person & Work) 303
Person of Christ 303
    — Orthodox Teaching 303
    — Ancient Heresies 308
    — Virgin Birth 312
    — Did Jesus Have Sin? 314
    — Was Jesus Born Again? 317
    — Was Jesus Only a Man While on Earth? 323
    — Are We One with the Father? 327
    — Did Jesus Empty Himself of His Deity? 328
Work of Christ 333
    — Orthodox Teaching 333
    — *Did Jesus Descend to Hell to Pay Off Satan?* 336
    — *"It Is Finished"* 340

Ch. 13: Another Gospel? (Why Believe in Jesus?) 345
New Birth 345
    — *Do We Partake of the Essence of God?* 345
    — What Is the New Birth? 350
Faith & Works: Their Distortions 351
    — Old Test. Justification: Works Without Faith 351
    — New Test. Justification: Faith Without Works 355
How Many Mediators? 357
What Comes After the Gospel? 358
Is Man Body, Soul, & Spirit? 360
    — Scriptural Refutation 361
    — Objections to the Biblical View 364
What Is the True Gospel? 367
How They Present the Gospel? 369

Table of Contents

   — Does Only One Sin Send to Hell? 369
   — Examples of Their Gospel 370
  What Is Grace? 373
Ch. 14: Conclusion 377
Appendix One: New Age & Word of Faith 381
Appendix Two: Baptism in the Holy Spirit 395
Appendix Three: Sovereignty of God in the New Birth .. 407
Appendix Four: Who Is Sovereign in Salvation? 413
Appendix Five: Did Jesus Go to Hell? 421
Bibliography 425
Index to Subjects & Persons 435
Index to Scripture 447

Foreword

by John F. MacArthur, Jr.

Curtis Crenshaw has done the body of Christ a great service in this thorough, careful review of the Health and Wealth Gospel. He has probed deeply into the movement's roots, examined their writings painstakingly to understand what they are saying, and listened attentively to hear why their message is so seductive — and ultimately so destructive — in the lives of thousands of professing Christians.

Dr. Crenshaw correctly sees that the Health and Wealth Gospel is nothing but latter-day gnosticism. He clearly demonstrates what that means and boldly calls all Christians who love the Lord to reject this deadly false teaching. He does not shrink from speaking plainly, yet it is evident that he writes in love that flows from a pure heart. He is driven by a deep commitment to Christ and an equally deep concern for the people of God who are confused by this dangerous false doctrine.

Some will claim otherwise, labeling a critique like this unloving and divisive. But remember that one of the solemn duties of every church leader is to expose and refute error (Titus 1:9). Much of the New Testament deals with these very issues, and the apostles were not reluctant to name those whose teaching and behavior undermined the truth of the gospel (cf. 1 Tim. 1:20; 3 John 9). Dr. Crenshaw maintains a careful biblical balance of love and truthfulness.

I know from experience, however, that the Health and Wealth teachers themselves are *not* usually loving to their critics. They frequently indulge in name-calling, threats, even cursing — conduct hardly fitting for people claiming to be Spirit-filled. One of them even prayed on a nationwide television network that God would kill me after I wrote a chapter questioning the biblical basis of their teaching.

How can people like that gain such a large following? They do it by intimidation, trickery, lies, and most powerfully of all, teaching that appeals to the common lusts of humanity. After all, who would not like to believe that health, money, affluence, and success are ours for the claiming? In a culture that is selfish, materialistic, and proud, the Health and Wealth message is bound to be popular. People with itching ears heap to themselves teachers who make the promises they want to hear. Meanwhile, the tolerance for sound doctrine is dangerously low (cf. 2 Tim. 4:3).

As Curtis Crenshaw clearly demonstrates, the Health and Wealth teachers are wolves among the flock. The church desperately needs to heed the warning he sounds here. I pray that this book will have a widespread influence.

Acknowledgments

My family and I took a vacation several years ago. As usual, when we stopped to rest, I gravitated to the book stores. I purchased a few Word of Faith pamphlets and booklets, which I read as my wife, Ruth, drove. I told her that I might read more and write something on it. She was expecting a 60 to 100 page book. Three years later, she is still waiting! She read through much of the manuscript and made helpful suggestions. I want to thank her for her encouragement, patience, and for putting up with me for 24 years of similar activity. Truly "an excellent wife is the crown of her husband" (Prov. 12:4) and a "prudent wife is from the Lord" (Prov. 19:14). I could not accomplish anything without her.

If this book is readable, one person deserves the credit: Nancy Osborne. With a master's degree in English, she persevered with undaunted courage through a maze of unclear paths, verbose sentences, and unnecessary paragraphs with sickle in hand. She rewrote, excised the manuscript from its original 550 pages to its current size, rearranged, and made numerous suggestions, which I took ninety percent of the time. She did all this in her "spare" time while she cooked, cleaned, washed, mothered four small children, and faithfully served her husband. Only the grace of God can account for such a woman. Any unclear parts are strictly mine (probably the other ten percent).

David Potts taught *himself* how to use computers and graphics software — no easy task! — and he did the cover design. His creative ability is much appreciated.

Other people have read the manuscript. A special thanks to Rev. Douglas Mills of Sevierville, TN, a former Word of Faith advocate, who read the manuscript and made many helpful suggestions. Thanks also to Thomas ("Pete") M. Frye who read it and helped with research in Chapter Ten.

Introduction

American culture is now pagan; not only is secular humanism dominant but all manner of cults and bizaare religions flourish. When the Gospel recedes, darkness encroaches, and darkness is moving across our land at alarming rates. All it takes for a new religion or movement to be successful is for someone to claim to be from God, to have visions and revelations, to be able to convince others that he can do miracles or some supernatural feats.

What is the Word of Faith movement and its teachings, and who are its leaders? Perhaps you have wondered why Kenneth Hagin, Kenneth and Gloria Copeland, Charles Capps and others have risen to leadership roles in Christianity, being so popular, and why so many people are mesmerized by them. Two reasons for their popularity stand out.

First, the movement appeals to man's two basest instincts: the love of power and the love of money.[1] Christians are being led to believe that they can control their own destinies, that they can create their own circumstances, that they can cause money, health, and objects to obey them, and that they can do anything God can by using the same spiritual laws and the same faith available to both them and Him. In the Age of Aquarius when New Age gurus, Shirley MacLaine, the occult, Satanism and many other "isms" are casting lures to secular people with promises of power, health, and money, the Word of Faith leaders are enticing Christians with the same appeals, using the same arguments. Many have taken the bait.

If their doctrine is so absurd, "How have they managed to acquire so many followers, even from among persons who earlier tasted the simple doctrine of the gospel?"[2] Calvin's reply is that the "Lord permits sects to emerge in order to test everyone's faithfulness and to distinguish the good from the evil."

Secondly, the doctrinal laxity that characterizes Christians

---

[1] Peter Marshall and David Manuel, *From Sea to Shining Sea* (Grand Rapids: Fleming H. Revell, 1986), p. 20.

[2] John Calvin, *Treatises Against the Anabaptists and Against the Libertines* (Grand Rapids: Baker Book House, 1982), p. 207.

makes them easy "fish" to catch. Few Christians are taught the basic truths of the Bible, and even fewer care. Modern Christianity has fallen on difficult times: infidelity and its offspring, humanism, capture many young Christians on the college campuses; most seminaries teach that the Bible is either full of errors or at best it *becomes* God's Word for the reader when he *encounters* it personally, making the Bible conform to each reader; and the pulpits reek with pleasing, pious platitudes that soothe hearers into soporific, self-satisfied complacency. Like most vacuums, this spiritual vacuum has been quickly filled with counterfeits. Thus when something new arises that seems to have answers, especially when vehemently proclaimed by those who claim to be directly called by the Lord with supposed visions and personal visitations from Him, the unwary listeners open their mouths and swallow the new doctrines, hook, line and sinker. Perhaps you have thought that something has tainted these new teachings from the Word of Faith leaders, but you have not been able to leach it out. This book, by God's grace, may help us to avoid Satan's attractive new hooks.

This book is *not* about the charismatic movement in general but only of the Word of Faith movement, sometimes called the health and wealth movement. Throughout the book, I also refer to this movement as the new charismatics, but I do not believe that most charismatics are health and wealth advocates. Therefore, I do not classify all charismatics in this new movement.

The goals of this book are three: (1) to demonstrate that the Word of Faith gospel is a form of transcendentalism or gnosticism (from which have come such metaphysical cults as Christian Science, Unity School of Christianity, and now the health and wealth cult), (2) to refute the new charismatics biblically point by point, and (3) to give the truth of Scripture in contrast to their errors. Repeatedly we shall demonstrate that the health and wealth leaders have borrowed their ideas from gnosticism, transcendentalism, or metaphysics. We shall do this not to engage in the fallacy of guilt by association but in the logical position that things equal to the same thing are equal to one another. In other words, if gnosticism is wrong and the new charismatics are gnostic, then the new charismatics are wrong. It is important not only to show that (1) they are gnostic but also (2) that they do not handle Scripture accurately, for many people think the leaders accurately represent what the Bible has to say. Finally, if they are wrong on so many points, (3) what does the Bible really say? Perhaps we can help cure some of the doctrinal laxity that has caused so much spiritual sickness.

Unfortunately, most evangelical Christians are unfamiliar with the metaphysical cults, their history, vocabulary, and way of thinking, which makes them easy prey. They are not aware that the New Age is not so much India in America as it is transcendentalism from America. Transcendentalism, which taught that "God" is all and man is "God," was popular in Boston in the 1800's but left the South and the Bible Belt in particular and evangelicals in general virtually untouched. Thus our ignorance in this metaphysical area has made us vulnerable to its subtleties. When one claims, therefore, to believe the Bible, using evangelical terms, but promotes health and wealth, the naive fall prey. Consequently, the Word of Faith movement is taking captive many otherwise evangelical Christians. The same arguments, backed by the same verses, have been promoted among the metaphysical cults for many generations and these arguments are based on Satanic assumptions. If most evangelicals knew what these assumptions were, they would run from the Word of Faith movement. This book attempts to expose and refute the Word of Faith movement and to some extent the metaphysical cults, for in dealing with one the others are also included.

I have classified the Word of Faith leaders as cultists, those who deny either the Person and/or the finished work of Christ (see "What Is Evangelicalism" below), but I quickly add that this does not apply to all the people who follow them. I think many of those who follow them are ignorant of what they are being taught. Most charismatics, though I disagree with them, are not cultists. They are our brethren in the Lord. Because most charismatics are long on experience and short on doctrine, however, they are easy prey for the Word of Faith movement, especially since they pretend to promote some of the same experiences such as speaking in tongues and the baptism in the Holy Spirit. A word to the wise is sufficient.

I have studied cults for twenty-three years. One thing I learned quickly is that they use the same terms we do but with different definitions. If you ask a Jehovah's Witness if he believes that Jesus is the Son of God, he will enthusiastically agree with you. What he means by the phrase "Son of God," however, is not the Bible's definition. The Bible teaches that He is equal with the Father (John 5:18), but they mean that He is less than God Almighty. Similarly, they claim to adhere to the "resurrection" of Christ, but they do not teach that the same body in which He tabernacled was raised, as the New Testament does (John 2:19ff; 20:27ff). We must be very careful, therefore, that we do not allow ourselves to be fooled by counterfeits simply because they look and sound similar to the real thing. It is the very nature of counterfeits to approximate the genuine as closely as possible. If the disparity were obvious to all at first glance, then the fabrication would not succeed. The closer to the original they are, the more dangerous they become. Remember, "Satan himself transforms himself into an angel of light. Therefore, it is no great thing if his ministers also transform themselves into ministers of righteousness, whose end will be according to their works" (2 Cor. 11:14, 15).

It is the essence of the charismatic movement that the Bible is not *sufficient* for life and godliness. It is *necessary*, but not sufficient. We hear much from the charismatics about the necessity of Scripture; but since they believe in new revelation in the form of dreams, visions, impressions on the heart, and statements like "God told me in my spirit man," they say nothing about Scripture *alone* being all we need. (See Chapter Nine.)

Since the Bible *alone* is either implicitly or explicitly denied as being sufficient, then the logical conclusion is to have new doctrines built on human experience, on visions, "Jesus told me," and such things. This is the logical conclusion of the Word of Faith movement, which preaches another gospel. Unfortunately, too many people are endorsing this new wave of Pentecostalism on the basis of common experiences without knowing how these men are defining their terms. They claim that Jesus is God, but then say we are, too. They claim to believe in His substitutionary death, but this was not on the Cross; it was when He went to hell to pay off Satan. They claim to believe in righteousness as a gift from God to us, but this righteousness is God's nature — not a forensic or legal righteousness that is credited to our account. These examples only reveal the tip of the iceberg, and these deceptions are what this book is exposing. Theirs is an easy gospel that promises riches, health, and a life of ease and demands virtually nothing. In our narcissistic society, is it any wonder that it is so appealing?

Who Are the New Charismatics?

E. W. Kenyon is the source. From him they have derived their new and unbiblical doctrines. I have read much of Kenyon's works, and I have not seen a single teaching the new charismatics promote that does not have its source in Kenyon. This is not my conclusion only, for D. R. McConnell's excellent book, *A Different Gospel*, extensively documents that Kenyon was the source of the Word of Faith movement.

Kenneth Hagin, who plagiarized Kenyon extensively (see *A Different Gospel*), has had more influence than any other person in the last half of this century in promoting the health and wealth gospel. He has heavily influenced his son Kenneth Hagin, Jr., Gloria and Kenneth Copeland, and Charles Capps. Others he may have influenced are Frederick K. C. Price (who founded the Crenshaw Christian Center of Inglewood, CA — no connection with me!), Jerry Savelle, Norvel Hayes, John Osteen, Robert Tilton, Bill Hamon, Paul and Jan Crouch of TBN (Trinity Broadcasting Network), and perhaps remotely Hobart Freeman. In South Korea there is Paul Yonggi Cho with his half million member church. Though his books, some of which have been translated into English, seem to be less radical than the others listed here, he still is very much influenced by the same background as the others. Others in the movement are Oral Roberts and his son, Richard. Pat Robertson is on the fringes of the Word of Faith movement. There are still others, but I have studied the main ones, which took two and a half years, thousands of pages of reading, and hundreds of hours listening to their broadcasts.

Other Movements

There are other movements that the new charismatics have spawned. One such movement is the Manifested Sons of God, in which the doctrine of the godhood of each believer is taught. I have not specifically analyzed this movement because the assumptions on which it rests are essentially the same as the Word of Faith movement and because the movement has blended with other movements. In other words, it does not exist, as far as I know, as a separate entity anymore.

Likewise the Shepherding movement, in which believers were subject to tyranny of overlords, has blended with other movements.

The Restoration movement, in which the claim is made that we are in the last days and God is restoring the miracle gifts to His church, such as prophets and apostles, is actually part of the Word of Faith movement. I have a few paragraphs on this movement in Chapter Nine (See The Restoration Movement on page 249; see also the paragraph beginning with "Consequently when anyone" on page 32.)

Why This Book Is Unique

This book is unique because it is the first book that I know of to take the movement to task in every major tenet of Christianity, to unmask their metaphysical theological roots by quoting New Age writers (see also Appendix One) and other modern metaphysical cults in comparison to their books, and to refute their arguments using detailed biblical arguments as well as their own arguments. I have tried to reproduce their best arguments for each point, quoting their books and sermons, and followed it with exegesis of Scripture. I have tried to show the assumptions of their arguments.

It is also the first book to connect them to Edward Irving, who also fell prey to the metaphysical cults of his day.

This book is unique because it not only refutes their heresies but also presents the biblical balance in each chapter. Heresy is truth out of balance. If there were no truth in any of their points, they would have been a passing fad long ago.

Finally, this book attempts to be Reformed in its flavor. I make no apology for this. To understand my beliefs in detail, read the Westminster Confession of Faith, the Thirty-Nine Articles, the Canons of the Synod of Dort, or the Heidelberg Catechism. I confess that these are not infallible, only the Bible is, but that these represent the best summary of biblical doctrine that man has written so far.

What Is Evangelicalism?

Since many Christians do not share my Reformed beliefs and yet are my brothers in Christ, it seems necessary to list the broad beliefs that make us members of one another. I consider the basics of evangelicalism to be the following. First, the sixty-six books of the Bible are the Word of the living God, inerrant in the whole and in the parts, without error on every subject of which it speaks, whether the subject is history, science, or theology. It is absolutely *necessary* and totally *sufficient* for the Christian life, being the only infallible standard for the world.

Secondly, God eternally exists as one God in three equal Persons, Father, Son, and Holy Spirit, co-equal, co-eternal, the same in substance, power, and glory, and unchangeable in every way.

Third, this God created all things out of nothing instantaneously, which places a permanent distinction between God and man. This Creator/creature distinction must be maintained at all times (which distinction the metaphysical cults violate by merging us with God). God created by omnipotence simply by speaking; He did not create by faith (as the Word of Faith leaders say).

Fourth, Jesus is the Christ, total God and total man in one Person forever with no mixture of the natures. He was, is, and always will be equal with the Father. When He came to the earth, He did not relinquish His deity but added to His divine Person a perfect human nature, yet was only one Person. While on earth, He functioned as both God and man.

Fifth, Jesus was born of a virgin by the power of the Holy Spirit in some way that kept Him free from sin. The mechanics of this miracle of conception are not revealed.

Sixth, the Lord Jesus Christ lived, died on the cross, and raised Himself from the dead as the *Substitute* for sinners. He lived a perfect life of obedience to God and His law and bore the wrath of God, the penalty of the law, while remaining free from personal sin. When He said "It is finished," the plan of redemption was completed.

Seventh, the Lord was raised *bodily* from the grave in the same body in which He tabernacled among men. Without this we are still in our sins.

Eighth, we are justified by faith *alone* in Christ *alone*. Justification is the forgiveness of our sins and the free gift of the righteousness of Christ. This is a legal righteousness that is entered to our account like an entry in a ledger. Therefore, we are adopted into the family of God *solely* on the basis of the Person and work of Christ, totally apart from any human works. The necessity of justification assumes, of course, that man is thoroughly sinful and incapable of doing anything to save himself.

Ninth, though we believe we are justified by faith *alone*, we also teach that the faith that saves is not alone, but is "ever accompanied by good works" (Westminster Confession of Faith). Obedience to God's Bible is the *necessary* evidence, though not the meritorious cause, of genuine faith, for "faith without works is dead." In other words, no true Christian will be without some good works in his life as the fruit of the new birth.

Finally, the Lord Jesus will literally return to the earth one day and judge mankind. Though evangelicals do not agree on the time or manner (amil, premill, postmill), we all agree that there is a Second Coming and a final judgment.

How To Read and Use This Book

Following the Introduction, read chapters one through four in sequence. Then you may read the other chapters in any order, though I think you will profit more by simply following the chapter sequence. The extensive cross referencing, expanded Table of Contents, and subject, personal, and biblical indices will help the reader to research quickly what he needs to study. I sincerely hope that this will be a research tool for pastors and lay people alike though many will want to read the book straight through.

The Tone of This Book

The reader may see strong statements occasionally throughout this book; it is by design. If someone objects that I am not engaging in Christian love, he should consider that love constrains me to be forceful. Furthermore, I am compelled to use strong language or the errors being countered might be construed as minor points of difference. The Apostle Paul did not mince words when opposing those in his day (1 Tim. 1:20), nor did John Calvin in his time.[3]

We are dealing with the eternal destiny of souls, which demands bluntness at times. We are not playing games. Truth takes precedence over unity, the Gospel over being nice. Paul in Galatians 1:8, 9 proclaimed that if anyone preached another Gospel, he would go to hell.

What Version of the Bible is Used?

I have used the New King James Version, which is very accurate to the Hebrew and Greek. I also prefer the majority Greek text of the New Testament. Both are published by Thomas Nelson and recommended.

For Whom Is This Book Written?

It is written for anyone. For the busy pastor, the extensive footnotes, internal cross references, and detailed Scriptural, personal, and topical indexes should prove helpful. For the layman who wants to study these things, I have tried to keep the language from being too technical by putting many of the technical matters in footnotes.

The book is especially for the lay person who may be in the Word of Faith movement and who does not know how far from the truth the leaders have ventured. It is my sincere desire that these people may be reached. I seriously doubt, though God is sovereign and can do as He pleases, that many of the leaders will be changed. Those who teach false doctrine and are widely held in high esteem seldom change. If you are a lay person in the movement, please do not take offense at the occasional strong statements. These are nearly always aimed at the leaders, not the lay people. The Lord Jesus did not mince words in Matthew 23 when He strongly blasted the Pharisees, the religious leaders of His day.

Chapter One is an exception, directed primarily at lay people. I thought that the followers should realize that the leaders could be "put out of business" if they had no followers, and Paul the apostle directed his comments to listeners who had "itching ears." If you will do the study and research, I

---

[3] Calvin, *Treatises Against the Anabaptists and Against the Libertines*, p. 203.

hope you will find that I have been fair, but straightforward. I am a pastor, and deal with people every week. I have a love for them, for their problems, and a desire to help them. I am not out to get anyone.

May the sovereign Triune God bless you as you study. "Come, let us reason together. . . ."

Curtis I. Crenshaw

1

What Do They Believe?

Assumptions of the Health & Wealth Gospel

For such are false apostles, deceitful workers, transforming themselves into apostles of Christ. And no wonder! For Satan himself transforms himself into an angel of light. Therefore it is no great thing if his ministers also transform themselves into ministers of righteousness, whose end will be according to their works (2 Cor. 11:13-15).

The new charismatics are the old gnostics of the early centuries, but what is gnosticism? This was a heresy opposed by the apostles in their writings and by the early church fathers. The gnostics counterfeited Christianity, and, like those today, wanted to be accepted as part of evangelical Christianity. Christian Science, Unity School of Christianity, Theosophy, and the Word of Faith movement are all descendants of gnosticism.

What do these sects teach? Not knowing the errors of church history, they have repeated the errors of gnosticism, adopting as their theology the ideas of the metaphysical cults that arose from 1830 to 1860 in New England and became very popular in the latter part of the 1800's.[1]

In America these cults began as transcendentalism, which gave rise to Christian Science (made popular by Mary Baker Eddy, having plagiarized Phineas Parkhurst Quimby), The Unity School of Christianity (popularized by Myrtle Fillmore after having been a Christian Scientist), and The Theosophical Society (made popular by Helena Blavatsky and Annie

---

[1]C. Gregg Singer, *From Rationality to Irrationality* (Phillipsburg, NJ: Presbyterian and Reformed Pub. Co., 1979), p. 423.

Besant). (The reader should notice that these cults were promoted by women, which will come up again in Chapter Two.) The reason for so many different metaphysical cults is given by Schaff: "The arbitrary and unbalanced subjectivity of the gnostic speculation naturally produced a multitude of schools."[2] Each of the following Word of Faith errors is rooted in gnosticism.

Pantheism

The early gnosticism of the second century, the teachings of Edward Irving in the early 1800's, and the present-day metaphysical cults have several things in common. First and foremost, *they deny the creator/creature distinction by either deifying man or humanizing God.* Man partakes of the nature of God in some mystical way, usually (though not always) through some form of identification with the right knowledge enabling him to realize his full potential as a lesser deity. This usually involves some sort of pantheism, "God" is all and all is "God," as Eddy says.[3]

Shirley MacLaine distills this quite well in her New Age mysticism in which she proclaims that she is "God in light."[4] Or again she confesses: "The more we are connected to higher resources, the more infinite we become as human beings."[5] How there can be degrees of "infinity" Ms. MacLaine does not explain, but she understands that by arrogating sovereignty to herself she participates in the being of "God." Of course her "God" is not the God of the Bible but of pantheism, in which all things and people are deity. The health and wealth leaders realize that to promote the sovereignty of man, to make man the creator of his own reality, to conceive of God's actions as dependent on man's initiations, is to make man share the nature or being of God. In other words, if man is the boss over God, he must be God. You will find this theme running throughout the writings of the new charismatics.

---

[2] Philip Schaff, *History of the Christian Church* (Grand Rapids: Wm. B. Eerdmans Pub. Co., 1910, 1979), 2:459.

[3] Mary Baker Eddy, *Science & Health*, p. 113.

[4] Shirley MacLaine, *Going Within* (New York: Bantam, 1990), p. 68.

[5] Ibid., p. 115.

The Word of Faith leaders would probably deny that they are pantheists. When they teach, however, that we are little gods, that we men are able to do things that only the sovereign triune God can do, that in the new birth man participates in the very nature and being of God, then their denial is meaningless. The point must be settled now: A denial does not mean one is not guilty of the accused heresy. The Jehovah's Witnesses deny that they are teaching heresy when they deny the deity of Christ and His bodily resurrection, but their denial is meaningless.

Dualism

"The affinity of gnosticism also with the Zoroastrian dualism of a kingdom of light and a kingdom of darkness is unmistakable. . . ."[6] In ancient gnosticism, it was taught that the kingdoms of darkness and of light are locked in eternal conflict.[7] We hear repeatedly in the health and wealth movement that God and Satan are locked in conflict, with God often losing. There is indeed a war, but in Scripture the outcome is sure and God controls evil, whereas in gnosticism evil and good are equal, each winning and losing according to its use of spiritual or metaphysical law. This law is not the moral law of the Ten Commandments but the neutral, spiritual laws that govern the universe (see Chapter Three).

The gnostics, were perhaps, the original environmentalists. They located sin in physical things, such as man's body,[8] and thought of it as metaphysical, instead of the biblical doctrine that sin is located in the heart of man, and that sin is ethical. Sin is disobedience to the law of God; it is rebellion. It is not located in physical things, such as alcoholic beverages, nor in the waste from factories. The problem in each case is the abuse, which lies in the heart of man. The Word of Faith leaders imply that sin is in man's body, misusing such verses as Romans 6:12, "Do not let sin reign in your mortal body." This obviously means that our bodies are to be used in His service, but Paul does not say that the body itself is sinful but that we are not to allow sin to dominate the body. Likewise

---

[6]Schaff, *History of the Christian Church*, 2:446, 504.

[7]Ibid., 2:454.

[8]Ibid., 2:457.

in Romans 7:18 when Paul says that no good thing dwells in his flesh, the word "flesh" means his indwelling sin, not his body.

In the old gnosticism of the second century, "Christ" was a demiurge, something less than God, and the docetic version taught that Christ did not have a real physical body. The reason Jesus did not have a body was that matter was evil and spirit good. Furthermore, since "Christ" was less than God, He was the One who created, for God was spirit and could not create something so evil as physical matter. Spirit was reality; not the Holy Spirit but that which is non-material. Matter was either an illusion (Christian Science) or real but something less than Spirit (Unity School of Christianity). Therefore, the spirit realm determined all truth. If something seemed to contradict the real world or spirit, it was ignored or brought into conformity by proper knowledge.

The spirit realm is the real world according to these new preachers. "We have to understand that man is a spirit, that he has a soul, and that he lives in a body,"[9] they often say. The Bible teaches that God is absolutely sovereign, but the health and wealth form of dualism presents a God who suffers at the hands of His enemy — Satan. Instead of the God Who does what He pleases, we have a God who must honor Satan, who must be just to the devil. He cannot do as He pleases. This dualism, therefore, is between matter and spirit and between God and the devil.

Knowledge is Salvation

The gnostics thought that *with the right knowledge they could conquer anything.*[10] In this scheme ignorance is sin. What must be gained at all costs is esoteric knowledge so that one can control his destiny, or at least his spiritual future.

Charles Capps says,

> Notice, it's not **just** the truth that sets you free. Everyone who has the Bible has the truth. But you must have **the knowledge of the truth**. You can't believe any further that [sic] you have knowledge. You have to **know the truth**

---

[9] Kenneth E. Hagin, *How You Can Be Led by the Spirit of God* (Tulsa: Faith Library Publications, 1989), p. 2.

[10] Philip J. Lee, *Against the Protestant Gnostics* (New York: Oxford University Press, 1987), p. 21.

before it can set you free [emphasis his].[11]

If you know what God will do, He'll do it. If you don't know what God will do, He's under no obligation [emphasis his].[12]

Kenneth Copeland is even stronger: "Knowledge of His will brings results. Once you know for sure that something is God's will, you should not be without it any longer."[13] Hagin agrees:

> All believers should thoroughly understand that their healing was consummated in Christ. When they come to know that in their spirits — just as they know it in their heads — that will be the end of sickness and disease in their bodies.[14]

E. W. Kenyon is the source for all these men:

> Until man is Righteous and **knows** it, Satan reigns over him, sin and disease are his masters. But the instant he knows that he is the Righteousness of God in Christ and **knows** what that Righteousness means, Satan is defeated.[15]

A favorite verse they use is Hosea 4:6: "My people are destroyed for lack of knowledge." Certainly Christians do not deny the importance of knowledge. There is no virtue in ignorance. As Thomas Manton said in the introduction to the Westminster Confession of Faith, the kingdom of Satan is built on ignorance and error. But the knowledge of which Manton spoke and of which Hosea speaks is not a secret knowledge only attainable to a select few who are the chosen prophets. It is a knowledge easily attained and available to all. Read the rest of Hosea 4:6: "Because you have rejected knowledge, I also will reject you from being priest for Me; because you have forgotten the law of your God, I also will

---

[11] Charles Capps, *Kicking Over Sacred Cows* (England, AR: Capps, 1983), p. 2.

[12] Charles Capps, *The Substance of Things* (Tulsa: Harrison House, 1990), p. 26.

[13] Kenneth Copeland, *The Laws of Prosperity* (Ft. Worth: KCP Publications, 1989), p. 45

[14] Kenneth Hagin, *Seven Things You Should Know About Divine Healing* (Tulsa: Faith Library Publications, 1987), p. 54.

[15] E. W. Kenyon, *Two Kinds of Righteousness* (Lynnwood, WA: Kenyon's Gospel Pub. Society, no date), p. 10. It is characteristic of metaphysical cults to capitalize unusual words, and Kenyon repeatedly does so.

forget your children." The knowledge they did not have was of the law of God. We have this law in our Bibles today, and it is there for anyone to read. We do not need men with special visions and revelations to say "God told me" or "Jesus said" to understand. There is nothing esoteric here.

Furthermore, in the new charismatic doctrine the "key" to the Christian life is simply knowledge. As B. B. Warfield so accurately expressed it, "Here, you see, is a truly rampant intellectualism, a pure gnosticism. To understand is to have and to be. In proportion as we understand, and understand intelligently, we possess."[16] By contrast, according to Scripture *one can know and not have*. Furthermore, if we needed some "key," certainly the Bible would have clearly told us.

E. W. Kenyon proclaims, "It is the amazing fact that there are two Kinds of Knowledge in the world today, and we have never contrasted them or compared them."[17] And what are these two kinds of knowledge? Kenyon tells us, "One is Knowledge that we have obtained through the Five Senses; the other is a Revelation from God." Of course Kenneth Hagin follows Kenyon in this: ". . . there are two kinds of truth: sense-knowledge truth and revelation truth."[18] This is pure gnosticism with its distinction between the physical and spiritual worlds. It is also Kantian, the philosophy that taught two kinds of knowledge from two realms: phenomenal (five senses) and noumenal (from God). Such an artificial distinction leads us to believe that we live in two worlds: a spiritual one and a natural one, and "the twain shall never meet." In Scripture the spiritual and the natural, the physical and the godly, are not separated. When God created, it is stated that man was a "living soul." By this we understand the unity of man, as both his body and soul are termed a single "living soul."

With this salvation by knowledge, which the gnostics had but the "normal" Christian did not, there came a spiritual

---

[16] B. B. Warfield, *Counterfeit Miracles* (London: Banner of Truth Trust, 1918, 1972), pp. 219, 220.

[17] E. W. Kenyon, *The Father and His Family: A Restatement of the Plan of Redemption* (Seattle: E. W. Kenyon, 1937), p. 16.

[18] Kenneth E. Hagin, *Prevailing Prayer to Peace* (Tulsa: Faith Library Publications, 1992), p. 3.

pride.[19] We see this in the sub-title of E. W. Kenyon's *Two Kinds of Righteousness*: "The Most Important Message Ever Offered to the Church."[20] Such pride is readily manifested by these leaders. Tilton calls himself a "modern-day prophet," saying that when he "prophesies God's Word, the storms of life are stilled, creative miracles flow, and the yoke of lack is broken."[21] Oral Roberts in *11 Major Prophecies for You in 1992* says, "I believe the Lord manifested the gift of prophecy through me," and this book "did not come out of my mind, but by the Holy Spirit."[22] He even copyrighted these eleven prophecies to make sure no other person could profit from them! (See "No one matches the pride. . . ." on page 38 for other examples.)

By contrast with ancient gnosticism which found favor primarily among the educated, modern gnosticism appeals to the educated *and* to the ignorant. That it appeals to the ignorant may seem strange until one remembers that twentieth century Christianity disparages education, learning, and knowledge in general, unless it is their particular brand. *They have substituted the supernatural for the rational quite deliberately, as if the two are in opposition.* We have, therefore, the irony of special knowledge both for the educated and the uneducated, with the educated taking pride in their learning and the uneducated taking pride in their ignorance. While the ignorant prefer the supernatural brand of gnosticism with its "Jesus told me," the educated prefer the more natural brand in Christian Science or Unity School simply because it is much less sensational and more esoteric.

In early gnosticism, "the highest source of knowledge . . . was a secret tradition," and the Protestant gnostic sects appealed to the Bible alone, "as understood by themselves," as their source of knowledge.[23] They neglected others outside

---

[19] Schaff, *History of the Christian Church*, 2:448, 506.

[20] One would think by the title that the book was about justification and sanctification, but it is not. The righteousness he speaks of "is the nature of the Father imparted to us" (pp. 10, 11, 39). He says that we partake of the very being of God.

[21] Robert Tilton, *God's Miracle Plan for Man* (Dallas: Robert Tilton Ministries, 1989), back cover.

[22] Oral Roberts, *11 Major Prophecies for You in 1992*, Introduction.

[23] Schaff, *History of the Christian Church*, 2:451

their group as sources of information, especially those in evangelical Christianity. The normal Christian was rejected as "traditional" and having only the usual sources of knowledge. So while they loved knowledge, especially something *new*, theirs was knowledge that came strictly from their sect.

Like the ancient gnosticism that sought to remove God from this world of evil, the new charismatics do the same. Instead of saying that God created the world through a demiurge, a lesser god, they have Him creating the world by faith through obedience to metaphysical laws, Satan being the ruler of this "mess," and God not having anything to do with sin in the sense of allowing or controlling it. Since God cannot control sin and He is governed by metaphysical laws, they have removed Him from direct involvement in the world.

Direct Revelation from Within

Gnostics were theosophists[24] who taught that *their own secret revelation was more important than the ordinary revelation they had in Scripture.* In this system of thought, man receives knowledge from God internally, within his spirit, apart from anything written. It is a direct, intuitive revelation. Kenyon, and Hagin following him, terms this "revelation knowledge." Consequently the mind of man is bypassed. Very often there is an antagonism to any written revelation, or else written revelation is twisted to support beliefs already held.

There were three kinds of people in gnosticism: (1) at the highest level were the *pneumatikoi* or the spiritual people; then (2) there were the *psychikoi* or the soulish people; and finally (3) the *sarkikoi* or carnal people. The first lived the truly victorious life, living above the mundane things of the physical world. The second group were those who were somewhat intellectual, above the last group but not having "arrived." The final category was where most people lived, enslaved to the physical and material world. Each level was determined by his level of knowledge. The more esoteric his knowledge, the higher his plane of existence.

Of course this led to the belief that man was composed of three separate parts: body, soul, and spirit, which conveniently corresponded to the three kinds of people. The health and wealth people strongly promote that man is body, soul,

---

[24]Ibid., 2:459.

and spirit. Through his physical body, man related to his physical and material environment and the world around him. With his soul, he affiliated with other humans, receiving "sense knowledge" through the five senses. With his spirit, the real self, he received spiritual knowledge, very often below the conscious level and directly from God.

Appealing to the Bible is very popular in Christian Science and in Unity School of Christianity. It is also very popular in the health and wealth movement to say that we must justify everything by the Bible. The problem, however, is that virtually no one reads the Bible except the leaders; and when someone does read Scripture, it is not to discover the argument of the human author of Scripture but to justify a position already held. The Bible is read through the new charismatic filter with the result that only their system is seen. Virtually none of the leaders have taken, for instance, the book of Romans and systematically worked through it verse by verse, seeking to understand what Paul was saying and teaching. Their metaphysical system would not survive this, for it is built on proof-texts taken out of context to support their favorite pretexts.

Along with this direct spirit revelation is the assumption that *Scripture is not sufficient in itself for the Christian life.* When the leaders repeatedly tell people that they have visions, dreams, things "God told me," and the like to guide them, obviously Scripture is not sufficient. When they tell how to be "led" by the Spirit in order to receive special guidance to know what God wants them to do, then Scripture is not adequate. They have made the fundamental Roman Catholic error of separating the Spirit of God from the Word of God by expecting the Holy Spirit to speak directly to them apart from Scripture. (See "The Holy Spirit and the Written Word" on page 235.)

Man Is Sovereign

As in the New Age teaching, people are encouraged by Word of Faith leaders to control their own destinies. Salvation from sin is rarely mentioned and certainly receives little weight in their writings. What is emphasized is how to get what you want by being your own god. "The quest for *metaphysical transcendence* rather than ethical transformation and repentance is a major source of the impetus to occultism" [emphasis his].[25] What Dr. North means is that the power man craves is to control his own destiny, to manipulate the forces of nature and other people, but not to control himself ethically. In other words, it is not the Gospel of the grace of God which forgives sins and enables one to be conformed to the moral image of Christ that is stressed but having one's own way by making God our debtor. Solomon said: "He who is slow to anger is better than the mighty, and he who rules his spirit than he who takes a city" (Prov. 16:32). He means that it is better to control oneself than to control others, but the health and wealth people promote the opposite. *They are after metaphysical control of others and their environment rather than the ethical control of themselves.* The same is found in transcendentalism, Christian Science, Unity School, and other gnostic sects.

Man becoming his own god leads logically to another problem: the search for power. Self-proclaimed power is a species of the genus of denying the creator-creature distinction, merging God and man. In the New Age and occultism, in black magic and white magic, in witches and Satanism, in humanism and Arminianism, we see man's desperate search for power, for metaphysical power rather than ethical power.

The reason man in his fallenness craves sinful power is because he still believes the lie Satan propounded to Eve: "For God knows that in the day you eat of it your eyes will be opened, and you will be like God, knowing good and evil" (Gen. 3:5). The Hebrew word for "knowing" here means to "determine"; Satan essentially said that Eve could be as powerful as God, determining her own morality. She could control her own destiny by creating her own ethic (the lie many in humanism today still believe).

The new charismatics teach that each Christian creates, through his own power, his own reality by what he confesses verbally. The search for power in itself is absolutely Satanic, participating in the rebellion of Satan. True power to change lives comes through the Gospel, in submitting to God through Jesus, in being changed by His grace to conform to the moral image of Christ. In short, *true power is ethical, in surrendering*

---

[25]Gary North, *Unholy Spirits* (Ft. Worth: Dominion Press, 1986), p. 64.

to Christ.

Furthermore, the magic arts in occultism, witchcraft, the New Age, Satanism, and so forth, promise power over one's enemies, and the ability to manipulate things and people to one's own end. They promise power through sharing in the being of God, which is a lie straight from hell. We will always be creatures and the sovereign Triune God will always be the Creator — for all eternity. We worship Him and love Him by faith and obedience to His Word (1 John 5:1-3), not by manipulating Him.

Controlling one's reality and circumstances, according to these new occultists, is a result of proper thinking. Because man allegedly partakes of the divine nature, he possesses a spiritual ability to control his circumstances by thinking. In the New Age, proper thinking comes through meditation. In Christian Science it is done by denying the real existence of the physical world. In Unity School of Christianity it is necessary to understand the primacy of Mind or Spirit. In the health and wealth gospel, one controls circumstances by knowledge, the force of faith, visualization, and confessing verbally. The particulars vary, but the substance is the same.

The example that applies to all three (New Age, Christian Science, health and wealth) is physical healing. There was a revival of physical healing among these metaphysical cults before it came into Christianity. All the metaphysical cults teach that one can be healed of any disease or problem by realizing that the spiritual controls the physical. In Christian Science the truth that empowers is that disease is an illusion. In Unity School you concentrate on Spirit and be in contact with "God." In New Age you can be healed by the proper adjustment of the chakras through meditation. In the new charismatic doctrine, one needs to have the knowledge that Satan is causing the problem and claim healing. In each system spiritual law determines the result, and we can determine our own spiritual adjustment by directing some personal energy or faith in conformity to the spiritual laws. Virtually everything they believe is governed by spiritual law.

Universe Governed by Spiritual Law

The metaphysical cults believe that the universe is governed by spiritual laws. These laws are metaphysical in nature, not ethical laws such as the Ten Commandments. From a book written by a leader in the Unity School of Christianity, we read: "The mental and spiritual world or realms are governed by laws that are just as real and unfailing as the laws that govern the natural world."[26] According to them, the spiritual laws have primacy over the natural ones. Thus God can do nothing except what we allow Him to do, for He is tied to these spiritual laws. *These laws bind God, and we can bind Him, too, if only we know how to use them.* According to them, knowledge is the key.

The new charismatic doctrine says there is spiritual law even above God, for when He created the world, He had to do so by faith. He "released faith in His words" so much so that the universe came into existence.[27] "Faith" is the law of the mind, or a "spiritual force," to use Kenneth Copeland's expression, that can use the spiritual laws to one's own advantage. Even as evolution supposedly operated according to some natural law, so do we in the spiritual realm.

Since the prosperity teachers have a low view of God's sovereignty and a high view of spiritual law, *they also have an almost non-existent view of providence,* the biblical teaching that everything that happens in our lives was planned by God before the world began for our good. In other words, "all things work together for good" (Rom. 8:28). These men strictly deny this. Even worse, it is the devil who plans "bad" things in our lives; and if we only had enough faith, we could prevent *any* problems from entering our lives. It is our use of spiritual law that determines what happens to us, not God's providence. Or as one of these people once said to me: "It is not possible for there to be any problems in my immediate family because I have faith." He believes that he is predestinating his life by his puny faith.

"The heart of occultism is its commitment to a universe

---

[26] H. Emilie Cady, *Lessons in Truth* (Unity Village, MO: Unity Books, no date), pp. 64, 65.

[27] Kenyon, however, did not believe in an instantaneous creation, but, like the metaphysical cultists, believed in a form of theistic evolution. Around the turn of last century, evolution was extremely popular, Darwin's *Origin of the Species* having come out. The metaphysical cults absorbed it into their system, as Kenyon did his, and Hagin, being ignorant of church doctrine, adopted Kenyon's system wholesale not knowing the heresies involved.

devoid of an ultimate sovereign."²⁸ In this world view there are many competing sovereigns, all operating according to some supposed spiritual law, all equally subject to this law, and all equally winning and losing, depending on how well they use the law. According to this system, God has placed certain spiritual laws in the world but has little or no power to alter anything. Each person "predestines" his own future by what he says verbally and by how well he uses spiritual law. Satan has power, demons have power, man has power, and God has power. What rules the world of the prosperity people, therefore, is chance, the old Greek god of Fate. As the reader will see, even the beloved Romans 8:28 ("all things work together for good") is reinterpreted to keep man at the center of his own destiny. *They* are at the center of their religion, a "Christian" humanism (an oxymoron if ever there was one). They argue tenaciously that God does not predestinate all things and then they present man as the predestinator, apparently having more confidence in man's ability to control the future than God's ability.

Faith Determines All

In the metaphysical cults, *faith is a spiritual energy or force* directed at "God" or at the spiritual laws governing the universe. Like Luke Skywalker in the Star Wars movies, one can control the forces of nature with the right technique. All it takes is concentration, a positive mental attitude, meditation, or some other formula. "Certain conditions of mind are so connected with certain results that the two are inseparable. If we have the one, we must have the other, as surely as the night follows the day. . . ."²⁹ According to them, we live in a mechanistic universe, not a personal one. In the words of the media, "We can do whatever we set our minds to accomplish." This is pure humanism.

Finally, as Rev. Douglas Mills so accurately observed, they believe in *directing* their faith, in believing *for something* rather than believing *in Someone* and relaxing in Him. By this means they think they can direct reality to conform to their thoughts and directions rather than trusting in the triune God and

---

[28] North, *Unholy Spirits*, p. 333.

[29] Cady, *Lessons*, p. 65.

relaxing in His providence.

Healing Is Available to All

Physical healing is a major emphasis in all the metaphysical cults. *They all look to healing as the validation of the truth of their systems.*

Elitism

The elite new charismatic preacher, like the gnostic of old, is "separated from his neighbor not only by his spiritual goals. He is separated also by the very spiritual experiences themselves. For with each experience the gnostic rises to a higher level of spiritual life. Above the mere believer he becomes a gnostic experiencer."[30] The elitism is rooted in supposed experiences he has had above the normal Christian experience, such as being "Spirit-filled" as opposed to a nominal Christian, a "Spirit-baptized" Christian as opposed to a "Spirit-filled" one, a "Spirit-baptized tongues speaking" Christian as opposed to only a "Spirit-baptized" one, and even one who talks to Jesus personally, visiting heaven and hell, and on it goes.

The assumption is that the Gospel is not enough. There is something more desirable than being redeemed, having your sins forgiven by the blood of the Lamb, receiving His legal righteousness as a free gift, and being conformed to His moral image. There are experiences that will elevate one above the mundane *if* — and that is the key word — the seeker will only *let* God give them to him and do what the insider tells him to do. You do not have to read and study Scripture when you can listen to instructions from one who has visions; why study when you can have an experience?

These gnostic experiences, this priority given to ever higher experiences rather than to "cold" theology, lifts one *over* his brother rather than *to* him.[31] Why should you be concerned with helping your sick brother when the right experience will eliminate the sickness? Why should you give money to the poor when the right experience will make the poor rich? Why should you be concerned with the worship of

---

[30] Frederick Dale Bruner, *A Theology of the Holy Spirit* (Grand Rapids: Wm. B. Eerdmans Pub. Co., 1974), p. 275.

[31] Ibid., p. 276.

God when the right experience will get what *you* want from God? This is a gospel of alienation. "If a man is sick, he does not need drugs; if poor, he has no need of money; if suffering, of material help or even sympathy. For the cure in all cases must be sought within."[32] Therefore, they constantly seek after various speakers and leaders, hoping to hear a new teaching or a new experience that will catapult them into a new plane of exhilarating experience, one in which they will never again wallow in the mundane things of each day, such as trials and problems with personal sins. Just one more experience, and they will have no more problems. It is a self-centered religion, one that makes the Christian rich and self-satisfied, not needy and dependent on the brethren. Such is the essence of the metaphysical cults and of the Word of Faith movement.

Individualism

In all the metaphysical cults there is little or no emphasis on the local church, for if knowledge is the key to life and one can have whatever he wants by the right confession or the right orientation, why should he be concerned with the worship of God? In this system, *God only works with individuals, not with groups such as churches*. The key to all of life is what you as an individual do, not what the church does in worship. They are taught to be individual-centered, man-centered, not God-centered. According to this, the electronic church can be a valid substitute for the local church since God only works with individuals. The morning church service, if there is one, is primarily for gaining more knowledge, for being taught by the "preacher," instead of the worship of God — all done so the person can have what he wants. In this individualism, "Man is a microcosm, consisting of spirit, body, and soul. . . ."[33] Likewise, there are three classes of people: the *spiritual*, in whom true knowledge and maturity are located; the *material*, carnal person; and the *psychical* who mediates between the other two extremes.[34] This has come over into Christianity as the carnal Christian, the spiritual Christian,

---

[32] Warfield, *Counterfeit Miracles*, p. 223.

[33] Schaff, *History of the Christian Church*, 2:456.

[34] Ibid., 2:456.

and the unregenerate.

Syncretism

Another characteristic of the metaphysical cults and the new charismatics is syncretism, which is the merging of many truths into one. These groups absorb what seems to be a threat to them, claiming to believe it or at least having modified it. *They are a mixture of many different and contradictory ideas.* Contradiction does not bother them. Chameleon like, these metaphysical cults use the same terms as evangelical Christianity, but with shades of meaning that are a different hue than the Bible's definitions. They can speak of Jesus as God manifested in the flesh, but then they claim the same for themselves.

Narcissism

I doubt that the new charismatics have given much thought to this but it *pervades* their writings. Narcissism is man turned toward himself. Everything in their writings is designed to teach the individual Christian how to get what he wants. From Kenneth Hagin's *How to Write Your Own Ticket with God* to Kenneth Copeland's *The Laws of Prosperity*, all is designed *to teach the Christian to turn inward, to orient himself to his wants and desires.* Not serving others but serving self is the orientation. Whatever happened to serving Christ by serving others? It is lost in selfishness.

Salvation

In creation man was made in the *image* of God, but the health and wealth teaching is that man partook of the *nature* of God. According to them, when man fell, he then lost the nature of God and took on the nature of Satan. This mistake, in turn, leads to heresy in their doctrine of salvation: When Christ came to the earth, He was simply a man operating in the power of the Holy Spirit. According to Edward Irving, He took on Satan's nature at His birth while the new charismatic doctrine maintains He did this when He went to hell for three days. In either case, Christ did not become sin for us but a sinner, indeed a demoniac, making payment to Satan. At His resurrection, they say Jesus was born again. His atonement was *not* done on the Cross but in hell for three days. *Since sin is spiritual, it was not possible for Him to atone for sin physically by a physical death* (dualism between spiritual and physical);

but He had to die spiritually in hell for three days. They speak of a substitution, but in their system Jesus was not a legal substitute bearing the wrath of God but a moral substitute, taking on Satan's nature so that at His resurrection He Himself was in need of the new birth!

Pragmatism

Pragmatism is the belief that the proof of truth is "if it works." Or someone may say, "If it works, use it."[35] Western Christians are so accustomed to pragmatism that many readers will not recognize it as a serious error. The test of truth is not "if it works" but rather what God says. By contrast if one does not adhere to the written Word as infallible, then he has no firm ground, and is like the man who built his house on sand. In pragmatism, infallibility gravitates to personal experience, which means that what works for me is right.

Likewise Unity writer Fox states: ". . . he tests the idea scientifically and judges only by results."[36] Ponder says regarding the "master plan": "It is scientific, it is practical, it is businesslike, and it works!"[37] Copeland and others think that the numerous followers they have means God approves them. Of course this further assumes that heretics cannot have large crowds, but a quick glance at the New Testament reveals that the Pharisees had numerous disciples. In our democratic America, we have been led to believe that voters or numbers determine truth so that the more people given to a cause the more credible we think it is. After all, fifty thousand people (or whatever number) can't be wrong, can they?

The danger is that human experience becomes the final authority in our lives rather than the written Word, the Bible. Thus, if something does not work, then we conclude that the Bible is wrong rather than conclude that our experience may need adjusting. We wrongly interpret the Bible through our experience rather than our experience through the Bible. Satan can produce virtually any human experience, but he will not

---

[35] R. C. Sproul, *Lifeviews* (Old Tappan, New Jersey: Fleming H. Revell Co., 1986), p. 77.

[36] Emmet Fox, *The Mental Equivalent* (Unity Village, MO: Unity School of Christianity, no date), p. 22.

[37] Catherine Ponder, *Dare to Prosper* (Marina del Rey, CA: DeVross & Co., 1983), p. 48.

produce the truth. The only objective guide to truth is the written Word of God, never our experience.

One example comes to mind. Kenneth Hagin claims to have been healed from a life-threatening disease when he was a teenager. He concludes from his own personal experience that healing is for everyone. Therefore, if one is not healed, then he does not have enough faith. However, for Christians like Joni Eareckson Tada, who broke her neck as teenager and is paralyzed from the neck down, to hear this must be very discouraging. Instead, she, like many other Christians, has concluded — not from her experience but from the Word of God — that though God does heal occasionally, yet healing is not for everyone, at least in this life.

No Old Testament

The gnostics either denied the Old Testament was the Word of God, or else they relegated it to the ignorance of a by-gone era. Whether denied or qualified, it had little if any application to those of the new revelation after Jesus. Many things the Old Testament prophets and people said were wrong and not for the people of today. We shall find the same in the Word of Faith movement, often stating that their ideas were wrong and of no value for today, even though the Lord (John 10:35; Matt. 15:3ff) and the Apostle Paul disagreed (2 Tim. 3:16, 17).

Conclusion

The essence of the movement is in the metaphysical ideas of pantheism, dualism, knowledge as salvation, direct revelation within the person apart from Scripture, and that spiritual or metaphysical law governs the universe and man's force of faith governs spiritual law. Without these there could be no Word of Faith movement. Like New Age pantheism, they claim some identity with God which enables them to do things that only a god can do. Like Christian Science, they have a dualism between two worlds: a physical and a spiritual one. Like all the metaphysical cults, they claim to receive direct revelation from God within themselves, that metaphysical law governs the universe, and that one's faith forces the laws to bring about what one desires. These metaphysical ideas are "proven" by physical healing and by verbally confessing things to happen. All these are mingled with a robust individualism and narcissism while pragmatism stirs up the "pot," seemingly making everything palatable. Tragically, we are only left with a poisoned "stew," which when eaten, kills the participant.

2

Where Did They Come From?

The Historical Roots of the Movement

Seek the Lord and His strength; seek His face evermore. Remember His marvelous works which He has done, His wonders, and the judgments of His mouth (Ps. 105:4, 5).

Christianity is an historical religion, tied to events in time and space, such as the exodus from Egypt, the life, death, and resurrection of Christ, and many other things. In the captioned verses, we see that God requires that we remember sacred history. He has commanded us to teach each succeeding generation, which will be able to teach the next (2 Tim. 2:2). The exalted Jesus has given gifted men to teach the church, and these men are not limited to our century. We are to learn from the great men of past centuries. Each generation is to remember, not to start over. We can still learn from an Augustine or from a Calvin. The gifted men were for all succeeding generations, not just for their own (Eph. 4:11-16).

Joshua commanded Israel to place stones on the banks of Jordan to remember (Joshua 4:1-7). We are to take the Lord's Supper "in remembrance of Him." For anyone to neglect the past is to repeat its failures, to deny that God has worked in previous generations, and to arrogantly think that all truth resides with one's contemporaries. Paul says in Ephesians 4:11-16 that God teaches His church and that it grows from generation to generation. The past is the key to the future, for we learn what to avoid, and we build on the shoulders of our predecessors. We learn which doctrines to shun and which are biblical. Ignoring the past is arrogant — and deadly.

But how interesting could the past be "when we are the 'terminal generation' awaiting 'the great escape' from 'the late great planet earth'"?[1] All truth is assumed to be in our generation, and if not, it does not matter since we are looking for the "upper taker" rather than the "under taker" to bail us out soon. This lack of a long term perspective has closed our eyes to the past and doomed us to failure in the future. We are existentialists, living in the "now," ships without anchor, sailing from nowhere and without destination, "tossed to and fro by every wind of doctrine" (Eph. 4:14). To ignore the past is suicide, and not planning for the future is to bury our talents.

Consequently when anyone brags that the Gospel is being restored for the first time in a thousand years or longer, we should quickly become skeptical. Christ has not been asleep, the gates of hell have not triumphed over His church, and the church has continued to advance in its understanding of God's Word. We do not need to go back and start over; we must continue to advance. The Jehovah's Witnesses with Charles Taze Russell, the Mormons and Joseph Smith, the Christian Scientists and Mary Baker Glover Patterson Eddy, and many others, all claim that the "gospel" was restored after centuries of being lost. The health and wealth preachers are saying the same today.

Essek William Kenyon (1867-1948), the father of the Word of Faith movement, boasts:

> Thinking men and women of this age have been rebelling against the orthodox interpretation of the Bible as represented in the denominational creeds. . . . A spirit of unrest has seized the heart of Christendom. Many of the old landmarks of Faith have been destroyed by modern Criticism. . . . These two basic facts of revelation have been covered by the verbiage of Theological speculation. The whole Plan of Redemption is: First, the Father God's Dream for a Family. Second, Redemption from a Sin Catastrophe. Third, the Dream Coming True.[2]

---

[1] Michael Scott Horton, *Made in America* (Grand Rapids: Baker Book House, 1991), p. 176.

[2] Essek William Kenyon, *The Father and His Family: A Restatement of the Plan of Redemption* (Seattle: E. W. Kenyon, 1937), p. 9-10. Kenyon has a propensity for capital letters, which is typical of those in metaphysical cults who see all kinds of things as God-like, such as Mind, Spirit (not the Holy Spirit), Cause,

> Theology . . . has never yet given a reason for Creation. . . . Her [church's] theologians have found more pleasure in abstract Theology than in personal dealings with God . . ., more pleasure in the opinions of men than in the Word of God.[3]
>
> The great body of the church does not see — as they have never seen — the issue squarely. . . .[4]

Kenyon asserts with bold independence:

> This book will blaze a new path in constructive interpretation of the Pauline revelation. It uncovers new veins of primary truths long covered by sense knowledge interpretation of the Word. . . . [5] There has been far too little growth in the knowledge of the Pauline Revelation since their [Reformers] day.[6] It is strange we never knew until recently that faith follows in the footprints of our confession.[7]

The Unity School of Christianity claims the same:

> I believe . . . the amazingly simple teachings of Jesus Christ were forgotten after a few hundred years. People build up creeds and ceremonies which they only half understand. Now, in this twentieth century, the secret things are being revealed and we are again having primitive Christianity.[8]

Someone will object that the Reformers restored the Gospel after centuries of lapse. The Protestant Reformers, however, did not want a new church; they wanted to purify the Roman Catholic Church. When the Roman church refused to be rectified, they had no choice except to establish new churches. They did not preach a new Gospel but the old one that many in the Roman church had preached for centu-

---

Intelligence, Principle, Consciousness, Soul, etc.

[3] Ibid., p. 24.

[4] E. W. Kenyon, *The Wonderful Name of Jesus* (Kenyon's Gospel Publishing Society), p. 17.

[5] E. W. Kenyon, *What Happened from the Cross to the Throne* (Kenyon's Gospel Publishing Society, 1969, fourth edition), p. 9.

[6] Ibid., p. 11.

[7] Ibid., p. 156.

[8] Florence Scovel Shinn, *The Power of the Spoken Word* (Marina del Rey, CA: DeVorss & Co., 1945), p. 75.

ries. John Wycliffe in the 1300's and John Huss in the 1400's had preached this Gospel, and they were in the Roman church, even when they died. The Roman church became corrupt, not the Gospel. We need to learn from our past, not ignore it.

Montanism or Déjà Vu

One who reads the health and wealth writers will be astounded by the similarity to ancient heresies. For example, in early church history there was a man by the name of Montanus who held to two of the tenets of the modern day health and wealth people: divine healing and prophetic utterances. Montanus himself was a new convert to Christianity, having been a priest of the pagan god Cybele,[9] having spoken in tongues at his baptism.[10] There are many parallels between the ancient and heretical Montanists and the modern Word of Faith leaders. "There is nothing new under the sun."

Prominence of Women

Montanism arose about the year A.D. 172, and like the modern movement *had women who were prominent in the movement.*[11] The women were Priscilla and Maximilla, and their leadership incurred the hostility of the early church fathers.[12] Furthermore, the women left their husbands to follow Montanus.[13]

Likewise, women in the modern movement claim to be prophetesses and especially to be co-pastors with their husbands. In a magazine of Robert Tilton's entitled *Signs, Wonders, & Miracles of Faith*, his wife, Marte, claims to be a pastor with him (pp. 2, 3). Annette Capps, the daughter of Charles Capps, says she "is an ordained minister, business-woman, and pilot. Since the age of 14, she has ministered in churches

---

[9] Philip Schaff, *History of the Christian Church* (Grand Rapids: Wm. B. Eerdmans Publishing Co., 1910), 2:418.

[10] Kenneth Scott Latourette, *A History of Christianity*, (New York: Harper & Row, 1953), p. 128.

[11] Walter A. Elwell, editor, *Evangelical Dictionary of Theology*, (Grand Rapids: Baker Book House, 1984), p. 732.

[12] *Evangelical Dictionary of Theology*, p. 732.

[13] Schaff, *History of the Christian Church*, 2:418.

and several foreign countries."[14] Paul says, however, that he did not allow women preachers (1 Tim. 2:11-3:5).

Required Recognition of Their Gifts

Montanus and his women prophetesses required that others recognize their so-called prophetic gifts simply based on their word.[15] Like so many of the modern leaders in the health and wealth "gospel," Montanus burned with fanatical zeal, "considering himself the inspired organ of the promised Paraclete or Advocate, the Helper or Comforter in these last times of distress."[16] The early church leaders were rightly concerned that new prophetic utterances would threaten the authority of the apostles and especially the New Testament Scriptures.[17] For once any person began proclaiming new revelations, where would they end?

The Word of Faith leaders often refer to themselves as prophets, adding that most Christians are defeated and are carnal, and that the millennium is near. Oral Roberts, in *A Daily Guide to Miracles*, boldly proclaims: "Don't fight me. Cooperate by simply reading it day-by-day. God has called me to be His servant and *prophet* to help you" [emphasis added].[18]

Robert Tilton has no subtlety. Repeatedly on TV he claims to be God's spokesman, able to prophesy, supposedly speaking the word of God to his audience. On the back of his book, *God's Miracle Plan for Man,* it states:

> Robert Tilton is a modern-day prophet, called and anointed [a word they love] by God to edify, comfort, and exhort the Body of Christ. . . . When Robert Tilton prophesies God's Word, the storms of life are stilled, creative miracles flow, and the yoke of lack [sic] is broken![19]

Not only is proclaiming oneself a prophet contrary to Scrip-

---

[14] Charles & Annette Capps, *Angels* (Tulsa, OK: Harrison House, 1984), p. 216.

[15] Schaff, *History of the Christian Church*, 2:418.

[16] Ibid.

[17] *Evangelical Dictionary of Theology*, p. 733.

[18] Oral Roberts, *A Daily Guide to Miracles* (Tulsa: Pinoak Publications, 1975), p. 16.

[19] Robert Tilton, *God's Miracle Plan for Man* (Dallas: Robert Tilton Ministries, 1987).

ture, but it is utter blasphemy to take God's name in vain by attributing something to God's name that is contrary to the Bible. (See Chapter Nine on Scripture.)

The Holy Spirit and the End of the World

These three "prophets," Montanus and his two women, went about *proclaiming the "true" Christian life, the age of the Holy Spirit, and the near millennial reign,* which reign they said would be in Pepuza, a small village of Phrygia.[20] They were date setters, claiming that the millennium would occur either in their life times or shortly thereafter. One of the prophetesses, Maximilla, said: "After me there is no more prophecy, but only the end of the world."[21] One historian points out, "The entire purpose, in fact, of the new prophecy was preparation for the approaching end."[22]

The Word of Faith leaders often proclaim that the Lord is coming back in our generation, that the "millennium" is almost here, and that most Christians are "carnal," not knowing what their heritage is or how to live correctly. They also proclaim that we are in the age of the Holy Spirit, the Old Testament being the age of the Father and Christ's incarnation as His time. Of course these "prophets" profess to know how to live correctly, and now for the first time in many centuries, they maintain, Christ is again raising up His "prophets" to help His people.

Oral Roberts says, "God told me this was in harmony with 1992 being a pivotal year of the end time. . . ."[23] Again he confidently asserts, "What is important in 1992 for the Body of Christ, is to get a *world view* . . . to see these prophetic events begin to take shape for what we believe will be the soon return of Christ Who will come in the Rapture" [emphasis and

---

[20] Schaff, *History of the Christian Church*, 2:418.

[21] Ibid., 2:425.

[22] Samuel MacAuley Jackson, *The New Schaff-Herzog Encyclopedia of Religious Knowledge* (Grand Rapids: Baker Book House, 1910), 7:486. Obviously, Maximilla was a false prophetess, for God says: "And if you say in your heart, 'How shall we know the word which the Lord has not spoken?' — when a prophet speaks in the name of the Lord, if the thing does **not** happen or come to pass, that is the thing which the Lord has not spoken; the prophet has spoken it presumptuously; you shall not be afraid of him" (Deut. 18:21, 22).

[23] Oral Roberts, *11 Major Prophecies* (Tulsa: Oral Roberts, 1992), p. 12.

ellipsis his].[24]

Gloria Copeland, wife of Kenneth Copeland, is confident:

> I believe that we are the generation which will usher in the coming of the Lord Jesus Christ. Before He comes, God will manifest Himself more intensely than He did in the time of Moses.[!] He will pour out His Spirit on all flesh. Think of it — the Spirit of God revealing Himself to flesh![25]

Like the women connected with Montanus, she says, "I believe that we are in the midst of the greatest outpouring of the Holy Spirit in the history of the human race."[26]

Miracles Are Normative

A fourth characteristic of Montanism was an insistence that *the miraculous gifts of the apostolic age should continue* and be a permanent part of Christianity.[27] They especially emphasized the continued gift of prophecy. Even the Montanists said that the miraculous gifts had ended with the apostles, but of course Montanus was restoring them. The cessation of the sign gifts was common knowledge even in the Second Century. Of course the modern health and wealth advocates also claim that the miraculous gifts are for today, especially the gift of prophecy, and that they are being restored through them.

Directly Called by God

A fifth characteristic of Montanism was the claim to be directly called by God without being confirmed by human agency.[28] In other words, they were called by God but not ordained by men. They had to say this since the early church did not accept them. Of course, these three "prophets" (Montanus and his women) referred to themselves as the *spiritual* Christians while all others were *carnal*,[29] very much like the new charismatics today. Schaff says,

---

[24]Ibid., p. 18.

[25]Gloria Copeland, *Walk in the Spirit* (Forth Worth: KCP Publications, 1984), p. 3.

[26]Ibid., p. 5.

[27]Schaff, *History of the Christian Church*, 2:423.

[28]Ibid., 2:424.

[29]Ibid., 2:419.

But they [Montanists] only brought another kind of aristocracy into the place of the condemned distinction of clergy and laity. They claimed for their prophets what they denied to the . . . bishops. They put a great gulf between the true spiritual Christians and the merely psychical; and this induced spiritual pride and false pietism.[30]

These self-proclaimed men pretend to be called by God, but they are not ordained. One needs both to be called and ordained to be legitimate. Christ grants the ministerial gifts to men, and they are confirmed by other godly men. This is the New Testament pattern: "Do not neglect the gift that is in you, which was given to you by prophecy with the laying on of the hands of the presbytery" (1 Tim. 4:14). The "laying on of hands" was the ordination, showing that the particular man had the approval of other Christians. This was — and is — the biblical way to keep the Gospel pure. In fact, there is a command not to lay hands on anyone too quickly lest Christians become partakers of the sins of new preachers who are ignorant. "Do not lay hands on anyone hastily, nor share in other people's sins; keep yourself pure" (1 Tim. 5:22).

No one matches the pride of Robert Tilton. Tilton said on his 11/02/90 nationwide TV broadcast, "Just as the widow was blessed by doing the anointed word of Elijah, so you must listen to what I say." He continued: "I want you to call me and make a $1,000.00 vow of faith." Again he stated: "This [his prophecy] is like a living Bible coming into your home."

Anti-Trinity

Montanists also had a tendency to deny the Trinity,[31] and the same tendency exists in the Word of Faith movement. They deny the deity of Christ (see Chapter Twelve), and proclaim themselves as gods (Chapter Eight). Therefore, ironically they exhibit both polytheism and pantheism. At the Synod of Iconium in A.D. 230, the church fathers refused to accept Montanist baptism, which effectively excommunicated them and they died out.[32]

---

[30]Ibid., 2:424.

[31]Ibid., 2:421; see also footnote 2.

[32]J. D. Douglas, *The New International Dictionary of the Christian Church* (Grand Rapids: Zondervan, 1974), p. 674.

The Anabaptists

The Anabaptists in the Reformers' days were opposed both to the Reformers and to the Roman Catholic Church, proclaiming that only believer's baptism (as opposed to infant baptism) was legitimate, and that only the New Testament was for today, not the Old Testament. Many also proclaimed that Jesus was not God, that all governments were of the devil so that no Christian should ever hold a government position, that Jesus was coming back in their generation, that salvation so freed one from the obedience to God that he need not show any evidence of conversion, and that all the sign gifts were still for today. Many of these beliefs are heretical and are also in the Word of Faith movement. Thus in the 1500's the Reformers often wrote against the Anabaptists. For example, John Calvin said, "If anyone replied to them by citing Scripture, they would respond that we shouldn't be subject to the 'letter that kills but to the Spirit who gives life.'"[33] Calvin said that they were always looking for "new revelations" and for "a better and more perfect wisdom than we find in [Scripture]."[34] Looking for more than Scripture is the essence of what the health and wealth leaders do.

The Anabaptists in the Colonial Era were more in the mainstream of Christianity, and Cotton Mather (1623-1728) stated that they "have been welcome to the communion of our churches."[35] On May 28, 1665, they formed their first church in New England.[36] They refused to worship with Cotton Mather even though he invited them, for they did not believe in infant baptism. Even though Mather would have allowed them to join his church and all the New England churches were exceedingly tolerant of them, they were intolerant of the Puritans and very exclusive. This same exclusive attitude is still among some of them today (Amish and Mennonites who will not join society). And some think *only* they are the bride of Christ (Landmark Baptists), even though they

---

[33] John Calvin, *Treatises Against the Anabaptists and Against the Libertines*, translated by Benjamin Wirt Farley (Grand Rapids: Baker Book House, 1982), p. 221.

[34] Ibid., p. 222.

[35] Cotton Mather, *The Great Works of Christ in America*, reprinted from the 1702 edition, (Banner of Truth), 2:532.

[36] Ibid.

allow that others may be Christians! We see this exclusive attitude among the prosperity gospel preachers. All others are sub-Christians, of a lower class, than they are.

Alongside the Anabaptists were the Libertines, whom Calvin and the Reformers opposed in the 1500's. Calvin says that they fulfill 2 Peter 2 and Jude in ensnaring the gullible in order to cater to their covetous desires, listening neither to God's law nor to reason.[37] As we shall see throughout this book, catering to covetousness and disparaging God's law and man's reason are characteristics of the Word of Faith movement.

The American Colonial Period

The Puritans came to a spiritually dark continent when they founded New England in the early 1600's. Much like the Israelites who entered Canaan, they encountered unbelievable savagery among the American Indians who were unceasingly murdering one another. The Indians also engaged in cannibalism, eating the raw flesh of their victims as the victims watched in horror and many other such things.[38] Satan would not relinquish this continent without a fight, and the Puritans, who preached a purer Gospel than most modern evangelicals today, encountered much Satanic opposition. Sometimes it was in the form of direct witchcraft.[39]

What Satan had done outwardly at the time of the witch trials in the late 1600's in Cotton Mather's day, he did secretly with false brethren a generation earlier in the early 1600's in John Cotton's day. There are two cases in particular that

---

[37] Calvin, *Treatises Against the Anabaptists*, p. 193.

[38] Peter Marshall, Jr., *The Light and the Glory* (Old Tappan, NJ: Fleming H. Revell Co., 1977), p. 77.

[39] Contrary to popular opinion, the Puritans did not kill hundreds of witches; they killed nineteen, and even then it was only after great pains were taken to prove their case in court. A hundred had been accused (Mather, *Great Works*, 2:477). The trials stopped when the ministers and the court directed that fasting and prayer be offered to ask the Lord to cause the Satanic activities to cease (Ibid., p. 472). God mightily answered their prayers: "The Lord so chained up Satan that the afflicted grew presently well . . . and for five years since, we have had no such molestation" (Ibid., p. 477). The molestations were spirits tormenting people, physically beating them, enabling them to cast spells on others, and many other such things. These things are returning as our nation again slides into demonic practices such as Satanism, witch craft, psychics, etc.

Where Did They Come From?

deserve our attention: Ann Hutchinson and the Quakers.

Ann Hutchinson, who is often the heroine of women's liberation groups and is considered as the first women's liberator, was the focus of considerable disturbance by those who think that sanctification has nothing to do with our assurance of salvation. (To put this in modern words, antinomians think Christ can be your Savior without being your Lord.) In the 1630's when John Cotton was preaching, some were saying — to Cotton's horror — that Christ by some immediate revelation to the heart would assure the Christian that he was saved.[40] Even further, as Cotton Mather[41] noted, some "... carried the matter on to a very *perilous door*, opened not only for new *enthusiastical revelations*, but also for a neglect of such *qualifications* in all *godliness* and *honesty*, as must be found in all who would be" discovered to be Christians [emphasis his].[42] Mather lamented that these people were playing with fire in their new revelations. The Puritans were obviously opposed to new revelations.[43]

Ann Hutchinson followed the great John Cotton to New England from England to hear his preaching. She began to repeat Mr. Cotton's sermons in her house on Sundays to a group of women, misrepresenting him badly, saying that one does not need to have any evidence in his life before assurance can be gained, that only an immediate revelation by the Spirit is necessary. Furthermore, she condemned all those who believed in "making their calling and election sure" as believ-

---

[40] Mather, *Great Works*, p. 2:509.

[41] John Cotton (1584 - 1652) and Increase Mather were contemporaries in New England, both ministers. Cotton Mather, the eldest son of Increase, apparently was named after John Cotton, and served as a minister in the same church as his father.

[42] Ibid., p. 508, 509. Today we have institutionalized such antinomian heresy, for a large "evangelical" seminary in Dallas, TX takes an official position that Christ can be your Savior without being your Lord, having proclaimed such in their doctrinal statement.

[43] Cotton Mather, referring to Hutchinson, insightfully revealed that one of the characteristics of false teachers is that they "seduce women into their notions." (Ibid., p. 509). Mather cites: "For of this sort are those who creep into households and make captives of gullible women loaded down with sins, led away by various lusts" (2 Tim. 3:6). Moreover, he pointed out that Simon Magus had his Helena, Montanus his Maximilla, and Arius, who denied the deity of Christ and was declared a heretic at the Council of Nicea in A.D. 325, had his several hundred virgins (Ibid., p. 516).

ing in a Gospel of works. From this she promoted her "immediate revelations about future events, to be equally infallible with the Scriptures."[44]

After many attempts to reclaim her for the Gospel, a church court was ordered and Mrs. Hutchinson was summoned (1637). She denied that she ever held to such heresies; and when many witnesses were produced confirming her beliefs, she was excommunicated for lying. She went to Rhode Island, which could be better named "Rogue" Island, for every heresy imaginable was permitted there. When excommunication was pronounced on her, she gave prophecies against John Cotton and the other ecclesiastical officials, pronouncing judgments on them, "which the Lord brought to me," she proclaimed. None of them came to pass,[45] clearly demonstrating that she was a false prophetess. They allowed her to stay until winter was over. Not long after her departure to Rhode Island, most of those where she lived were murdered by the Indians, including her and her family. The judgment she proclaimed on others came on her, which ended her influence and her "revelations."

With Ann Hutchinson, we see women taking a leadership role that God reserves for men and leading others astray into such heresies as works are not a necessary result of salvation, the local church is not important, and new revelations apart from the Bible, which the Word of Faith leaders are repeating.

The Quakers, who began in New England in 1657,[46] went further in their heresies than Hutchinson. These novel people (who sometimes called themselves Friends) denied the Trinity, repudiated the human and divine Christ, cursed the Bible and the Puritans, and caviled that "justification by that righteousness which Christ fulfilled in His own person without us is a doctrine of devils."[47] Again they stated: "We deny thy Christ! We deny thy God, which thou callest Father, Son and Spirit! Thy Bible is the word of the devil!"[48]

---

[44]Ibid., p. 517.

[45]Ibid., p. 518.

[46]Ibid., p. 523.

[47]Ibid., p. 524.

[48]Ibid., p. 526.

They received their name from the "odd symptom of quaking" their bodies.[49] They especially enjoyed shocking the Puritans of the day, who endured them with uncommon grace. (The Puritans were not the ogres and tyrants that modern "historians" caricature them as being.) Cotton Mather reports that "two women of their sect, who came stark naked as ever they were born into our publick [sic] assemblies, and they were (baggages that they were!) adjudged unto the whipping post for that piece of devilism."[50] It is difficult to imagine the shock that such an event would have had on these godly people. The "publick assemblies" were probably the churches.

Again we see the dominance of women in the movement.[51] Throughout history women have had a prominent part in what may be called "enthusiasm" or the tendency to emotional Christianity, which tends to be a Christianity not supported by the Bible, given over to direct revelations, "baptism in the Holy Spirit," and tongues. We do not mean to imply that God hates emotion or that women are inferior to men but that prophecy, healing, and tongues can have an unhealthy emotional emphasis and that women, who are more given to emotion, are easily deceived. "And I do not permit a woman to teach or to have authority over a man, but to be in silence. For Adam was formed first, then Eve. And Adam was not deceived, but the woman being deceived, fell into transgression" (1 Tim. 2:12-14). Some women, when made to feel good or needed, often fall prey to heresies. Enthusiasm in itself can be good if channeled in the right direction, but the movement called "Enthusiasm" was not good. There is an unusual number of women in the tongues and healing movements of today.[52]

The real danger of Quakerism, though, was its theology. All the basic tenets of the faith were denied, and the heresies

---

[49]Ibid., p. 528.

[50]Ibid., p. 527.

[51]Ibid., p. 530.

[52]Sometimes Galatians 3:28 is used to justify women preachers, but this verse says nothing about officers in the church. Paul is teaching that in justification that God makes no difference between men and women, both being justified by faith alone in Jesus alone.

came from one error: the teaching on "inner light." This belief was the mother of all their other errors. Like New Age mysticism, and most of the Eastern religions, inner light was "the mystical dispensations of the light within, as having the whole of religion."[53] This "light" was only the natural conscience, unsanctified by the written Word, by which they judged every standard. It was a sort of special revelation to the conscience so that they did not need the external Bible. They had an "internal Christ" who led them to deny the "carnal Christ" or physical, external Christ, of the Puritans. They are quoted as saying, "The greatest error in the world, and the ground of all errors, is to say, the Scriptures are a rule for Christians."[54] Rejecting the sufficiency of Scripture is an extremely dangerous and Satanic heresy, for once one denies the written Word of God and seeks inner light, he exposes himself to doctrines of demons. The written word is the only objective check against such subjectivity.

This inner light sounds ominously similar to the modern New Age concept of "going within," in Shirley MacLaine's words, of meditating, of trying to clear the mind of all thoughts so that one may contact the "God" within himself. Another New Age term for this is an "altered state of consciousness" or "higher consciousness." One has to reverse his thinking when reading New Age books, for common words have muddled meanings. "Meditating" does not mean using the mind to think but "removing all thoughts and interferences from the mind, which, when emptied, can be filled with 'God feeling.'"[55] Ms. MacLaine loves to remind herself that "I am God in light,"[56] that "we are all of God and God is part of us,"[57] that "The higher self is . . . your personal expression of the Divine within you."[58] One way to remove all thoughts is to concentrate on "a small object — a button, a flower, or

---

[53] Ibid., p. 523.

[54] Ibid., p. 524.

[55] Shirley MacLaine, *Going Within* (New York: Bantam Books, 1989), p.68. See also Lawrence LeShan, *How To Meditate* (New York: Bantam Books, 1988), pp. 1-12.

[56] Ibid., p. 68.

[57] Ibid., p. 77.

[58] Ibid., p. 79.

... my navel"![59]

The great mission of Ms. MacLaine is to help us remember that we are God, we just forgot that we were God. Some gods who cannot remember their own deity! If we could only remember to contact this Higher Self within, this inner light, this Divine Oversoul, the God within, the inner Christ, the spirit man (as the new charismatics term it), then we could have tremendous power over our lives, over our own destinies, over our own physical healing and emotional health.[60] If we learn to "tap into" the Universe within, knowing that we are "a spark of God," then we can learn to create our own circumstances.[61] When a person "goes within," he contacts spirit guides, which are nothing less than demons, who lead the gullible into doctrines of demons. Mrs. MacLaine has a spirit guide.[62]

The New Age "going within" and the Quaker inner light are not different from the "revelations" and learning to "listen" to one's human spirit that Kenneth Hagin and his disciples promote. Like Montanus of old, like Ann Hutchinson and the Quakers, and like the New Age movement, these new charismatics promote revelations apart from the written Word, the Bible (see Chapter Nine).

Edward Irving (1792-1834)

Edward Irving in England became a leader of the "ecstatic" and "prophetic" movement. From him came the Shakers.[63] "During his last five years his doctrinal position was virtually that of the Pentecostal body of today."[64] Though he shared beliefs with Pentecostalism, he also held to heresies that they reject.

In his younger years, Irving proved to be a good student,

---

[59] Ibid., p. 73.

[60] Ibid., pp. 83, ch. 15.

[61] Ibid., pp. 69, 91.

[62] Ibid., p. 89.

[63] B. B. Warfield, *Counterfeit Miracles* (London: The Banner of Truth Trust), p. 131. This is an excellent book on so-called miracles done today; must reading.

[64] Arnold Dallimore, *Forerunner of the Charismatic Movement, The Life of Edward Irving* (Chicago: Moody Press, 1983), p. 7.

especially loving Milton's *Paradise Lost* (no easy task to read!). He received a master of arts degree and won commendations from his professors.[65] Irving apparently experienced a "conversion" and became the assistant to the famous Thomas Chalmers of St. John's Church in Glasgow.[66] However, "There is no evidence he had ever known an experience of conversion like that of Chalmers,"[67] who had been converted out of his liberalism. Chalmers' preaching, as a result of his true conversion, was filled with power and evangelical piety. But Irving's preaching was different, like that of Oral Roberts, making no clear statement about salvation and being without power.[68] This is not to say that Irving's preaching was not well received; like Oral Roberts' preaching, it was. He was a good orator and spent much time developing his vocabulary and pulpit skills. After a short period under Chalmers, he was called to the Caledonian Chapel in London, which he accepted with great enthusiasm.[69]

The philosopher Samuel Taylor Coleridge was a regular attender at Irving's preaching in London, and was a free spirit and Unitarian, though he left Unitarianism for transcendentalism. Transcendentalism was the pantheistic philosophy that "God" is all, that especially nature untouched by man was a truer revelation of "God" than most other avenues. Thoreau, Orestes and Amos Brownson, Margaret Fuller, and especially Emerson were the leaders of this movement in the USA. In 1836 when Emerson published *Nature*, he became the unofficial leader of transcendentalism. These men claimed a direct access to "God" unmediated by Scripture or Christ. All one had to do was go within himself to find this divine nature.[70]

Yet Irving loved nothing better than to drink deeply from the well of Coleridge's "wisdom," often spending many long evenings conversing with him. It would seem, as we shall see

---

[65] Ibid., p. 27.

[66] Ibid., p. 35.

[67] Ibid., p. 37.

[68] Ibid., p. 39.

[69] Ibid., p. 42.

[70] Elwell, *Evangelical Dictionary*, p. 1107.

Where Did They Come From?

later when we study Irving's view on the person of Christ (see Chapter Twelve), that he drank too deeply. Coleridge promoted transcendentalism in England, that revolt against the Enlightenment of the eighteenth century, in which intuition and pantheism became the norms of truth.[71] Man's reason as the measure of all things was being replaced by "going within" or by intuition. In transcendentalism one listened to "God" within or within nature rather than to man's reason. In the Protestant Reformation, God speaking in Scripture was the standard by which all things were measured. There were, therefore, three standards all vying for final authority: man's reason (Enlightenment), intuition (transcendentalism), and the Bible, and these three are still with us today. Of course, it is the latter that is the true standard.[72]

It was Coleridge's mysticism that led Irving to espouse the sinful nature of Christ, to reject the substitutionary death of Christ, to deny the Bible alone as sufficient for life and godliness, and to maintain "salvation" by imitating Christ. He taught that there were spiritual laws that governed the universe just as there were physical laws, and each man must learn how to use his faith to manipulate these laws for what he wants. (See paragraph beginning with "What do these sects teach" on page 11 and following for a summary of what transcendentalism, gnosticism, and the metaphysical cults teach.)

The great Christian preacher Thomas Chalmers went with Irving to visit Coleridge, but he observed that Coleridge was full of "German mysticism and transcendental poetry." Chalmers offered to help Irving in his thinking about these things,

---

[71]C. Gregg Singer, *A Theological Interpretation of American History* (Phillipsburg, NJ: Presby. & Reformed Pub. Co., second edition, 1981), p. 56.

[72]In this country, Ralph Waldo Emerson and Henry David Thoreau (along with Walt Whitman, and Parker) made popular the works of Coleridge, especially his *Aids to Reflection* (Ibid., p. 59). Also Dr. Singer has an excellent book on the topic of the change in thinking from the Reformation to the present entitled *From Rationality to Irrationality*. I highly recommend it. Singer demonstrates that transcendentalism and the metaphysical cults can be traced back to Hegel, and the dualism of "sense knowledge" verses "revelation knowledge" traced to Kant. In England, Wordsworth, Scott, Coleridge, Byron, Shelley, and Keats carried the metaphysical and transcendental ball, and many such people often attended Irving's church. That they enjoyed his preaching reveals that Irving must have catered to them.

but Irving refused.[73] The intellectual community of the day, however, thought that Coleridge was a man of great wisdom and to have his favor was considered a great honor. Coleridge said of Irving's preaching that he was a "super Ciceronian."[74] This mutual admiration between Irving and Coleridge — and Irving wanted the admiration of his fellowman more than anything — moved Irving to adopt too much of this philosopher's views. Indeed, Irving stated that "he had learned more of the 'orthodox doctrine' from Coleridge than from 'all the men with whom I have entertained friendship and conversation.'"[75] Apparently this meant he had not learned much from Chalmers.

In three significant areas, Coleridge influenced Irving.[76] First was in the Person of Christ. Christ's nature was presented as something less than divine, for all men have a spark of divinity in them (pantheism), which in turn led Irving to promote the idea that Jesus had a sinful nature. The reason Jesus never sinned, according to Irving, was because He used the same Holy Spirit available to us to overcome indwelling sin, and this overcoming personal sin Irving considered to be the essence of salvation. Jesus, therefore, was a way-shower by His example but not the way, contrary to John 14:6.

Secondly, according to Coleridge the world would get worse, not better, which led Irving to adopt the pessimistic millennial view of premillennialism and to prophesy the end of the world. Irving left the postmillennialism that was considered the basic orthodoxy of his day. Like the Montanists of old, Irving promoted the idea of a premillennial and imminent return of Christ.[77] Like many today, He repeatedly proclaimed that Christ would soon return, and he often spoke of the signs of the times.[78] Of course since the Lord did not return, it is obvious that his views were wrong. Irving even spoke of "being baptized into the assurance of the gift of the

---

[73] Dallimore, *Forerunner*, pp. 60, 63.

[74] Ibid., p. 60.

[75] Ibid., p. 60.

[76] Ibid., p. 61ff.

[77] Warfield, *Counterfeit Miracles*, p. 7.

[78] Dallimore, *Forerunner*, p. 136.

Holy Ghost."[79]

Thirdly, and in my opinion most significantly, was Coleridge's doctrine of the Holy Spirit. The "Spirit" was not a person but a universal Spirit that indwelt all people, and the preacher was the greatest embodiment of this. When he preached, "God" was speaking. Even further, one could "learn" from this Spirit directly, apart from the written revelation and apart from the mind, by "listening" inwardly to intuition. It is my opinion that this mysticism led Irving to his views of continuing revelation and prophecy, though it is not clear if Irving rejected or accepted the Holy Spirit as a Person. Even further, if one could receive direct revelations, what would keep the Spirit from giving other gifts as He had during the age of the apostles? Here we see a man who minored in Scripture and majored in the transcendental human philosophy of the day.

It has been noted by biographers of Irving that he had an over-active imagination, being given to emotional arguments and to sensationalism, rather than to sound arguments based on the Scriptures.[80] This, along with his popularity, created an unstable Irving convinced that he was destined for some great purpose in the plan of God. As Thomas Carlyle said of Irving's mental ability: "I received a copy of Irving's defence before the Annan Presbytery, and read it with a mixture of admiration and deep pain: the man is of such heroic temper, and of head so distracted."[81] Carlyle was referring to Irving's defense of his ministry; in 1832 he was deposed as a Presbyterian minister. A year earlier he indignantly walked out of the Presbytery when it had accused him of heresy because of his doctrine of the "sinful substance" of Christ's human nature, maintaining that Jesus avoided sinful acts because of the power of the Holy Spirit, not because He was sinless. But in 1832 he was deposed. This emotionalism, sensationalism, illogic, and slippery exegesis are very much characteristic of the modern health and wealth movement.

Once again, as with Montanus of old, a number of women

---

[79] Ibid., p. 137.

[80] Ibid., p. 70ff.

[81] Ibid., p. 160.

gathered around him and became the chief "prophetesses" of his movement. Irving quickly became infatuated with himself, thinking that some great world wide mission had been committed to him.[82] Irving's baby, however, became ill and in spite of much prayer and confession the child died, and Irving admitted that he never received the gifts.[83]

An honest man served as Irving's assistant, one David Brown. "Witnessing tongues that required so much human inducement and seeing many attempted healing that failed, Brown found he could not identify himself with those things and therefore resigned his position."[84] This David Brown became the famous Brown in the widely acclaimed *Jamieson, Faussett and Brown Commentary on the Bible*. Referring to tongues as requiring "so much human inducement," he meant that initiates were given instructions in "releasing" their tongues and in uttering sounds, an artificial practice still in vogue.[85]

"In a long discourse, later printed with enlargements . . . [Irving] preached at the anniversary of the Continental Society in 1825, . . . and foretold the Second Coming of the Lord for the year 1864." Obviously, Irving was wrong. In 1827 he also published a work attributed to a Jesuit priest (named Lacunza) on the coming of Christ, entitled *The Coming of Messiah in Glory and Majesty*. (Some at Dallas Theological Seminary considered the origin of the pre-tribulation rapture theory to come from this priest.) As time went on, Irving became more and more heretical, "speaking of the 'sinful substance' of the body of Christ."[86] Like the health and wealth people today, the minors became majors; thus tongues and prophecy became the focal point of his "worship" services.

On December 4, 1834 at the age of forty-two, Irving died of tuberculosis, having been deposed from the ministry, unable to get healing for himself, opposed by most of his own

---

[82] Ibid., p. 135.

[83] Ibid., p. 153.

[84] Ibid., p. 174.

[85] For an eye witness of Irving's church service, see Warfield, *Counterfeit Miracles*, p. 297ff. The witness was the great semitic scholar of Princeton, Joseph Addison Alexander.

[86] *New Schaff-Herzog*, 6:33.

who had previously claimed to have the miracle gifts but now renounced them, burned out.[87] It was the great theologian B. B. Warfield who said that Irving chose to play with fire and got burned; and if it had not been this fire, given Irving's temperament, it would have been some other.[88]

Though the Irvingites died out rather quickly, the Catholic Apostolic Church was spawned from Irvingites in Scotland around 1835.[89] They maintained all the offices of the New Testament, apostles, prophets (and others) and all the gifts of the Spirit, especially tongues and continued revelation in prophecy, though they repudiated the label of being Irvingites. This denomination was "particularly characterized by an insistence on the nearness of Christ's return, and that teaching was especially fruitful in attracting public attention."[90] By 1900 their movement had all but died out.[91]

John Alexander Dowie (1847-1907)

John Alexander Dowie, an immigrant from Melbourne, Australia, established the Christian Catholic Apostolic Church in Zion[92] in 1896 in Chicago.[93] He claimed to be Elijah III, John the Baptist being Elijah II,[94] and strongly promoted prophecy and tongues. He is often considered a father of the miracle movement. "He loudly lumped doctors, drugs and devils in the same category and outlawed all three of them...."[95] His life ended in disgust: his daughter died in a

---

[87] Ibid., pp. 187, 188.

[88] Warfield, *Counterfeit Miracles*, p. 153.

[89] *New Schaff Herzog*, 2:457.

[90] Dallimore, *Forerunner*, p. 191.

[91] Charles Hodge discusses some of the excesses in the First Great Awakening in *The Constitutional History of the Presbyterian Church in the United States of America* (Philadelphia: Presbyterian Board of Publication, 1851), 2:11-101. These are interesting though not directly pertaining to the health and wealth gospel.

[92] The names of churches get progressively worse!

[93] *New Schaff-Herzog*, 3:40.

[94] Ibid.

[95] Bruce Barron, *The Health and Wealth Gospel* (Downers Grove: InterVarsity Press, 1987), p. 42. I recommend reading his chapter on the "Roots of the Health and Wealth Gospel." Very informative.

fire (which he said was for her disobedience); he was charged with misuse of funds and with bigamy in 1906; and he became paralyzed, dying a year later.[96]

The Twentieth Century

Smith Wigglesworth (1859-1946)

Smith was born and lived his early adult life in England. He professed faith in Christ at an early age, and the first person he "won to Christ" was his mother.[97] In reading his biography, one is impressed with the man's apparent genuineness and love for souls. He married a Polly Featherstone, who had been given a commission in the Salvation Army by William Booth.[98] Polly left the Salvation Army after their marriage, and she taught her new husband how to read and write — but not how to spell.[99] Polly "was a popular preacher for women's services and quite a favorite with men's Bible classes."[100] At this time Mrs. Wigglesworth did most of the preaching while he made a living as a plumber.

While in Leeds, England purchasing plumbing supplies, he happened on a healing meeting. He was so impressed with it that he began to send people to Leeds to be prayed for. His wife went there and was allegedly healed from an ailment which made both of them strong advocates for healing the rest of their lives. From then on the Wigglesworths taught that medicine was only for the weak in faith.[101]

Years later he came across some Pentecostals who were receiving the "baptism in the Holy Ghost." For weeks he longed for this new experience and prepared himself to receive it. Earlier he thought he had received the "baptism," but he had not spoken in tongues. He was informed that it was not the Pentecostal baptism if he had not spoken in

---

[96] Ibid., p. 43.

[97] Stanley Howard Frodsham, *Smith Wigglesworth: Apostle of Faith* (Springfield, MO: Gospel Publishing House, 1948), p. 13.

[98] Ibid., pp. 19-21.

[99] Rev. Douglas Mills says that one popular but apocryphal story is that when Smith picked up a Bible that God instantly taught him how to read.

[100] Frodsham, *Smith Wigglesworth*, p. 23.

[101] Ibid., p. 24.

tongues. Finally it came.

> I could speak no longer in English but I began to praise Him in other tongues as the Spirit of God gave me utterance. I knew then, although I might have received anointings previously, that now, at last, I had received the real baptism in the Holy Spirit as they received on the day of Pentecost.[102]

Thus healing and tongues became focal points in their (his and his wife's) ministry. We must observe how he knew that he had received the true baptism — an experience.

The Smiths went all over the world: to the USA, Australia, New Zealand, and Europe, proclaiming this "new-found" truth:

> God knew that I should have to go all over the world and proclaim this glorious truth, that all could receive the baptism in the Holy Ghost in exactly the same way as they received on the Day of Pentecost with the speaking in other tongues as the Spirit of God gives utterance.[103]

Their ministry continued for many years. Most of the modern health and wealth people have drunk deeply from the Wigglesworths' well, though only occasionally quoting them.

Essek William Kenyon (1867-1948)

In Boston mystical transcendentalism was replacing Unitarianism which emphasized human reason. There is no proper focus without understanding how popular transcendentalism was. It virtually dominated the intellectual circles with its rejection of human reason as authoritative and the acceptance of inward intuition by "going within" to seek the divinity inside ourselves. This is why the emphasis on nature was so prominent among some of the poets, for since "God" was all and all was "God," we could find "Him" (or "It") in the pureness of nature where man had not corrupted things or by going within oneself.

It was in this philosophical milieu that P. P. Quimby developed his ideas of metaphysical healing, which Mary Baker Eddy, according to Warfield, plagiarized in the founding of Christian Science. From Christian Science came The-

---

[102]Ibid., p. 44.

[103]Ibid., p. 47.

osophy and the Unity School of Christianity movements. When Kenyon attended college in Boston, which was the center of this activity, the intellectual community was buzzing with such metaphysical talk. Even more significant, the college Kenyon attended was founded to promote transcendentalism and the metaphysical ideas of the day. Kenyon drank heavily from this cup as he began his college career in 1892 at the metaphysical Emerson College of Oratory. In Kenyon we have the merging of second century gnosticism, eighteenth century German mysticism, ninteenth century transcendentalism, and the metaphysical cults.

In their zeal to demonstrate the truth of their metaphysical systems, all these cults looked to physical healing as proof of their teachings. The modern revival of faith healing did not begin with charismatics but with transcendentalism and the metaphysical cults. There was much enthusiasm for this new found truth that one could be healed by "faith" in obedience to the spiritual laws of the universe, and this healing is more popular than ever among the metaphysical cults of today as seen in the New Age movement, Edgar Casey, Christian Science, Theosophy, and Unity School Christianity. One can attend a Wednesday night service at any Christian Science church to hear testimonies of healing, or read of them in the back of *Science and Health*.

E. W. Kenyon is the twentieth century father of the Word of Faith movement, even more so than Kenneth Hagin. Kenyon is the source of their theology, and Hagin is the popularizer. The importance of Kenyon, however, is not realized by many of those who have written about the Word of Faith movement. His importance cannot be over stated. There is no idea in the Word of Faith movement (except tongues and the baptism in the Holy Spirit) that does not come directly from Kenyon.

After completing my research, I discovered D. R. McConnell. He did graduate work at Oral Roberts University, and has chronicled long comparisons between Hagin and the other Word of Faith leaders, demonstrating that virtually all the doctrines of the new charismatics come from Kenyon through Hagin to the others.[104] He has demonstrated that

---

[104] D. R. McConnell, *A Different Gospel* (Peabody, MA: Hendrikson, 1988).

Where Did They Come From?

Hagin plagiarized long sections from Kenyon, thereby impugning the integrity of Hagin. Kenyon says, "Righteousness means the ability to stand in the presence of the Father God without the sense of guilt or inferiority."[105] Hagin has said "Righteousness means the ability to stand in the presence of God without an inferiority complex, without a consciousness of sin."[106] Hagin does not give Kenyon credit.

McConnell cites a master's thesis done at Oral Roberts University by Dale H. Simmons, proving that one of Hagin's best selling booklets that has gone through twenty-one printings, *The Authority of the Believer*, plagiarized as much as seventy-five percent of John A. MacMillan's work by the same title.[107] In later editions Hagin changed the title to *The Believer's Authority* and in the foreword he says: "I came across a wonderful pamphlet entitled *The Authority of the Believer* by John A. MacMillan."[108] Coming across the pamphlet and writing a book based on it without giving credit are not the same. So much for Hagin's integrity.

In the latest edition of Hagin's book, *The Believer's Authority*, and in the latest edition of MacMillan's book, *The Authority of the Believer*, things have been changed to some extent. MacMillan's book is now a composite of his former books, *The Authority of the Believer* and *The Authority of the Intercessor*. Both Hagin and MacMillan deal primarily with Ephesians, both have chapters on prayer with similar ideas (Hagin, ch. 1; MacMillan, ch. 5). Hagin "borrows" MacMillan's definition that "authority is delegated power" (Hagin, p. 7; MacMillan, p. 12), that the source of authority is His resurrection (Hagin, p. 13; MacMillan, p. 14), and that the believer's authority is over demons, not over wills of men (Hagin, p. 57; MacMillan, p. 47), and many other such things.

A few more illustrations will demonstrate how dependent on Kenyon the Word of Faith leaders are. The distinction

---

[105] E. W. Kenyon, *Two Kinds of Righteousness*, p. 9; see also E. W. Kenyon, *The Father and His Family*, p. 281.

[106] Kenneth Hagin, *The Present Day Ministry of Jesus Christ* (Tulsa: Faith Library Publications, 1983), p. 13.

[107] McConnell, *A Different Gospel*, p. 69.

[108] Kenneth E. Hagin, *The Believer's Authority* (Tulsa: Faith Library Publications, 1992), Foreword.

between "sense" knowledge and "revelation" knowledge comes from Kenyon.[109] Charles Capps has a book entitled *Authority in Three Worlds* which comes from Kenyon.[110] Capps's bizarre explanation that Jesus was kept free from sin in the Virgin Birth because no fetus has his father's blood is from Kenyon.[111] Kenneth Copeland denies that Jesus ever claimed to be deity, which Kenyon also denied.[112] The distinction between *Zoe* life and other kinds of life that Kenneth Hagin promotes is from Kenyon.[113] The idea that Old Testament saints were not born again that Capps and Hagin promulgate is from Kenyon.[114] Hagin boldly proclaims that Christians are in the same class as God, which came from Kenyon.[115] Capps and the rest promote positive confession which imitates Kenyon;[116] says man has three parts, body, soul, and spirit;[117] maintains that the Christian is an incarnation of God (Hagin);[118] that Jesus died two deaths, physically and then spiritually when He went to hell;[119] and many other such things.

In Kenyon's writings, he did not espouse tongues or the "baptism in the Holy Spirit." It appears that the Word of Faith movement has combined Kenyon's metaphysics and Wigglesworth's Pentecostal gifts to form a new theology and a new movement.

A few more names will help us put the twentieth century in perspective. Charles Finney, who rejected every major doctrine of Christianity,[120] promoted an "experience sub-

---

[109] E. W. Kenyon, *What Happened from the Cross to the Throne*, p. 11.

[110] Ibid., p. 15.

[111] Ibid., p. 19ff.

[112] Ibid., p.25.

[113] Ibid., pp. 42, 146.

[114] Ibid., pp. 51, 75.

[115] Ibid., pp. 62-64; *The Father and His Family*, p. 41.

[116] Ibid., pp. 108, 110, 158.

[117] *The Father and His Family*, p. 56.

[118] Ibid., p. 129.

[119] Ibid., p. 162, 175ff.

[120] I have read and studied most of the works of Finney, including his *Systematic*

sequent to conversion which he called the baptism of the Holy Ghost."[121] Finney's emotional revival methods have been with us through others since his "evangelistic" campaigns, and he has done more harm to Christianity than almost any single person. Many of his human-centered ideas are in the Word of Faith movement, especially the sovereignty of man, the ability of man to obey God, and God waiting for man to *let* Him do something.

The Keswick Convention was born in England in 1875 and came to the USA under Asa Mahan, Walter Palmers and others.[122] A. J. Gordon, F. B. Meyer, A. B. Simpson, Andrew Murray, D. L. Moody and especially R. A Torrey, all promoted the idea of a second work of grace.[123] The latter two termed this second work "the baptism in the Holy Ghost."

Adoniram Judson Gordon, the pastor of the Clarendon Street Church in Boston from 1869 to 1895, wrote a book that has since been very popular with the health and wealth men, *The Ministry of Healing*. Most of the modern Word of Faith leaders have been influenced by this work and still use it today.

Hobart E. Freeman (1920-1984) was a key figure in the 1970's. Dr. Freeman received his doctorate from Grace Theological Seminary and became an instructor in Old Testament and Hebrew in 1961. I have Dr. Freeman's book, *An Introduction to the Old Testament Prophets*, published by Moody Press in 1968 (6th printing in 1973), and it is a fairly good work. But his theology began to falter, and he was asked to leave the seminary after a year and a half. He went to Chicago and started his own ministry, where he strictly forbade anyone from going to a doctor. As a consequence of this, many in his church died from unnecessary medical problems. By 1984 "the number of documented, unnecessary deaths" attributed

---

Theology, which is neither systematic nor a theology. In the first few chapters, Finney presents his gospel of human works. Later in the book he rejects the substitutionary work of Christ, maintains that we are justified by our obedience, and other heresies.

[121] Frederick Dale Bruner, *A Theology of the Holy Spirit* (Grand Rapids: Wm. B. Eerdmans Publishing Co., 1970), p. 41; see also B. B. Warfield, *Perfectionism* (Philadelphia, PA: Presbyterian and Reformed Pub. Co., 1959), p. 52ff.

[122] Ibid., p. 44.

[123] Ibid., p. 45.

to his ministry were 90.[124] And even though he himself is now dead, his church still conducts services and the deaths are still mounting. The Lord Jesus said you would know them by their fruits (Matt. 7:16).

Oral Roberts

Oral Roberts is the Pentecostal Holiness evangelist turned Methodist who is known world wide. His ministry has extended to millions. His son, Richard, seems to be the heir apparent even though he has been divorced and flunked out of Oral Roberts University. At age twenty Richard had already been hired by his father and was elected president of the Oral Roberts Association.[125] Oral also has two daughters.

Roberts sends out millions of pieces of mail each year and receives hundreds of thousands of calls annually.[126] He claims that the ministry to which God has called him is healing. It is to his credit that he does not disparage doctors and medicine as most do, and he has built a hospital in Tulsa (though it since has gone out of business). Wayne Robinson, who worked closely with Oral Roberts for years, wrote a biography entitled *Oral*. In it he says Oral Roberts was known as the "praying" evangelist while Billy Graham was known as the "preaching" evangelist.

Robinson states that few — if any — of the people who came to him for healing were ever healed. They would say they were healed to keep from hurting Oral's feelings or his ministry.[127] Even Mr. Robinson who worked with him went to doctors and did not believe in healing.[128] This does not mean, though, that the people he prayed for were not helped, says Robinson. "At least fifteen percent were helped in a tangible way,"[129] (whatever that means).

Does Oral Roberts preach the Gospel? I have listened to him for twenty years, and I have never once heard him preach the Gospel. The music is good, and the atmosphere always

---

[124] Baron, *Health and Wealth Gospel*, p. 23.

[125] Ibid., p. 130.

[126] Wayne A. Robinson, *Oral* (Los Angeles: Acton House, 1976), pp. 2-3.

[127] Ibid., p. 9.

[128] Ibid., p. 11.

[129] Ibid., p. 30.

positive — but no Gospel. I listened all those years with the express purpose of seeing what "gospel" he preached, and it has always been "seed-faith" or occasionally healing for the body. Not once have I heard him preach Jesus and Him crucified, that one receives forgiveness of sins by trusting in the death and resurrection of Christ. Perhaps Oral has preached this when I was not listening, but at best the true biblical Gospel, receives poor priority next to "seed-faith" and healing.

In fact Patti Roberts, who was married to Richard Roberts and later wrote a book about the Robertses, stated that she became disillusioned with her part on the Oral Roberts TV show and called the president of the Oral Roberts Evangelistic Association. Here is the conversation:

> "Al," I said, "in the forty shows that we taped last year, how many times did we give people the plan of salvation?"
>
> "The plan of salvation? Gosh, Patti, I don't know. I'm sure we must have given it to them at least once," he said.
>
> "And how many times did we give them the principles of Seed-Faith?"
>
> He laughed. "Patti, you know the answer to that. We give the principles of Seed-Faith on every show."
>
> "Al, in the letters that you received from viewers, how many of them thought that maybe if they gave money to Oral, they had bought a little place in the Kingdom? How many may have thought that swayed God's opinion about their eternal destiny?"
>
> He didn't answer for a long time. When he finally replied he lowered his voice and said soberly and a bit hesitantly, "A whole lot of them did, Patti."[130]

What the "plan of salvation" is Patti does not say, but at least she was extremely concerned. This concern cost her her marriage, as Richard and especially Oral would not allow dissidence and encouraged Richard to get a divorce for the sake of the "ministry." Richard asked Patti for the divorce, stating that he would give her the children but that he would have to remarry for the sake of his image in the Oral Roberts

---

[130]Patti Roberts, *Ashes to Gold* (New York: Jove Books, 1987), p. 122.

"ministry."[131]

What is Oral Roberts' theology? Does he believe the Bible? It is painful to say that his theology is unclear. Mr. Robinson said that he taught Oral theology, especially from such contemporary "theologians" as Reinhold Neibuhr, who was anything but orthodox. At one point Roberts wanted Robinson to give a series of lectures on contemporary theology to the seminary connected with Oral Roberts University. Here is what Robinson said:

> Oral had come to believe there was a correlation between his beliefs and those of several celebrated contemporary thinkers. We had talked about theology for hours on our travels. He was especially impressed with the existentialists, and his sermons began to speak to the importance of relating one's beliefs to one's own experience and existence.[132]

This is disturbing, obviously, for existentialists do not believe the Bible. Robinson does say, though, that "There was never a hint of Oral's forsaking his beliefs; he had simply found a new language to express them." But what beliefs? Robinson does not say. In listening to Oral Roberts for years and reading ten or so of his books, I still don't know what he believes about the Virgin Birth, the infallibility of Scripture, the deity of Christ, heaven, hell, or anything else. At best we can say that Oral is not very perceptive to have a Robinson working closely with him for years who (Robinson) loved contemporary theology, thought of heaven as "a mode of talking about the external worth of all creation," and could not give a satisfactory answer about the Virgin Birth.[133] We hope that Oral has not succumbed to this, but when one listens and reads another for years and cannot state clearly what he believes, then the communicator is either incompetent, a liberal, or has something to hide.

One may wonder where Oral Roberts got some of his techniques; according to Robinson they came from Gene Ewing, a slick communications man. Mr. Roberts sought his advice when things started going badly financially for him in

---

[131] Ibid., p. 137.

[132] Robinson, *Oral*, p. 95.

[133] Ibid., p. 97.

1968. What techniques? Here is what Mr. Ewing suggested to Oral: (1) Go to the prayer tower and make it central in his appeal to the people; (2) send a letter to millions and tell them he was going to pray for them; (3) he (Oral) would take their letters with him to the prayer tower; (4) there should be no requests for money.[134] Mr. Ewing suggested a picture of Oral Roberts to be in the letter, smiling, with Bible in hand with this caption: "Something good is going to happen to you." Now you know where this slogan came from, a marketing genius! Also Christian prosperity was advised, called the "Blessing Pact." "Give God a dollar and He'll bless you with two" was the idea.[135] Of course it was strongly suggested that the money be given to God by giving to Oral Roberts. Oral took all these suggestions, except that he called his prosperity message "Seed-Faith."

Patti Roberts commented that though at one time the ministry was oriented toward helping people now it existed to serve itself. "We used sophisticated marketing techniques to sell Jesus," she confesses.[136]

Does God use Oral Roberts to heal? He wears glasses, has had sinus surgery, and constantly takes allergy medicine. His daughter in law, Patti Roberts, almost died in the birth of their second child even though Oral had prayed for her personally.[137] The answer is obvious.

Others

Kathryn Kuhlman was very popular at one time. She began her preaching career in 1923.[138] She traveled with a fellow evangelist, Burroughs Waltrip, who left his wife to marry Miss Kuhlman, but the marriage only lasted six years.[139] She had a CBS television program that lasted from 1950 to 1976, the year she died. Mr. Barron says of her: "She never made high-pressure appeals for financial support. She constantly attributed any and all miracles to the power of the Holy

---

[134]Ibid., p. 106.

[135]Ibid., p. 107.

[136]Roberts, *Ashes to Gold*, p. 119.

[137]Ibid., p. 81.

[138]Barron, *The Health and Wealth Gospel*, p. 51.

[139]Ibid.

Spirit, not to any power within herself. She insisted on medical verification of healing before she would include the stories in her books. Her services were dramatic but not hysterical."[140] From my reading of her, this much seems to be accurate.

Her doctrinal statement in *I Believe in Miracles*[141] is inoffensive. She appears to be Trinitarian, which is certainly biblical, and she also believes that the Holy Spirit is sovereign: "It was foreordained from before the foundation of the world, that the Holy Spirit should be dominant and controlling in the church." This is more than Charles Capps would say.

She is, however, ambiguous regarding the Gospel. She speaks of "salvation" being a definite experience (whatever that may mean), "by simple faith, belief in God's Son, and acceptance of Him as Divine Saviour, the guilty sinner is *made* righteous" [emphasis mine]. She does not explain what she means by "experience" or by "salvation." In Scripture the words for "salvation" sometimes mean "justification," "sanctification," or "glorification" or all the above. It would appear that she means "justification," in which case she is either careless, ignorant, or heretical. In justification the sinner is not *made* righteous; he is *declared to be* righteous.

The whole essence of the Gospel turns on her statement that "the guilty sinner is *made* righteous." This is what Roman Catholics teach while Protestants, reflecting the Bible, have emphasized and taught that we are *declared* to be righteous. If the difference sounds like picky theology, then there is a desperate need for some careful thought. If we are accepted by God only when we are *made* righteous, then when are we made righteous? The answer is, not in this life, and the answer of Roman Catholicism is by our works. They say that we earn our acceptance by our works as we strive to be made righteous enough to be accepted by Him. (See Chapter Thirteen.)

Bill Hamon, a so-called modern day prophet, says that the modern day prophets "prepare the way for the Second Coming of Christ."[142] A familiar theme, isn't it? He states that

---

[140] Ibid., p.52.

[141] Kathryn Kuhlman, *I Believe in Miracles* (New York: Pyramid Books, 1970), pp. 220ff.

[142] Bill Hamon, *Prophets and Personal Prophecy* (Shippensburg, PA: Destiny

healing and prophecy were restored to the church in the 1880's,[143] obviously admitting that these gifts were not practiced for many centuries. He even claims that the Aaronic priesthood was restored in 1948.[144] The Mormons would not like to hear that as they claim it was restored under Joseph Smith last century! Hamon approves of women pastors.[145] He goes even further by stating that apostles are back.[146] There is no end to the eccentric, unbiblical practices one finds when one opens the "Pandora's box" of new revelations in addition to the Bible.

Conclusion

Irenaeus (A. D. 130-200) described the gnostic interpreters of his day: ". . . every one of them generates something new every day, according to his ability; for, among them, no one is considered mature who does not develop some enormous fictions."[147] "There is nothing new under the sun"! So the Word of Faith leaders are always inventing some new truth, which seals new followers to them as they hear a new idea that was supposedly never known in church history. The more bizarre it is, the more the inventor is required to say God told him the "truth" in visions or dreams, or maybe that Jesus Himself appeared to him/her and related this astonishing new truth. He must proclaim it vehemently and with a martyr's complex to disarm in advance any criticisms.

An excellent summary of our historical survey is provided by theologian Frederick Bruner:

> The ancestral line of the Pentecostal movement [gifts movement] could appear to stretch from the enthusiastic Corinthians (1 Cor. 12-14) or even the Old Testament anointed and ecstatic (Num. 11; 1 Sam. 10), through the gnostics of all varieties, the Montanists, the medieval and the pre-Refor-

---

Image, 1987), p. 23.

[143] Ibid., pp. 37, 38.

[144] Ibid., p. 56.

[145] Ibid., p. 84.

[146] Ibid., p. 61.

[147] Elaind Pagels, *Adam, Eve, and the Serpent* (New York: Vintage Books, 1989), p. 64.

mation spiritualists, [which we did not cover] the so-called radical, left-wing, or Anabaptists movements, the **Schwärmer** of the Reformation period [not covered], the post-Reformation Quakers and, when given fresh new parentage through the Pietist, Wesleyan, and revivalist movements of the seventeenth and eighteenth centuries in Germany, England, and the United States, continuing in the first half of the nineteenth century briefly but very interestingly through Edward Irving in England, and lengthily and very influentially through Charles Finney in America, issuing in the latter half of the nineteenth century in the higher-life and holiness movements which gave birth to their twentieth-century child, the Pentecostal movement.[148]

Every discipline builds on the shoulders of its predecessors, but these self-proclaimed theologians are starting over. What would you say if your doctor said that he had thrown out all his training, in fact had not been trained, that all those who attended medical school were those who had "a big education but knowing nothing about" medicine? Would you let him do open heart surgery on you? That is precisely what these men are doing! They are doing spiritual surgery on the hearts of their followers, and then they pre-prejudice their admirers against those who have learned from the past with statements like the one from Kenneth Hagin. No one doubts that the Bible — not history, theologians, nor any one person's theology — is the final authority, but the Lord commanded us to learn from others: "And the things that you have heard from me among many witnesses, commit these to faithful men who will be able to teach others also" (2 Tim. 2:2). Why did He give us gifted men to the church down through the centuries (Eph. 4:11ff.) if not to equip His church? Ignorance is not to be gloried in. The best way to avoid theological pot holes is to know where they are, not to be ignorant of them.

In all candor, the Word of Faith people probably do not

---

[148]Frederick Dale Bruner, *A Theology of the Holy Spirit* (Grand Rapids: Wm. B. Eerdmans Publishing Co., 1970), p. 35. This is an excellent book on the "gifts" movement throughout history as well as an excellent exegetical analysis of virtually all New Testament passages on the gifts, especially the baptism of the Holy Spirit. It is definitive, and absolutely unanswerable. If you read only one book listed in my notes, this is it. Not for those who do not like to think.

realize that their heresies are, for the most part, not new. They do not know that they have severely departed from the faith, for they have not (in all probability) studied the errors of the past. This does not excuse them, and it demonstrates with what arrogance they pursue their doctrines when they refuse to be instructed from the great men of former centuries. As Calvin said of the Libertines of his day: "[They] introduce nothing new with respect to the principal articles of all their teachings, but rather since the time of the apostles there have existed similar heretics . . . ."[149]

A few basic questions must be faced by the modern "Montanists": How do we explain the absence of the miracle gifts and of their distinctives for so many centuries? If the church matured and grew over the centuries without such "gifts" and especially without the health and wealth gospel, then why are they needed now? Furthermore, if they are necessary for Christian growth, then how did the church grow for centuries without them? How did the world's greatest revival, under the Protestant Reformers, change the course of the Western world without the health and wealth formulas? If the Holy Spirit brought millions into the fold without these, and there can be no question that He did, then why are these things necessary now? Why is the restoration of the Word of Faith emphases any different than the restoration of the Gospel, which is claimed by so many cults today, such as the Jehovah's Witnesses, Mormons, Christian Scientists, and others? As R. L. Dabney rightly stated, "Such arrogance [in ignoring the past] is the surest sign of heedlessness and superficiality."[150]

---

[149]Calvin, *Treatises Against the Anabaptists*, p. 191.

[150]R. L. Dabney, *Christ Our Penal Substitute* (Harrisonburg, VA: Sprinkle Publications, 1978), p. 100.

3

What Governs the Universe?

Metaphysical Law

O Lord of hosts, God of Israel, the One who dwells between the cherubim, You are God, *You alone*, of all the kingdoms of the earth. You have made heaven and earth (Isa. 37:16).

Everything the health and wealth people believe is based on their concept of spiritual or metaphysical law. Therefore, an understanding of their belief about this law is eminently important. Several of their most important doctrines arise from metaphysical law. Man is identified with God in some metaphysical way that enables him to manipulate his circumstances by obedience to spiritual law and to receive new revelations in his "spirit man." This new knowledge enables him to be healed, get wealthy, control the weather, and get just about anything he pleases. In other words, *he becomes a little god.*

What Is Spiritual Law?

According to the metaphysicians, spiritual law is basically a metaphysical law that is neutral and perfunctory.[1] It is neutral because it is impersonal and can be used for good or for evil. It is perfunctory because it will work automatically, every time we engage it. Spiritual law functions as naturally as day follows night. According to this theory, we relate to the metaphysical laws more than to a personal God. In the metaphysical cults, there is no personal God. The new charismatics have adapted the concept by teaching that though the laws are impersonal, the personal God of the Bible has bound

---

[1] Robert Russell, *God Works Through Faith* (Marina del Rey, CA: DeVross & Co., 1957), p. 85.

Himself by these laws. Thus both metaphysics and the Word of Faith theology state that impersonal, metaphysical law rules the universe and that "faith" governs impersonal law.[2] For example Kenneth Copeland says:

> We must understand that there are laws governing every single thing in existence. Nothing is by accident. There are laws of the world of the spirit, and there are laws of the world of the natural. . . . We need to realize that the spiritual world and its laws are more powerful than the physical world and its laws. Spiritual law gave birth to physical law. The world and the physical forces governing it were created by the power of faith — a spiritual force. God, a Spirit, created all matter . . . with the force of faith.[3]

These statements by Copeland reveal the gnostic dualism between matter and spirit that is so dominant in the Word of Faith writings. Furthermore, Fred Price says: "There has to be another world, another realm where faith is the law."[4] Again he states: "You need to know that there is a law of words."[5] We shall see in Chapter Eight that the law of words is positive confession, or "you get what you say."

Furthermore, this neutrality of spiritual law is very much like the *Star Wars* movies in which "The Force" could be used for evil or good. The Force was neutral, perfunctory, and impersonal. Luke Skywalker and Yoda used it for good, but Darth Vader used it for evil. If you confess properly with your mouth, the Force or law will be with you; if not, it will be against you.

Obviously, such a system does not have God's moral or ethical laws but metaphysical laws. By contrast, God's moral laws are not metaphysically neutral but ethically good and personal since God is personal. In the Bible we relate to a personal God based on pure grace, not to impersonal laws based on one's works or verbal confessions.

---

[2] Russell, *God Works Through Faith*, p. 17.

[3] Kenneth Copeland, *The Laws of Prosperity* (Ft. Worth: KCP Publications, 1974, 1989), p. 15.

[4] Frederick K. C. Price, *Living in the Realm of the Spirit* (Tulsa: Harrison House, 1989), p. 17.

[5] Ibid., p. 27.

If we understand their concept of spiritual law, then it is clear why they think miracles are normal. Mrs. Eddy, the foundress of Christian Science, says, "The miracle introduces no disorder, but unfolds the primal order, establishing the Science of God's unchangeable law."[6] If the world is governed by impersonal spiritual laws, then the only hindrance to having a modern miracle is your faith.

On the other hand, if Jesus and His miracles were unique, then miracles are not normative. If God is personal and governs the world personally, not like some deistic God who made laws and left the world to work out its own fate, then spiritual law is moral and personal. Only God can alter physical laws and perform miracles. Only God is in charge of what happens.

Other statements from the metaphysical writers confirm these things:

> [Man] had need for the spiritual laws of God.[7]

> We know that we live in a mental world, and to know this is the key to life. . . . If children could be taught only one thing, they should be taught that this is a mental world. I would let all the other things go and teach them this. . . .[8] The universe is governed by law, and there is no such thing as a broken law.[9]

According to them, it is the mental world that controls the physical world, spiritual law that controls physical law.

How Do These Laws Work?

These spiritual laws allegedly work by our mental processes, such as knowledge, faith, and visualization.

Knowledge

To them sin is ignorance (metaphysical) rather than dis-

---

[6] Mary Baker Eddy, *Science and Health*, p. 135.

[7] Agnes Sanford, *The Healing Power of the Bible* (San Francisco Publishers, 1984), p. 31. Unfortunately, her books are sometimes recommended by otherwise orthodox Christian writers, demonstrating how easily one can be taken in. Her books are undiluted from the occult, magic, and New Age teachings.

[8] Emmet Fox, *The Mental Equivalent* (Unity Village, MO: Unity School of Christianity, no date), p. 4.

[9] Ibid., p. 21.

obedience (ethical), and if a person has right knowledge then he can get what he wants.

> As we understand the laws that govern this world and work in agreement with them, then we can reap the harvest God has provided in the spirit world. . . .[10]

> Jesus Christ was the greatest of metaphysicians and gave us definite rules for controlling conditions through word and thought. You must answer every negative thought with a word of authority . . . The army of the aliens will chant: "Business is dull and money is scarce." Immediately you reply, "My supply comes from God and now appears like mushrooms overnight."[11]

> With all your getting, get understanding; understanding of the working of Spiritual Law, so that we distribute this power within us in a constructive way.[12]

> Every right thought that we think, our every unselfish word or action, is bound by immutable laws to be fraught with good results.[13]

> The mental and spiritual world or realms are governed by laws that are just as real and unfailing as the laws that govern the natural world. Certain conditions of mind are so connected with certain results that the two are inseparable. If we have the one, we must have the other, as surely as the night follows the day. . . .[14]

> It is a mental law that any idea held firmly in the mind expresses itself in the body and affairs. . . .[15] The greatest force in his life is his consciousness of Oneness with God.[16]

Man controls conditions by a knowledge of Spiritual law.

---

[10] Charles Capps, *The Substance of Things* (Tulsa: Harrison House, 1990), p. 34.

[11] Florence Scovel Shinn, *The Power of the Spoken Word* (Marina del Rey, CA: DeVross & Co., 1945), p. 26.

[12] Ibid., p. 36.

[13] H. Emilie Cady, *Lessons in Truth* (Unity Village, MO: Unity School of Christianity, no date), p. 10.

[14] Ibid., pp. 64-65.

[15] Russell, *God Works Through Faith*, p. 99.

[16] Ibid., p. 140.

> Suppose your problem is lack or limitation. Your urgent need is supply. Link with this God-power within, and give thanks for your immediate supply.[17]

We see that either the simple acquiring of knowledge guarantees power or else that great knowledge leads to massive metaphysical power. Either way knowledge is the key to unlock "secret" powers of the metaphysical laws governing the world. According to Scripture, knowledge is indeed important but only because it leads to an ethical understanding of the triune God, to a *personal* relationship with Him based on grace, not because it gains us power over Him.

Faith Is a Spiritual Force

There is no separate chapter on faith in this book though the Word of Faith leaders speak and write on faith more than any other subject. Because their concept of faith is connected with spiritual law, we have included it here. (A further discussion of faith is found in the subject appendix.)

The faith that is taught by these men is not personal faith in a loving God but a "magnetic" force directed *at* these laws to control them. They often say that "faith is a force," by which they mean that faith controls, directs, and manipulates the metaphysical laws to the end the person has mentally directed them. If one wants prosperity, he must use faith to harness the laws which will create circumstances that bring in money. Likewise, if one is healed, he is only using his faith to exploit the laws to his own advantage. Notice these confirming quotes:

> If Jesus hadn't known that the man with the palsy could get up and walk, he couldn't have walked even when Jesus commanded him to walk. The power was not in the command, **Arise**, but in the belief or mental equivalent that Jesus held.[18]

> Trust in Spiritual law and "it will be given to you."[19]

> Another truth is that the demand must be made before the supply can come forth to fill it. . . that our asking is simply our complying with an unfailing law which is bound to work; there

---

[17] Shinn, *The Power of the Spoken Word*, p. 21.

[18] Ibid., p. 150.

[19] Ibid., p. 15.

is no escape from it.[20]

In its static form, faith is neutral and impersonal. Anyone can use it for any purpose. It has no choice or desire of its own.... But the requirements of faith must be met. There must be absolute conformity to its Law.[21]

A numinous quality, an emanation of that kind of spiritual energy that we call faith, seems to connect with the very book [Bible] itself.[22]

Help me to use my faith to set in motion the power that transforms nothing into something and zero into everything.... Now be with me and help me to release my faith to You that needs may be met in my life.[23]

Faith ... is a superior force over fear and it brings about miracles.[24]

The new charismatics also have much to say about these so-called metaphysical laws. Bob Buess wrote *The Laws of the Spirit* in which he taught that Jesus always "operated" as a man while on earth, using the same spiritual laws by faith in God like you and I have to do.[25] Charles Capps discusses the laws pertaining to healing and other things as we shall see throughout the book.[26] Likewise Copeland agrees that the spiritual force of faith must be "released" to manipulate spiritual laws:

... spiritual law would be useless if the force of faith were not a real force; but faith *is* a real force. Faith is a spiritual force, a spiritual energy, a spiritual power. It is this force of faith which makes the laws of the spirit world function.[27]

---

[20] Cady, *Lessons*, pp. 66-67; see Capps, *Angels*, p. 91ff.

[21] Russell, *God Works Through Faith*, pp. 130-131. Rev. Doug Mills says that a Word of Faith pastor in Birmingham said that the rankest unbeliever could use the name "Jesus" to get whatever he wanted.

[22] Sanford, *Healing Power*, p. 7.

[23] Oral Roberts, *Prayers for Seed-Faith Living* (Tulsa: Oral Roberts, 1970), p. 87.

[24] Oral Roberts, *Seed-Faith Scriptures with Personal Commentary* (Tulsa: Oral Roberts, 1972), p. 23.

[25] Bob Buess, *The Laws of the Spirit* (Van, TX: Bob Buess, 1968), p. 36.

[26] Charles & Annette Capps, *Angels* (Tulsa: Harrison House, 1984), p. 91ff.

[27] Copeland, *The Laws of Prosperity*, pp. 15, 16.

What Governs the Universe: Spiritual Law

This last quote reveals why the Word of Faith movement is so preoccupied with faith and man, and not with the object of faith, the Triune God. God has done all He can, the Universe is governed by spiritual law, and now one must learn how to use his faith according to these laws to get what he wants. One can get *anything* he wants by faith, they are constantly telling their followers; and when things inevitably do not work out the way they were told, endless books roll off the presses explaining how the follower did not use his faith properly. Constant frustration is the inevitable result.

Instead of preaching the object of faith, the sovereign Triune God, they preach faith itself to allegedly sovereign man who supposedly has the moral power to pump-up faith from a totally sinful heart (Jer. 17:9; Gen. 6:5). (See paragraph beginning with "The point being made" on page 372.) Since sinful man has the innate ability to create faith in his own heart, the only hindrance is for him to realize that and do it. Thus, endless books are written to show man how to manipulate himself properly so he can have "faith" and in turn manipulate the metaphysical laws to his advantage. Instead of faith being a *moral* persuasion in the infinite personal God, it is a *metaphysical force* directed at metaphysical laws. Just as rising and falling magnetism will induce current in a coil, so our rising or falling metaphysical magnetism ("faith") will induce the spiritual laws to bring about what we have "decreed," whether that is health, wealth, or something bad we have inadvertently brought on ourselves. In lieu of faith being *submission* to God it is *control* over Him and the metaphysical laws that allegedly control the universe. Thus the myriad books on faith tell man how to analyze himself to determine why his faith is not working, not to trust in the God who makes all things work together for the saint's good. Man controls, not God. (There is no providence, according to them.) Faith, therefore, according to the Word of Faith leaders *originates* within man; its *nature* is metaphysical; its *object* is the metaphysical laws to manipulate the "force" for one's desires; and its *purpose* is for selfish ends. In Scripture faith is *created within* by God (Phil. 1:29; Acts 13:48; 16:14; 18:27), its *nature* is moral and submissive, its *object* is the Triune God, and its *purpose* is to glorify God and to serve Him. We could not have more contradictory concepts of faith.

According to Paul Cho, the pastor of the half-million member church in Seoul, South Korea, there are four principles of faith to correctly harness spiritual law.[28] Because leaders like Cho promise the impossible to their people, they are continually being embarrassed, having to devise new rules to make sure one used his faith correctly and to explain the failure of their followers. Cho had to rationalize that the reason three girls from his church drowned when they tried to use their faith to cross a swollen, raging river is that they did not understand the difference between a *logos* word from God and a *rhema* word from God. (See paragraph beginning with "Oral Roberts says" on page 217.) It is incredible that people choose to believe such nonsense.

Hagin and his followers have written most of their books on faith and the myriad "rules" to make it work. They guarantee the moon to their followers, but one must follow precisely the "rules" of the leaders. Since "rules" vary according to the leader, the followers are habitually frustrated and constantly seek the leaders to "adjust" their faith.

Visualization

Not only knowledge and faith but also visualization is very important in harnessing so-called spiritual laws. Visualization is the metaphysical technique of using what one sees, imagines, or intensely desires in his mind to create the corresponding reality in the physical world. The Word of Faith leaders rarely use the word "visualization" in their writings (the metaphysical cults regularly use it), but it can be recognized as "desiring intensely," using a mental image, picturing the results in your mind as you pray, using your imagination to picture the goal, proclaiming to others that you have something (such as physical healing) even when the symptoms scream the opposite, and many other such things. The point is that one cannot expect results unless he can "believe" (visualize) that the outcome is sure. This "believing" is picturing the end result.

Cho says we must "envision a clear-cut objective."[29] He explains: "There are laws in the spiritual realm, and you have

---

[28] Paul Yonggi Cho, *The Fourth Dimension* (South Plainfield, NJ: 1979), p. 9ff.

[29] Ibid., p. 9.

endless resources in your heart."[30] He elaborates: ". . . the only way for us to incubate [create what we want] is through our imaginations, through our visions and dreams." He quotes Proverbs: "'Where there is no vision the people perish.' If you have no vision, you are not being creative. . . ."[31] The Proverbs passage, however, is better translated: "Where there is no revelation, the people cast off restraint; but happy is he who keeps the law" (Prov. 29:18). The Hebrew word for "vision" means "special revelation," the law of God, not a goal or one's imagination. Typically, a weak view of the original languages leads to unbiblical conclusions.

Cho says that Abraham, Jacob, Joseph, and others had to use the metaphysical law of imagination or visualization to bring about changes in their lives. He cites Jacob's acquiring spotted cattle as a prime example of using visualization to create what is desired. According to him, this is using your "fourth dimension" imagination to make changes in the "third dimension" physical realm, or using the metaphysical laws to make changes in the physical world.[32] If we do not present the proper mental blueprint to God, there is nothing He can do; but if we do present the proper imagination, then He *must* give us what we ask, Cho explains.

Hinduism, New Age, occult practices, mind sciences, and others have used this technique for centuries. Mary Baker Eddy in *Science and Health* repeatedly proclaims that illness is a product of incorrect thinking, and one can get rid of the symptoms by visualizing his own health. Visualization would not be effective if man were not assumed to be God-like with creative powers. Thus the assumption of visualization is that the mind of man is creative. In New Age, occultism, Christian Science and other metaphysical cults man is considered either God or God-like, which is pantheism, which is straight from hell. We see these same beliefs in the Word of Faith movement.

Robert Schuller wrote the foreword to Cho's *The Fourth Dimension*, stating that even unbelievers can learn how to use their inward spiritual strength. Spiritual law works well for

---

[30] Ibid., p. 30.

[31] Ibid., p. 44.

[32] Ibid., p. 53ff.

both Christian and non-Christian, indicating that one relates to God through spiritual law rather than through the Gospel. Cho agrees: "Now unbelievers, by exploring and developing their inner spiritual being in such a way, can carry out dominion upon their third dimension, which includes their physical sickness and diseases."[33] The fourth dimension controls the third dimension and the third the second, and so on. Each writer tends to develop his own vocabulary, but the essence of what they say is the same.

Allegedly God told Cho that this is how Pharoah's magicians in Moses' day did miracles; that is, they used their inner spiritual strengths (fourth dimension) to exercise dominion over the physical world (third dimension), changing their circumstances and healing people. Cho uses the same explanation for the physical healings among the Buddhists and Sokagakkai in South Korea. He commends non-Christians all over the world for using the laws of the fourth dimension to determine their own realities.

It is a serious departure from Scripture to attribute spiritual strengths to unbelievers, who are dead in their sins. Indeed, this is to promote spiritual, metaphysical law that is available to everyone, Buddhist, Shintoist, New Ager, and all others, who can control their circumstances and their bodies, if only they will learn how to "tap into it." What need then is there for a personal relationship with God? What need is there of forgiveness of sins and the Gospel if one can determine his own station in life, his prosperity, circumstances, and bodily healing by his own use of spiritual law through visualization?

In contrast to neutral metaphysical laws, God's moral laws can only be used for good, and the one who violates them suffers both His temporal (read Deut. 8 and 28) and eternal judgment (Rom. 6:23). His moral laws are not morally neutral but positive, and they are not metaphysical laws governing the whole world in some neutral way — God personally governs the world (see Chapter Ten).

Similar to visualization is positive confession, the former being mental and the latter verbal. Both are supposed to engage certain spiritual laws that will "manifest" (cause to

---

[33]Ibid., p. 40.

happen) in our lives what we have "decreed" mentally or verbally. The metaphysical cults speak primarily of mental visualization while the Word of Faith teachers usually refer to verbalizing. As Unity writer Shinn puts it, "Science is discovering the power within the atom; metaphysics teaches the power within thoughts and words."[34] When one confesses the right words verbally, he allegedly invokes a spiritual law that works automatically. Just as electricity is *provided*,[35] so God's laws are only potential until we "plug into" His power. The laws are always there and always *potentially* operative, but it is up to us to use them properly.[36] If we confess rightly, using the right words and keep on using them over and over (vain repetitions!), then the spiritual laws will work *for* us; but if we confess wrongly, then they will work *against* us.

Kenneth Hagin, the primary Word of Faith leader, speaks of this supposed metaphysical law: "Our confession will either imprison us or set us free. Our confession is the result of our believing, and our believing is the result of our right or wrong thinking."[37] Again, "It is our confession . . . that creates the reality, and then it becomes real in our lives."[38] Oral Roberts thinks that our confessions, especially as manifested in seed-faith, will cause us, by spiritual law, to reap what we sow.[39] If you are negative, according to Roberts, you "block the flow of God's intervention in your behalf."[40] Likewise Capps: "Whether you realize it or not, you frame your world with your words daily."[41]

---

[34] Shinn, *The Power of the Spoken Word*, p. 49.

[35] A key buzz word in Arminianism is *provided*. God's grace, promises, and laws are only potential until we actuate them. It is all up to us.

[36] Charles Capps, *Dynamics of Faith & Confession* (Tulsa: Harrison House, 1987), p. 63ff.

[37] Kenneth Hagin, *Right and Wrong Thinking* (Tulsa: Kenneth Hagin Ministries, 1989), p. 7.

[38] Ibid.

[39] Oral Roberts, *Miracle of Seed-Faith* (Tulsa: Oral Roberts, 1970), p. 125.

[40] Ibid., p. 148.

[41] Capps, *The Substance of Things*, p. 10.

Who Is Subject to Spiritual Law?

According to Word of Faith teachers, God Himself is subject to spiritual law and works through it. In both metaphysics and the new beliefs of the new charismatics, we and God create our own reality by this law[42] so we must learn all we can about it.

> Even though God had the image inside Him and the Spirit of God was there to cause it to come to pass, **it had to be released out of His mouth before any changes could take place** [emphasis added]. . . .[43] God used His words to bring the image into manifestation. He filled His words with the spiritual force of faith. . . .[44]

> Even Jesus could not have done it in any other way because this is a cosmic law.[45]

> So if we decree or affirm unwaveringly, steadfastly, we hold God by His own unalterable laws to do the establishing or fulfilling. . . .[46] There are some things that God has so indissolubly joined together that it is impossible for even Him to put them asunder. They are bound together by fixed, immutable laws; if we have one of them, we must have the other.[47]

Cho states[48] that God used the law of the fourth dimension — in cooperation with Abraham since God can do nothing without our using the spiritual laws — to bring about the renewal of Abraham's body to have a child at the age of one hundred. It follows then that we are a god, in the same basic class as God Almighty, with access to the same forces that He uses. This is precisely the lie of the devil to Eve when he deceived her that she could be like God by taking the fruit, that there was a law above God that both she and God were subject to, and that God knew that if she took the fruit she

---

[42] Russell, *God Works Through Faith*, p. 68.

[43] Charles Capps, *God's Image of You* (Tulsa: Harrison House, 1985), p. 48.

[44] Ibid., p. 51.

[45] Fox, *The Mental Equivalent*, p. 23.

[46] Cady, *Lessons*, p. 52.

[47] Ibid., p. 64.

[48] Cho, *The Fourth Dimension*, pp. 48-49

would be in His class, determining her own reality. God promptly demonstrated, however, that there were no laws above Him when He judged Adam, Eve, and the serpent for disobedience to Him!

Conclusion

It is clear how firmly rooted in metaphysics the health and wealth movement is. I have not seen *anything* in the Word of Faith that is not also in metaphysics except tongues and the baptism in the Holy Spirit. The Word of Faith people make minor adjustments in the metaphysical terms and concepts to make the teaching seem biblical, even using evangelical terms, but the content is basically the same. Even the particular verses both groups use to support health, wealth, and positive confession are essentially the same.

If man is made in God's image and the world is governed by spiritual law, laws that even God is subject to, then man can do nearly anything God can do. This is the theology and assumption of those both in the metaphysical cults and in the health and wealth movement. If spiritual laws control the world, then they take precedence over the physical laws. Therefore, we can by "faith" command sickness to leave our bodies (Chapters Four through Six), money to come in (Chapter Seven), trials to abate — in short, we can create our own realities. Any problems we have are self-inflected because we have not used the spiritual laws correctly, such as the law of positive confession (Chapter Eight). We are a part of "God" and He is part of us, therefore, we can discover for ourselves which spiritual laws govern the universe (Chapter Three). It is "up to us," to use one of their favorite expressions, to have success. This means that man is sovereign over "God" and the world (Chapter Ten). If all these things are true, how do these beliefs affect the Person and work of Christ (Chapter Twelve) and the Gospel (Chapter Thirteen)? "Faith," as formed by the proper knowledge and expressed in a spiritual force through visualization and positive confession, is the alleged key to all blessings. "Faith," thus defined, controls the metaphysical forces to our advantage.

According to this scheme, God is either not needed or irrelevant. In the metaphysical cults, He is not needed. Therefore, "God" may be a force, the Universe, man or whatever. What we may call Him/It is not important. In the Word of Faith movement He is practically irrelevant, for man must learn how to use the spiritual laws properly to receive what he wants. God has established the laws, and there is little else He can do. Now "it is up to man" to learn how to use these laws to his advantage.

The opposite of all this is the verse at the beginning of this chapter which declares that God *alone* is Creator and Ruler, that there are no impersonal laws. The universe is infinitely personal because God is infinite and Personal. We relate to Him by personal faith in Christ, and He relates to us according to our needs, giving and withholding as He thinks best.

4

Are Miracles Normal?

Miracles: Who, When, & Why

"A wicked and adulterous generation seeks after a sign, and no sign shall be given to it except the sign of the prophet Jonah." And He left them and departed (Matt. 16:4).

There are two extremes regarding miracles: God never performs miracles, or miracles are normal. Our generation craves miracles. Christians are not satisfied with ethical Christianity, with a religion that transforms the sinner to a saint by sovereign grace; they want more, wickedly seeking signs (1 Cor. 1:22). The Lord blasted the religious leaders of His day for not being satisfied with ethical Christianity and demanding a power religion based in metaphysics. He said He would give them the signs of Jonah and of Solomon. Jonah's sign was the preaching to the people of Ninevah, who repented, and Solomon's sign was the wisdom he displayed to the queen of the South, both signs being ethical (Matt. 12:38ff).[1]

Our generation assumes that miracles necessarily reveal genuine Christianity, contrary to the Lord's teaching:

> Many will say to Me in that day, "Lord, Lord, have we not prophesied in Your name, cast out demons in Your name, and done many wonders in Your name?" And then I will declare to them, "I never knew you; depart from Me, you who practice lawlessness!" (Matt. 7:22, 23)

The magic word with which the health and wealth leaders lure their followers is "miracle." It is like a mantra, repeated over and over so that the hearers are hypnotized to respond favorably to the Tiltons, Oral Roberts, and other charmers. They tell people that God is just waiting to give them *their* miracle, all they have to do is . . . . The conditions vary with

---

[1] The three days and nights Jonah spent in the fish were a sign to Jonah, not the Ninevites who had no knowledge of this.

the speaker, but most of them have one thing in common: money. They may not say it, though many do, but they at least imply that to get their miracle, they need to send money to the one preaching.

If you listen to Robert Tilton, you will not be able to count the numerous times he uses the word "miracle." After the audience is thoroughly mesmerized, not only with "miracles" but also with testimonies of success he *always* has, then the plea to make a "vow" by sending him money is made. It is psychological manipulation by using repeated words, testimonies, and emotional ups and downs. It is cheap. It is a mass con game.

The health and wealth leaders program their followers to expect a miracle, in blatant disregard of the Lord's teaching in Matthew 16:4. The real test for truth, however, is not miracles but the Gospel. Is the Gospel of grace preached and emphasized, the Gospel that says that all men are sinners, that Jesus is almighty God (John 1:1; 5:18; 8:24, 58; 10:30; 20:28) and perfect humanity (John 1:14) in one glorious Person (Col. 2:9) who obeyed God's law perfectly and died on the cross as a substitute for His people, bearing their sins (Mark 10:45), that He arose bodily from the grave in the same body in which He tabernacled among men (John 2:21, 22; 20:28), and that the sinner will receive the free gift of forgiveness of sins when he turns from his sins and trusts in Christ alone for forgiveness (Acts 10:43)? If this is not the preaching, then the person is not of God.

Miracles in the Early Church

The cessation of the miracle gifts is simply a record of early church history, which denied that prophets, tongues, new revelation, and healing continued. If the sign gifts were only for the beginning church, they are not for today. The record of their cessation is extensive. As one historian has noted: "Their opponents [opponents of Montanism] . . . declared that prophecy ended with John the Baptist and was sealed by the passion of Christ, also urging the words of Christ and the apostles against false prophets (Matt. 7:15; 2 Thess. 2:9; 1 John 4:1-3; and especially 1 Tim. 4:1-3)."[2] The following quotes are

---

[2] *The New Schaff-Herzog Encyclopedia of Religious Knowledge*, 7:487.

representative of the early church fathers that the gifts had ceased.

Eusebius (265-339), writing as an eye witness, states that though Montanus claimed that prophecy should continue until the Second Coming, yet only fourteen years after the death of Maximilla no prophet existed even in their own group. Again Eusebius says about Montanus:

> There is said to be a certain village of Mysia in Phrygia, called Ardaba. There . . . one of those who was but a recent convert, Montanus by name, when Cratus was proconsul in Asia, in the excessive desire of his soul to take the lead, gave the adversary occasion against himself. So that he was carried away in spirit, and wrought up into a certain kind of frenzy and irregular ecstasy, raving, and speaking, and uttering strange things, and proclaiming what was contrary to the institutions that had prevailed in the church, as handed down and preserved in succession from the earliest times. But of those who happened to be present, and to hear these spurious oracles, some being indignant, rebuked him as one under the influence of demons and the spirit of delusion, and who was only exciting disturbances among the multitude. These bore in mind the distinction and the warning given by our Lord, when he cautioned them to be vigilantly on their guard against false prophets.[3]

> For he [Montanus] excited two others, females, and filled them with the spirit of delusion, so that they also spake like the former, in a kind of ecstatic frenzy, out of all season, and in a manner strange and novel, whilst the spirit of evil congratulated them, thus rejoicing and inflated by him, and continued to puff them up the more, by promises of great things.[4]

Eusebius, writing about the year A.D. 325, stated that prophecy had ceased and that it was the practice of the church in his day to rebuke those who claimed to give prophecies. Observe that the one they rebuked was none other than Montanus and his two women! Eusebius again mentions this in a work by a historian, Miltiades, quoting a brother in Christ by the name of Alcibiades, ". . . in which he demonstrates the

---

[3] *Eusebius' Ecclesiastical History*, translated by Christian Frederick Cruse (Grand Rapids: Baker Book House, reprinted from the 1850 edition), p. 200.

[4] Ibid., pp. 196, 197.

impropriety of a prophet's speaking in ecstasy."[5] Apparently he is speaking of those who claim to speak in tongues while prophesying, both of which were considered wrong.

Furthermore, Eusebius observed that the canon of Scripture had been closed for some time, listing the books of the Bible which the church accepted as infallible. These are the same as our Protestant Bibles.[6] If the canon were closed, they argued, there was no more need for special revelation via tongues, prophecies, or other ways.

There were many other godly men in the early church who stated that the sign gifts had disappeared, but only a few more need mentioning.

Justin Martyr, writing about A.D. 155, claimed to have seen some miracles, though these seem to be limited to demons being driven out and perhaps some healing. Irenaeus (120-202) asserted that raising the dead and speaking in tongues were still around in his day; but when Theophilus challenged him to produce one, he could not. Neither Eusebius nor Papias (60-130) were familiar with miracles in their own day.[7] John Chrysostom (347-407) writes on the extraordinary gifts: "This whole place is very obscure: but the obscurity is produced by our ignorance of the facts referred to and by their cessation, being such as then used to occur but now no longer take place."[8] Likewise, Augustine (354-430) says of tongues:

> In the earliest time the Holy Ghost fell upon them that believed: and they spake with tongues, which they had not learned, "as the Spirit gave them utterance." These were signs adapted to the time. For there behooved to be that betokening of the Holy Spirit in all tongues, and to show that the Gospel of God was to run through all tongues over the whole earth. That thing was done for a betokening and it passed away.[9]

---

[5] Ibid., p. 199.

[6] Ibid., pp. 110, 244ff. Eusebius included 1 & 2 Esdras, but this was often the designation for Ezra and Nehemiah with 3 & 4 Esdras being the Apocryphal books.

[7] B. B. Warfield, *Counterfeit Miracles* (London: Banner of Truth Trust, 1918, 1972), pp. 11, 14.

[8] John Chrysostom, *Homilies on First Corinthians*, Vol. XII of *The Nicene and Post-Nicene Fathers*, Hom. 29.2.

[9] Augustine, "Ten Homilies on the First Epistle of John," Vol. VII, *The Nicene*

Even Edward Gibbon (1737-1794), who wrote *The Decline and Fall of the Roman Empire,* observed that miracles had ceased very early in Christian history. He states, though, that some fanatics still maintained that miracles continued: "They still supported their pretensions after they had lost their power."[10] What modern Christianity has forgotten is that "the primitive Christian demonstrated his faith by his virtues,"[11] and that the real power of God's grace is in forgiving sin and in ethically changing a person so that the sin he once loved he now hates and the ethical laws of God he once hated he now loves.

If the miracle gifts ceased, then health, wealth, signs, and writing Scripture ceased. We do not mean that God cannot do miracles today but that He has not given men the ability to do so as He did the apostles.

Assumptions

One of the assumptions of this miracle-mentality is that God is a genie in a bottle waiting to jump out and grant any wish as long as the lustful wisher "rubs the bottle" (read: fulfills the conditions) correctly. And the conditions vary according to the preacher, and yet each preacher is emphatic that his conditions are the true ones because "Jesus told him so." It is blasphemous to consider the sovereign God of the Bible as a slave to be used to satisfy one's wishes. If the sovereignty of man were not their assumption, then they could not say that the only hindrance to gaining a miracle is their stubborn wills. This assumption presents man in control and God wanting to grant miracles, but man will not let Him. If God decided who would be given a miracle and when he would get it, then the whole healing, tongues, prosperity movement would never have arisen (see Chapter Ten).

In aberrant Christianity the search for power is in miracles rather than in ethics or obedience to Scripture. People want to be served, not to serve; they want to create their own little worlds in which to live, and the health and wealth preachers

---

and Post-Nicene Fathers, VI, 10.

[10] Edward Gibbons, *The Decline and Fall of the Roman Empire* (New York: Harcourt, Brace and Co., 1960), 1 vol. edition, p. 162.

[11] Ibid., p. 163.

are telling a generation that they can do just that. By contrast the Gospel, especially as seen in light of the sovereignty of God, is the only cure. To pursue raw power directly is to come under judgment; we must pursue *ethical* power indirectly, through submission to King Jesus by believing His Gospel and obeying His written Word, the Bible.

We must not glibly pass over this. Paul Crouch says that miracles must be used in evangelism.[12] To seek miracles as a means of power evangelism is to turn the Gospel on its head. In fact, he said he felt sorry for those who did not do miracles because this hindered their ability to win the lost. Miracles were being used, according to Crouch, in crusades to convince people of the Gospel. He quoted Acts 8:6 as proof: "And the multitudes with one accord heeded the things spoken by Philip, hearing and seeing the miracles which he did."

He has misunderstood miracles. They do authenticate the man and his message *if and only if* the Holy Spirit opens one's eyes to see. In Luke the Lord said: "If they do not hear Moses and the prophets, neither will they be persuaded though one rise from the dead." In Acts 4:16 the religious leaders admitted regarding the lame man Peter healed, "What shall we do to these men? For, indeed, that a notable miracle has been done through them is evident to all who dwell in Jerusalem, *and we cannot deny it*." But this did not convince them to believe in Jesus, for they still commanded the disciples not to preach Him (v. 17ff). When Jesus raised Lazarus from the dead, did this convince the Jews that Jesus was the Messiah? "The chief priests plotted to put Lazarus to death" (John 12:10).

The implication of Crouch and others is that man's hindrance in coming to Christ is a metaphysical one instead of a moral one, that man needs physical power and not moral power to become a Christian, that man will indeed believe if presented with enough physical evidence, all of which is the opposite of what the Lord said. In Romans 1:18ff. Paul clearly reveals that man will not believe, not because of lack of evidence, but because he suppresses the truth. He suppresses the truth because he loves his sin and does not want to come to the light lest his deeds be exposed as immoral (John 3:20).

---

[12] 04/23/92 at 11:30 P.M., TBN, Memphis, TN.

The problem is ethical and suppression of knowledge, not metaphysical or a lack of knowledge. No amount of miracles will make one a Christian, because he is not objective, not open to truth, hates God, and loves his sin. It is the preaching of the Gospel that exposes this rebellion, the Gospel being the power of God for salvation (1 Cor. 1:18ff.), not miracles in themselves.

We need a return to ethical Christianity to cure all these evils, not a falling prey to the same by assuming that physical or metaphysical changes in circumstances will change these ethical sins. It is the essence of liberalism to think that our problems lie within our circumstances and that if we fix the circumstances, then the problems will be solved. That is environmentalism, a belief that rearranging physical things or cleaning up the outside of the cup will renovate the inside. The Gospel, though, cleans up the inside, and then the circumstances reflect the change.

Another assumption is that miracles are a normal part of life. If this were true, then how could we define a miracle, which is usually thought of as something abnormal? From the Scripture quoted at the beginning of this chapter, Jesus denounced those seeking miracles. He would not have said that if miracles were normal. In that case seeking them would be commended.

Definition of a Miracle

One might think that the definition of a miracle were obvious. If so, then why don't the health and wealth people define it? They repeatedly use the word but do not define it. This equivocation gives an aura of legitimacy to what they say, since the listeners accept such use of the word as biblical, but the word is applied to every unusual circumstance as well as to genuine miracles in the Bible. In other words, if a miracle is something unusual, then a coin falling on the floor and remaining on its rim is a miracle. A. J. Gordon, for instance, in his book *The Ministry of Healing* published in the 1880's, was very hesitant to define a miracle.

If one does not define it, then he can point to anything as a miracle and most will believe it. This confuses people who think that if they get money after they have given to a Word of Faith preacher it is a "miracle." Then the genuine miracles of the Lord and the apostles tend to lose their special significance. For example, Oral Roberts thinks that the growing of a seed into a tree or plant is a miracle.[13] We must see how miracles are defined in the Lord's ministry.

The early church recognized that the miracles of the Lord were anything but commonplace, that they were unique to Him. Indeed, an early church father named Gregory of Nyssa (330-395) stated: "His [Jesus'] very miracles have convinced us of His deity."[14] Another father, Athanasius (296-373) said: "it may be known from His works that He who can do these things is not man, but the power and Word of God."[15]

The signs in John's Gospel all point to some spiritual truth in Jesus (see paragraph beginning with "We can also see" on page 92); therefore, the "greater works" that we shall do (John 14:12) must be spiritual works — not miracles. The whole point of the sign-miracles was to testify of salvation. We cannot feed five thousand people, turn water into wine, raise the dead, etc., but we can point people to the bread of life, to the light of the world, and to the resurrection and the life. We shall see many converted whereas the Lord saw few. These are the "greater works" the Lord had in mind.

With this blurring of the definition of miracle, the modern peddlers of miracles claim they have proven the truth of what they preach. They point to all the "miracles" accomplished through their ministries. Yet they have leveled the definition of miracle to include virtually everything. Every answer to prayer and every "unusual" providential circumstance is labeled a "miracle."

Later in his book A. J. Gordon does give a definition: "A miracle is the immediate action of God, as distinguished from His mediate action through natural laws," to which the great theologian B. B. Warfield adds: "no definition could be clearer or better."[16] Does this mean the laws of nature are suspended, that they are overruled by a higher law, that God simply does it directly and contrary to nature? Does God

---

[13] Oral Roberts, *Miracle of Seed Faith* (Tulsa: Oral Roberts, 1970), p. 73.

[14] Colin Brown, *Miracles and The Critical Mind* (Grand Rapids: Wm. B. Eerdmans Pub. Co., 1984), p. 4.

[15] Ibid.

[16] B. B. Warfield, *Counterfeit Miracles* (London: Banner of Truth, 1972), p. 161.

accelerate the laws of nature, or is there any difference in any of these? We doubt that God contradicts the laws of nature, as there is no law higher than God to which He is accountable. We doubt that He accelerated the laws of nature so that the natural healing process was sped up to light speed as it were, because some people, like the man born blind (John 9), would never have gotten better no matter how much time was involved. God simply suspends the normal way He works and does things differently. Whatever the details, several things are sure: they are done *directly* (without normal human means) by Him and in the case of healings they are done *instantaneously* and *perfectly*.

A distinction between miracles and the supernatural should also be observed. There are many supernatural things in our world, such as angels, séances, demon possession, and so forth. These are not, however, to be considered miracles. They are abnormal, unusual, and not believed by many in our culture. Sometimes God's providence is so unusual that we think of it as a miracle, but normal means are used so that perhaps it is not a miracle. For example, in Memphis, Tennessee, certain members in a church were attacked by the U. S. Justice Department on false charges. The circumstances looked insurmountable — even impossible — since the government had lying witnesses, a seemingly predisposed judge, years of investigation and millions of dollars to spend. Those charged had little if any money, told the truth, and were defenseless. Yet God performed a "miracle" in that the jury saw through the government's subterfuge. This was most unusual, but not a miracle in the technical sense. Supernatural? Yes. A miracle? No. Wonderful? Absolutely!

The Purpose of Miracles

The purpose of miracles in Scripture was not simply to help someone, though people were often helped. Some miracles did not help anyone, such as Moses' staff becoming a snake and Elijah calling down fire from heaven. The ten plagues Moses commanded were judgments against the Egyptians and harmed most of them. *The main purpose of all miracles, however, was to validate God's man with God's message.* Let's survey Scripture on this point.

From the creation of the world to the coming of Jesus,

there have been only three periods of miracles: Moses and Joshua, Elijah and Elisha, Christ and the apostles. In each case, God gave *men* the authority to perform miracles, not that the men actually did the miracles but that when they commanded, things happened (no doubt by the power of God). We are not denying that God has done miracles at other times and can do one whenever He pleases, but *there are only three times in history that He has given men the authority to perform them in His name basically whenever they chose to do so.* The rest of the time God does one occasionally without the agency of men.

When God commissioned Moses to go to Pharoah and command him to let His people go, Moses asked the Lord: "But suppose they will not believe me or listen to my voice; suppose they say, 'The Lord has not appeared to you.'" Remember that the Lord enabled Moses to turn a rod into a snake and water into blood (Ex. 4:29). Can you see Moses' point? "Pharoah will think I'm loony if I tell him God sent me; I need some proof." So God gave it to him, and for the next forty years Moses, by the authority and power of God, performed miracles. Joshua, as his successor, had similar authority. The miracles validated Moses and Joshua as God's men with God's message.

The next time in Scripture that *men*[17] have the authority from God to perform miracles was in the days of Elijah and Elisha. Israel was so apostate that the Lord commissioned Elijah to perform miracles to validate His Gospel, bringing the people back to Him by His grace. Remember Mt. Carmel, the fire from heaven, and the killing of the prophets of Baal? Remember the widow woman, the oil in the barrel and her food? Elijah also raised her son. Temporarily, at least, Israel returned to the Lord, and the miracles categorically validated that Elijah was God's man with God's message. When the fire fell from heaven and burned up Elijah's offering, the people said: "The LORD, He is God! The LORD, He is God!" (1 Kings 18:39). When Elijah revived the widow's son, she exclaimed: "Now by this I know that you are a man of God, and that the word of the Lord in your mouth is the truth" (1 Kings

---

[17] I may be wrong, but I cannot recall a woman in Scripture doing a miracle. Deborah was a prophetess, but she did not do a miracle in the technical sense.

17:24).

In the time of Jesus' incarnation, many were proclaiming to be the Messiah. How were people to know that Jesus was the One? Again God validated the Man and His message with signs and wonders. When the Lord forgave the paralytic, the scribes said within themselves: "This Man blasphemes." So the Lord validated His Gospel with these words: "'But that you may know that the Son of Man has power on earth to forgive sins' — then He said to the paralytic, 'Arise, take up your bed, and go to your house'" (Matt. 9:6). This is so often repeated in the synoptic Gospels that other references are not needed.

In the book of Acts, do we see thousands of miracles? No. The main point emphasized throughout the book is the Gospel preached by the apostles, though miracles are done occasionally. In Acts chapter three, Peter heals a crippled man. Did he do this simply to heal the man? No, Peter used it as an occasion to preach Jesus and the resurrection (3:11-26); the miracle validated that he (Peter) was God's man with God's message.

In each of the three time periods, once the men and the message had been validated, the miracles ceased. Again we emphasize that God can perform miracles anytime He chooses, but in only three periods in human history has He given *men* the authority to perform miracles. Daniel had to ask God with much prayer and fasting (Dan. 9:3), and God often answered him with the miraculous. But in the case of the three Hebrew children, they confessed that they did not know if God would deliver them from the fiery furnace or not but they would still not worship the golden calf (Dan. 3:18).[18]

---

[18] It is wicked to think that death is defeat for the Christian; this is the view of the world. The three Hebrew men were confessing that their deliverance was in the Lord's hands and that they were satisfied with that. If God delivered them, they would not serve false gods; and even if it meant they would face death, they still would not serve. According to Charles Capps (I heard this on his radio program over KSUD from West Memphis, AR, 01/31/91) the expression "If it be so" (Dan. 3:17) means if the king throws them into the fire, and the expression "But if not" in verse 18 means if not thrown into the fire. In other words, the three young men knew that God would not allow them to be hurt because they had faith. Therefore, *if* the king threw them into the fire, they would survive and not serve the king; or *if* the king did not throw them into the fire, they still would not serve the king. This interpretation does not conform to the Aramaic. (This section of Daniel is not Hebrew but Aramaic.) Here is a

Someone may object that God is not limited to these three time periods, that a fourth may yet come. This could be true except for one thing: Jesus was the *final* prophet, priest, and king. He did miracles in fulfillment of prophecy, which pointed to Him as the One to come Who would *perfectly* reveal the Father, *perfectly* fulfill the Old Testament, and offer a *perfect* sacrifice. If a man had the gift of miracles, this would imply that more revelation is needed, that Jesus did not reveal all that the Father intended us to know about Himself, and perhaps that another Jesus should be known or at least more of the Gospel should be known than God has told us — all of which disparage the Lord and His mission.[19]

As we have said, miracles validate the man and his message. We say *validate* or confirm, not prove, for the proof is from God Himself through sovereign grace. Miracles by themselves will convert no one. Miracles were a catalyst, a visual aid of the Gospel, which were unanswerable in themselves. The interpretation of them would be according to one's heart. Someone morally threatened by them as the Pharisees were would attribute them to the devil. If he were not threatened, he would give God the glory. In short, if his heart was prepared by grace (like the blind man in John 9), he would rejoice and believe the Gospel. If his heart was not prepared, he would harden his heart against the miracles as the Pharisees did who talked to the man born blind.

We can also see from the various Greek words used for "miracle" that God's purpose was to validate the man and the message. There are several Greek words used for miracles but

---

literal translation of these two verses: "If it is that our God Whom we serve is able to deliver us from the furnace of burning fire and from your hand, O king, He will deliver. But if not, let it be known to you, O king, we will not serve your god." Of course, this translation causes some to question the theology it presents, the problem being that it seems that God may not be able to deliver the three. The interpretation of E. J. Young seems to be the best when he states that it is not a question of God's absolute ability in omnipotence but of His ethical ability (Edward J. Young, *The Prophecy of Daniel* (Grand Rapids: Wm. B. Eerdmans Pub. Co., 1975), p. 91; Keil and Delitzsch agree). In other words, if God thought it would be consistent with His plan and with His righteousness, He would deliver them. If it were not consistent, then He would take them home with Himself. We have never seen a commentator who knew the original languages take Capps's interpretation.

[19] Other fringe reasons for miracles were for edification (1 Cor. 14:5), for healing the sick.

Are Miracles Normal?

three deserve our notice.[20] These are translated wonders, sign(s), and power(s), and are not three different kinds of miracles, but three ways of viewing the same miracles. They are *wonders* to inspire and awe the viewer, physical *signs* that point to some spiritual truth, and the *power* of God. The word for *wonders* is never used alone but always with another Greek word for miracle, usually with *signs*.[21]

In the Gospel of John, which uses *sign* primarily, we can understand the purpose of all His miracles. "The basic meaning of [*sign*] is a sign by which one recognizes a particular person or thing, a confirmatory, corroborative, authenticating mark or token."[22] A few examples from John will help us to understand why the definition just given is correct.

In John 2:11 the Lord changed water into wine — and good wine at that. Why was it done? Here is John's answer: "This beginning of *signs* Jesus did in Cana of Galilee, and manifested His glory; and His disciples believed in Him." The miracle showed Who He was, that He was God in the flesh, and faith followed. The miracle validated the Man and His message. Again we see John saying: "Now when He was in Jerusalem at the Passover, during the feast, many believed in His name when they saw the *signs* which He did" (John 2:23). Peruse these other verses in John:

> This man came to Jesus by night and said to Him, "Rabbi, we know that You are a teacher come from God; for no one can do these **signs** that You do unless God is with him" (3:2).

> Then Jesus said to him, "Unless you people see **signs** and wonders, you will by no means believe" (4:48).

> Then a great multitude followed Him, because they saw His **signs** which He performed on those who were diseased (6:2).

> And many of the people believed in Him, and said, "When the Christ comes, will He do more **signs** than these which this Man has done?" (7:31).

---

[20] The Greek words are: τερας, σημειον, δυναμις.

[21] The advanced student is encouraged to read Trench's *Synonyms of the New Testament* (pages 339ff.) for a good treatment.

[22] Colin Brown, *The New International Dictionary of New Testament Theology* (Grand Rapids: Zondervan Publishing House, 1975), 2:626.

> Therefore the people, who were with Him when He called Lazarus out of his tomb and raised him from the dead, bore witness. For this reason the people also met Him, because they heard that He had done this **sign** (12:17, 18).
>
> And truly Jesus did many other **signs** in the presence of His disciples, which are not written in this book; **but these are written that you may believe** that Jesus is the Christ, the Son of God, and that believing you may have life in His name (20:30, 31).

When Jesus claimed to be the bread from heaven and then fed the five thousand from a few fish, the people believed in Him (John 6). When He proclaimed He was the light of the world and healed the man born blind, many believed Him (John 9). When He argued that He was the resurrection and the life and raised Lazarus from the dead, who could deny this (John 11:25ff.)? In each case, the miracle or sign was done to show who Jesus was, to validate the Man and His message, to give a visual object lesson of the Gospel — not just to heal someone. In fact John stated at the end of his Gospel that His signs were done "that you may believe that Jesus is the Christ, the Son of God."

His miracles pointed to Himself.[23] They were done to show that Jesus cures the greatest of all maladies: sin. In the *Theological Dictionary of the New Testament*, Rengstorf has rightly concluded of John's use of *signs*:

> The word [sign] has taken over the role which [power] plays elsewhere in the New Testament and especially in the Synoptics [the other three Gospels]. . . . John's [signs] and the person of the One Who does them cannot be separated. In some way the [signs] also bear the nature of Him Who is at work in them. Concerning the [signs] of Jesus Nicodemus says that no one can do them unless God be with Him, John 3:2. . . . The decisive thing is not the quantity of [signs] or the greatness of the individual [sign]; it is the quality, which depends on the quality of their author.[24]

We argue that the miracles in John are unique, pointing

---

[23] Gerhard Kittel, *Theological Dictionary of the New Testament* (Grand Rapids: Wm. B. Eerdmans Pub. Co., 1964), 7:243.

[24] Ibid., 7:245.

to a unique Person. He did most of the miracles in His own name, and they showed creative power. Turning the water to wine was an act of creation; feeding the five thousand demonstrated His creative power to make many fish out of a few and to feed spiritually His people; healing the man born blind necessitated that He create eyes to work and therefore He could open the spiritual eyes of those blinded by sin; and especially the raising of Lazarus proved that He was the Creator in the flesh and that He could give spiritual life to dead sinners. Jesus was unique; His miracles were unique, pointing to Him, demonstrating that He *only* is the Savior. If someone else could do His miracles, then he would also be a savior.

The apostles had power to work miracles to validate and confirm who they were: Jesus' special men. Did not Paul argue that he was an apostle based on his miracles: "Truly the *signs* of an apostle were accomplished among you with all perseverance, in *signs* and *wonders* and *mighty deeds*" (2 Cor. 12:12)? Paul uses all three Greek words for "miracle," and the "signs and wonders and mighty deeds" proved that he was an apostle.[25] If anyone can do the same miracles, then how were these miracles proofs of his apostleship? Once his apostleship was validated, why should miracles continue? There would be no more need for them, and as we have already seen the early church testified that they ceased. (See the paragraph on page 82, "The cessation of miracle gifts".) John MacArthur boldly and rightly proclaims that "after the church was born at Pentecost, no miracle ever occurred in the entire New Testament record except in the presence of an apostle or one directly commissioned by an apostle."[26]

---

[25] One man (Sam Storms) has suggested that since the word "signs" is in the nominative case and "in signs and wonders and mighty deeds" in the dative case that Paul did not mean the authentication of an apostle was miracles but only that miracles happened to attend the "signs." The "signs" were the fruit from preaching the Gospel. This is nonsense, for the same Greek word for "signs" is used in "signs and wonders and mighty deeds," indicating that the latter three words are an explanation of the former word. Indeed, Paul thought of miracles as simply "signs" that could be viewed in three ways. Secondly, I know of no place in the New Testament where "sign" refers to the fruit of preaching but is used primarily of miracles and occasionally of a mark that indicates something else (Matt. 16:3; 24:3, 30; Rom. 4:11).

[26] John F. MacArthur, *The Charismatics* (Grand Rapids: Zondervan, 1979), p. 80.

Often the "miracle workers" of today loudly proclaim Acts 1:8 and conclude that all of us should receive power to be His witnesses and to do miracles. When the Lord said to the eleven in Acts 1:8, however, that they would be witnesses to Him and would receive power, He was referring to their being eye witnesses of His bodily resurrection. In other words, the word "witness" became a technical Greek word in the book of Acts for one who was an eye witness of the Lord's bodily resurrection, something no one today could claim. The power or authority they waited for was to preach the Gospel, not to do miracles. In 1 John 1:1-3 John spoke of having seen the Lord's body and handled it after His resurrection. Notice also the verses in Acts that speak of their "witness:"

> This Jesus God has raised up, of which we are all **witnesses** (Acts 2:32).
>
> And killed the Prince of life, whom God raised from the dead, of which we are **witnesses** (Acts 3:15).
>
> And with great power the apostles gave **witness** to the resurrection of the Lord Jesus. And great grace was upon them all (Acts 4:33).
>
> Him God has exalted to His right hand to be Prince and Savior, to give repentance to Israel and forgiveness of sins. And we are His **witnesses** to these things, and so also is the Holy Spirit whom God has given to those who obey Him (Acts 5:31, 32).
>
> And we are **witnesses** of all things which He did both in the land of the Jews and in Jerusalem, whom they killed by hanging on a tree. Him God raised up on the third day, and showed Him openly, not to all the people, but to **witnesses** chosen before by God, even to us who ate and drank with Him after He arose from the dead (Acts 10:39-41).
>
> Then he said, "The God of our fathers has chosen you that you should know His will, and see the Just One, and hear the voice of His mouth. For you will be His **witness** to all men of what you have seen and heard" (Acts 22:14, 15).
>
> Am I not an apostle? Am I not free? **Have I not seen Jesus Christ our Lord?** Are you not my work in the Lord? (1 Cor. 9:1)

Only the apostles were chosen to be eye-witnesses of His

resurrection so we should not expect to do the signs they did. Their miracles were unique because Jesus chose them for a unique mission, but even then their miracles bore witness of Jesus.

Jesus' Miracles Versus Those of Today

Some miracles only the Lord could do; neither the apostles nor anyone today can match them. And should we expect anything less? Did anyone else ever do nature miracles like His, such as stilling the storm, or riding on a donkey on which no man had ever sat without being bucked off (try it!). Or how about raising a man whose flesh had already begun to decay, or healing a man born blind? Each of these miracles, as we have already seen, testify to some aspect of the Person and work of the Lord Jesus. No one else did these: "If I had not done among them the works *which no one else did*, they would have no sin; but now they have seen and also hated both Me and My Father" (John 15:24). If we could do the same, then Jesus' statement would lose its significance.

Furthermore, in this verse He stated that *He Himself* had done the miracles. Thus it is definitely not true that the Lord *only* did miracles in the power of the Holy Spirit so that we can do all He did by the same Holy Spirit. His miracles testified in a unique way to His unique Person and mission. We are not God in the flesh who came to be a substitute for His people. Charles Capps completely missed the point when he said that Jesus did not come "to prove He was the Son of God."[27] Maybe "prove" is too strong a word, but the Lord did demonstrate who He was and even stated that if the people did not believe His words then they should at least believe His works (John 5:36; 10:25-42; 14:11). Likewise, Kenneth Hagin claims that Jesus did not do miracles to demonstrate His deity or His mission.[28] John says He did. Who is right, the Apostle John or Capps and Hagin?

One miracle in particular Jesus uniquely performed in His deity. In John 18 a Roman cohort of soldiers (about 500) came to arrest Him. John tells it best: "Then — when He said to them, 'I am *He*' — they drew back and fell to the ground"

---

[27] Charles Capps, *Authority in Three Worlds* (Tulsa: Harrison House, 1964), p. 95.

[28] Kenneth Hagin, *Hear and Be Healed* (Tulsa: Faith Library Pub., 1987) p. 14.

(John 18:6).[29] The "He" is in italics indicating that it is not part of the Greek so that the Lord claimed to be the I AM (Ex. 3:14; John 8:58). When He made this manifestation of His deity, the soldiers went backward and fell to the ground. Did any apostle ever do this? No! Only God in the flesh was capable of this. Warfield sums up well the uniqueness of Jesus:

> Because Christ is all in all, and all revelation and redemption alike are summed up in Him, it would be inconceivable that either revelation or its accompanying signs should continue after the completion of that great revelation with its accrediting works, by which Christ has been established in His rightful place as the culmination and climax and all-inclusive summary of the saving revelation of God, the sole and sufficient redeemer of His people.[30]

To claim that visions or miracles are still for today and also normal would be to destroy the uniqueness of the Person and work of Christ and the uniqueness and authority of Scripture. Therefore, when Mary Baker Eddy proclaims that miracles are still to be expected, which she and Christian Scientists give as the proof of their teaching,[31] they are taking away from Jesus. Jesus was the final Prophet, the final Priest, and the final King. To expect more revelations and more miracles would be to dishonor Him as the final One to whom all Scripture pointed. We do not look for another priest to die for us, another king to rule us, so why do we look for another prophet to reveal God to us? Was not Jesus enough? What did He omit about God? What is lacking that needs to be supplemented by someone today?

The Roman Catholic Church promotes continuing miracles that are allegedly performed by its saints and priests as a chief proof that it is God's true church; and if the Protestants could not produce miracles, Rome charged, they were not of

---

[29] Rev. Douglas Mills says that this verse and 2 Chronicles 5:14 are used as proofs of being "slain in the Spirit." John 18 says nothing of the kind, for the ones who fell backwards were the enemies of God, not those filled with the Spirit. Furthermore, John does not say they became unconscious, as Benny Hinn does to his audience when they come forward. Second Chronicles 5:14 is speaking of ministering to God, not falling unconscious.

[30] B. B. Warfield, *Counterfeit*, p. 28.

[31] Mary Baker Eddy, *Science and Health*, p. 123.

God. They claim that some of their honored saints are filled with the power of God in their bodies, in their clothes, and in their remains.[32] John Calvin's response to the miracle-working Catholics of his day is still apropos:

> In demanding miracles of us, they [Roman Catholics] act dishonestly. For we are not forging some new Gospel, but we are retaining that very Gospel whose truth all the miracles that Jesus Christ and his disciples ever wrought serve to confirm.
>
> Perhaps this false hue could have been more dazzling if Scripture had not warned us concerning the legitimate purpose and use of miracles. For Mark teaches that those signs which attended the apostles' preaching were set forth to confirm it (Mark. 16:20). In like manner, Luke relates that our "Lord . . . bore witness to the word of his grace," when these signs and wonders were done by the apostles' hands (Acts 14:3).
>
> When we hear that these [so-called miracles] are the seals of the Gospel, shall we turn to the destruction of faith in the Gospel? When we hear that they were appointed only to seal the truth, shall we employ them to confirm falsehoods?
>
> The Lord made us wary of these miracle workers when he predicted that false prophets with lying signs and prodigies would come to draw even the elect (if possible) into error (Matt. 24:24). And Paul warned that the reign of Antichrist would be "with all power, and signs, and lying wonders" (2 Thess. 2:9).[33]

Miracles were given to confirm the Gospel, but no amount of miracles can confirm false doctrines. These miracles of Christ and the Apostles are facts of church history and belong to the church so why repeat them? Columbus discovered America, but does this need to be repeated for each new generation? This heritage now belongs to all Americans. If we are starting a new religion or founding a new country, we may need to repeat these events, otherwise we do not. The written Word of God has now been given to teach us the true from the false so that miracles are no longer needed to establish the Gospel (though God can perform one anytime He chooses). The men

---

[32] Warfield, *Counterfeit Miracles*, p. 97.

[33] John Calvin, *Institutes of the Christian Religion*, editor John T. McNeill (Philadelphia: Westminster Press, 1975), Prefatory Address, pp. 16, 17.

and their message have been forever recorded in Holy Scripture. This has been preserved for all generations. The "kind of Christian life that is ever seeking spiritual novelties and that places high emotionalism ahead of biblical understanding"[34] is extremely dangerous. The life of faith lived in quiet obedience to God is the life of power.

Pat Robertson makes God sound so perfunctory, for to get *our* miracle we only have to know the "rules" of miracles.[35] The "rules" are:[36] (1) take our eyes off the circumstances, (2) we are not to doubt in our hearts, (3) God's will must be transmitted by the Holy Spirit to our spirits, (4) we must verbally speak the words we want to accomplish as the verbal, literal speaking into the air engages God's spiritual laws, (5) we must forgive others or "we block the flow of miraculous power." How frustrated his followers must become when things do not work out as Pat told them. Did they believe enough? Was there someone they have not forgiven? Did they speak loudly enough? Pat tells of one miracle that enabled him to go into debt,[37] which is contrary to Scripture (Rom. 13:8; Prov. 22:7), so we have to question where this "miracle" came from.

Are today's "miracles" validated? In the case of our Lord and His apostles, there were many witnesses to confirm the miracle. As to the "miracle workers" today, one usually has to be content with others who have "seen" them. The eye witness is always just around the corner but never found. A physician named William L. Nolen wrote a book about the "miracles" of Kathryn Kuhlman, *Healing: A Doctor in Search of a Miracle*. He really wanted to believe but he was not able to verify any "miracles." They were always testified to by others who had seen them, but when he searched them out, very few if any had actually seen them first hand. They had heard of them from others. The ones that he could verify never quite turned out to be miracles.

---

[34] Arnold Dallimore, *Forerunner of the Charismatic Movement: Life of Edward Irving*, p. 158.

[35] Pat Robertson, *The Secret Kingdom* (New York: Walker and Company, 1982), p. 269, large print edition.

[36] Ibid., p. 269ff.

[37] Ibid., p. 290.

Conclusion

A miracle is special. It is done by God without normal human means and done instantaneously. The Lord's miracles testified of Him and His message. So did the apostles' miracles. Jesus did miracles by His own power as well as by the Holy Spirit. Once the Gospel was established through these unique miracles, there was no more need for them. Real, lasting power is in the Gospel to forgive sins and to change men's lives, which is why the Lord came. He did not come to establish perpetual miracles but to establish the kingdom of God through the Gospel. Miracles were like the first stage of a rocket; once they had served their purpose, they fell away. The problem with the health and wealth gospel is that people want God to serve them; they seek a sign and believe that power is in the miracle rather than in the Gospel. The opposite is the truth: We are to serve God, not seek the miraculous but seek His ethical power in our lives through the Gospel (1 Cor. 1:18ff.) as we are gradually changed into Jesus' moral image (2 Cor. 4:16-18).

If the miracles of Jesus were not unique, then what is so special about Jesus? If His miracles were unique, how can they be repeated? The miracles of the Lord were little Epiphanies, revealing the majesty of His Person, testifying to His deity, His humanity, and His mission. Many want to believe in miracles rather than in Jesus Himself, wanting something to make them happy rather than forgiveness of sins with the holy and wrathful God. Many have been made to feel weak and unspiritual because they cannot do great miracles like Jesus and the modern leaders. Feigning great miracles is how Word of Faith leaders maintain their elevated positions.

If anyone can do miracles, then "miracle" has lost its meaning; it is not something unusual by an unusual Person but becomes commonplace and capable by all men. If we have the same power as Jesus and can do all the miracles He did, then He has lost His uniqueness and thus His meaning. Within this false teaching, miracles happen according to some higher law that even God is subject to, and man can manipulate this metaphysical law with his own mind. If all men can do this, then Jesus was certainly not extraordinary.

Finally, miracles are no absolute proof that one is of God. "It is tempting to believe that if one can have a spectacular experience it must be a divine experience."[38] One who performed miracles *and* preached the Gospel was of God. True power is ethical, not metaphysical, in submitting to Christ: for when we are weak, then He is strong.

---

[38] Frederick Dale Bruner, *A Theology of the Holy Spirit* (Grand Rapids: Wm. B. Eerdmans Pub. Co., 1974), p. 223.

5

Natural Healing

The Bible, Doctors, and Medicine

> And in the thirty ninth year of his reign, Asa became diseased in his feet, and his malady was [very] severe; yet in his disease he did not seek the Lord, but the physicians (2 Chronicles 16:12).

The healing revival began with the metaphysical cults. Edward Irving thought that miraculous healing proved his beliefs. Mary Baker Eddy, the foundress of Christian Science, claimed the same proof and has a large section in the back of *Science and Health* on miraculous healing. Mrs. Eddy said, "If mankind would relinquish the belief that God makes sickness, sin, and death, or makes man capable of suffering on account of this malevolent triad, the foundations of error would be sapped...."[1] Likewise, Unity writer Robert Russell says, "We will prove through the Scriptures that bodily healing is just as much a part of the Divine plan as spiritual development."[2] Man can heal anything according to Unity writer Emmet Fox: "Realizing Divine Life heals a sick person, and, or course, you can heal animals and plants too."[3] Fox further proclaims that sickness is never sent for a good purpose.[4]

Kenneth Hagin, like Christian Scientists, teaches people to deny their physical symptoms, and is defensive: "They think I am teaching Christian Science. However, this is not Christian Science but Christian sense. We do not deny pains and other symptoms, for they are real. Instead, we look beyond

---

[1] Eddy, *Science and Health*, p. 357.

[2] Robert Russell, *God Works Through Faith* (Marina del Rey, CA: DeVross & Co., 1957), p. 129.

[3] Emmet Fox, *The Seven Main Aspects of God* (Marina del Rey, CA: DeVross & Co., 1942), p. 12; see also Robert Russell, *God Works Through Faith*, p. 13.

[4] Ibid., p. 12.

them to God's promises."[5] Hagin for once is partially right; Christian Science does teach its people that the symptoms do not exist while Hagin teaches they do. The difference is minor. The concept, however, is still metaphysical and not biblical. Both the Unity School and Hagin believe the symptoms are a result of personal failure and can easily be overcome. Hagin would say the *Christian* can believe for his healing while Unity teachers would say *anyone* can. In both cases the sick person pretends the illness does not exist, relying only on "spiritual" means for healing.

There are two extremes: those who think that doctors are of the devil, or that only those weak in faith go to them, and those who do not seek the Lord at all in their sicknesses. One uses only the spiritual means and the other only doctors.[6]

The 2 Chronicles verse presents the correct view. It is not wrong to go to physicians, but it is wrong to seek them *only*, which is what Asa did. We are to seek God first and then the physicians. And by seeking God first, we do not mean that the temporal order has to be God and then the physician, but Scripture is clear that our faith looks *primarily* to the Lord and *secondarily* to His common grace in physicians. In the end, it is always God who heals, whether He does so directly (rare) without doctors or indirectly (common) through His common grace by means of doctors and medicine.

Common Grace and Medicine

The health and wealth preachers *do not understand common grace.* By common grace God causes the sun to shine on the just and on the unjust (Matt. 5:45). By common grace God elevates a culture from devastating disease and economic depravation to one of health and prosperity. We in the United States live a long time, more than most cultures. God has blessed us with knowledge about germs, cleanliness (as also revealed in Leviticus), vaccinations, and many other things.

---

[5] Kenneth E. Hagin, *Faith Edition Bible* (Tulsa: Kenneth Hagin Ministries, 1972), p. xiv.

[6] It is not my purpose to explain every possible passage on this topic. A very fine book on the single topic of healing is by a fellow seminary student, C. Samuel Storms, *Healing and Holiness* (Phillipsburg, NJ: Presbyterian and Reformed, 1990). I highly recommend it. The foreword is by J. I. Packer.

Thus our whole society has been elevated to a level of health unknown by most cultures. Indeed, by common grace through doctors and vaccinations, God has granted us cures from most diseases that ravage other cultures.

If we listened to the "healers," we would think that healing is always a spiritual matter, devoid of any physical reality, that germs do not exist or do not matter. If we had enough faith, we would never be sick and never have accidents that would cause physical harm. Therefore, since only those with faith would be well and only those without faith would be sick, doctors, vaccinations, and medicine would not be needed. Society as a whole, however, would never advance by common grace for only Christians could be healed. Norvel Hayes agrees: "Every one of our sick folk today should be healed, *if* they are believers" [emphasis added].[7] According to Mr. Hayes, we should even expect Jesus to heal our washing machines![8] This is pure magic. Likewise, Oral Roberts has stated that God only heals Christians: "God will not give healing . . . to people who do not love and worship Him."[9] Again, "You may get saved without getting healed, but you cannot get healed without getting a blessing for your soul."[10]

But our society has advanced medically to such a degree that some diseases, like small pox, leprosy, and several types of measles, are virtually unknown. It is the common grace of God that unbelievers as well as Christians have God's medical blessings. Cultures that follow the teaching of the "faith healers," believing in divine and miraculous cures for every problem, become stagnant, such as in Haiti and some cultures in Africa, Brazil, and others. The medicine man has the cure, otherwise the situation is hopeless. The cures, however, of modern doctors work virtually every time with or without faith, for medicine and science are objective.[11]

---

[7] Norvel Hayes, *God's Power Through the Laying on of Hands* (Tulsa, OK: Harrison House, 1982), p. 28.

[8] Ibid., p. 44.

[9] Oral Roberts, *If You Need Healing, Do These Things* (Tulsa: Healing Waters, Inc., 1950), p. 60.

[10] Ibid., p. 130.

[11] Certainly nothing is entirely objective; there are presuppositions which determine how a person views science. But the point is that these diseases and the cures exist

For a person to neglect using these medical means for his health is to tempt God. When the Lord Jesus was on top of the temple, the devil told Him to jump down because God's angels would take care of Him (Matt. 4:6). The Lord said that to do so would be to tempt God (Matt. 4:7). In other words, if there are normal means we can use, we are obligated to do so. To neglect doctors is no different than jumping from the temple instead of walking down, no different than expecting God to take care of us while we play on the expressway.

Likewise Shirley MacLaine, who prefers New Age healers to doctors, speaks of the inability of a New Age healer to heal because of the presence of negative energy in a witness.[12] Such, however, is magic, not medicine, with the result that if this were really true then only those without "negative energy" would be healed. If there were only miracle healing, then babies, who do not have faith that can be instructed as an adult, could not be healed. Everything would be subject to magic, to "witch doctors" who could cure *if* the patient did all the right spiritual things. Ms. Maclaine documents many healings by those in the New Age, and I do not doubt these. The problem is that the healings are done by Satan and often lead to moral bondage in the lives of those healed.

On the other hand, we do need childlike faith in God's providence in which "all things work together for good" and in which God is praised for giving us the polio vaccine that prevents us from catching the crippling disease, whether those inoculated believe in it or not.

The great theologian of early 20th century, B. B. Warfield, accurately states that we must reject superstition "because it hindered fighting against physical ills with the weapon with which they should have been fought — that is, by God-trusting labor."[13] Magic is manipulation of God and/or the forces of nature by means of incantations and beliefs; true healing is by God's help and using the normal means of science to discover a cure. Superstition is seeing a demon as the cause of everything; understanding providence means seeing God's

---

whether people have faith in Christ or not and that a whole culture can be elevated.

[12] Shirley MacLaine, *Going Within* (New York: Bantam Books, 1990), pp. 275-76.

[13] B. B. Warfield, *Counterfeit Miracles* (Banner of Truth, reprinted in 1972 from the 1918 edition), pp. 65-66.

hand behind everything and using normal means to change things. Superstition is thinking that one can control God with the right words; prayer is humble submission to the God Who controls all things. A magical faith is thinking that one can create his own reality and so does not have to use normal means; biblical faith prays and then works to accomplish the desired end, knowing that it is only as the Lord wills that desirable circumstances come about.

But in the "healing movement," every bad thing is from a demon. There is the demon of lust, the demon of cigarette smoking, even the demon of Christian Science. (Smith Wigglesworth claimed that he cast out the "demon of Christian Science" from a lady.)[14] If everything bad is caused by a demon, then it is not my fault and I do not need to repent: "The devil made me do it." Little is seen to be the result of personal sin, germs allegedly do not exist, and vaccinations therefore are for the weak.

The "miracle workers" assure us that the kingdom of God is advanced primarily by miracles, whereas God's Word teaches us that His kingdom is advanced by the Gospel. The battle of the ages is ethical and concerning the Gospel, not about who can cast the most spells. Without exception, whenever a culture substitutes supernatural miracles for the Gospel and natural means (doctors, medicine, etc.), it becomes oriented to magic, to its own presumed sovereignty, and it turns inward with Satanic arts becoming dominant. Welcome to America in the 1990's!

God does occasionally perform miracles, but at His choosing. A culture falls or stands by its ethics, not by its miracles, and the preaching of the Gospel determines ethics. (Read Deut. 28 to see how ethics apply to nations.) We must realize that God blesses or curses nations in direct proportion to their obedience to Scripture. When a nation obeys God, He even removes diseases from it. In this sense healing is spiritual, but also by common grace unbelievers are helped in the culture that honors the Gospel. The preaching of the Gospel, therefore, which leads to obedience, is the method that God has ordained to have diseases removed, not direct miracles.

---

[14]Stanley Howard Frodsham, *Smith Wigglesworth: Apostle of Faith* (Springfield, MO, Gospel Publishing House, 1948), p. 81.

"If you diligently heed the voice of the Lord your God and do what is right in His sight, give ear to His commandments and keep all His statutes, I will put none of the diseases on you which I have brought on the Egyptians. For I am the Lord who heals you" (Ex. 15:26).

God gave or withheld disease in proportion to Israel's obedience to Scripture so that ethics — not metaphysics — determined healing.

The Extremes

It is very common in this late twentieth century for some people to have an almost divine view of doctors. Most people, even Christians, never think of going to God for healing. They view it as the superstition of a by-gone era. They have overreacted to the other extreme of only seeking the supernatural in healing. They equate praying to God for healing with healing lines, fainting, and fanaticism. In their diseases they "do not seek the Lord but the physicians." They view the Lord as not interested in healing except in a general way that draws out vague prayers.

The other extreme, of course, is in the healing movement. Unity writer Florence Shinn considers doctors only for the weak in faith when she says that "filled with doubts" we may have to "go to a Practitioner."[15] Though a "practitioner" is not a doctor in her belief, the idea is still that weakness in faith is the reason for the lack of healing. Kenneth Copeland agrees: "The doctor is a man's best friend if the man does not know how to use his faith."[16] Smith Wigglesworth viewed those who had to use doctors as weak in faith,[17] and he and his wife made this commitment: "From henceforth no medicine, no doctors, no drugs of any kind shall come into our house."[18]

Charles Capps allows some treatment: "If doctors can help

---

[15] Florence Scovel Shinn, *The Power of the Spoken Word* (Marina del Rey, CA: DeVross & Co., 1945), p. 21.

[16] Kenneth Copeland, *The Force of Faith* (Fort Worth: KCP Publications, 1989), p. 7.

[17] Stanley Frodsham, *Smith Wigglesworth: Apostle of Faith*, p. 24.

[18] Ibid., p. 36.

you, don't be condemned over going to a doctor. God wants you alive and well. If medical care can help you, get some medicine. Get well. Get in the Word and stop the next attack with God's Word and your faith."[19] Capps cautions people against throwing away their medicines "when their faith was not developed to that level."[20] He has a detailed discussion concerning not taking the immature in faith off their medicine.[21] He states that "medicine won't heal you,"[22] indicating that it is for the immature who *think* it can heal and so it helps them by giving them a measure of belief.

The Balance: James 5:14-16

(14) Is anyone among you sick? Let him call for the elders of the church, and let them pray over him, anointing him with oil in the name of the Lord. (15) And the prayer of faith will save the sick, and the Lord will raise him up. And if he has committed sins, he will be forgiven. (16) Confess [your] trespasses to one another, and pray for one another, that you may be healed. The effective, fervent prayer of a righteous man avails much.

This practical section of God's Word requires these: confession to the elders (if necessary), forgiveness, healing, and accountability. The confession is not the auricular confession of Roman Catholics to priests for every sin. James 5 is an unusual circumstance, and the person may be sick from his sin. Once confession is made, the elders, who represent Christ, forgive him. Then the person will be healed. If confession is not necessary, the anointing and healing are still promised. Accountability to the elders is very important: The sick person recognizes his responsibility to seek out their prayers for his healing and also their support and oversight if he confesses sin. The elders will require repentance if the person confesses sin.

---

[19] Charles Capps, *Dynamics of Faith & Confession* (Tulsa: Harrison House, 1987), p. 88.

[20] Ibid., p. 155; see also T. J. McCrossan, *Bodily Healing and the Atonement* (Tulsa: Faith Library Pub., 1989), pp. 79, 80.

[21] Ibid., pp. 196-205.

[22] Ibid., p. 155.

This passage is an embarrassment to many people. It embarrasses the health and wealth leaders for they do not like to think that James considered the possibility of the saints becoming sick. Kenneth Hagin says, "The fact that James asked the question infers there should *not* have been any sick among them" [emphasis his].[23] In another place Hagin says these people in James cannot act for themselves; for if they could they would use Matthew 8:17 ("He took our infirmities") rather than James 5:14-16.[24]

The passage also embarrasses those in the broad stream of evangelicalism as they do not want to be associated with something so "weird" as anointing a person with oil and then asking the Lord to heal him. They try to say that the passage is medicinal only and not for today since we have better healing techniques than anointing with oil. Or they say that this particular ministry ceased with the other sign or miracle gifts. We must use all means available, however, such as doctors and medicine, but the proper order, unlike that of Asa, who sought only the physicians, is God and then man. A closer look at the James passage may be helpful.

First, the sick person should call for the elders of the church; if the office of elder is still valid (and it is; cf. 1 Tim. 3:1ff, Titus 1), we should expect that this rite continues. One person suggested that since the sick person calls for the elders that the elders should not go to him first. This is not correct. The assumption in the individual calling the elders is simply that he is too sick to go to them. It is no more wrong for the elders to go to the sick person than for the elders to go to one involved in sin. The text does not say how many elders should go, but since the plural is used we assume at least two. It was the common practice of the Jewish elders, from whom we derive the Christian elders, to visit the sick, praying for them and anointing them.[25]

Secondly, the elders pray and anoint the person with oil.

---

[23] Kenneth Hagin, *Seven Things You Should Know About Divine Healing* (Tulsa: Kenneth Hagin Ministries, 1987), p. 24.

[24] Ibid., pp. 45, 24; Rev. Douglas Mills of Gatlinburg, Tennessee says that he was taught the same thing about James 5 while in the Word of Faith movement.

[25] Alfred Edersheim, *Sketches of Jewish Social Life* (Grand Rapids: William B. Eerdmans Pub. Co., 1974), p. 167ff.

Natural Healing: Doctors and Medicine

The grammar indicates that praying and anointing go together.[26] The term for oil is often used of olive oil in rites (Isa. 1:6; Jer. 8:22). An almost exact parallel is Mark 6:13: "And they cast out many demons, and anointed with oil many who were sick, and healed [them]." It is not the oil that heals any more than the water in baptism regenerates, but God normally uses some visible sign to accompany His grace. Oil sometimes had medicinal value, though, as seen by the Good Samaritan who poured oil on the wounded man (Luke 10:34), but the point here in James seems to be associational, not medicinal. "Oil was no doubt beneficial, but no one claims it was appropriate for *every* illness. Also, if the purpose of the oil was exclusively medicinal, why was it necessary for the elders to do the anointing?"[27]

Furthermore, there is nothing in the passage that indicates that the healing is miraculous. It could be, but it may also be the body healing itself through the recreating process that God designed, which process normally is aided by doctors and medicines.[28] Nor is there any mention that these elders have the gift of healing, but we see the power of their abiding office. This passage was regularly practiced in the early centuries of the church without thought of a miraculous healing.[29]

---

[26] An aorist participle ("anointing") must be either simultaneous with or antecedent to the main verb ("pray").

[27] C. Samuel Storms, *Healing & Holiness* (Phillipsburg, NJ: Presbyterian and Reformed Pub. Co., 1990), pp. 112, 113.

[28] See B. B. Warfield, *Counterfeit Miracles* for a discussion of this, p. 169ff.

[29] See Peter Davids below, p. 194. See also J. B. Mayor who has a long discussion of the early centuries and those who practiced this in *The Epistle of James* (Minneapolis: Klock & Klock Christian Publishers, 1892, 1977), p. 170ff. At our church we practice the rite, anointing the sick and asking God to heal. Then we encourage the sick person to seek out medical help if he has not already done so. This is not a sacrament as the Roman Catholic Church teaches. First, there are only two sacraments in the Old Testament: circumcision and Passover, which come over into the New Testament as baptism (Col. 2:11, 12) and the Lord's Supper (1 Cor. 5:7; Matt. 26:2, 17-20). Secondly, there is nothing in this passage that suggests that the oil or the healing is a sign or a seal of God's covenant grace or that it relates to His covenant with His people. Even the Roman church did not accept this passage as a sacrament until the Council of Trent in the 1500's, though it was sanctioned in 1439 at the Council of Florence. (*The New Schaff-Herzog Encyclopedia of Religious Knowledge* [Grand Rapids: Baker Book House, 1977], 4:252.)

Thirdly, some who are embarrassed about healing do not want to see sickness but only forgiveness of sins. That James means illness may be seen from the terms used: (1) *astheneō*, which the standard Greek lexicon renders "sickness";[30] (2) *kamnō*, also translated "sick" by the lexicon;[31] (3) and *iaomai*, which most understand to mean "physically heal" in this passage.[32] Moreover, there is a word that often means to "save" in the sense of salvation: *sōdsei*. Here it means to "save" in the sense of healing the sick.[33] Peter Davids sums up the evidence well: ". . . the need to call the elders to him, the use of oil, and the two terms [save and sick] indicate that illness is indicated."[34] There is another significant word used: *egeirō*, which is translated "will raise up." In Mark 1:31; 2:9-12; 9:27; Matthew 9:5-7; Acts 3:7 it means to "raise up" in the sense of physical healing. The context is the same here.[35]

Fourthly, notice that the elders exercise the faith, as seen in their praying for the sick person; there is only an inference that the one who called the elders had faith. The sick person demonstrates faith when he calls the elders, for he believes that God will honor this part of His Word. If the sick person is in a coma, he cannot pray or consciously exercise faith. (The relatives, in this case, would call for the elders.) Isn't it interesting that James did not tell the sick person to pray for healing, though this would not be wrong, nor did James instruct him to call for someone with the gift of healing or attend a healing service?[36] This healing rite comes under the jurisdiction of the local church through its elders, whereas the modern "healers" are often independent of the local church.

Fifth, James says, "and *if* he has committed sins, he will be

---

[30] Bauer, Arndt, Gingrich, 2nd edition, p. 115(b). So Moulton and Milligan (p. 84) state that in the papyri it often means sickness.

[31] Ibid., p. 402(b).

[32] A. T. Robertson, *Word Pictures in the New Testament* (Nashville: Broadman Press, 1933), 6:66.

[33] See also Matt. 9:21ff. and Mark 6:56.

[34] Peter Davids, *New International Greek Commentary: James* (Grand Rapids: William B. Eerdmans Pub. Co., 1982), p. 192.

[35] See Bauer, Arndt, and Gingrich lexicon, 2nd edition, p. 214(c).

[36] Storms, *Healing & Holiness*, p. 111.

forgiven." The person may be sick and sin may not be the reason! At least some specific sin may not have caused his sickness though we know that all sickness comes from Adam's original sin. Those who believe that a lack of faith is the only reason a person is not healed make some personal sin the cause of every sickness.

Unity author Shinn states: "Fear is man's only adversary. You face defeat whenever you are fearful!"[37] Similarly, Mrs. Eddy declares: "When fear disappears, the foundation of disease is gone."[38] Fox says, "There can be no sickness without fear."[39] Unity writer Russell is even stronger: "The failure is *always* within the person seeking healing. He does not meet the requirements of healing; he has not cooperated sufficiently with the Grace of God" [emphasis added].[40] The Word of Faith leaders constantly say the same about fear.

James flatly contradicts that illness is always from personal sin when he states that one may be sick but not have sinned. The Lord Himself made it clear that not all sickness is the result of personal sin (John 9:1ff; 11:4) as did Paul (2 Cor. 12:1ff.) and even Job (Job 1-2). If sin is the cause, however, healing will extend to the soul as well. So we see healing of both body and soul, especially in verse sixteen (see also vv. 19, 20). Confession, prayer, and healing often go together in Scripture (1 Cor. 11:30-32; 1 John 5:16, 17).

The Bible and Medicine

We should not have to state the obvious, but the Bible approves of doctors: "But when Jesus heard that, He said to them, 'Those who are well have no need of a physician, *but those who are sick*'" (Matt. 9:12; see Mark 2:17; Luke 5:31). "Luke the *beloved* physician" (Col. 4:14). The word "beloved" is often used of those loved by God (1 Cor. 4:7; 2 John 2, 5, 11) and is applied to Luke *the physician.* Job designates his "friends" as worthless physicians, implying that they should have been good ones: "But you forgers of lies, you are all

---

[37] Shinn, *The Power of the Spoken Word*, p. 24.

[38] Eddy, *Science and Health*, p. 368.

[39] Emmet Fox, *The Mental Equivalent* (Unity Village, MO: Unity School of Christianity, no date), p. 24.

[40] Russell, *God Works Through Faith*, p. 120.

worthless physicians" (Job 13:4). Even if the Bible never said anything positive about doctors, we would still use them since God always requires us to use normal means in every area of life. We use the normal means of transportation today, cars and planes, even though neither is mentioned in Scripture. When we obey Scripture by using normal humans means, such as seeking physicians, then we are seeking the Lord. The Lord Himself has commanded us to use doctors and medicines; therefore, the one who refuses to do so is not seeking the Lord's healing — he is tempting the Lord.

Likewise, the Bible has many verses about medicine. Repeatedly we see people in Scripture instructed to trust in God *and* take medicine. The Lord *never* deprecated physicians or medicine, not once. Sometimes alcoholic beverages are prescribed: "Give strong drink to him who is perishing, and wine to those who are bitter of heart" (Prov. 31:6). "No longer drink only water, but use a little wine for your stomach's sake and your frequent infirmities" (1 Tim. 5:23).[41] Isaiah prescribed figs:

> Now Isaiah had said, "Let them take a lump of figs, and apply [it] as a poultice on the boil, and he shall recover" (Isa. 38:21).

Because of the sins of Israel, God indites them that they "have no healing medicines" (Jer. 30:13). God takes it for granted that medicines are used for diseases. God speaks of His blessings on the righteous:

> Along the bank of the river, on this side and that, will grow all [kinds of] trees used for food; their leaves will not wither, and their fruit will not fail. They will bear fruit every month, because their water flows from the sanctuary. Their fruit will be for food, **and their leaves for medicine** (Ez. 47:12).

The process of cleansing from leprosy in Leviticus was a healing process applied with normal means by the priests (Lev. 13 & 14). In fact, most of the cleansing laws were to keep

---

[41] The television show *Sixty Minutes* reported that French people have four times less incidence of heart problems even though they eat five times richer food. The answer from several medical doctors was that red wine kept one's veins clear and cut the rich food, and the French drink red wine with their meals. The area of highest incidence of heart problems because of wrong eating, according to *Sixty Minutes*, was the "Bible Belt" where people are told not to drink any alcohol but eat terribly.

one clean and thus healthy (Lev. 15). God knew about germs long before modern science, and He gave instructions for cleansing the hands, especially after handling the dead. We can conclude, therefore, that God expects us to use medicine and doctors as the normal part of life, but our hope is always ultimately in the Lord, not in these means.

Does God Want You Healthy?

One assumption of the health and wealth leaders is that God *always* wants His people well and that God never uses diseases to discipline His people. If they are right, we should expect that His people would never get sick, especially from the hand of God. What does the Scripture say?

All through the Bible, especially in the Old Testament, we find God purposefully using disease and sickness. First, observe that the Lord promises to sustain, not necessarily heal, His people when they are sick: "The Lord will strengthen him on his bed of illness; You will sustain him on his sickbed" (Ps. 41:3).

God warns and promises His people that He will place diseases on them for disobedience and remove them for obedience. Notice how often that judgment for sin is sickness:

> If you diligently heed the voice of the Lord your God and do what is right in His sight, give ear to His commandments and keep all His statutes, I will put none of the diseases on you which I have brought on the Egyptians. For I [am] the Lord who heals you (Ex. 15:26).

> But if you do not obey Me, and do not observe all these commandments, and if you despise My statutes, or if your soul abhors My judgments, so that you do not perform all My commandments, [but] break My covenant, I also will do this to you: ***I will even appoint terror over you, wasting disease and fever which shall consume the eyes and cause sorrow of heart.*** And you shall sow your seed in vain, for your enemies shall eat it (Lev. 26:14-16).

> So the anger of the Lord was aroused against them, and He departed. And when the cloud departed from above the tabernacle, suddenly **Miriam became leprous**, as [white as] snow. Then Aaron turned toward Miriam, and there she was, a leper. So Aaron said to Moses, "Oh, my lord! Please do not lay

[this] sin on us, in which we have done foolishly and in which we have sinned. Please do not let her be as one dead, whose flesh is half consumed when he comes out of his mother's womb!" So Moses cried out to the Lord, saying, "Please heal her, O God, I pray!" Then the Lord said to Moses, "If her father had but spit in her face, would she not be shamed seven days? Let her be shut out of the camp seven days, and after that she may be received [again]." So Miriam was shut out of the camp seven days, and the people did not journey on till Miriam was brought in [again] (Num. 12:9-15).

So Moses said to Aaron, "Take a censer and put fire in it from the altar, put incense [on it], and take it quickly to the congregation and make atonement for them; **for wrath has gone out from the Lord. The plague has begun.**" Then Aaron took [it] as Moses commanded, and ran into the midst of the congregation; and already the plague had begun among the people. So he put in the incense and made atonement for the people. And he stood between the dead and the living; so the plague was stopped. Now those who died in the plague were fourteen thousand seven hundred, besides those who died in the Korah incident (Num. 16:46-49).

Then it shall come to pass, because you listen to these judgments, and keep and do them, that the Lord your God will keep with you the covenant and the mercy which He swore to your fathers. **And the Lord will take away from you all sickness, and will afflict you with none of the terrible diseases of Egypt which you have known, but will lay [them] on all those who hate you** (Deut. 7:12, 15).

If you do not carefully observe all the words of this law that are written in this book, that you may fear this glorious and awesome name, **THE LORD YOUR GOD, then the Lord will bring upon you and your descendants extraordinary plagues** — great and prolonged plagues — and serious and prolonged sicknesses. **Moreover He will bring back on you all the diseases of Egypt**, of which you were afraid, and they shall cling to you. **Also every sickness and every plague, which [is] not written in the book of this law, will the Lord bring upon you until you are destroyed** (Deut. 28:58-61).

We see specific instances where the LORD used sickness for judgment:

> And a letter came to him from Elijah the prophet, saying, "Thus says the Lord God of your father David: 'Because you have not walked in the ways of Jehoshaphat your father, or in the ways of Asa king of Judah, but have walked in the way of the kings of Israel, and have made Judah and the inhabitants of Jerusalem to play the harlot like the harlotry of the house of Ahab, and also have killed your brothers, those of your father's household, [who were] better than yourself, behold, the Lord will strike your people with a serious affliction — your children, your wives, and all your possessions; and you [will become] very sick with a disease of your intestines, until your intestines come out by reason of the sickness, day by day.'" **After all this the Lord struck him in his intestines with an incurable disease** (2 Chron. 21:12-15, 18).

> Therefore I will also make [you] sick by striking you, by making [you] desolate because of your sins (Micah 6:13).

These passages are so clear that it would take very sophisticated twisting to evade their force. So what do the health and wealth people do with these? Listen to this: "A general belief in those days [Old Testament days] was that everything that happened came from God."[42] What Mr. Capps means is that the Old Testament people mistakenly believed that these things were done by God, but since the New Testament was written we now know that the devil did them. He justifies this fallacy with a meaningless distinction: "Yes, *all scripture is given by inspiration of God*, but not all scripture is inspired of God" [emphasis his].[43] What he seems to be saying is that it was true the Old Testament writers wrote these things but what they said was not true. Such a distinction in itself could be valid. (It is true that Satan told Eve that she would not die if she ate of the tree, but the content of the statement was not true.) Since God Himself is speaking in many of the Old Testament passages mentioned above, Mr. Capps is absolutely wrong. If Jesus does not change, then He still deals with people the

---

[42] Charles Capps, *Kicking over Sacred Cows* (England, AR: Charles Capps), p. 27.

[43] Ibid., p. 29.

same way today as in the Old Testament (Heb. 13:8). These cases of accurately recording a lie (Satan to Eve) are not very common, and one better not claim that God Himself is lying when *He* speaks! This is taking God's name in vain.

In a letter Mr. Capps sent out in 1991 (not specifically dated) entitled "Did God Create Darkness and Evil?" (Isa. 45:7), he states: "In the Hebrew many times the active voice only grants permission of something rather than being the cause of it. But yet [sic], the people under the Old Testament believed that everything that happened came from God. Their theory was: if God allowed it, He did it; which is not true." This typical statement is so mixed up and entangled that one despairs of making sense of it. He often tries to sound scholarly by making statements about the biblical languages, but it is patently obvious that he does not understand the grammar of either Hebrew or Greek. Such a general statement about the active voice in Hebrew grammar is virtually worthless as one would have to take each Hebrew verb in its context to test his theory — no small task![44]

Secondly, Capps states that the Old Testament people *believed* that God caused everything but that their theory was incorrect. This is the fallacy of a hasty generalization, which means that he has devised a general rule by which to interpret the whole Old Testament without looking at each instance. He wants to demonstrate how the Old Testament can harmonize with a theory already devised rather than allowing the Old Testament to develop his theory. We call this circular reasoning, assuming what one wants to prove. Reread the above passages and see if you can honestly conclude that all

---

[44] Most of the time the active voice means that the subject is indeed causing the stated action. One example: "In the beginning God created the heavens and the earth." The word "created" is the Qal tense, active voice. Does this mean that He allowed them to be created? Obviously Mr. Capps's theory falls. Mr. Capps probably got this from Hagin who says of the Old Testament statements of God's sovereignty: "The original Hebrew of these Scriptures was in the permissive tense, but because the English language has no corresponding tense, the verbs were translated in the causative" (Kenneth E. Hagin, *Redeemed from Poverty, Sickness, and Spiritual Death* (Tulsa: Faith Library Publications, 1983), p. 13.). Hagin is just plain wrong as both Hebrew and English have a sense of permission. For example, English: "I will *permit* you to go to the store." Hebrew: "And you did not *allow* me to kiss my sons and my daughters" (Gen. 31:28). Hebrew also has a causative tense (Hiphil), and this is often used of God causing things to happen.

those Old Testament saints were ignorant fools who did not know what they were talking about.[45] And what about the death of David's child?

> Then David said to Nathan, "I have sinned against the Lord." And Nathan said to David, "The Lord also has put away your sin; you shall not die. However, because by this deed you have given great occasion to the enemies of the Lord to blaspheme, **the child also [who is] born to you shall surely die.**" Then Nathan departed to his house. **And the Lord struck the child that Uriah's wife bore to David, and it became [very] ill.** David therefore pleaded with God for the child, and David fasted and went in and lay all night on the ground. So he said, "While the child was [still] alive, I fasted and wept; for I said, 'Who can tell [whether] the Lord will be gracious to me, that the child may live?' But now he is dead; why should I fast? Can I bring him back again? I shall go to him, but he shall not return to me." Then David comforted Bathsheba his wife, and went in to her and lay with her. So she bore a son, and he called his name Solomon. And the Lord loved him (2 Sam. 12:13-16, 22-24).

We see that the Lord took David's child even though David pleaded in prayer. If someone says that David only thought the Lord killed his child but he was mistaken, was David also mistaken that he had sinned, that the child would not come to him and that he would go to the child? You can see how arbitrary it is for Capps to take statements made by David and attribute some of them to ignorance and some to wisdom. Notice also that David's attitude after the child died was one of comfort that God always does right. He did not attribute blame toward God, but he accepted the death as what God wanted and therefore what was best.

Furthermore, in both the Old and New Testaments many of God's people have had sicknesses:

> **Elisha had become sick with the illness of which he would die.** Then Joash the king of Israel came down to him, and wept over his face, and said, "O my father, my father, the chariots of Israel and their horsemen!" (2 Kings 13:14).

---

[45] Sometimes Word of Faith leaders say that under law things were worse but under grace Christians do not have to get sick. See Chapter Thirteen for their view of Old Testament salvation.

In those days **Hezekiah was sick and near death**. And Isaiah the prophet, the son of Amoz, went to him and said to him, "Thus says the Lord: 'Set your house in order, for you shall die, and not live'" (2 Kings 20:1).

And **I, Daniel, fainted and was sick for days**; afterward I arose and went about the king's business. I was astonished by the vision, but no one understood it (Dan. 8:27).

Then immediately an angel of the Lord struck him, because he did not give glory to God. **And he was eaten by worms and died** (Acts 12:23).[46]

And lest I should be exalted above measure by the abundance of the revelations, a thorn in the flesh was given to me, a messenger of Satan to buffet me, lest I be exalted above measure. Concerning this thing I pleaded with the Lord three times that it might depart from me. And He said to me, "My grace is sufficient for you, for My strength is made perfect in weakness." Therefore most gladly I will rather boast in my infirmities, that the power of Christ may rest upon me. Therefore **I take pleasure in infirmities, in reproaches, in needs, in persecutions, in distresses, for Christ's sake. For when I am weak, then I am strong** (2 Cor. 12:7-10).

Yet I considered it necessary to send to you Epaphroditus, my brother, fellow worker, and fellow soldier, but your messenger and the one who ministered to my need; since he was longing for you all, and was distressed because you had heard **that he was sick**. Indeed I have all and abound. I am full, having received from Epaphroditus the things [which were sent] from you, a sweet smelling aroma, an acceptable sacrifice, well pleasing to God (Phil. 2:25, 26; 4:18).

For to you **it has been granted on behalf of Christ**, not only to believe in Him, **but also to suffer for His sake**, having the same conflict which you saw in me and now hear is in me (Phil. 1:29, 30).[47]

---

[46] Some say this happened to Herod because he was an unbeliever, but still God did it and the other New Testament examples of sickness are of believers.

[47] Word of Faith leaders sometimes state that "for His sake" never means sickness but persecution. The English "for His sake" has several Greek equivalents (*huper autou, dia* with the accusative, etc.), and none of them exclude physical

Elisha, Hezekiah, Daniel, the Apostle Paul, (Timothy earlier), and Epaphriditus had sicknesses but not these health and wealth people. The Lord said to Paul that He would not remove the ailment but that He would give him strength to bear it. The health and wealth folks think they can avoid what Paul boasted in — infirmities! That God would give Paul grace is the same as 1 Corinthians 10:13, which is so often misunderstood: "No temptation has overtaken you except such as is common to man; but God is faithful, who will not allow you to be tempted beyond what you are able, but with the temptation will also make the way of escape, *that you may be able to bear it.*" Though certainly God does remove many of our trials, Paul says the way of escape is *"that you may be able to bear it."*

Paul's Thorn

Dr. Philip Hughes, now with the Lord, has a lengthy discussion of the various views of the "thorn" in history.[48] We may infer from these considerations that Paul's "thorn" was a physical problem. First, most of the early church fathers' explanations of the "thorn" favored some kind of physical problem (see Hughes). Secondly, the Greek seems to say "a thorn *in* the flesh," not *for* the flesh, which favors something literal. Thirdly, the parallel in Galatians 4:13ff. specifically states a physical infirmity. Some dispute that this is parallel to 2 Corinthians 12, but reading both contexts seems to indicate they are related. If this is so, Scripture would interpret Scripture.

> You know that because of physical infirmity I preached the gospel to you at the first. And my trial which was in my flesh you did not despise or reject, but you received me as an angel of God, [even] as Christ Jesus. What then was the blessing you [enjoyed]? For I bear you witness that, if possible, you would have plucked out your own eyes and given them to me (Gal. 4:13-15).

---

illness. Furthermore, the Greek word for suffer here means to suffer death, to suffer from one's enemies, and many other such things (Arndt and Gingrich Greek Lexicon, second edition, p. 634).

[48] For a brilliant discussion of Paul's "thorn" in 2 Cor. 12, I recommend two sources: *Healing and Holiness* by Samuel Storms (p. 102ff.) and especially the commentary on 2 Corinthians by Philip E. Hughes (p. 440ff.), published by William B. Eerdmans Publishing Company.

Do not these verses indicate that Paul had some kind of physical problem, perhaps with his eyes? The Greek words in the expression "physical infirmity" are the same Greek words that Paul uses in 2 Corinthians 12:7-10.

Fourthly, the word for "buffet" tends to indicate something physical. In the *Shorter Lexicon of the Greek New Testament* by F. Wilbur Gingrich, it is stated of "buffet" in 2 Cor. 12:7 that it is "figurative of attacks of illness" (p. 118).

Fifthly, the word for "weakness" is used five times in this context (four times as a noun and one as a verb) and is the same word used in Matthew 8:17 of sicknesses or infirmities. This does not necessitate that it means the same here, but it is probable.

Sixthly, whether it is physical or not, the point is still the same: Paul had some pressing problem that the Lord refused to remove. Moreover, the problem was from Satan but controlled by the Lord Jesus for Paul's good. In verse eight Paul says "concerning *whom*"[49] he asked the Lord to remove him (Satan), but consider the Lord's response: "My grace is sufficient for you." And what was Paul's response to this? Did he think that he did not have enough faith for the problem to be removed? Did Paul become depressed and discouraged? Read for yourself: "I will not boast, except in my infirmities" (v. 5). The prosperity teachers do the opposite; they hate their afflictions and consider those who have them as not walking in faith and obedience.

Finally, Satan was not the ultimate cause of Paul's suffering though he was the immediate cause; Christ was the ultimate cause. Paul prayed to Jesus to remove the problem; he did not command Satan to be gone. Therefore, Paul knew that Jesus held the key to his trial and that Satan was controlled by Him. Christ used Satan to sanctify Paul! The health and wealth people wrongly maintain that if Satan does something then God had nothing to do with it, or if God does something then Satan had nothing to do with it, which is gnostic dualism in which opposing powers constantly fight one another with each one winning and losing.

T. L. Osborn comments on the thorn: "It seems so unrea-

---

[49] The Greek is υπερ τουτου, not περι τουτου. The former preposition is usually used with persons and the latter with things or events.

sonable to me that such broad and diverse ideas should be passed from one to the other, when Paul so clearly states exactly what his *'thorn' was* — *'a messenger of Satan'"* [emphasis his].[50] We have already admitted that Satan is a source, just not the ultimate one. And because Satan is a source and is a person does not mean that the thorn was not something physical, as Osborn gnostically assumes.

Osborn maintains that the word for thorn never means an illness but only some kind of "blow" to "buffet" him (as the King James says) such as the blows of life Paul received from Satan. The early church fathers, whose first language was Greek, disagreed with Osborn. If the reader peruses Dr. Hughes's commentary, he will find that the fathers had no problem with the idea that Paul's ailment could have been an illness.

Furthermore, that the Greek word for "buffet" often literally means to beat someone (Matt. 26:67; Mark 14:65; 1 Peter 2:20) supports the idea that this may have been something physical, and that Satan did it lends credence to the idea that it may not have been literal fists that did the beating. If the "buffeting" were only the trials of life that Paul went through, then it would seem odd that Paul would indicate that the "thorn" stayed with him. In other words, Paul was in and *out* of many trials so why would this one be any worse? Whatever this "thorn" was, it stayed with Paul from one circumstance to another. Finally, that the Greek word translated "infirmities" often means a sickness or some permanent physical malady, supports our idea better than Osborn's.

God has often used Satan to distress His people to produce humility. We see this in the case of Job clearly. In 2 Samuel 24:1 God made David number Israel and then judged him for it. In the parallel passage in 1 Chronicles 21:1 we see that Satan caused David to number Israel. Which one is accurate? Did God or Satan cause David to number Israel? They both did. God used Satan to accomplish His purpose, but the prosperity preachers want to say that the 2 Samuel 24:1 passage is mistaken and that *only* Satan did this. We agree that Satan did it, but not only him. We believe both passages; they believe only one. The health and wealth leaders adjust

---

[50]T. L. Osborn, *Healing the Sick* (Tulsa: OSFO International, 1959), p. 170.

the meaning of the texts to their theology while we adjust our theology to the meaning of the texts.

The most wicked event of all history, the crucifixion of Jesus, was accomplished by Satan but was controlled by God to do precisely what He wanted:

> For truly against Your holy Servant Jesus, whom You anointed, both Herod and Pontius Pilate, with the Gentiles and the people of Israel, were gathered together **to do whatever Your hand and Your purpose determined before to be done** (Acts 4:27, 28).

> But we speak the wisdom of God in a mystery, the hidden [wisdom] which God ordained before the ages for our glory, which none of the rulers of this age knew; for had they known, they would not have crucified the Lord of glory (1 Cor. 2:7, 8).

Did not Satan enter into Judas to make sure the betrayal went according to his plan (Luke 22:3), and yet God had determined that this would happen (Luke 22:22)? Satan wanted Jesus dead, so did God. Satan did precisely what he wanted to do; no one made him crucify the Lord of glory. Yet the Lord was the Lamb crucified *before the foundation of the world* (Rev. 13:8). If God could not control Satan and overrule his plans against Christ and His people, we would be in hell, or at least most miserable. It is a wonderful comfort to know that Satan's schemes are overruled by God for our good!

The health and wealth leaders completely misunderstand those with whom they disagree. For instance, Kenneth Hagin quotes a friend:

> And recently he's been baptized with the Holy Ghost, speaking in other tongues. He has nine children, and he said to me, "Brother Hagin" — very humble man. He was here, you know, and his wife for several days. He said, "Brother Hagin, I'm just new in this, but I know that it's real. I pray with tongues every day," and I prayed with him in tongues. Praise God! "And it enriches me. I found out that." But he said, "You know, I've been trained for thirty years." He said, "I've preached against all of this. It takes me a little time to readjust my thinking. I've preached that healing has been done away with, or that God uses sickness." But he said, "We have nine children." And I [Hagin] saw this boy in San Francisco, one of their boys, thirteen years, who has polio and he's in a wheelchair. And he said, "I

Natural Healing: Doctors and Medicine

> got to thinking, just common reasoning. Now I'm a psychologist, I have counseling classes, I'm a psychiatrist[51] as well as a minister." But he said, "Just common reasoning — I got to reasoning: If sickness is a blessing and God is using this to bless my boy and to deepen his piety and to deepen him spiritually, then I ought to pray that all nine of my kids get paralyzed. I ought to pray that God send polio to all of them so that they will all be deepened."
>
> —Oh, somebody said "that's silly." That's no more silly than to claim that God does it . . . Well, you see, he got to thinking, the utter fallacy of what he had been preaching himself for years. "Just be patient," he'd teach, you know, and preach. "God sends those things, you know, and he uses that to deepen you spiritually," but he woke up. Well, he said, "If that's the case, if it's a blessing, if sickness is a blessing, then polio would be a blessing 'cause it's a sickness. Then I ought to pray that God'll bless all nine of my kids, the other eight - give all of them polio."[52]

This passage demonstrates how the health and wealth leaders argue. First, notice the method in "refuting" the idea that God uses sickness: ridicule. This is not a logical approach; it is an emotional approach, a gimmick, propaganda and demagoguery — very effective with the ignorant. No one wants to be ridiculed, so if one does not agree with Hagin, then he is subject to this treatment. It is like grade school boys on a play ground and several say, "Ha, ha, look at Johnny's trousers." Johnny may change his trousers and never know why. People mistake deriding for truth.

Secondly, it is evident that Hagin does not understand our position, or else he does understand it and cannot handle it. Either way he is wrong. In logic this is called the straw man's argument, which is a theory invented that seems to represent us but actually does not, and consequently is easily "blown over." Since he cannot refute the real idea, he invents one that somewhat similar to the real idea and then claims to be triumphant when he refutes it.

Thirdly, we do not believe that we should pray for God to

---

[51] Apparently Hagin does not know the difference between a psychiatrist and a psychologist, using the two words synonymously.

[52] Quoted by Thomas "Pete" Frye from a message preached by Kenneth Hagin.

give us sickness; no one believes that. We do pray that God would mature us, and we leave the "how" to Him. Indeed, God disciplines all His children with trials of all kinds (Heb. 11:30-12:11) as seems best to Him, and our part is to humbly submit to them and to Him, not to rebel by pouting and demanding that He do things our way.

Fourthly, when Hagin says God does not use sickness, he is directly contradicting all the Bible passages quoted above. These are clear enough for the reader to determine who is accurately representing Scripture.

A few more passages will suffice.[53] In Genesis 32:22-32, Jacob wrestled with the Angel of the Lord (the pre-incarnate Lord Jesus) Who dislocated his hip, which lasted the rest of his life. It was physical, of God, and remained.

When Moses stood before the burning bush, God asked him to put his hand in his breast (Ex. 4:6ff.), and it became leprous. Then Moses was commanded to do it again, and his hand was healed. Thus we see that God made Moses' hand leprous in order to heal it. Miriam and Aaron sinned against God and the Lord made Miriam leprous (Num. 12:10ff.). In 1 Kings 15:1-5 the Lord afflicted King Azariah with leprosy *until the day he died* (2 Kings 15:5). Did the Old Testament people mistakenly believe that these were sicknesses? No; the LORD Himself is presented as the Speaker.

We see the same thing in the New Testament:

> Now as [Jesus] passed by, He saw a man who was blind from birth. And His disciples asked Him, saying, "Rabbi, who sinned, this man or his parents, that he was born blind?" Jesus answered, "Neither this man nor his parents sinned, but that the works of God should be revealed in him" (John 9:1-3).

The passage does not explicitly say that God caused the blindness, but neither does it say that the devil did. Certainly Adam's original sin played a part, for if Adam had never sinned, no one would ever have been born blind. However, we can reasonably see that God is the One who caused the man to be born blind.[54] He was born blind "in order that" (v.

---

[53] Most of these verses were culled by Thomas "Pete" Frye. Thanks, Pete!

[54] Grammatically and contextually, it would seem that verse three modifies the word "born" in verse two so that he was born blind to display the works of God.

3)[55] God's works might be displayed. In other words, the blindness happened with the express purpose of giving opportunity for the manifestation of God's work. How could Jesus show Himself strong to heal unless He had the occasion? Which was the cause and which the effect? Did the blindness cause God's works to be manifested or did God's glory cause the blindness? The Greek implies the latter. This interpretation is consistent with Scripture: "So the Lord said to him, 'Who has made man's mouth? Or who makes the mute, the deaf, the seeing, or *the blind*? Have not I, the Lord?'" (Ex. 4:11).

Like Hagin, McCrossan says if we believe that God sends sickness to help us, then it is inconsistent for us to call for a physician to help us dispose of God's affliction. We should just submit to it. If God willed it, why should we "unwill" it?[56] The answer is not very difficult. First, God requires that we use human means to remove trials, for we do not know if God has designed for us *to endure* the trial or not until we seek to remove it. If the affliction remains, it is God's will (see Chapter Ten on God's sovereignty). Secondly, we have already seen that God limits our trials (1 Cor. 10:13). If God limits them, He could stop them. Of course someone will say that God does not tempt anyone (James 1:13), and this is true. God *personally* does not do this. But He does allow it:

> Lead us not into temptation (Matt. 6:13).

> And you shall remember that the Lord your God led you all the way these forty years in the wilderness, **to humble you [and] test you**, to know what [was] in your heart, whether you would keep His commandments or not (Deut. 8:2).

> Then Jesus was led up by the Spirit into the wilderness to be tempted by the devil (Matt. 4:1).

In this last verse, Jesus insisted on normal human means to meet His needs, not the miraculous! He refused to turn stones into bread or to jump off the temple, but He did use normal human means to remove His trial. It was not removed until the Father was ready to remove it.

---

[55] The Greek is a *hina* purpose clause. Often *hina* clauses are epexegetical or result.

[56] T. J. McCrossan, *Bodily Healing and the Atonement*, p. 79.

When all means to remove the trial have been exhausted, we must submit to it as the Lord did in going to the Cross. It was God's will for Him to be crucified. Paul submitted to his trial after praying three times for it to be removed (2 Cor. 12:7-10). Job still trusted God and submitted.

Conclusion

We see that God commands us to trust Him primarily but also to use doctors and medicines. Christians should be healthy if they obey God's Word. Finally, God uses sickness in the lives of His children and for judgment on unbelievers. If He heals us directly, we call this a miracle; if indirectly through doctors and medicine, we have the normal means of healing. If He does not heal us, we still trust in Him, knowing that He always does what is best for us.

6

Supernatural Healing

Healing and the Atonement

Surely He has borne our griefs and carried our sorrows; yet we esteemed Him stricken, smitten by God, and afflicted (Isa. 53:4).

Is there healing in the atonement?[1] Absolutely. Where else would it be? All sickness is a result of sin, and sin is what the Lord came to bear. All benefits without exception come from His death and resurrection. The curse on the earth and the universe will be lifted as a result of the atonement (Rom. 8:18-23; Col. 1:19, 20). Just as the curse on the earth is a result of sin, so sickness is a result of sin. In addition, no one can be completely free of sickness in this life without being completely free of sin. Conversely, to be sickless implies that one is sinless.

The Essence of the Atonement

Did the Lord bear our sicknesses in the atonement? Yes and no. It depends on what is meant by this, and it is a crucial point. No, Christ did not literally bear our diseases. Yes, He did bear the *cause* of our illnesses, which is sin. Furthermore, He did not literally become a sinner for us; this teaching is rank heresy. But He did bear the *curse* of sin for us: "Christ has redeemed us from the curse of the law, having become a curse for us, for it is written, 'Cursed is everyone who hangs on a tree'" (Gal. 3:13). Again, "For He made Him who knew no sin to be sin for us, that we might become the righteousness of God in Him" (2 Cor. 5:21). Christ could be sin for us when He "knew no sin" because He bore the *wrath* of God for our sin, not the moral corruption of sin itself. The Lord bore the curse of sin, the punishment of sin, the guilt of sin, but surely no one would claim that He became a sinner for

---

[1] Though the word *atonement* is not used in the New Testament, theologians have used it to refer to what Jesus accomplished in His life, death, and resurrection. This is the theological use of the word, not the strict biblical usage.

us.

For the Lord to literally bear our diseases would imply that He became a sinner for us, for the only way one can be sick is to be a sinner. There is no guilt in having diabetes, nor does the Bible say "Do not commit cancer" or "Forgive us our colds as we forgive those who flu against us." Sickness is the *result* of sin, not the sin itself. Can you imagine the police charging a man in a car wreck with a broken arm? The broken arm is the *result* of the wreck, not the cause.

Jesus took our guilt in His *official* capacity as our legal Head and legal Representative. In His *personal* capacity, He took neither our sins nor our diseases.[2] Officially He took our punishment; personally He took nothing. If He personally took our sins, then we have no savior for He would be a sinner; it is that simple. It is vitally important that we understand that *in the atonement* **the Lord Jesus officially took our punishment** that was due sin; He took our hell, as it were.

R. L. Dabney explains the distinction between official and personal guilt this way. A treasurer, Mr. Smith, obtains a bond covering him in his work. Mr. Jones agrees to put up the bond. Later Mr. Smith runs off with the money and is nowhere to be found. Legally Mr. Jones has assumed the liability for Mr. Smith's action and pays the creditors, but does anyone imagine that the embezzler's meanness or personal sinfulness is imputed to Mr. Jones? Not at all. Mr. Jones *voluntarily* assumed the responsibility for Mr. Smith, yet only in an official or legal capacity.[3] As Dabney rightly says, any other consideration "may be named Christianity . . . but it will be another building, his own handiwork, not that of God — another Gospel."[4] Similarly, Jesus voluntarily and legally took our guilt but was never personally a sinner.

When Jesus took our sins, which ones did He take? To ask this question is to misunderstand the atonement. He did not take specific sins; He bore the penalty of sin, the guilt of sin, our punishment. Likewise, to say that Jesus took every specific

---

[2] Robert L. Dabney, *Christ Our Penal Substitute* (Harrisonburg: Sprinkle Pub., 1978), pp. 10-19. See also George Smeaton, *The Doctrine of the Atonement According to Christ* (Winona Lake, IN: Alpha Publications, 1979, from the 1871 edition), p. 158ff.

[3] Ibid., p. 13ff.

[4] Ibid., p. 15.

disease makes the atonement meaningless in two ways: in quantity and in reference to Whom atonement was made.

In quantity, it took an infinite Person (Jesus) to satisfy an infinite Person (the Father). The Father imputed our sin to Christ and thus poured out His infinite wrath on the infinite Son. Thus to quantify the atonement into a finite number of illnesses means absolutely nothing. Sin does not have finite implications; it has infinite implications. That is why a sinner must remain in hell forever; namely, it takes an infinite amount of time for a finite sinner to satisfy an infinitely righteous Being. Christ, being infinite, could execute perfect and infinite justice in a finite amount of time. He took our infinite punishment.

The word "propitiation" in Scripture means a satisfaction of infinite wrath by taking punishment. Propitiation has reference to God. The word "redemption" refers to sin, that our sin was "paid for" by Christ. The word "reconciliation" refers to the sinner, who was placed in a righteous relationship with the holy God. All of this was accomplished legally by the Substitute, the federal or covenant Head who represented His people. Our guilt was imputed[5] to Him and His satisfaction to us. These three biblical words accomplished by substitution reveal the essence of the atonement.

Since Jesus' atonement was made to the Father, He could not have borne our literal diseases. In early church history, it was popular for some of the fathers to say that atonement was made to Satan. (See heading "Did Jesus Descend to Hell to Pay Off Satan?" on page 332.) It did not take long for the church to see the fallacy of this. It was God the Father to Whom atonement was made. Not that His love for us had to be won, but the Son came *because* the Father loved us (John 3:16; 1 John 4:10) and *because* the Father has uncompromising justice or righteousness. But the point is that when Adam sinned, two things happened: (1) God's law was broken, and (2) a penalty was exacted for breaking the law. When the Lord came, (1) He obeyed the law perfectly for His people and (2) He took their punishment on the cross. Both of these have

---

[5] Word of Faith people do not seem to recognize the distinction between "imputing" and "imparting." "Imputing" is a legal transfer to another person but does not in itself affect the person morally. "Imparting" is a moral concept that changes the person's character. The former is justification and the latter sanctification.

reference to the Father. These passages on the satisfaction of His death and in reference to Whom it was made may help:

> But He [was] wounded for our transgressions, [He was] bruised for our iniquities; **the punishment for our peace [was] upon Him,** and by His stripes we have been healed. All we like sheep have gone astray; we have turned, every one, to his own way; and the Lord has laid on Him the iniquity of us all (Isa. 53:5, 6, my translation).
>
> But now the righteousness of God apart from the law is revealed, being witnessed by the Law and the Prophets, even the righteousness of God [which is] through faith in Jesus Christ to all and on all who believe. For there is no difference; for all have sinned and fall short of the glory of God, being justified freely by His grace through the redemption that is in Christ Jesus, **whom God set forth [to be] a propitiation by His blood, through faith, to demonstrate His righteousness**, because in His forbearance God had passed over the sins that were previously committed, to demonstrate at the present time His righteousness, that He might be just and the justifier of the one who has faith in Jesus (Rom. 3:21-26).
>
> Much more then, having now been justified by His blood, **we shall be saved from wrath through Him**. For if when we were enemies we were reconciled to God through the death of His Son, much more, having been reconciled, we shall be saved by His life. And not only [that], but we also rejoice in God through our Lord Jesus Christ, through whom we have now received the reconciliation (Rom. 5:9-11).
>
> For Christ also suffered once for sins, the just for the unjust, that He might **bring us to God**, being put to death in the flesh but made alive by the Spirit (1 Peter 3:18).
>
> For even the Son of Man did not come to be served, but to serve, and to give His life a ransom for many (Mark 10:45).

The Lord had to be man to identify with our sin problem (Heb. 2:14-18), and He had to be God to satisfy infinite righteousness (Heb. 9:14; Acts 20:28; John 20:28). The result of the atonement is that those for whom He died do not go to hell. Or as our Arminian brothers would say, those who trust in Him are saved. We are justified, declared righteous, adopted as sons, on the basis of the Person and work of Jesus, who is "the LORD our righteousness." This is the quintessence of the atonement. The Word of Faith leaders, however, make a fruit of His death, healing diseases, the essence of the atonement. They miss the whole point of sin, judgment, and Jesus' death, for God has not charged us with diseases but with sin, with disobedience to His moral laws. Diseases are the *result* of sin, not the sin itself, and Jesus bore our sin, not the result. The atonement for sin was in answer to the attribute of righteousness in God. His righteousness demanded that sin be punished, and it was punished in Christ. What attribute in God would diseases answer to? There is none.

There are other benefits that we receive from the atonement such as our sanctification or daily conformity to the moral image of Christ (2 Cor. 4:16-18), and glorification, when we will be made completely into His moral image to sin no more. While in this life though, we shall always have some sin and thus some sickness. It is only when we are glorified that we shall no longer sin (1 John 3:2). Just as we do not expect sinlessness in this life, neither should we expect perfect health. One day we shall be sinless and free of sickness, and one day the curse from the earth shall be removed, all as a result of the atonement, but not now. We will not be morally perfected until glorification, and we shall not be physically perfected until the resurrection (Rom. 8:23; Phil. 3:21).

Some of the other benefits of the atonement are that Satan is defeated, our enemies are defeated, the works of the devil are destroyed, the world is conquered by Jesus as He is Lord of lords and King of kings, and many other such things. But all these are benefits flowing from the essence of the atonement; they are not the atonement itself.

Isaiah 53:9 and Two Deaths

Charles Capps completely misunderstands that Jesus did not take our diseases when he says: "I am convinced every diabolical disease known to man ravaged Jesus' body as He hung on the cross."[6] Not only does he misunderstand the nature of the atonement, but he also misunderstands Isaiah 53:9 from which he concludes that Jesus took our diseases.

---

[6]Charles Capps, *Authority in Three Worlds* (Tulsa: Harrison House, 1982), p. 134.

The verse says: "And they made His grave with the wicked — but with the rich at His *death*, because He had done no violence, nor [was any] deceit in His mouth." He comments on the word for death: "The Hebrew word for *death* is plural — not *one* death, but *two*. 'He made His grave with the wicked in His *deaths*.'"[7] It would seem that Capps ultimately got this idea of dual deaths from E. W. Kenyon.[8]

By two deaths, Capps means He died for our sins and also for our diseases. Capps used the word "plural" regarding death, and in English "plural" means two or more, not just two. Secondly, Hebrew nouns have three endings: singular, dual (only two), and plural (two or more). When Capps used the word "plural," therefore, he confused the dual with the plural.

Furthermore, it would be extremely unusual, if not unique, for the word "death" here to be dual, indicating two deaths. First, Hebrew words that indicate a dual are bodily parts such as hands, eyes, feet, or pairs of things such as pants, etc., not a word such as "death." Secondly, nowhere in the Old Testament does "death" indicate a dual. Furthermore, "death" in Isaiah 53:9 is a plural,[9] not a dual, and the plural is intensive[10] which means "it is applied to violent death, the very pain of which makes it like dying again and again."[11] The plural is qualitative, not quantitative, emphasizing the pain in the death, a very common device in Hebrew which all the grammars discuss. (For other examples of the intensive use of "death," see Ez. 28:8, 10; Jer. 16:4.) Thirdly, in verse twelve, only three verses away and in the same context, the same word for "death" is used and it is singular, indicating that only one literal death is in view.

---

[7]Ibid., p. 131.

[8]E. W. Kenyon, *The Father and His Family: A Restatement of the Plan of Redemption* (Seattle: E. W. Kenyon, 1937), p. 162, 175ff. Capps does not give credit to Hagin, from whom he apparently got this idea of two deaths, and Hagin in turn does not give credit to E. W. Kenyon.

[9]Brown, Driver, Briggs, *Hebrew & English Lexicon of the Old Testament*, p. 560(d).

[10]Edward J. Young, *The Book of Isaiah* (Grand Rapids: Wm. B. Eerdmans Co., 1972), 3:353, footnote 35.

[11]Keil and Delitzsch, *Old Testament Commentary* (Grand Rapids: Associated Authors and Publishers), 5:361.

Matthew 8:17

What about Matthew 8:17, which quotes Isaiah 53:4 that says Jesus carried our diseases or sicknesses and His death heals us? We shall have to do some word studies. First, let us look at Isaiah 53. The Hebrew word for "sickness" (*hôlî*) is interesting. Sometimes Hebrew words have one meaning in narrative sections (as in Genesis through 2 Chronicles) and another meaning in poetry (wisdom literature of Psalms through Solomon and most of the prophets). It seems to be slightly true of this word. It is used twenty-four times and only twice is the meaning "sickness" with no judgment of God associated with it.[12] In all the other narrative sections, it means a literal illness which was caused by the Lord's judgment.[13] In Deuteronomy 7:15 the removal of the sickness is a sign of God's blessing so that the sickness may have been the result of His curse, and in 1 Kings 17:17 it is not clear whether the sickness is judgment or not.

In poetry the meaning varies a little, becoming a little less literal with more emphasis on the accompanying judgment by God. For example, in Ecclesiastes 6:2 it is figurative for "useless" with no judgment indicated. This is the only place in biblical poetry where judgment is not associated with the word for "sickness." In the remaining passages, it is figurative of God's judgment.[14]

In the poetry of Isaiah 53, everything is centered around the life, death, and resurrection of Messiah, not around diseases. Notice also the words surrounding "sickness." First, it is associated with "sorrows" (*mak'ôb*) in verses three and four, which means "mental pains."[15] Secondly, "borne" (*nâsâ'*) is used of one bearing the guilt of sin or punishment of the sin of others.[16] Thirdly, in verse eight the word for "stricken" (*nega'*) occasionally means illness but by consistent

---

[12] 2 Kings 8:8, 9; 13:14.

[13] Deut. 7:15; 28:59, 61; 2 Kings 1:2; 2 Chron. 16:12; 21:15, 18, 19.

[14] Isa. 1:5; Jer. 6:7; 10:19; Hosea 5:13; Ps. 41:4). It is probably literal in Eccl. 5:16 (v. 17 in English).

[15] Brown, Driver, Briggs, *Hebrew and English Lexicon of the Old Testament*, p. 456.

[16] Lev. 5:1, 17; 16:22; 17:16; 24:15; 17:17; 7:18; 19:8; 20:17, 19, 20; Num. 14:19; Isa. 53:12 as quoted in Brown, Driver, Briggs, p. 671; Koehler & Baumgartner, *Lexicon in Veteris Testamenti Libros* (Leiden: E. J. Brill, 1958), p. 636.

usage it speaks metaphorically of divine judgment.[17] The word is so commonly used this way that only a few references need be given.[18] Finally, the word for "healed" in verse five (*râpâ'*) is nearly always used in a figurative sense of healing one's distresses or sins.[19] It is used of the "healing" and forgiveness of Gentile nations.[20] A partial conclusion may be drawn. If the word for "sickness" in Isaiah 53:3-5 often means a judgment, and if the words surrounding it in the Isaiah 53 context often mean "judgment" or the "bearing of sin," then "sickness" means a judgment for sin.

But let us continue our study of the word "sickness." In the Septuagint (the Greek translation of the Old Testament done about 200 B. C.) the translation of Isaiah 53:4 is: "He bears our *sins*[21] and is pained for us." Therefore, the Septuagint translators understood the "sickness" as sin, not diseases, and surely they knew their Hebrew quite well.

We may conclude, therefore, that the word for "sickness" in Isaiah 53:3-5 means a judgment of some kind because of sin, which is its consistent usage in the Old Testament, the meaning of the defining terms around the word, and even the Septuagint understood it this way. Furthermore, that the word for "sickness" can be of the soul and "healing" also of the soul is clearly seen in Psalm 41:3, 4: "The Lord will strengthen him on his bed of illness; You will sustain him on his sickbed. I said, 'Lord, be merciful to me; *Heal my soul*, for I have sinned against You.'" In Isaiah 53 we see the Lord Jesus judged for our sins, and the judgment is "sickness." This is not to say that the literal meaning of "sickness" in Isaiah 53 is ruled out, but only that Isaiah uses the word to infer "sin" and "judgment." Now let's look at Matthew 8:17.

Matthew 8:17 says: "He Himself took our infirmities and bore our sicknesses." The word for "infirmities"[22] does not

---

[17] Brown, Driver, Briggs, p. 619.

[18] Gen. 12:17; Ex. 11:1; 2 Sam. 7:14; 1 Kings 8:37, 38; 2 Chron. 6:28, 29, etc.

[19] Ps. 30:2; 41:3, 4; Isa. 19:22; 57:18, 19 as quoted in Brown, Driver, Briggs, pp. 950, 951.

[20] Isa. 19:22; 57:18 as quoted in harris, Archer, Waltke, *Theological Wordbook of the Old Testament* (Chicago: Moody Press, 1980), 2:857.

[21] The Greek is αμαρτια.

[22] The Greek word is ασθενεια.

Supernatural Healing

denote bodily sickness in every case though it is sometimes used that way.[23] The word for "sicknesses,"[24] however, normally means diseases, always meaning such in the New Testament. The context in Matthew 8 clearly indicates literal diseases.

Now we may ask what is the relationship of Matthew 8:17 to Isaiah 53:4? Matthew quotes Isaiah and says Jesus healed people "that it might be fulfilled which was spoken by Isaiah the prophet, saying, He Himself took our infirmities and bore our diseases."[25] Matthew, unlike Isaiah, used verbs that do not denote atonement. For example, he uses a very common word for "took"[26] and a not so common word for "bore."[27] Furthermore, there is nothing in Matthew's context that speaks of atonement, rather he applies Isaiah 53:4 to the public ministry of our Lord. Nor does Matthew quote the last half of Isaiah 53:4, where atonement is definitely in view, but only the first half of the verse. Yet Matthew says the Isaiah passage is "fulfilled."

The word "fulfilled" has a variety of meanings in Matthew. In 2:15 there is a "fulfillment" by type, in 2:17 a "fulfillment" by analogy (similar circumstances), in 2:23 a "fulfillment" by reference to the prophets in general, and in 2:5 a "fulfillment" literally. The point is that just because Matthew used the word "fulfill" does not mean this was the only idea in mind in the Old Testament.

So what is the relationship of Matthew 8:17 to Isaiah 53:4? Isaiah uses words that emphasize atonement though he also uses words for disease, while Matthew uses words that *only* denote disease. Isaiah emphasizes the suffering the Lord went through by using words that denote the *effect* of sin: "a man

---

[23] Arndt and Gingrich, *A Greek English Lexicon of the New Testament and Other Early Christian Literature*, first edition, p. 114.

[24] νοσος.

[25] Matthew did not quote the Septuagint but made his own translation of the Hebrew.

[26] Greek is λαμβανω.

[27] βασταζω. This latter word is only used four or five times in the Septuagint and never means atonement. Likewise, in the New Testament it never means to bear sin but to bear one another's burdens or literally to carry an object. The atonement word for bearing sin is αιρω (John 1:29; Col. 2:14; 1 John 3:5; Isa. 53:8 in the Septuagint).

of sorrows and acquainted with grief" (v. 3), "borne our sicknesses and carried our sorrows" (v. 4).[28] Then in verse five Isaiah surfaces the root or the cause of the suffering: "He was wounded for our transgressions, He was bruised for our iniquities; the punishment for our peace was upon Him, and by His stripes we have been healed."[29] Judgment against Messiah is implied in verses 3 and 4 and is stated explicitly in verse 5; He was judged because of our sins. Thus Isaiah argues from the effect to the cause, from sickness to sin, from grief to guilt.

Putting the effect (disease) for the cause (sin) is called metonymy of the effect, a very common device throughout Scripture. For example, in Genesis 25:23 we read: "Two *nations* are in your womb," in reality two infants whose seed would become two nations, the effect (nations) put for the cause (infants). Psalm 18:2 says: "O, LORD my *strength*," the effect (human strength) is put for the cause (the Lord's strength). Many examples could be compiled.[30] Using a metonymy emphasizes dramatically what is said. It is more effective when a John Wayne says, "Your buildings will be rubble" than if he were to say, "We may alter your town."

While Isaiah gives the cause, Matthew appeals only to the effect, the sicknesses, but with words that do not imply atonement. Isaiah uses words that denote atonement; Matthew the effect, illness. Isaiah speaks of the cause, sin; Matthew does not. Isaiah uses "sicknesses" to emphasize His suffering and to point to sin, speaking of His atoning death, while Matthew uses the word to show the Lord's compassion during His earthly ministry.

Thus Matthew and Isaiah complement one another. Isaiah applies his words to the atoning death of our Lord while Matthew takes them to apply to the life of the Lord without any mention of His atoning death. When Matthew says Isaiah is "fulfilled," he means fulfilled not in the sense that this is

---

[28] Matthew reverses the Hebrew word order and puts the clearer word for sickness last whereas Isaiah has it first.

[29] "Have been healed" is a better rendering than "are healed" as the Hebrew is emphasizing the finality and completeness of the work of Messiah.

[30] There are seven pages of examples from Scripture in E. W. Bullinger, *Figures of Speech Used in the Bible* (Grand Rapids: Baker Book House, 1968, originally printed in 1898), p. 560ff.

what Isaiah primarily had in view but in the sense that the Hebrew allows the literal meaning of "sickness." Christ indeed healed people, not by having the flu for them, but by dismissing diseases by the spoken word. *There is not the slightest hint in Matthew eight that Jesus literally had the flu or literally got sick with someone else's disease.* He "bore" their diseases by feeling compassion for them, which is the way "bore" is used, as we have seen.

Is there healing in the atonement? Certainly, and in exactly the way Matthew used the Isaiah passage. From Isaiah we learn that Jesus definitively and once for all removed the cause of sickness by atonement in bearing sin. From Matthew we learn that He occasionally removed the effects of sin during His earthly ministry by miracles. We have already seen that He did miracles to demonstrate Who He was, and once this was done, there was no reason to expect them to continue. The purpose for them had been completed. Since the healing aspect of the Isaiah passage was "fulfilled" in the life of the Lord, why should we look for it to be fulfilled again today?

What about 1 Peter 2:24?

Peter described Christ as the One "who Himself bore our sins in His own body on the tree, that we, having died to sins, might live for righteousness — by whose stripes you were healed." The word for "healed"[31] is used many times in the Septuagint. Often it has a figurative meaning so that even stones can be "healed" (i. e., restored; Neh. 4:2), one's soul can be "healed" (i. e., forgiven; Ps. 41:4), and one's distresses "healed" or healed in the sense of being forgiven.[32] In Psalm 60:2 the earth is "healed" (restored or corrected). A verse that we often hear — and one badly needed in our ungodly generation — is 2 Chronicles 7:14: "If My people who are called by My name will humble themselves, and pray and seek My face, and turn from their wicked ways, then I will hear from heaven, and will forgive their sin and *heal* their land." To heal the land means to restore it to its fruitfulness, to remove sin from it, to make things right and liveable again.

---

[31]The Greek is ιαομαι.

[32]Jer. 3:21, 22; 6:14; 15:18; 17:14; 19:11; 2 Chron. 6:30; 7:14; Ps. 6:2; 29:2; 102:3; 146:3.

In Deuteronomy 30:3 the Septuagint reads "heal your *sins*"! The Greek word in 1 Peter 2:24 is also used literally of healing diseases many times in the Septuagint.[33]

Likewise in the New Testament the same two meanings dominate, the literal[34] and the figurative.[35] Most of the figurative meanings refer to the healing of the soul (and are used when the Old Testament is quoted in the New Testament).

Without documentation but with dogmatism, T. J. McCrossan, the so-called Greek and Hebrew scholar for these Word of Faith leaders, states that the word for "heal" (*iaomai*) "without one exception in the New Testament refers only and always to physical healing, never to spiritual healing."[36] We have already seen that this is decidedly not true in the Septuagint, and also the Greek lexicons do not support this. For example, Colin Brown in *The New International Dictionary of New Testament Theology* states of this verb that it "is used in the literal sense as a medical term, and also metaphorically and figuratively: to free from an evil . . . or some intellectual shortcoming."[37] Likewise Dr. Oepke in the *Theological Dictionary of the New Testament* (ten volumes), quoting 1 Peter 2:24 and Hebrews 12:13 says, "In such passages [*iaomai*] denotes the restoration of divine fellowship through the forgiveness of sins, and all the saving benefits which accompany it."[38] The standard Greek lexicon states that in the early church fathers and in the New Testament it is used figuratively of "deliverance from other ills of many kinds" such as a healing "from sin and its consequences," quoting Matthew 13:14; John 12:40; Acts 28:27; Luke 4:18; Hebrews 12:13; 1 Peter 2:24.[39]

---

[33] Gen. 20:17; Ex. 15:26; Lev. 14:3, 48; Num. 14:13; Deut. 28:27, 35; 32:39; 1 Kings 6:3; 4 Kings 20:5, 8; (The Septuagint does not label 1 and 2 Samuel; it calls them 1 and 2 Kings so that 3 and 4 Kings are what we would call 1 and 2 Kings.) Job 5:18 (perhaps); 12:21 (maybe); Ps. 103:3; 106:20; Eccl. 3:3; Isa. 19:22 (maybe).

[34] Matt. 8:8, 13; 15:28; Mark 5:29; Luke 5:17; 6:17, 19; 7:7; 8:47; 9:2, 11, 42; 14:4; 17:15; 22:51; John 4:47; 5:13; Acts 3:11; 28:8; 9:34; James 5:16.

[35] Matt. 13:15; Luke 4:18; John 12:40; Acts 10:38 (maybe); 28:27; Heb. 12:12, 13.

[36] T. J. McCrossan, *Bodily Healing and the Atonement* (Tulsa: Faith Library Pub., 1989), p. 62.

[37] Volume 2, p. 166.

[38] Volume 3, p. 214.

[39] Walter Bauer's *A Greek Lexicon of the New Testament and Other Early*

For the sake of thoroughness here are some New Testament passages where the lexicons state that the healing is figurative or healing of the soul:

> For the heart of this people has grown dull. Their ears are hard of hearing, and their eyes they have closed, lest they should see with their eyes and hear with their ears, lest they should understand with their heart and turn, so that I should **heal** them (Matt. 13:15; see also John 12:40; Acts 28:27).

> The Spirit of the Lord is upon Me, because He has anointed Me to preach the gospel to the poor. He has sent Me to **heal** the brokenhearted, to preach deliverance to the captives and recovery of sight to the blind, [to] set at liberty those who are oppressed (Luke 4:18).

> Therefore strengthen the hands which hang down, and the feeble knees, and make straight paths for your feet, so that what is lame may not be [dislocated], but rather be **healed** (Heb. 12:12, 13).

The Old Testament usage disagrees with the modern healers, the New Testament usage contradicts them, the lexicons oppose them, the New Testament scholars disagree with them, but they still believe that "heal" (*iaomai*) only means physical healing! Everyone is wrong but them.

Now what about 1 Peter 2:24? "Healing" must be figurative, referring to the healing of the soul for these reasons. (1) It is a permissible meaning of the word both in the Old Testament and in the New Testament. (2) Peter is quoting Isaiah 53:5 and we must see the entire verse: "But He was wounded for our transgressions, He was bruised for our iniquities; the chastisement [punishment] for our peace was upon Him, and by His stripes we have been healed." The contexts in both Isaiah and Peter are clearly atonement, sin, and forgiveness.

Furthermore, the Hebrew word for healed (*râpâ'*) that Peter translates from Isaiah 53:5 can mean to heal literally (Gen. 20:17; 50:22; Num. 12:13; 2 Kings 20:5, 8), but usually it means to heal the hurts of a nation in the sense of restored favor and forgiveness (Hosea 6:1; 11:3; Ex. 15:26; Isa. 19:22; Jer. 33:6; 30:17; 51:8, 9) or to heal individual distresses

---

Christian Literature (second edition), p. 268.

(Jer. 7:14; 19:11; 51:9; Ps. 41:5; 147:3; Isa. 61:3). There is no question that in Isaiah 53:5 the word "healed" means to heal the soul in the sense of forgiveness of sins. Likewise the Greek word in 1 Peter 2:24 means to heal the soul in the sense of forgiveness. Virtually no scholar debates this. The problem is that the health and wealth leaders have read an English meaning into the Greek and Hebrew words. Indeed, healing in the sense of remission of sins is often used in the Old Testament and in the early church fathers, such as Philo, who was close to the New Testament and understood the Greek language.[40] Therefore, we conclude that "healing" in 1 Peter 2:24 means to heal the soul.

Objections to the Orthodox View

Objection: "All sickness comes from the devil. Christ destroyed the works of the devil so all sickness must be destroyed." There are several answers to this. First, who said all sickness was from the devil? They use Acts 10:38 for their proof: "God anointed Jesus of Nazareth with the Holy Spirit and with power, who went about doing good and healing all who were oppressed by the devil, for God was with Him."[41] They have committed an elementary logical fallacy. Healing "all who were oppressed" does not mean that this includes all who were healed. Perhaps some were healed who were not oppressed. Consider this example: John gave one hundred dollars to all those who wore red coats. Does this mean that no other class of people exists except those who wear red coats?

Even if all sickness were of the devil, the question is *when* will God remove all sickness? The answer is not until all sin is removed. Also, we may even grant for argument's sake that all sickness is of the devil but this would not preclude God from using it (see Chapter Ten on the sovereignty of God).

Objection: "Jesus Christ is the same yesterday, today, and forever" (Heb. 13:8). "If He healed yesterday, then He must heal today or He has changed." In context the verse refers to the *nature* of Jesus, not to the way He *administers* things. Also the new charismatics prove too much. If Jesus or God never

---

[40] Gerhard Kittel, *Theological Dictionary of the NT*, 3:203.

[41] McCrossan, *Bodily Healing and the Atonement*, p. 35.

changes His way of administration, then we must still have the animal sacrifices of the Old Testament, the temple, and the tabernacle. Samuel Storms, a Dallas Theological Seminary graduate, is excellent:

> ... God's nature or character does not change.... What He has been from eternity past He will be into eternity future. However, to say that because God's **nature** is immutable, He must **do** in every age what He does in one age is erroneous. The immutability of God's nature simply means that what He **is** He will always be. But the **way** in which God manifests Himself to men and women and deals with them undoubtedly varies.
>
> There is no indication in Scripture that the spiritual gift of tongues ... was in operation prior to Pentecost. Does this mean that we are justified in charging God with being changeable?
>
> To assert flatly that God must perform the same works in every age is both theologically naive and simplistic.... It exposes a failure to distinguish between who God is and what God does.... It is a matter not of God's power but of His purpose [emphasis his].[42]

Objection: "Just as we have an immaterial part and a material part so Jesus had to die to save our souls (forgiveness of sins) and also die to save our bodies (healing)."[43] McCrossan says: "If Christ is our Passover lamb, His blood was most assuredly shed to save us from the wrath of God through the forgiveness of our sins, and His flesh was bruised and broken for our physical benefits."[44] The logical conclusion to such reasoning is that if one gets sick, he really has not had his sins forgiven. To evade this logic, they make a distinction between forgiveness and healing, which is the gnostic dualism we spoke of in Chapter One. (See heading "Dualism" on page 13.) God did not create us in two separate acts but in one act and called man a "living soul," which statement included both body and soul (Gen. 2:7). Man is a monad, a unit, composed

---

[42] C. Samuel Storms, *Healing and Holiness*, pp. 14, 15; see also John F. MacArthur, Jr., *The Charismatics* (Grand Rapids: Zondervan Pub. House, 1979), p. 52ff.

[43] McCrossan, *Bodily Healing and the Atonement*, pp. 42, 55, 62.

[44] Ibid., p. 62.

of body and soul. When man died, he died spiritually and then physically, both as a consequence of his one sin. As we have already seen, the one atonement for sin included the redemption of the body and the lifting of the curse from the world. By restoring man to righteousness, his sins are forgiven and his body redeemed. In other words, since physical death is the consequence of sin, physical restoration is the consequence of redemption from sin.

McCrossan makes an objection regarding Isaiah 53:4 and Matthew 8:17. He quotes the great Semitic scholar Delitzsch as saying that this verse states that Christ bore *"not our sins, but our sicknesses and pains"* in an atoning sense. He quotes about two paragraphs from the Keil and Delitzsch Old Testament commentary, but what most readers do not realize is that he quotes these two "paragraphs" as if they were consecutive in the commentary; they are not. McCrossan has picked out several sentences that promoted his idea and skipped over others.[45] Keil and Delitzsch say that Jesus in Matthew 8:17 was concerned with the consequences of sin, but that He did not bear the consequences separately in an atoning sense. Jesus did bear our sin in an atoning sense by substitution and McCrossan quotes these scholars to this effect. McCrossan did not realize that the part of the commentary he quotes is not dealing with the consequences of sin in sicknesses but of sin itself.[46]

---

[45] Here are two sentences that he left out: "In 4a it is not really sin that is spoken of, but the evil which is consequent upon human sin, although not always the direct consequence of the sins of individuals (John 9:3)." In other words, Keil and Delitzsch are stating exactly what we said earlier of this verse, the sicknesses are the consequences of sin, the effects put for the cause, not a separate category from sin called sickness. Either McCrossan has misunderstood these men, not knowing how to read the technical language, or he deliberately misquoted them. One other sentence he left out (among others): "But in the fact that He [Jesus in Matt. 8:17] was concerned to relieve this evil [consequences of sin as sicknesses] in all its forms, whenever it came in His way in the exercise of His calling, the relief implied as a consequence in v. 4a was brought distinctly into view, *though not the bearing and lading that are primarily noticed here*" [emphasis added].

[46] "It is not meant that the Servant of Jehovah merely entered into the fellowship of our sufferings, but that He took upon Himself the sufferings that we had to bear." Again, he has misunderstood the scholars. McCrossan concludes from this latter quote: "Now when one takes sufferings upon himself which another had to bear, and does this, not merely in fellowship with him, but in his stead,

Supernatural Healing

E. W. Hengstenberg, another great Semitic scholar, states the same idea of Isaiah 53:4 as Keil and Delitzsch but with greater clarity:

> He [Messiah] has not only **put away** our sicknesses and pains, but He has, as our substitute, **taken them upon Him**; He has healed us by His having himself become sick in our stead. This could be done only by His having, . . . as a substitute, appropriated our **sins**, of which the sufferings are the **consequence**.[47]

J. A. Alexander, a great Semitic scholar of last century, asserts of Matthew 8:17 and Isaiah 53:4:

> The application of these words by Matthew (8:17) . . . is [not] an exposition of the passage [Isa. 53:4] quoted it its full sense, but, as Calvin well explains it, an intimation that the prediction had begun to be fulfilled, because already its effects were visible, the Scripture always representing sorrow as the fruit of sin.[48]

Another outstanding Semitic scholar of this century was E. J. Young. On Isaiah 53:4 he comments:

> It should be noted that the consequences of sin and not sin itself are mentioned. Nevertheless, when it is said that he bore our sicknesses, what is meant is not that he became a fellow sufferer with us, but that he bore the sin that is the cause of the evil consequences, and thus became our substitute.[49]

Finally, the classic work on the atonement was done by A. A. Hodge last century, and he discloses that

> The New Testament writers quote the Old Testament freely, accommodating the sense to a present purpose. Isaiah affirms that Christ bore our sorrows — that is, bore them on himself in order to remove them. Isaiah uses the technical words . . . but Matthew substitutes "took" [for bear]. There is no contradiction; only Isaiah emphasized the **carried**, and Matthew

---

we call this Substitution." Ibid., p. 22. Thank you, Mr. McCrossan, for making the same point that we did earlier.

[47] E. W. Hengstenberg, *Christology of the Old Testament* (MacDill, FL: MacDonald Pub. Co.) 1:593.

[48] J. A. Alexander, *The Prophecies of Isaiah* (Grand Rapids: Zondervan Pub. House, 1974), p. 294.

[49] E. J. Young, *The Book of Isaiah*, 3:346.

emphasized the **removed**. The first pointed out the means, the other the result effected [emphasis his].⁵⁰

Must We Have Faith to be Healed?

The answer is an emphatic No. Even from human experience we know this. We have already seen that vaccinations work whether one believes in them or not.

The ultimate sickness is death. Did Lazarus believe for his healing after he had been dead four days? Of course not. Lazarus was sick "for the glory of God, that the Son of God may be glorified through it" (John 11:4). Can you see Lazarus calling out to Jesus from the tomb and saying, "I believe, heal me and raise me from the dead!" If one does not need to have faith in the most extreme case, then he may not have faith in the lesser illnesses.

In Luke 17:12-19 all ten lepers were healed but only one had faith (see v. 19 where the "your" is singular referring to the *one* leper who returned with faith). Faith itself is the gift of God to His people: "For to you it has been granted on behalf of Christ, not only to believe in Him, but also to suffer for His sake" (Phil. 1:29). Notice that two things have been granted: faith and suffering. Thus if one believes, it is because God has enabled him to do so.

There is no specific mention in James chapter 5 that the sick person believes; the faith is that of the elders of the church. Sometimes healing is the result of faith; sometimes it is not. One cannot establish a certain pattern. In Acts 3 there is no indication that the man lame from his mother's womb expected to be healed or exercised faith in Jesus for healing. Indeed, he seemed quite surprised that he was healed and

---

⁵⁰A. A. Hodge, *The Atonement* (Memphis, TN: Footstool Publications, republished in 1987, first published in 1907), p. 178. One may object that Matthew 8:17 does indeed speak of an atoning work as in the Septuagint, using the same word for "take" in "take our infirmities" as the Septuagint used the word of one "taking sin" for another (Lev. 5:1; chapter 17; 16:22; 19:8, 17; 22:9; 24:15; Num. 5:31; 9:13, etc.). This word "take" (λαμβανω) translates the Hebrew (*nasa'*) which means to "bear" in an atoning sense. If the Septuagint and the Hebrew used the word in the sense of atonement, then Matthew does too. Our response is that there is a significant exception: Matthew says He took our *infirmities* while the Septuagint says He took our *sin*. The Greek word "take" has many meanings, and it is very appropriate for the non-atonement idea or "taking our sorrows" in Matthew 8:17.

rejoiced exceedingly.

Here is a partial listing of people healed or of a miracle performed with no mention of the receiver having faith: feeding of the five thousand (Matt. 12:13; 14:13ff); feeding of the four thousand (Matt. 15:32); healing of Simon's mother in law (Mark 1:31); quieting the storm (4:39); casting demons out of a man (Mark 4:13); raising the little girl (Mark 5:41); healing the deaf mute (Mark 7:35) and the blind man (Mark 8:22ff); casting demons out of the demoniac (Luke 8:26ff); healing of deformed woman (Luke 13:10ff); turning water into wine to the people's surprise (John 2:9); curing of the nobleman's son, where belief followed the healing (John 4:46ff); the healing of the man born blind (John 9:1ff) when the man came to faith only some time later — v. 35); the raising of Lazarus (John 11:36ff), and others.

Even Kathryn Kuhlman had to admit that some people were healed without faith. She relates one man's story whose ear was healed: "My ear has just opened and I do not believe!" She comments that she questioned him thoroughly, but he adamantly maintained his unbelief. She gives her analysis: ". . . all that I can tell you is that these are mercy healings. They have been healed through the mercy of the Lord."[51] At other times people are healed in answer to faith (Matt. 9:2, 22, 28, 29; Mark 1:41; 5:29; 9:24, etc.).

The healers correctly state that at death we shall all be healed of all diseases instantaneously and permanently. The questions we would like to ask are, "Suppose someone does not have enough faith for this? Suppose someone does not want this at that time? Suppose someone has had wrong teaching and thinks this will never happen, that we shall always have to battle sickness? What happens then?" If the healer says that God completes His work anyway, we would agree. If God can complete His work at death whether the justified person knows about healing or agrees, cannot He heal people now who do not have faith or lack proper knowledge? If God makes the saint want healing and righteousness perfectly at death, is He unable to do so now? What makes the difference between the moment of death and the

---

[51] Kathryn Kuhlman, *Never Too Late* (Minneapolis: Bethany Fellowship, 1975), p. 76.

saint's whole life? Obviously nothing; God does what is best for us whether we agree, like it, or don't like it. Do not we as parents do what is best for our children without their permission?

Some may object that in Matthew 13:58 it is stated of Christ: "He did not do many mighty works there because of their unbelief." McCrossan believes that unbelief kept Christ from healing these people.[52] The answer is so simple that we wonder how this verse was ever used wrongly. The verse does not say that Jesus *could* not do miracles because of their unbelief but that He *did* not because of their unbelief. Perhaps one of the reasons He refused is that "an evil and adulterous generation seeks after a sign" (Matt. 12:39). The parallel passage in Mark 6:5 says: "Now He could do no mighty work there, except that He laid His hands on a few sick people and healed [them]." Here it is stated that He *could* not do mighty works, but it is not stated why He could not. From the latter part of the verse it would seem that only a *few* came to Him. The problem was not Jesus' lack of ability because of unbelief but lack of occasion. Jesus was angry *at* unbelief, not immobilized *by* it. Their unbelief kept them from coming where Jesus was, thus not affording opportunity.

The modern healers incessantly speak about "having a point of contact" so that the person can "release his faith." Hagin says, "That was my point of contact when hands were laid on me."[53] What is a "point of contact"? "It's the point when you release your faith and start believing for your healing."[54] With Oral Roberts the definition is similar: "Remember this, a point of contact is something you do, that when you do it, it helps you to believe."[55] This is magical and very dangerous. It is magical because it presents God as Someone Who can easily be manipulated by the right formula. It is dangerous because a point of contact leads very quickly to idolatry. For centuries Roman Catholics have claimed that people are healed by their points of contact,

---

[52] McCrossan, *Bodily Healing and the Atonement*, p. 44.

[53] Kenneth Hagin, *Seven Things You Should Know About Divine Healing* (Tulsa: Kenneth Hagin Ministries, 1987), p. 49.

[54] Ibid., p. 50.

[55] Oral Roberts, *Miracle of Seed-Faith* (Tulsa: Oral Roberts, 1970), p. 165.

which were relics. A relic could be an alleged piece of bone from a martyr, a lock of hair, a piece of cloth, a picture, just about anything. Eventually the relic takes on mystical powers and becomes the object of worship in place of God, which is a violation of the second commandment: "No graven images."

Our modern society is only slightly more sophisticated, but the substance is the same. The radio, a color photograph, handkerchiefs, holy oil and all manner of gimmicks are used as the "point of contact." Those who sell these sink lower than snakes, selling indulgences to poor people. (See the paragraph beginning with "Asking for money" on page 162 for more on indulgences.)

In the Word of Faith movement, faith in faith rather than faith in God is what is promoted. Both Kenneth Hagin and Charles Capps have books entitled *Having Faith in Your Faith* and *How to Have Faith in Your Faith* respectively, and this idea appears many times in their literature. Dave Hunt beautifully summarizes this idea: "If a person is healed *merely because he believes he will be healed*, then the power is in his mind and God is merely a placebo to activate his belief" [emphasis his].[56] According to Hunt, the new charismatics believe they are healed because they have decided it so. If they respond to their symptoms, then they have not believed. This circular reasoning is like trying to lift up oneself by his boot straps, invoking the mind as the initiator of some magical spiritual law that will heal. Once again, here is occult magic in the manipulation of things for man rather than a humble submission to God's sovereignty Who always does things well. Faith has no power in itself; it is no better than its object. (See paragraph beginning with "The point being made" on page 372.) To think that what we believe must come to pass is to place ourselves and God on the same plane.

Health Problems the Healers Avoid

The faith healers will not tackle organic diseases such as slipped discs, broken bones, congenital deformities, correcting eyesight (Oral Roberts wears glasses), filling teeth, lacera-

---

[56] Dave Hunt & T. A. McMahon, *The Seduction of Christianity* (Eugene, OR: Harvest House, 1985), p. 25.

tions from wrecks, gallstones, kidney stones, hernias, burns — in short anything that affects the body directly and obviously. Ailments that are hidden and cannot be easily verified they claim to cure.

Fred Price, who is the pastor of a large Word of Faith church in California and has a TV show, said there is a distinction between healing and a miracle. If your hand is mangled, you can demand healing and God must do it. If your hand is cut off, however, you need a creative miracle and God has not promised to do this.[57] This is a very convenient distinction, getting them off the hook for healings that could be easily verified. Furthermore, Price said that it is God's decision whether He recreates or not, which is exactly the point we have been making concerning all healing. Here is a major concession by one of their leaders.

By contrast Jesus could heal anything. He could recreate eyes that had never seen, limbs that had never walked, and even the whole decayed body of Lazarus! He made no excuses nor engaged in any such casuistry or fine distinctions.

The Lord and the apostles performed healings of organic things that were easily verified. Peter healed the man lame from birth, a fact verified even by his enemies (Acts 4:16). The Lord healed a man born blind, again verified by His enemies (John 9:17-21). But the "miracles" of the modern faith healers are not organic and are gradual, in other words, not miracles at all. Most of their "healings" could be self-healing in the sense of positive thinking, not that positive thinking cures all things. Some "diseases" are psychosomatic, being induced by one's mind and attitude. These, along with their symptoms, are therefore easily removed mentally. We know that the "will to live" often sustains a person who is facing death. Likewise one's attitude in self-healing is very strong: "The spirit of a man will sustain him in sickness, but who can bear a broken spirit?" (Prov. 18:14).

There is no doubt, however, that occasionally God does heal miraculously; the option, however, is His, not ours. We respond with child-like faith, resting in Him that He will do what is best for us.

---

[57] 07/20/92, TV, TBN, Memphis, TN.

Supernatural Healing

How Did the Lord Heal?

Jesus' healings were like His miracles that we have already discussed. They were instantaneous, perfect, and permanent. None were too hard for Him; He healed all the ones He attempted. The healings of the Word of Faith people are almost never instantaneous but gradual,[58] partial instead of perfect, and not permanent but subject to loss. If the Lord's healings had been such, who would have called them miracles and why would people have been in such awe of them?

Gradual Healings?

The metaphysical people, from whom the health and wealth derive most of their ideas, said that "miraculous" healing could be gradual.[59] There are three healing miracles that they and the Word of Faith leaders think were gradual: John 4:52; Luke 17:11-14; Mark 8:22-26.

How does one infer that the healing in John 4:52 was gradual? "Then he inquired of them the hour when he got better. And they said to him, 'Yesterday at the seventh hour the fever left him.'" There is nothing to suggest gradual healing. Jesus told the man that his son lived, and *at the very hour* that Jesus said this, the son was healed.

The second so-called gradual healing is from Luke 17:14 which states: "So when He saw [them], He said to them, 'Go, show yourselves to the priests.' And so it was that as they went, they were cleansed." Hagin's interpretation is ridiculous: "Someone once said to me, 'Brother Hagin, in Bible days, people always got healed instantly.' I replied, 'What about the 10 lepers? The Bible says that they were healed *as they went*'" [emphasis his] (Luke 17:14).[60]

Hagin has read neither the English nor the Greek accurately. The progressive aspect is the *going*, not the healing. This is seen in the English tenses but especially in the Greek tenses.[61] The present tense is used with the "going" but the

---

[58] Charles Capps, *Dynamics of Faith & Confession* (Tulsa: Harrison House, 1987), p. 236ff.

[59] Russell, *God Works Through Faith* (Marina del Rey, CA: DeVross & Co., 1957), p. 57.

[60] Kenneth Hagin, *Seven Things You Should Know About Divine Healing*, p. 63.

[61] In the Greek, "as they went" is an articular infinitive with εν, which Luke often used. The infinitive uses a present tense, but the word for "cleansed" is the

aorist tense with the "cleansed." Thus the "going" is progressive but the "cleansed" is not. In other words, *as they went* or walked along they were *instantly* healed.

In the Mark 8:22 passage, the Lord spat on a blind man's eyes and the man claimed to see people as trees walking. Then the Lord put His hands on his eyes, and he saw clearly. The new charismatics adduce this as a gradual healing. However, there are two miracles here, and both instantaneous.

Some years ago I watched a Moody science film that graphically illustrated this passage. The Moody scientist wanted to illustrate that we see with the brain, the eyes being the instrument. We know that we see things upside down, and the brain reverses the image for us. For several weeks the scientist wore special glasses that reversed images which caused him to see things upside down. Eventually his brain re-adjusted so that he saw things properly, thus proving that the brain was doing the seeing. When he removed the glasses, his brain adjusted again so that he saw things right-side-up though it took several weeks to re-adjust.

In healing a blind person, two things are necessary: the physical eyes must receive light and the brain must interpret properly. Thus when the Lord healed this man, He did two miracles, each one instantly. First, He healed the eyes, and then He healed the brain so that he interpreted properly. It did not take several weeks for his brain to adjust; his brain began to interpret correctly immediately. Even if one rejects this interpretation, it should be obvious that if time did expire in this healing, it was only a few seconds at most, not the days, weeks, or months that modern healers tell their people to expect.

Making the Exception the Rule

There is a passage in Acts (19:12) where diseases were healed and demons cast out by the handkerchiefs of the apostles. This was certainly unusual and not something that should be normalized, but the health and wealth preachers have made this one verse a major basis for their healing techniques. Regularly Robert Tilton and Oral Roberts and others send out cloths that supposedly have the power of God

---

aorist tense indicating instant healing.

in them. Based on a misunderstanding of this passage, they say that God's healing power is a substance. When a "gifted" preacher blesses the cloth, the substance of God's power enters the cloth. Neither the verse nor the context says anything about a substance; they merely draw an inference to justify their practices. Likewise the context says nothing about charging money for the cloths.

The healers may object to the word "charge," saying that they do not charge for cloths. This is only playing with words. In a letter I received from Oral Roberts, there is the ubiquitous color photo of him looking concerned, holding letters and looking up toward heaven. He promises to pray for us in "seven hours of intense prayer." He wants me to send him my "seed money," and he will return "a handkerchief that [he has] saturated with prayer up in the Prayer Tower to use as my point of contact for my miracle." A return envelope without a stamp is provided.

The metaphysical cults also believe that healing is a substance. Like Norvel Hayes in *God's Power Through the Laying on of Hands* (pp. 6-8), New Age author Ric A. Weinman teaches that God's power is transmitted through hands. He wrote *Your Hands Can Heal: Learn to Channel Healing Energy* with a picture of hands on the front. Unity author Agnes Sanford states that physical contact between persons makes healing more powerful as a substance is transferred.[62] Likewise Unity writer Robert Russell states that God's power flows when we lay hands on people.[63] Hagin says the Lord told him "the healing anointing is in your hands."[64]

That healing is considered a substance makes sense in light of the metaphysical roots of Unity, New Age, and the Word of Faith leaders. This power can be transferred from one person to another. According to Oral Roberts, it can also be transferred through a "point of contact."[65] Apparently it is easier to believe God if you have something physical to

---

[62] Agnes Sanford, *The Healing Power of the Bible* (San Francisco: Harper & Row Publishers, 1969), pp. 164-65.

[63] Robert Russell, *God Works Through Faith*, p. 107.

[64] Kenneth Hagin, *Hear and Be Healed* (Tulsa: Faith Library Publications, 1987), p. 5.

[65] Oral Roberts, *If You Need Healing* (Tulsa: Healing Waters, Inc., 1950), pp. 30-38.

relate to, such as a radio, a prayer cloth, and so on.

Someone is sure to object: "How do you know these miracles with handkerchiefs in Acts 19:12 were not normative and thus unusual?" Look at the context: "Now God worked *unusual* miracles by the hands of Paul, so that even handkerchiefs or aprons were brought from his body to the sick, and the diseases left them and the evil spirits went out of them" (Acts 19:11, 12). One Apostle on one occasion had unusual miracles happen, and these modern self-made apostles want to make it normative.

The "Rules" for Healing

The rules for healing vary from preacher to preacher, yet each preacher is emphatic that his rules are the necessary ones. As an example, here are those of T. J. McCrossan:

> (1) We must make an absolute surrender to God: a 100 percent consecration.
>
> (2) Our hearts must be pure.
>
> (3) We must realize that our bodies belong to God.
>
> (4) We must exercise a genuine expectant faith in the promises of God.[66]

If a person can meet all these conditions, he will merit God's healing. Where do we see these conditions being met by those in the Gospels? We do not. Where do we see them met in the epistles? We do not. Furthermore, the conditions are impossible. There is no one alive who is one hundred percent surrendered to God. There is no one alive whose heart is pure; it is only when we see the Lord that our hearts will be completely pure (1 John 3:2).

And notice what kind of faith the person must have: not just faith, but *expectant* faith, and not just expectant faith but *genuine* expectant faith! Who knows what this is or when he has it? But it is necessary for them to advance such a faith so that they can have an answer to those who claim to have faith for healing but are not healed: "You only had faith; you must have genuine, expectant faith." Rarely does the New Testament give qualifiers for "faith" in the sovereign God of the

---

[66]McCrossan, *Bodily Healing and the Atonement*, p. 65.

Bible.[67] In other words, we do not find true faith, or genuine faith or expectant faith in the Bible. What we do find is simply faith in Him.

Conclusion

"Word of faith theology makes the healer a hero when miraculous cures are claimed, but always blames the seeker for a lack of faith when a healing does not happen."[68] This imbalance does not promote Christian love and charity but places more guilt on those who are not healed.

And praying for healing is a curious event. It seems that the unwritten rules require that the one praying do so with great emotion and waving of hands, bind Satan with spoken words, punctuate his sentence with several crescendos, and end with a double "Amen, and amen." Why would not a simple "be healed" be sufficient as it was in the Gospels?

The health and wealth leaders speak of progressive healings while Jesus and the apostles did instantaneous healings. The health and wealth people discourage taking medicine while the writers of Scripture, from the Old Testament to the New Testament, encouraged it.

The consequences of a wrong view are grave. Remember the two extremes. In never seeking the Lord, many may be missing healing. At least they are not giving God the glory for their healing, which certainly violates the verse at the beginning of chapter 5.

The other extreme of thinking all sickness is of the devil and that all healing is spiritual with enough faith, means that many people are kept in a state of discouragement and despair. Why are they not healed? They do not have enough faith, which only makes them worse. In others who are healed there is a spiritual pride that says, "Look at me! I had enough faith."

The difference for some may be death, when healing from physicians and medicine are not sought and death ensues, a situation chronicled in *We Let Our Son Die*. The boy's death

---

[67] The exceptions are 1 Tim. 1:5; 2 Tim. 1:5. Both speak of Timothy who had true, saving faith as opposed to those who had hypocritical faith.

[68] John F. MacArthur, *Charismatic Chaos* (Grand Rapids: Zondervan Pub. House, 1992), p. 283.

was easily preventable; the parents followed the advice they had, which turned out to be deadly theology. These faith healers undermine true faith while producing guilt in their followers.

Another negative result is the lack of care for the sick and especially for the terminally ill. Fred Price said, "You're suffering because you're stupid."[69] Price elaborated by saying that if they knew Christ had taken the curse of the law for them (that is, poverty and diseases) then why were they allowing Satan to curse them any more with illness? You can see how destructive this would be in the life of someone who was sick or in poverty.

As Bruce Barron accurately expressed, "I am not aware of any passage in faith literature that specifically addresses the problem of how to care for the terminally ill and dying."[70] They have no theology for this except "believe and get well." They are coldly incapable of ministering to such a class of people. Certainly this demonstrates their terrible theology, and with such discouraging beliefs, they do more damage then good.

Furthermore, the Lord's healing miracles were also far different than those today. The Lord never had healing services; He healed very casually as the need arose. He also never turned anyone away, like we see today in the so-called healing meetings. He healed all who came to Him: "Now when the sun was setting, all those who had anyone sick with various diseases brought them to Him; and He laid His hands *on every one of them and healed them*" (Luke 4:40). There were none too hard for Him, not one. Furthermore, the Lord's healing miracles were always instantaneous, perfect, and permanent.

The excuse that some use today for not healing all that come to the meetings is that God allegedly leads them to the ones He wants the healer to help, which is to admit that God only wants certain ones healed, at least on that particular day.

We ask our health and wealth friends a question: If God

---

[69] Broadcast on the TBN TV network 05/04/92, 12:00 A.M. to 1:00 A.M., Memphis, TN.

[70] Bruce Barron, *The Health and Wealth Gospel* (Downers Grove, IL: InterVarsity Press, 1987), p. 197.

wants everybody healthy, why does everybody without exception die? Death is the result of sin (Rom. 5:12ff.) and so is sickness. If sickness can be eradicated in this life, why not death? It is obvious that God has willed this form of sickness on all, even babies. When one dies who thinks that all forms of sickness can be eliminated with enough faith, did he die because of lack of faith? Getting old and dying is a form of sickness, and all the health and wealth people are getting old and will die. They have wrinkles on their faces, their skin gets loose, their eyes lose their sharpness and they need glasses. Observe that Paul says that it is his spirit that is being renewed day by day while his body is dying (2 Cor. 4:16-18).

If all the works of Satan were destroyed by Jesus — and they were — then why do people die, since death is the work of the devil (Heb. 2:14)? The answer is that God will not destroy this work of the devil until the Last Day: "The last enemy that will be destroyed is death" (1 Cor. 15:26; see also Rev. 20:14). If God will not complete the application of Jesus' work regarding death until the Last Day, then why is He obligated to make us sickless now?

E. W. Kenyon stated: "He is the Lord of all. He has conquered Satan, sin and disease."[71] If Satan is conquered — and he is — why is he still here on the earth? Why do we have to fight him? If sin is conquered — and it is — why do we sin? If disease is conquered (and it is), why do we get sick? In all three cases, it is because God has not removed these *yet* — it is a matter of timing. If we could be free of sickness, then why can't we be free of Satan's attacks and our sin?

Does sickness bring us closer to God? It can, or it can drive us away, depending on how we respond. It is never the actual sickness that draws us closer to God, but the sickness gives us a reason to look to Him, which does bring one closer to Him. Or as Pete Frye says,

> Now suppose the Word of Faith position is correct. Suppose that the sickness I am experiencing results from some sin I committed. Suppose further that I confess that sin and claim Christ's healing by faith. Does not the potential exist that I have been brought nearer to God in holiness because of

---

[71] E. W. Kenyon, *The Blood Covenant* (Lynnwood, WA: Kenyon's Gospel Pub. Co., 1969), p. 41.

confessed sin and claiming the blessings of God? Could I not have learned more about the effects of sin in my life as a result of my encounter with it?[72]

Finally, as J. I. Packer beautifully expressed it, health and life is not something we die *out of* but something we die *into*.[73] Only when we leave this world and go where there is no more sin can we expect not to have sickness, Satan, and death.

---

[72] Quoted from a personal letter.

[73] Storms, *Healing*, p. 35, footnote 15.

7

Does God Want Us Rich?

God, Wealth, and Faith

The blessing of the Lord makes one rich, and He adds no sorrow with it (Prov. 10:22).

A faithful man will abound with blessings, but he who hastens to be rich will not go unpunished (Prov. 28:20).

Like the modern healing revival, the prosperity movement appeared first in the metaphysical cults and then in the Word of Faith through Kenyon. Metaphysical and Unity author Emmet Fox states, "It is your duty to be healthy, prosperous, and free."[1] Catherine Ponder, also a metaphysical writer, wrote the book *Dare to Prosper!* to her Unity School of Christianity friends to teach them how to prosper.[2]

In contrast to the simplistic and deceptive teaching by many like Kenyon and Ponder, the Bible has much to say that is both cautionary and promising. Having riches is not wrong, but pursuing get-rich-quick schemes is sin. There are extremes among Christians. Some think that money itself is evil, not the *love* of money, so they glory in their poverty.[3] Others

---

[1] Emmet Fox, *The Mental Equivalent* (Unity Village, MO: Unity School of Christianity, no date), p. 20.

[2] She wrote others: *The Millionaires of Genesis, The Millionaire Moses, The Millionaire Joshua, The Millionaire from Nazareth.* Each book has this subtitle: "His Prosperity Secrets for You." She also wrote *Open Your Mind to Receive, Pray and Grow Rich, The Prospering Power of Prayer* and others.

[3] Some Christians condemn those who are productive and use guilt manipulating gimmicks to relieve the person of his money. Ronald Sider in *Rich Christians in an Age of Hunger* is a classic example of the first extreme. The definitive answer to Sider is David Chilton's excellent work entitled *Productive Christians in an Age of Guilt Manipulators*. He shows the balance: being productive over a period of time by hard work, enjoying the fruit of one's labor, and helping the

think that the lack of money is evil so they pursue get-rich-quick schemes to show other Christians how much faith they have. God condemns both.

Prosperity preachers imply that "the *lack* of money is the root of all evil." In 1974, I heard Reverend Frederick J. Eikeren Koetter (commonly referred to as Reverend Ike) say on the radio: "Paul did not mean to say that the *love* of money is the root of all evil but that the *lack* of money is the root of all evil." He continued: "You can't lose with the stuff I use, and the stuff I use is mind power." "Mind power" is metaphysical power. But in 1 Timothy 6:10 God inspired Paul to say it His way. Another idea these leaders promote is "faith without cash is dead." In other words, if you have faith, you will have cash and no money problems. If you have money problems, it is because you do not have faith.

Rev. Douglas Mills,[4] a pastor in the Gatlinburg, Tennessee, area, was in a Word of Faith church in his early Christian experience. He points out that in the Word of Faith movement biblical mandates are distorted, not clarified. One example he used was concerning giving. The Bible commands us to give money to the Lord's work, but the Word of Faith people declare that we are to give in order to get. They change the motivation for giving from pleasing God to pleasing self, from giving out of love to God to giving because we will receive more than we gave. Rev. Mills explains that the Word of Faith leaders present giving as if it were investing in a stock; you will get back more than you put in. Though stocks are risky, God guarantees a "dividend" if you did it "right." God's commands are nearly always pressed on the people with a selfish motive.

Rev. Mills tells of a pastor's wife in Alabama who, during testimony time at church, stated that she did not shop at Sears or K-Mart. Since England's princess did not shop at these places because she is royalty, and since she herself was royalty in being a child of God, she shopped only at the best places. The attitude that God owes us the best material things tends

---

brethren (1 Tim. 6:17-19).

[4]Rev. Mills came out of the Word of Faith movement and took a Charismatic church. He exegeted Scripture until he came out of the Charismatic movement into the Reformed Faith, bringing his church with him. It is an unusually good leader who can take his church with him. May God continue to bless him and his ministry.

to characterize many in the movement.

Patti Roberts, the first wife of Richard Roberts and daughter-in-law of Oral Roberts, admits that she and Richard lived the "jet-set lifestyle" for years. Richard drove a Mercedes and she a Jaguar, and they took vacations in Palm Beach at expensive hotels, eating only the best.[5] Richard and Patti believed that money showed God's approval, according to her own admission.[6]

Giving, however, is qualitative as well as quantitative. The Lord commended the widow who gave all she had (two mites). Others gave from their abundance but she gave from the heart without thought of return (Mark 12:42, 43).

Profligate Prosperity Preachers

Each of the Word of Faith preachers has his own scheme, each was supposedly told it by the Lord (apart from Scripture), and each one is different.

On his magazine that Tilton sends free entitled *Signs, Wonders, & Miracles of Faith*, a large color picture of him adorns the front cover. Questions on the cover include: "Who is this man? What is his mission?" In twenty-four pages there are forty-seven pictures of him and twenty-six pictures about the Robert Tilton Ministries. Two hundred and three times his name or some form of it is used, which is 8.45 times per page. Only sixty-three times is the Lord Jesus' name used. There is one picture of Tilton standing in a crowd with dozens of people around him, reaching out their hands to touch him; a picture of him demonstrating his "humility" by washing a man's feet. The caption to this latter picture says: "This man who has visions and big dreams always has time to do the humblest task if it will show a man how much God loves him" (p. 10).

Numerous pictures show Tilton "healing" others with great concern on his face. Of course there are testimonies throughout the magazine to impress you with the many wonderful miracles that occur through this "anointed servant of God." Along with the magazine there is a packet with a color picture of him on the front, and inside there is a life-size

---

[5] Patti Roberts, *Ashes to Gold* (New York: Jove Books, 1987), p. 82.

[6] Patti though repented and has come out of the movement.

picture of him with his eyes closed holding his hand up. The reader is supposed to place his hand on Tilton's and ask any request. Inside is a "prayer of agreement miracle cloth" that is to be sent back to him for "anointing." (Why was it not "anointed" before it was sent? Because it had to be sent back with money and *then* he would pray over it, anointing it.) Tilton says:

> I'm going to lay my hands on this cloth, and it will become a Miracle Cloth filled with the Presence of God for you to receive your miracle. When I am literally saturated with His power — His anointing — for you, I will touch this cloth and His miracle-working power will flow into this cloth for you. Then I'll return it to you.

Notice how many times Tilton says "you": four times. Most people are incurably selfish, and he is tenaciously appealing to this motive.

Asking for money for prayer cloths is tantamount to selling indulgences, peddling the Word of God. In the Protestant Reformation, Tetzel, a Roman Catholic leader, went about selling indulgences to finance the Pope's building projects in Rome. An indulgence is a grant by the church to lessen the amount of time one will have to burn in purgatory before he suffers enough for his sins to go to heaven. Of course, purgatory is purely fictional. But this is not much different than what Tilton (and others) is doing in selling the blessings of God for profit. See what God says about men like this:

> If anyone teaches otherwise and does not consent to wholesome words, even the words of our Lord Jesus Christ, and to the doctrine which is according to godliness, he is proud, knowing nothing, but is obsessed with disputes and arguments over words, from which come envy, strife, reviling, evil suspicions, useless wranglings of men of corrupt minds and destitute of the truth, **who suppose that godliness is a means of gain.** From such withdraw yourself. But godliness with contentment is great gain (1 Tim. 6:3-6).

While Oral Roberts *appears* on television to be more legitimate than Tilton, his mail-outs are virtually identical to Tilton's. If one were to place Tilton's and Roberts' ads adjacent to one another, the two could not be distinguished except for the ubiquitous color pictures of each man. In July of 1992, I received a packet from Oral with four prayer cloths inside, each a different color with corresponding envelopes of the same colors. The instructions say to send money in each envelope with the appropriate color cloth matched to envelope, one envelope per week for the four weeks of July. There is a large calendar for the month of July enclosed with three color pictures of Oral on it. On each Monday, there is a reminder to send in the appropriate color prayer cloth. On each preceding Sunday there is the reminder to send in the "SEED-FAITH GIFT."

Patti Roberts lamented that the "flow of dollars into the prized ministry" and the public image were more important to Richard and Oral than her marriage.[7] She further bemoans in her biography about her life with the Robertses:

> The Seed-Faith theology that Oral had developed bothered me a great deal because I saw that, when taken to its natural extremes, it reduced God to a sugar daddy. If you wanted His blessings and His love, you paid Him off. Over and over again we heard Oral say, "Give out of your need." I began to question the motivation that kind of giving implied. Were we giving to God out of our love and gratitude to Him or were we bartering with Him?[8]

> Of course, Oral was more subtle. He never promised salvation in exchange for gifts to his ministry, but there were still many people who believed that God was going to look at them in a kindlier way and perhaps their son would get off drugs or they would get their drunken husband into heaven if they gave money to Oral Roberts.[9]

Charles Capps says, "Good news to the poor is: You don't have to be poor anymore!"[10] He has two principles to get what you want from God. First, you must give: "When you give, you set a law in motion. Every time you give to God's work for Jesus' sake and the gospel's, it will come back multi-

---

[7] Patti Roberts, *Ashes to Gold*, pp. 21, 22.

[8] Ibid., p. 119.

[9] Ibid., pp. 120, 121.

[10] Charles Capps, *Authority in Three Worlds* (Tulsa: Harrison House, 1982), p. 98.

plied."[11] Giving is certainly important, but if we think we can make God our debtor, if we believe that we can force God to respond by our works, we have misunderstood the Gospel of grace. Sometimes God gives when we do not deserve it, and other times He withholds because we need to learn perseverance or some other virtue. He alone decides what is best for us.

Capps's second principle is to confess, which means to verbalize what you want. It is very important that we say it over and over, and out loud. Here is what Capps did when he wanted a piece of property:

> After I made the offer, I went out and walked around the piece of property. I talked to it. I spoke to it, just like Jesus said in Luke six [verses 47, 48]. . . . So I walked around that piece of property and talked to it. This is the principle of the Kingdom — calling things that be not as though they were. I said, "Ground, I'm talking to you. I call you into the ministry" [sic].[12]

Don't laugh, the man is serious. This is why some call it the "blab it and grab it" prosperity gospel.

Kenneth Copeland has yet another formula for getting rich. His concept is: ". . . let me share this little formula. It has worked consistently for us and will work for you if you commit yourself to it."

> 1. Decide on the amount you need. Be careful not to cheat yourself. God is not a skinflint.
>
> 2. Get in agreement according to Matthew 18:19. This is very important. The best and most powerful situation on earth is a husband and wife who can agree together in these areas.
>
> 3. Lay hold on it by faith. Use the principles set out in Mark 11:23, 24. Believe it in your heart and confess it with your mouth.
>
> 4. Bind the devil and his forces in the name of Jesus.
>
> 5. Loose the forces of heaven. Hebrews 1:14 refers to the angels

---

[11] Charles Capps, *Dynamics of Faith & Confession* (Tulsa: Harrison House, 1987), p. 143.

[12] Ibid., p. 210.

as ministering spirits "sent forth to minister for those who shall be heirs of salvation."

6. Praise God for the answer.[13]

Copeland thinks that we can receive an hundredfold return on all our gifts, which he bases on Mark 10:30: "Who shall not receive a hundredfold now in this time — houses and brothers and sisters and mothers and children and lands, with *persecutions* — and in the age to come, eternal life." He takes the "hundredfold" quite literally, and if consistent we should expect an hundredfold return not only in our houses but also in our persecutions! The verse means, however, that the one who leaves all for the kingdom of God can expect dividends in all areas of life, but how much and when is left to Him, not to us.

Kenneth Hagin has yet another set of steps, boldly proclaiming that Jesus appeared to Him and gave him four conditions "to get what you want." Jesus allegedly told him: "If anybody, anywhere, will take these four steps or put these four principles into operation, he will always receive whatever he wants from Me or from God the Father."[14] The four steps are: 1. Say it out loud with your mouth. 2. Do it. Take a step of faith. 3. Receive it. Plug into God's electrical outlet by faith to receive from Him. 4. Tell it to others.

This latter step is what confuses people who are not familiar with the health and wealth movement. How can one tell others that he has money when he is poor or that he has been healed when the disease is still manifesting itself in his body? They answer that by confessing to others (visualization; see page 73 for more on visualization) then they will receive what they want. Conversely, if one states that he is not rich or not well, then he is doubting and will not receive from the Lord. He must believe that God has already given to him even though he does not have it yet. By this method God will be forced to grant the wish.

Robert Tilton has made a career of telling people that they need to make a vow to give money to God, and that He will

---

[13] Kenneth Copeland, *The Laws of Prosperity* (Ft. Worth: KCP Publications, 1974, 1989), pp. 87, 88.

[14] Kenneth Hagin, *How To Write Your Own Ticket With God* (Tulsa: Kenneth Hagin Ministries, 1979), p. 5.

then send them more money than they imagined. Tilton probably got this technique from Oral Roberts.[15] Virtually every program of Tilton's in 1991 was dedicated to making a vow to God and then giving money to God by sending it to Tilton.

Ironically, Tilton does not say to send money to Oral Roberts for your blessing, and Oral Roberts does not say to send money to your local church for your blessing. Each televangelist wants the money sent to him.

In a letter from Oral Roberts dated March, 1992, he says, "Get your seed of faith, your love-gift, working for you. None of us ever gets something for nothing." This is legalism and works-righteousness, trying to make God obligated to us by our gifts. He is wrong; we do receive something for nothing, such as righteousness from God: "Now to him who works, the wages are not counted as grace but as debt. But to him who does not work but believes on Him who justifies the ungodly, his faith is accounted for righteousness" (Rom. 4:4, 5). Such a horrendous statement reveals that Mr. Roberts does not understand grace.

Roberts goes on to say, "SOW a generous love-gift of Seed-Faith out of your need to God into this good soil, then expect your miracle (Luke 6:38)" [emphasis his]. At the bottom of the letter which was graced with two color pictures of Oral, there were suggested amounts to send: "$100.00, $35.00, $75.00, $250.00, other."

There is no end to the creativity of these men whose apparent motive is to enslave. Richard Roberts gets money from the seed-faith sowers and enslaves them to debt in one easy step: "Sow a seed on your MasterCard, your Visa or your American Express, and then when you do, expect God to open the windows of heaven and pour you out a blessing."[16]

John Osteen has yet a different formula. 1. Be absolutely specific about what you want. 2. Have a burning desire for the thing that you want, not simply a vague want. Desire it intensely and never give up. 3. Believe that you receive it. Envision yourself possessing your desires. 4. Call the things

---

[15] Oral Roberts, *Miracle of Seed Faith* (Tulsa: Oral Roberts, 1970), p. 45.

[16] John F. MacArthur, *Charismatic Chaos* (Grand Rapids: Zondervan Pub. House, 1992), p. 286.

that are not as though they were (Rom. 4:17).[17] Oral Roberts has three principles. 1. Realize that God is your source. 2. Give that it may be given to you. 3. Expect a miracle.[18] The Unity School of Christianity, which had its own prosperity gospel before the health and wealth preachers, has yet different formulas. There are six steps by Russell,[19] and Catherine Ponder has six things different from Russell.[20]

How can there be so many differences in the formulas? How can Jesus appear to Osteen, giving him four steps, appear to Hagin to give instructions on the same topic, but the instructions are not the same? Roberts and Tilton have also been "told by Jesus" their formulas which are also different. Someone is lying, and it is not the Lord.

A major problem is that these formulas encourage covetousness. Osteen's "burning desire," which is so intense that "God will pay attention to you," sounds like coveting. It is also visualization. (See page 74.) Osteen further says, "What would make you happiest? . . . God delights in making you happy."[21] Instead of "glorifying God and enjoying Him forever," He is to glorify us and make us happy. God is the genie in the bottle who wants to grant your wish. All you have to do is what Capps says, or Hagin's four steps, or Copeland's six instructions, or was it Osteen's four prong program? To get your wish granted, do everything just "right" and maybe, just maybe, you will get what you *want*. The Reformation had men who preached a God-centered Gospel, as did the apostles, but today we have a man-centered one.

God says that we are to be content with food and clothing; these people say the opposite. God says that those who desire riches and who love money are sinful; they praise it. God says that those who use godliness as a means of financial gain are wicked and that we should stay away from them. But these

---

[17] John Osteen, *Four Principles in Receiving from God* (Houston: John Osteen Publications, no date given), see whole booklet.

[18] Roberts, *Miracle*, p. 13ff.

[19] Robert Russell, *God Works Through Faith* (Marina del Rey, CA: DeVross & Co., 1957), p. 102.

[20] Catherine Ponder, *Dare to Prosper* (Marina del Rey, CA: DeVross & Co., 1983), pp. 3, 7, 11, 13, 18, 20.

[21] Osteen, pp. 31, 32.

people encourage their followers to send them money, feigning sincerity and holiness to swindle people out of their money. If they cannot be trusted with money, God will not commit to them the true riches (Luke 16:11).

What constitutes covetousness? You can ask for something and be satisfied when God does not give it, which would not be covetousness, while another demands, like a spoiled child, that God give him what he *wants*. You may say, "Lord, I need a new car. Please bless me to obtain one, but if not I'll still love you and be satisfied. You know what is best for me." That is the attitude of Job who loved God for Who He is. That is not coveting. Another person may say, "Lord, I want a new car and nothing short of that will satisfy. If You want to make me happy, these are the terms." He confesses verbally, demands, fumes, and stops at nothing to get what he wants. This person loves God for what he can manipulate out of Him. He is coveting. Satan told the Lord that Job loved Him for what He gave him, but take all that away and Job would curse Him. Today we have a new twist: The prosperity preachers are saying that Satan was right, we should love the Lord for what we get from Him.

The prosperity preachers seem to have conveniently forgotten these verses, (which, by the way, they seem never to quote):

> Do not overwork to be rich; because of your own understanding, cease! Will you set your eyes on that which is not? For riches certainly make themselves wings; they fly away like an eagle toward heaven (Prov. 23:4, 5).

> Two things I request of You (deprive me not before I die): remove falsehood and lies far from me; **give me neither poverty nor riches** — feed me with the food You prescribe for me; lest I be full and deny You, and say, "Who is the Lord?" Or lest I be poor and steal, and profane the name of my God (Prov. 30:7-9).

> Though the fig tree may not blossom, nor fruit be on the vines; though the labor of the olive may fail, and the fields yield no food; though the flock be cut off from the fold, and there be no herd in the stalls — Yet I will rejoice in the Lord, I will joy in the God of my salvation (Hab. 3:17, 18).

If Scripture were any clearer, we would not understand it. Our age is narcissistic to the extreme, and now we have a "theology" to justify this selfishness. Agur, however, in this passage from Proverbs only wanted enough to meet his needs, leaving the rest to the Lord, and Habakkuk said he could be satisfied with less.

Who in Scripture Did Not Have Money?

The greatest Person who ever lived, Jesus the Son of God, was not rich: "And Jesus said to him, 'Foxes have holes and birds of the air have nests, but the Son of Man has nowhere to lay His head'" (Matt. 8:20). He said that those who would follow Him must be willing to give up all for Him (Matt. 16:24, 25). The Lord Jesus commanded us to seek first the kingdom of God and then all our material needs would be met (Matt 6:33).

Even the Apostle Paul had problems:

> For I think that God has displayed us, the apostles, last, as men condemned to death; for we have been made a spectacle to the world, both to angels and to men. We are fools for Christ's sake, but you are wise in Christ! We are weak, but you are strong! You are distinguished, but we are dishonored! **Even to the present hour we both hunger and thirst, and we are poorly clothed,** and beaten, and homeless. And we labor, working with our own hands. Being reviled, we bless; being persecuted, we endure it; being defamed, we entreat. We have been made as filth of the world, the offscouring of all things until now (1 Cor. 4:9-13).

> Not that I speak in regard to need, for I have learned in whatever state I am, to be content: I know how to be abased, and I know how to abound. Everywhere and in all things I have learned both to be full and to be hungry, both to abound and **to suffer need** (Phil. 4:11, 12).

Paul had *learned* — and it does take time to learn this — to be content. He had learned it because he had been hungry and in need. The assumption is that God, not Paul, was in control of his circumstances, that he needed to adjust to His providence, not that he could create his own providence by speaking words.

Charles Capps tries to circumnavigate this passage. He

says, "Paul is not saying, 'I'm just going to be content with what I have, and I can't do anything about it.'"[22] Capps wants the passage to mean that Paul was "independent" of his circumstances. Capps is right and wrong. It is correct that Paul did not say that there was nothing he could do about his financial condition, but he most emphatically said that he would learn to adjust to it, which is the only way to be independent. If one is not content, then he is controlled by his circumstances.

Then Capps strongly feels the force of Hebrews 13:5: "Let your conduct be without covetousness, and be content with such things as you have. For He Himself has said, 'I will never leave you nor forsake you.'" Capps weasels: "Is this really saying we ought to be content with what we have, and not want anything else? Is this talking about finances? If so, why would Jesus say, *give and it shall be given unto you*? If we should be content with what we have, then we should not want to receive anything more."[23] Capps concludes that Paul really meant ". . . don't covet someone else's wife [v. 4]."[24]

Kenneth Copeland thinks that poverty is of the devil.[25] If so, then the Lord and Paul were not living by faith! The Lord said that we would *always* have the poor with us (Matt. 26:11; Mark 14:7; John 12:8) so apparently He did not intend to completely rid the world of the poor until the curse is lifted from the world (Rom. 8:22ff). Copeland also asserts that if we say words that are not positive, such as speaking against government taxes,[26] we will bring woe on ourselves instead of weal. He should have been present in 1776 to instruct the founding fathers of our nation, whose revolution was founded on a tax rebellion, but which God still blessed.

Does God Want You Wealthy?

What About 3 John 2?

Third John 2 says: "Beloved, I pray that you may prosper

---

[22]Charles Capps, *Kicking Over Sacred Cows* (England, AR: Charles Capps), p. 124.

[23]Ibid., p. 125.

[24]Ibid.

[25]Copeland, *Laws of Prosperity*, p. 54.

[26]Ibid., p. 86.

in all things and be in health, just as your soul prospers." The word for "prosper"[27] means literally "to have a successful journey" but the derived meaning that is often used in the papyri and in the New Testament is "to be successful" or "to prosper."[28] We must ask the question, "Prosper in what sense?" The prosperity preachers assume that the word means to prosper *financially*, but there is nothing in the context to indicate this.

In the Septuagint (Greek translation of the Old Testament done about 200 B. C.) the Greek word for "prosper" is used almost exclusively for the Hebrew word *zsâlêah*, which in turn has many meanings. Here are two of them and notice how different they are: to "prosper morally" (Isa. 53:10; 54:17; Num. 14:41), and the Spirit of God "coming upon" someone (Judges 14:6, 19; 15:14, etc).[29] (We shall return to this in a moment.)

The literal meaning of the Greek word "be in health"[30] refers to the health of one's body, which is used quite often at the beginning of "private letters."[31] This is a classic case of the opening statement of a private letter using the formula "I wish you good health." This would be somewhat equivalent to our "I hope you're doing fine."

Does John mean that God intends for Gaius to be well physically and to prosper financially? There are several reasons that indicates he does. First, even though this is a customary greeting, God providentially used it and preserved it, as He has done in many cases in the New Testament. Secondly, John says that he prays to God that he (Gaius) will be in good health and prosper. Unless we think that John was lying or exaggerating, we should take him at face value.

---

[27] ευοδουσθαι.

[28] Moulton and Milligan, *The Vocabulary of the Greek New Testament* (Grand Rapids: Wm. B. Eerdmans Pub. Co., 1972); Arndt and Gingrich, 2nd edition, p. 323(d).

[29] See Brown, Driver, Briggs, *Hebrew and English Lexicon of the Old Testament* (Oxford: Clarendon Press, 1972), p. 852(b); Richard Harris, Gleason L. Archer, Jr., Bruce K. Waltke, *Theological Wordbook of the Old Testament* (Chicago: Moody Press, 1980), p. 766.

[30] υγιαινω.

[31] Moulton and Milligan, *The Vocabulary of the Greek New Testament*, p. 647; see also Arndt and Gingrich Greek lexicon, second edition, p. 832(b).

Does that wish apply to all Christians and not only to Gaius? This is more difficult. Probably it does. John's desires for Gaius would not be different than his desires for other Christians. However, it does not follow that all of God's people will be healthy and rich in this life. Such a conclusion goes far beyond what John says. It will be true, one day, that all of God's children will have new bodies not subject to disease and that the meek will inherit the earth. Paul taught the former (Phil. 3:20, 21) and the Lord promised the latter (Matt. 5:5), yet neither will occur in fulness until the resurrection at the Last Day.

The second primary meaning for the Greek word for "health" is "sound" as in "sound" doctrine (1 Tim. 1:10; 6:3; 2 Tim. 1:13; 4:3; Titus 1:9, 13; 2:1, 2, 8). Obviously that is not what John had in mind in his context.

The phrase "above all things" in 3 John 2 probably does not modify the word "pray" ("I pray above all things") but the word "prosper" ("prosper above all things"). The best translation, therefore, of 3 John 2 would seem to be: "I pray that you may prosper above all things and that you may be in good health."

Since John says that Gaius's soul already prospers, it seems that he intends financial gain. It would be redundant for John to pray for him to prosper spiritually and add that he is already prospering spiritually. But consider the balance of Scripture. John prays that Gaius may prosper and be in health. The health here is indeed physical, but the prospering may be financial and if so it is an inference, not the inherent meaning of the word. John is saying, therefore, that he wished Gaius to be in good health and to prosper financially, though the amount is not stated.

There are other passages regarding the word "prosper" the prosperity preachers use, and many of these are in the Old Testament. One Hebrew word for "prosper" is *sākal*. It has at least three *nuances*: (1) To act wisely (Ps. 36:3; 64:9; Prov. 1:3); (2) to prosper, often in a moral sense (Jer. 10:21; 20:11; Isa. 52:13); and (3) to understand (Prov. 21:16; Isa. 44:18; Jer. 3:15).[32] The prosperity preachers cite the English word "prosper" and assume a financial meaning for it. The

---
[32] Brown, Driver, Briggs, p. 968; Harris, Archer, Waltke, p. 877.

unwary and ignorant who hear this think he is right, not knowing that the English, the Greek, and the Hebrew words for "prosper" have various meanings. This is what is called an equivocation, changing the meaning of a word without telling the audience, or, as Webster says, "to express one's opinions . . . in terms which admit of different senses, in order to deceive or mislead."[33]

Consider the English word "trunk." Does this mean the back of a car, the front of an elephant, the base of a tree, or something that you find in your attic? The context determines. The same is true of the Hebrew word "prosper." It rarely, if ever, means to prosper financially, but to prosper spiritually.

What About 2 Corinthians 9:6?

This verse says: "But this I say: He who sows sparingly will also reap sparingly, and he who sows bountifully will also reap bountifully." In context this verse means that we can expect to receive back financially in proportion to our giving. Some abuse the passage by expecting God mechanically and necessarily to respond to us. Personal relationships, however, are very complex, and Christians are in a personal relationship with God. A person may claim that he has given much but has not received anything, not realizing that God reads the heart. Maybe the person is not mature enough to handle money, or maybe his heart is not right toward God but is giving only to receive.

What About Luke 6:38?

"Give, and it will be given to you: good measure, pressed down, shaken together, and running over will be put into your bosom. For with the same measure that you use, it will be measured back to you." This verse does say to give, but it does not stipulate how much to give nor how much we shall receive back. Again, how much and when we are blessed is in the Lord's hands. Moreover, in context the verse tells us to give without thought of receiving back.

What About Deuteronomy 8:18?

Moses said: "And you shall remember the Lord your God,

---

[33] *Webster's New Twentieth Century Dictionary*, Unabridged, Second Edition, p. 618.

for it is He who gives you power to get wealth, that He may establish His covenant which He swore to your fathers, as it is this day." All things being equal, Christians should be prosperous. Acquiring wealth involves time — lots of it — work, prayer, honesty, and many other things. Some look at this verse and think they can get rich by "claiming" the verse.

The Hebrew word for "wealth" means just that in this context.[34] God gave Israel strength to gain wealth not because they deserved it nor because of something they did but out of grace. They are warned to love Him or else they will be judged with economic disasters.

Deuteronomy 28 also has many other promises of financial benefit to those who are faithful to God. We see this in the balance of Scripture: giving and working with faithfulness to God over a period of time may produce some measure of wealth.

What About Psalm 118:25?

"Save now, I pray, O Lord; O Lord, I pray, send now prosperity." The broader context reveals that this is a messianic Psalm so that the word for "prosperity" means to "send success"[35] in a spiritual sense.

What About Philippians 4:19?

The verse says: "And my God shall supply all your need according to His riches in glory by Christ Jesus." This verse is often quoted by the prosperity preachers, but it is nearly always taken out of context. Paul promises that God will supply all of our needs, but Paul also revealed a few verses prior that he had learned to be content with little or much (vv. 11, 12). Furthermore, Paul commended the Philippians for giving to the needs of others (vv. 15-17). Verse 19, therefore, is not a blanket promise that God will make you rich, but that we must learn to be content, give to others, and then God will grant all our *needs* — not all our greeds.

Conclusion

What difference does it make if we believe that money is

---

[34]Brown, Driver, Briggs, p. 298, 299; Koehler and Baumgartner, *Lexicon in Veteris Testament Libros*, p. 295.

[35]Brown, Driver, Briggs, p. 852(c).

evil or if we believe that only Christians without faith have financial problems? Plenty. On the one hand, money is an excellent means for furthering the kingdom of God. If money is evil or Christians should never have much, then how is the kingdom going to advance? It takes money to be on TV or radio or to print books, and it takes money to have a church. One of the best ways to advance the kingdom is for rich Christians to raise godly children who use their inheritance for God's glory. This is long term covenant strategy, and the way God usually does things. He did this with Israel for generations. On the other hand, we should not respond like spoiled children, being frustrated and angry at God if He does not make us rich. The balance is work and being content.

If Christians have money problems because of lack of faith, then the only hope these prosperity preachers can offer their followers is to have more faith and to give more (to them, of course). There is little if any ministry to the poor by prosperity preachers in the form of food, money, or other things. In addition, Christians who are poor are made to feel guilty for their poverty. They add additional burdens to their already heavy ones.

Does God want you wealthy? Sometimes, but not always and not necessarily now. When we compare our standard of living to the rest of the world, you probably are wealthy. Is it possible to become wealthy with God's blessings? Yes. There will be a time when all God's children will inherit the earth, but for now becoming wealthy involves time, work, giving, faithfulness, and leaving the result to Him.

Finally, the Word of Faith movement appeals greatly to the selfish and to the ignorant. The selfish are too lazy to study in order to validate the bizarre twisting of Scripture, too lazy to work, to obey God or to attend church so it tickles their ears to hear that they can have money by moving their lips. The ignorant do not know how to confirm the teachings of the leaders and are easily led astray. Lazy and selfish people want to be deceived. We hope this book will help them.

8

Man as God: Verbally Directing Reality

Positive Confession

Then He Jesus said to them, "My soul is exceedingly sorrowful, even to death. Stay here and watch with Me" (Matt. 26:38).

For I Paul am already being poured out as a drink offering, and the time of my departure is at hand (2 Tim. 4:6).

Computer users have a saying: WYSIWYG, "What You See Is What You Get." According to prosperity preachers, "What you *say* is what you get."[1] They actually believe that we can create our own reality or circumstances by what we verbalize aloud. We begin now to see the more radical beliefs of the health and wealth preachers — and this one is indeed radical.

What Is Positive Confession?

This particular doctrine reveals their roots in the metaphysical cults even more clearly than some of the other doctrines. Both the health and wealth and the metaphysical cults promote the belief that there are metaphysical spiritual laws governing us which can be invoked. These laws are engaged by positive confession: saying positive words while thinking positive thoughts. By doing this, the law must work to bring about whatever we have confessed. If we speak negative things, then metaphysical law will bring them to pass. Consequently what we have in our lives is the result of our confessions. We create our own circumstances by what we say.

The ability to control one's environment or create one's

---

[1] Charles Capps, *How You Can Avoid Tragedy* (Tulsa: Harrison House, 1980), p. 152.

own reality assumes that man is like God, that man has enough of God's characteristics that he can, with his words, create his own private world. The Word of Faith leaders have fallen into the lie of Satan to Eve: "You shall be like God." Without this assumption of their "theology," there could be no positive confession. Furthermore, it is pantheism: man partaking of the essence of God, God and man are merged, and the Creator/creature distinction is compromised. Most cults either pull God down or lift man up, and the Word of Faith movement does both. Agnes Sanford even says that God's life is in rocks.[2]

The desire to control one's private world — or the world at large — is the essence of the sin of rebellion. Since Satan's offer of the fruit to Eve, man has wanted the power to be his own god, a metaphysical power over his environment, not the ethical power over himself that the Gospel brings. "Rebellion is as the sin of witchcraft, and stubbornness is as iniquity and idolatry. Because you have rejected the word of the Lord, He also has rejected you. . . ." (1 Sam. 15:23). The desire to be master of one's own fate is to reject the word of the Lord, to be engaged in witchcraft, and brings about rejection by the Lord. Instead of God's providence is man's magic, in lieu of God's Word is man's word; replacing God's moral laws are the metaphysician's so-called spiritual laws that supposedly control the physical laws of the world.

The metaphysical writers say things like "God is the Source of my supply,"[3] which is much like Oral Roberts' TV statements. Of course God is our supply for everything, but *He* determines the timing and dispensing. They maintain that *we* determine this. Fred Price says: ". . . you are going to create the reality of them [problems] with your own mouth. That is a divine law."[4] Rev. Douglas Mills, who has left the movement, reports of one Word of Faith preacher who said: "I don't care if you are a drunk and unsaved, if you say something and add 'in Jesus' Name,' it has to come true." Rev. Paul Yonngi Cho

---

[2] Agnes Sanford, *The Healing Power of the Bible* (San Francisco: Harper & Row Publishers, 1984), p. 18.

[3] Ponder, *Dare To Prosper* (Marina del Rey, CA: DeVross & Co., 1983), p. ix.

[4] Frederick K. C. Price, *Living in the Realm of the Spirit* (Tulsa: Harrison House, 1989), p. 29.

states that our "word actually goes out and creates." "Your word is the material which the Holy Spirit uses to create."[5]

The Random House Dictionary, reflecting *Webster's New Twentieth Century Unabridged Dictionary*, defines magic as "the use of various techniques, as spells, charms, etc., that presumably assure human control of supernatural powers."[6] Faith is used as the magic that "assures human control of supernatural powers." If done properly — and "properly" varies according to the Word of Faith leader — God will have no choice but to grant the incanter's wish.

Charles Capps also loves magic. He says, "The Word of God . . . spoken out of the mouth releases the ability of God." But "if it's the devil you are quoting, you are releasing the ability of the devil. It's just that simple."[7] Again he states, "With words you bind things, or you loose other things. Sometimes you think you are just being honest, and you loose the devil against your finances by saying things like, 'Well, we just never can get ahead.' 'If I ever do get a good job, I lose it.'"[8] Obviously, this is a classic definition of magic, which is nothing more than a form of the occult. By contrast God looks at our hearts and attitudes; He is not manipulated by mere words. We live in a personal world, not a magical one.

E. W. Kenyon often promotes magic by saying that if we mouth the name "Jesus" we shall have anything we want, and nature and demons will obey us. You recall, however, that when someone tried to use the name of Jesus by magic, but who did not *know* Jesus, he was overpowered and beaten by the demons (Acts 19:13-16). So much for the magical use of the name Jesus.

Robert Tilton goes further: "You can tell God on the authority of His Word what we would like Him to do. That's right! You can actually tell God what you would like His part of the covenant to be!"[9] This kind of activity increases with

---

[5] Paul Yonggi Cho, *The Fourth Dimension* (South Plainfield, NJ: Bridge Publishing, Inc., 1979), p. 31.

[6] 1980 edition, desk top size, p. 527.

[7] Charles Capps, *Dynamics of Faith & Confession* (Tulsa: Harrison House, 1987), p. 33.

[8] Ibid., p. 64.

[9] Robert Tilton, *God's Miracle Plan for Man* (Tulsa: Robert Tilton Ministries,

the advent of each new century, and especially of each new millennium. As we approach the second millennium after Christ, we shall see accelerating magic, occultism, New Age, and every kind of nonsense imaginable, both inside and outside Christianity. I am no prophet — neither is anyone else — but I predict that after the year 2000 much of this hysteria will cease, though it may take a few years. Of course the Lord Jesus will literally return to the earth one day, but that will certainly not occur on *our* timetable.

Both the metaphysical cults and the health and wealth leaders assert that to possess something you must desire it intensely. In other words, covetousness helps. As Osteen says one must have a "burning desire" which is so intense that "God will pay attention to you." You must visualize what you want and keep on confessing that you will receive it. Osteen continues, "What would make you happiest? . . . God delights in making you happy."[10] Likewise, Unity author Robert Russell says that to get what we want we must desire it with "deep feeling."[11] Bob Buess says of visualization: "When you meditate on it, then visualize or imagine it happening, you actually believe before it is manifested. Then you begin to move into the gift."[12]

Rev. Douglas Mills gives a personal example of how positive confession worked in a church. Doctors gave one member only a short time to live. The congregation was asked to "pray in agreement for his healing." The agreement was the joined faith force of the congregation. Those who could not believe for his healing were told not to speak about the matter in any form lest their negative confession outweigh the positive. The man died, and the church leaders told the people that even speaking about it would be a negative confession that might spread to others. In this church, the brethren could not ever

---

1989), p. 36.

[10] John Osteen, *Four Principles in Receiving from God* (Houston: John Osteen Publications, no date given), see whole booklet; see also Cho, *The Fourth Dimension*, p. 23.

[11] Robert Russell, *God Works Through Faith* (Marina del Rey, CA: DeVross & Co., 1957), p. 63.

[12] Bob Buess, *The Laws of the Spirit* (Van, TX: Bob Buess, 1968), p. 23. This also sounds very much like Amway, which encourages its participants to visualize by putting pictures of things they want on the refrigerator.

share problems with others and thus bear one another's burdens.

What Do They Mean?

They think that we determine our financial station, our health, and whether we have trials or not by the actual words we speak. If we speak the right words, then we will never have trials. Only those who do not speak the right words are the ones who have trials or afflictions, so if you are having trials then it is your own fault. God never brings a trial on anyone for any reason. The devil may try to afflict you, but you can avoid all tragedy by speaking the right words.

Pat Robertson says, "We simply speak the word aloud."[13] Again he states: ". . . the Law of Dominion . . . depends on the spoken word. We are to take authority by voicing it, whether it involves the devil or any part of the creation."[14] Hagin declares: "It isn't just a matter of faith going out of your heart toward God, without your saying anything. That won't work. Nowhere in the Bible do we read that."[15] Capps says, "The Lord is going to say, 'That was your trouble on earth. *You kept saying what you had, and I said you could have what you said*'" [emphasis his].[16]

The Unity School of Christianity also promotes visualization and verbal confession:

> Supply yourself with a mental equivalent, and the thing must come to you. . . . The doctrine of the mental equivalent is the essence of metaphysical teaching; the doctrine that you will receive that for which you provide the mental equivalent.[17]

> The only weapon you can use against your lions [problems] is your word. Your word is your wand, filled with magic and power. . . .[18]

---

[13] Pat Robertson, *The Secret Kingdom* (New York: Walker and Company, 1986), p. 312.

[14] Ibid., p. 311; see Capps, *How You Can Avoid Tragedy*, p. 133.

[15] Hagin, *Faith Edition Bible* (Tulsa: Faith Library Publications, 1972), p. xix.

[16] Charles and Annette Capps, *Angels* (Tulsa, OK: Harrison House, 1984), p. 136.

[17] Emmet Fox, *The Mental Equivalent* (Unity Village, MO: Unity School of Christianity, no date), pp. 5, 19.

[18] Florence Scovel Shinn, *The Power of the Spoken Word* (Marina del Rey, CA: DeVross & Co., 1945), p. 25.

You cannot control your thought but you can control your words, and eventually the word wins out.[19]

Emmet Fox also encourages us to pray aloud to get better results.[20] Metaphysical writer Russell says that we ought to speak out loud.[21]

How Does It Work?

The health and wealth preachers proclaim that at least three things are necessary: (1) Words must enter the human spirit, (2) spiritual law must be invoked, and (3) we must use the "force" of faith.

(1) Charles Capps instructs about the human spirit:

> What you receive in your heart will get into your mouth; and what you have in your mouth will get into your heart. It starts in the mouth![22]

> When it [spoken word] gets into your heart, your human spirit works night and day to find a way for it to come to pass.[23]

> Your spirit will guide you into a position to cause what you are saying to come to pass. This may explain why you have been misled at times. You have deceived your heart with words.

> Your spirit worked night and day to bring you into a position to cause to come to pass things you really did not want.

> But you spoke wrong words into your spirit day in and day out. You prayed wrong words. You **prayed** the problem. Your heart received that as being your will and worked day and night to bring you into a position where the things you were saying would come to pass [emphasis his].[24]

Thus Capps and others believe that what we say enters our human spirit, and the human spirit engages the metaphysical laws.

---

[19] Ibid., p. 45.

[20] Emmet Fox, *The Seven Main Aspects of God* (Marina del Rey, CA: DeVross & Co., 1942, 1970) p. 8.

[21] Robert Russell, *God Works Through Faith*, p. 95.

[22] Capps, *How You Can Avoid Tragedy*, p. 135.

[23] Ibid., p. 139.

[24] Ibid., pp. 141, 142.

Verbally Directing Reality

The transcendentalists agree; Agnes Sanford says that our words instruct our inner man: "But our prayers seem to be more powerful if they are expressed in words that more correctly instruct the inner being of the person."[25] Here are some other Unity School writers:

> People joke destructively about themselves and the subconscious takes it seriously. It is because the mental picture you make while speaking impresses the subconscious and works out on the external.[26] . . . When an idea is once registered in the subconscious, it must objectify [come true].[27]
>
> How often have you used the law of decrease and talked problems, difficulties, failure, limitation, ill health, confusion, inharmony?[28]

What the Word of Faith teachers refer to as the human spirit, the Unity School leaders say is the subconscious. Though the terms are different, the ideas are the same.

The Word of Faith leaders proclaim the identical ideas: *"God's Word in your mouth produces a force called 'faith' in the human spirit"* [emphasis his].[29] "God's will must first be transmitted by the Holy Spirit to our spirits."[30] Another passage Capps used is John 6:63 where the Lord says: "the words that I speak unto you, they are spirit and they are life." This means, according to Capps, that it is necessary to say good words for anything good to happen to you.

This whole process is fraught with bad theology. First, if these things are true, then the deaf and dumb person must be going to hell. And if he can be saved, he has no hope of anything in this life since he cannot speak. He cannot produce much faith in his human spirit because he cannot verbally confess anything for the human spirit to receive.

Secondly, most of the Bible verses used to support their theory have nothing to do with positive confession. They

---

[25] Sanford, *The Healing Power of the Bible*, p. 159.

[26] Shinn, *The Power of the Spoken Word*, p. 48.

[27] Ibid., p. 71.

[28] Ponder, *Dare to Prosper*, p. 14.

[29] Capps, *Dynamics of Faith & Confession*, p. 65.

[30] Robertson, *Secret Kingdom*, p. 270.

claim that the parable of the sower in Mark 4 and Matthew 13 means that we sow words into our hearts by what we verbalize,[31] that the words determine what kind of heart or spirits we will have.[32] The parable of the sower is speaking of the Gospel which an evangelist or Christian proclaims, not to the mechanics of speaking. A deaf person could receive the Gospel by sign language and become a Christian. Furthermore, Capps states that the words determine the heart, but the Lord says the heart determines the words. If one has a good heart, then the words or the Gospel will take root; if the person has a bad heart, the seed will perish. This is exactly the opposite of what Capps says. Likewise in John 6:63, the *ideas* the Lord speaks are life, not the mechanics of tongue and throat.

They counter the charge of being mechanistic by programming their people to expect criticism: "There is probably no other principle in the Bible that will cause you to be criticized more than this one."[33] In logic this is called "poisoning the well," prejudicing the hearer to respond a certain way without dealing with the force or logic of the objection. It is also called demagoguery or prejudice in lieu of reason. By making their followers martyrs, they reinforce their error.

Thirdly, the method of interpretation they use, if one can call it a method, is definitely unpredictable. We used to live in the country, and each spring we would purchase a dozen ducklings. The local retriever would swim into the water to catch them, but just as the dog would get close, the duck would submerge. You never knew where the duck would surface (one time right under the dog's chin!). The same is true of these people. Since they have no knowledge of language in general or of Greek and Hebrew in particular, you never know what kind of answer will surface or how. They will take some passages extremely literally and others extremely figuratively with no discernable method as to how they determine their meanings. It is arbitrary nonsense. To make matters worse, they glory in this ignorance; when you try to point out the failure of their logic, they conveniently

---

[31] Capps, *How You Can Avoid Tragedy*, p. 144.

[32] Capps, *Dynamics of Faith & Confession*, p. 57.

[33] Ibid., p. 282.

say "Jesus told me this was right."

Mary Baker Eddy in Christian Science teaches the same. She says that a mother by a negative confession ("My child may get hurt") governs her child's response, and it is better for the mother to say, "You're not hurt, so don't think you are."[34] Again Mrs. Eddy says, "You say that you have not slept well or have overeaten. You are a law unto yourself. Saying this and believing it, you will suffer in proportion to your belief and fear."[35] The Unity School of Christianity agrees: "If you tell a friend about [your problem], you strongly affirm the existence of the problem, which is the very thing you are trying to get rid of."[36]

These responses promote alienation from one's friends and personal hurt since one cannot unburden himself to a brother for help. To do so would be to speak the problem, which only makes things worse. Even an injured child cannot count on sympathy from his mother. Rev. Douglas Mills says a Word of Faith pastor in Birmingham forbade his congregation to come to him with their problems because this was a negative confession.

Romans 10:17 says, "So then faith comes by hearing, and hearing by the word of God." According to Capps, this means that you put faith in your own human spirit by hearing your mouth confess the right things. So Capps advises that if you want to sell your car, "Say, 'Car, I am calling you sold. Someone loves your paint job. They are impressed with you. By faith I call you sold, in Jesus' name.'"[37] You can do this for your check book, for your health, or for anything that you want. Similarly, Unity author Fox tells of "blessing" a store for its success,[38] and Russell recommends the following confession when things are not going right: "Subconscious mind of me, I am tired of your lies, and I command you to tell the truth. I command you to restore my courage and faith, and I command you to do it now."[39] The health and wealth people could

---

[34] Mary Baker Eddy, *Science and Health*, pp. 154-55.

[35] Ibid., p. 385.

[36] Fox, *Mental Equivalent*, p. 28; see also Russell, *God Works Through Faith*, pp. 26-27.

[37] Capps, *Dynamics of Faith and Confession*, p. 34.

[38] Fox, *Seven Main Aspects of God*, p. 30.

[39] Russell, *God Works Through Faith*, p. 45.

use Russell's "prayer" except that they would add "in Jesus' Name" at the end. If one wants to remove a stain from a dress, Shinn suggests to say this: "Evil is unreal and leaves no stain."[40]

Furthermore, the Greek in Romans 10 refutes Capps's understanding. In verses 14 and 15 we do not have "how shall they believe *in* Him *of* whom they have not heard" but "how shall they believe *Him whom* they have not heard."[41] Thus Christ Himself is preaching through His preachers to those who hear, not that each person is talking to himself.

Also the word for "hearing"[42] in verse 17 is a pregnant word. It is the same word as "report" in v. 16.[43] In this context, the idea in "hearing" is *what* they heard, the *message*, with the mechanics of hearing being in the background.[44]

In Romans 10 preachers proclaim the Gospel message; when they do, those who are able hear *Him* speaking — not some gibberish about selling a car. And when they hear Him speaking, they hear the *content* of the message, the death and resurrection of Jesus the Almighty Lord, not simply some sounds that magically enter their human spirits.

(2) The second step in making positive confession work is invoking spiritual law. Since we have seen in Chapter Three that these laws supposedly control results, elaboration is unnecessary. Suffice it to say that our verbalizing allegedly engages these laws to bring about in our lives what we have said.

(3) The force of faith is another key to positive confession. According to metaphysics, faith is a spiritual force that en-

---

[40] Shinn, *The Power of the Spoken Word*, p. 19.

[41] ". . . the thought is of their hearing Christ speaking in the message of the preachers. (To explain [this] as meaning 'about whom they have not heard' is not really feasible; for the use of ακουω with the simple genitive of the person meaning 'to hear about someone' would be very unusual)" (Cranfield in the ICC Romans Commentary; John Murray in his commentary on Romans agrees).

[42] ακοη.

[43] See Heb. 4:2; 1 Thess. 2:13; Gal. 3:2, 5 for the same usage of the word for "hearing."

[44] F. F. Bruce on *Galatians*; *New International Dict. of the NT*; *TDNT*; Godet, Liddon, John Murray on Romans, Cranfield on Romans in the ICC series. The message heard is what the Lord often said: "The one who has ears to hear, let him hear" (Matt. 11:15; 13:9, 43; Mark 4:9, 23; Luke 8:8; 14:35; Rev. 2:7, 11, 17, 29; 3:6, 13, 22; 13:9). The Lord was not questioning that they had ears but was emphasizing the acceptance of His *message*.

gages the metaphysical laws with the directions given by our inner spirits. Faith is very much like a switch for electricity: turn it on and the light burns; turn it off and it does not. In either case, positive or negative, it is very mechanical. Faith is not directed so much toward a Person in humility, submission, and love as it is directed at laws to manipulate them for one's desires. Thus they present believing *for something* rather than believing *in Someone*.

A practical problem is the bondage this brings to its adherents. There is no end to the bizarre steps required to follow properly in order to reap God's blessings. The person wonders if he has done enough. Were ten steps enough, did he do them just right, did he practice them often enough?

By contrast, in a *personal* relationship with the God of all grace through Jesus, God the Son, the sinner trusts the Lord to do what is right, knowing that he could never be perfect enough to receive anything from Him. The saint knows that God accepts what he does for Christ's sake, not because he has merited it; and even when his practice is not what it should be, the loving personal God may grant his requests anyway, or withhold them since He always knows what is best. In other words, God is not democratic; He does not treat each child exactly alike but personally, according to need, and always on the merits of Christ. One may need to learn perseverance and patience so God allows the trial to continue. Another may need encouragement so He grants what is asked even though the child does not deserve it. God is not a computer that we program by our "correct" steps, but He is a person with Whom we relate on the basis of the merits of Jesus' blood and righteousness.

Do We Create Our Own Realities?

The health and wealth people say: ". . . I have learned the powerful force of the spiritual world that creates the circumstances around us is controlled by the words of the mouth. This force comes from inside us."[45] "We live in an environment of our own making — one that we have largely created by our own words."[46] "*Whatever you can conceive, and believe,*

---

[45] Kenneth Copeland, *The Laws of Prosperity* (Forth Worth: KCP Publications, 1989), p. 83.

[46] Kenneth Hagin, Jr., *God's Irresistible Word* (Tulsa: Kenneth Hagin Ministries,

you can do!" [emphasis his].⁴⁷ And Hagin says, "You will find that faith's confession creates reality."⁴⁸

The metaphysical writers agree:

> Whatever enters into your life is but the material expression of some belief in your own mind.⁴⁹

> . . . we recognize matter as the obedient servant of our word and receive abundantly from Spirit.⁵⁰

> You can and should create your world accordingly, because you are created in the image and likeness of God, and you, too, have the power to form substance through your definite, spoken decrees for good.⁵¹

> . . . man was to continue the work of creation.⁵²

We see, therefore, that both the metaphysical writers and the Word of Faith leaders teach that we can and must create our own little worlds, that our circumstances are our making, and the ability to do such assumes that we are like God.

Does God Answer All Prayer?

The prosperity people proclaim that God must grant *any* prayer request they ask in faith. Is this correct? Absolutely not. Then what does the Lord mean when He said, "Whatever you ask in My name, that I will do" (John 14:13)? It is not a promise without balancing it with other Scripture. If it were an unqualified promise, then one could ask for revenge on all his enemies as he watched, a million pounds of gold, a thousand beautiful wives, and the continent of Europe, and demand these now. You rightly say that these requests are not allowed by *other* passages of Scripture, which proves that there are limitations to the promise. In other words, we must ask

---

1989), p. 6.

⁴⁷Oral Roberts, *Miracle of Seed-Faith*, p. 7.

⁴⁸Hagin, *Faith Edition Bible*, p. xlv.

⁴⁹Emmet Fox, *The Mental Equivalent*, p. 4.

⁵⁰Robert Russell, *God Works Through Faith*, p. 143.

⁵¹Catherine Ponder, *Dare to Prosper*, p. 14.

⁵²Sanford, *Healing Power*, p. 30.

according to His will as it is revealed in Scripture (1 John 5:14). If our small son asked us for a scorpion, would we give it to him simply because he asked genuinely? No; we would only do what is best for the child. Can we expect God to be any different? He does what is best, and what is best is revealed in the whole Bible, not just in one verse.

The Lord Jesus prayed: "Father, *if it is Your will*, remove this cup from Me; nevertheless not My will, but Yours, be done" (Luke 22:42). It was not the Father's will, and Jesus went to the Cross.

Someone may object: "Why pray for something if God has already promised it in His Word?" Answer: "Would we want to ask for something He has not promised?" He said: "Yet you do not have because you do not ask" (James 4:2). God delights in His people showing dependence on Him by asking.

Furthermore, it may be God's revealed will in the Bible that we have something, but the timing may not be right. For example, we shall have a resurrection body, but this will not happen until the Last Day. It would make no sense for us, nor do any good, to pray to have it now.

There are other qualifications to prayer: We must have a sincere heart (Mark 12:40); we must have love for Him and mankind (Mark 12:31, 32; Matt. 5:43-48); we must persevere (Luke 18:1-8); we need to have submission to His sovereign will (Matt. 6:10b; 26:39); and ask through Christ alone (John 14:6; 15:16; 16:23; 1 Tim. 2:5). Even the Lord Jesus prayed having met all these qualifications.

Another condition for prayer is that we must be in obedience: "If I regard iniquity in my heart, the Lord will not hear" (Ps. 66:18); "And whatever we ask we receive from Him, *because* we keep His commandments and do those things that are pleasing in His sight" (1 John 3:22); "One who turns away his ear from hearing the law, even his prayer shall be an abomination" (Prov. 28:9). That may shock modern antinomians, those who think grace means that good works are optional in our lives. Good works do not save us nor keep us saved, but the one who knows God perseveres by the irresistible grace of God in a faith that manifests itself by good works.

Have We Asked God Properly?

Does God keep His promises and does He stand by His Word? Absolutely; we are not disputing this. How do we know if we have asked properly? The Word of Faith people think *they* determine whether they have asked properly, but the truth is that *God* determines this. Observe James 4:3: "You ask and do not receive, *because* you ask amiss, that you may spend it on your pleasures."

Secondly, we can never make God our debtor for we always sin. Our relationship with Him is always one of grace. Our constant indwelling sin guarantees that we never ask for anything with pure motives or solely for His glory, but He gives us what we need — and more — for Jesus' sake. God knows what we need before we ask, but we must ask rightly (James 4:3) and we must ask (James 4:2), both of which show dependence, trust, and humility.

Thirdly, we must ask for things that glorify Him, that promote His kingdom, and not just for personal lusts (James 4:3). It is not wrong to ask for our needs; indeed, we are instructed to do just that in the Lord's prayer (Matt. 6:11: "Give us this day, our daily bread"). Remember, though, that Solomon did not ask for riches but for wisdom (1 Kings 3:6-14). Solomon's concern for God and His people was genuine so that God gave him more than what he asked for, including riches. This was God's option, not Solomon's demand. Too often the health and wealth leaders think that God *must* do what they demand, so they ask for things for themselves rather than for wisdom to promote God's glory and His kingdom. Their mentality seems to be expressed in the bumper sticker: "He who dies with the most toys wins." If we seek first God's kingdom and His righteousness, all our needs will be supplied (Matt. 6:33); but only He knows if we are doing that. We do not know ourselves very well; He knows us perfectly.

The Prayer of Agreement

The new charismatics think they can control God by the prayer of agreement: "Again I say to you that if two of you agree on earth concerning anything that they ask, it will be done for them by My Father in heaven" (Matt. 18:19). Perhaps they got this from Unity School of Christianity.[53] All you need

---
[53] Shinn, *The Power of the Spoken Word*, p. 21.

is one other person to agree with you, and God has no choice but to grant your wish. The context of this particular verse, however, is concerning church discipline. The Lord is saying that if a church has two witnesses against an individual for some sin, that they can pray to the Lord and He will grant their request, whether for binding or loosing the individual. This is judicial process, not a meeting concerning personal wishes.

The Word of Faith leaders demand that God give them the things that they *want* rather than the things they *need*. We must be careful about pushing for something that is not good for us as He may give it: "But [Israel] lusted exceedingly in the wilderness, and tested God in the desert. And He gave them their request, but sent leanness into their soul" (Ps. 106:14, 15).

Passages Used for Positive Confessionism

Joshua 1:8

Capps finds "saying" with the mouth all through the Bible. In Joshua 1:8 the LORD said: "This Book of the Law shall *not depart from your mouth*, but you shall meditate in it day and night, that you may observe to do according to all that is written in it. For then you will make your way prosperous, and then you will have good success." According to Capps "not departing from the mouth" means to speak,[54] but the Hebrew and the context simply mean for the Word to be a part of one's life, to be obedient to the Word.[55] If we adhere to Capps's interpretation, the word would *not* be spoken, for the verse says it must not leave our mouths ("not depart from your mouth").

Mark 11:22-24

(22) So Jesus answered and said to them, "Have faith in God. (23) For assuredly, I say to you, whoever **says** to this mountain, 'Be removed and be cast into the sea,' and does not doubt in his heart, but believes that those things he **says** will come to pass, he will have whatever he **says**. (24)

---

[54] Capps, *Dynamics of Faith & Confession*, p. 267

[55] Keil and Delitzsch, *Old Testament Commentaries* (Grand Rapids: Associated Publishers and Authors), 1:1191.

Therefore I say to you, whatever things you ask when you pray, believe that you receive them, and you will have them."

This is the most popular passage used for positive confession, and even the Unity School people often refer to it as proof of positive confession. Russell says of these verses: "Who is it that is going to speak the word that will cast this mountain of trouble into the sea? Why YOU, of course" [emphasis his].[56] Notice, however, the obvious similarities of the verses:

Verse 23	Verse 24
Truly I say to you	Therefore I say to you
whoever	whatever
says	you pray
does not doubt but believes	believe
shall be (done) for him	shall be (done) for you

Is it not obvious that "saying" in verse twenty-three is the same as "praying" in verse twenty-four? The word for "prayer"[57] in v. 24 is almost always used in the New Testament of prayer to God, not to binding circumstances by metaphysical laws. Though it is certainly not wrong to pray verbally, God can also answer prayer that is silent, as He did when Hannah prayed for a son: "Now Hannah spoke in her heart; only her lips moved, but her voice was not heard. Therefore Eli thought she was drunk" (1 Sam. 1:13).

Mark is not promoting mere verbalizing but believing, trust in God (v. 22). The words for "saying" do not mean the actual sound from one's mouth but the content of what is said or believed.

Removing the mountain is figurative for removing the "giant problems" of our lives (see Zech. 4:7; 14:4), and it was a common expression of the Rabbis of Jesus' day to speak of the *mountain* of difficulties we all face.[58]

---

[56]Russell, *God Works Through Faith*, p. 50; see also Cady, *Lessons in Truth* (Unity Village, MO: Unity Books, no date), p. 60.

[57]προσευχομαι.

[58]Henry Sweet, *Commentary on Mark* (Grand Rapids: Kregel, 1977), p. 259.

Deuteronomy 28:1

In Deuteronomy 28:1 ("If you *diligently hearken* to the voice of the LORD your God, to observe carefully all His commandments which I command you today, that the Lord your God will set you high above all nations of the earth"), Capps says the Lord told him to look up the Hebrew words for "hearken" and for "diligently," and this is what he found: *"Hearken* first means 'to hear intelligently.' It also means 'to be obedient,' and 'to declare.' . . . *diligently* means 'wholly, completely, far, fast, and louder and louder.' The word could be used that way."[59] Then Capps paraphrases the verse:

> It shall come to pass, if you shall hear intelligently, be obedient to, declare wholly, completely, far, fast, louder and louder what God has said, to observe and to do all His commandments, then all these blessings will come upon you and overtake you.[60]

It appears that Capps got all these definitions from the back of *Strong's Concordance*. But Strong's Hebrew lexicon was not designed to give in-depth definitions of Hebrew words, as its introduction states, but to help with some basic meanings. Most people do not know how to use Strong's and do not understand that it has very limited value. People have become dangerous by abusing Strong's.

First, it seems that Capps looked up the word "diligently" and found no number for the word under Deuteronomy 28:1. He saw that Deuteronomy 24:8, the reference just above 28:1, had the number 3966 for "diligently." Thus he looked up this word — which is not even used in Deuteronomy 28:1! — and copied down the meanings he *liked*. We say *liked* because it is not possible that "diligently" could simultaneously have all those meanings he gives the word, and Capps leaves out other meanings. Strong's uses semicolons to separate major meanings of words, which Capps conveniently ignored, combining several major meanings into one broad meaning while over looking other major meanings. One would have to do an in depth word study to determine which of Strong's meanings

---

[59] Capps, *Dynamics of Faith & Confession*, p. 132.
[60] Ibid.

— if any — would apply in any particular context. Capps says Jesus told him to look up the meaning of the Hebrew word in Deuteronomy 28:1, but apparently Jesus did not know His Hebrew well enough to know the word Capps looked up did not appear.

Secondly, the word translated "diligently" in the KJV in Deuteronomy 28:1 is not the 3966 word (*me'ôd*) but a form of the verb "hearken."[61] This is a Hebrew idiom that woodenly reads "*obeying* you shall obey," which in English means "*carefully* or *diligently* obey." One can easily see from this that Capps does not know how to do Hebrew exegesis or even understand the basics of the language.

When questioned about his method of exegesis, he said in a letter dated 09/14/92:

> If I was incorrect in what the specific context of that actural [sic] word said, it does not change the truth that I got from that particular context which I believe the Lord gave me understanding of. Now I might be ignorant enough not to know that that's exactly what the text said, but that is what the Holy Spirit said to me . . . through that verse [Deut. 28:1]. . . .

Essentially Capps admitted that my analysis of his use of Strong's was correct: "I am certainly not a Greek or Hebrew scholar but the Strong's Concordance gives you the ways this Hebrew word can be used. Whether or not that is specifically the way the word is used in that particular instance does not rule out the truth of what I stated." In other words, it makes no difference what the Hebrew says or that the word does not even occur in that verse, he receives his meanings directly from the Lord.

Furthermore, Capps says in the letter that the rest of the Bible supports his positive confession ideas, making this concession: "Now if what I stated [about confession] could not be found in other parts of the Bible, then we would have to say that would be prosumption [sic] on my part." My heart goes out to this man who cannot spell or do exegesis, but he is convinced that he is right and is teaching others these metaphysical doctrines. He should never have been ordained

---

[61]The form is the infinitive absolute, which is commonly used adverbially with the main verb to intensify the meaning of the main verb.

as a minister, if he ever was. The rest of the Bible does not teach his doctrines, and he is presumptive. Unfortunately, he and the other leaders will probably not read a book like this because it would be a "negative confession." May God have mercy on those who follow such presumption and proud ignorance.

Finally, Capps did not respond in his letter to the obvious problem that Jesus allegedly told him to look up a Hebrew word that did not occur. This casts serious doubt on anything Capps supposedly receives directly from the Lord, indicating that Capps is lying or some spirit did tell him something, but not Jesus.

Hebrews 1:3

Another blunder Capps makes is from Hebrews 1:3 where God says that Jesus is "upholding all things by the word of His power." Capps comments that "God's power is in His Word,"[62] making the analogy that when we speak we can invoke this same power. Commenting on the Greek word for "power" he says: "The [Greek] word is the source of our [English] words *dynamite* and *dynamo*. The idea present here is that *God has given us a dynamo that will produce spiritual power* [emphasis his]."[63]

Capps makes several errors. First, the text does *not* say that God's power is in His Word though it does say His Word is powerful. The power is in God Himself. The reason Jesus' Word is all-powerful is that Jesus is all-powerful. As Philip Hughes insightfully declares: "The word of the Word is infallibly effective precisely because it is one with the word of the Father."[64] Jesus is revealed to be one in essence with the Father in verses 1-3a, and this is why His word is infallible, not because He functions according to some metaphysical spiritual law that is above Him. There is nothing above Him, nothing He is subject to, being the Creator of all things, which is what Hebrews chapter one is about.

Secondly, because we derive an English word *dynamo* from

---

[62] Capps, *Dynamics of Faith & Confession*, p. 135.

[63] Ibid.

[64] Philip Edgcumbe Hughes, *A Commentary on the Epistle to the Hebrews* (Grand Rapids: Wm. B. Eerdmans Pub. Co., 1977), p. 46.

the Greek does not mean the Greek means what the English does. This is getting the cause and effect reversed, using the English to determine the Greek. The English word *nice* comes from a Latin word that means *ignorant*. Certainly that doesn't make the Latin mean *nice*. This misuse of the biblical languages is typical among Word of Faith leaders.

Romans 4:17

Another very important passage that Capps and others use is Romans 4:17 from the King James Version. (Unity writer Robert Russell also uses this verse in the same way that new charismatics do.)[65] Capps says:

> As much as I admire Kenneth Hagin and Kenneth Copeland, they were not the ones who wrote Mark 11:23-24, or who came up with the method of using God's words as creative power. Neither was I. . . . It was God Himself Who started it all. Romans 4:17 says God ". . . quickeneth the dead, and calleth those things which be not as though they were."[66]

Capps's assumption is that we can do what God can do, for the verse states that it is *God* who "quickens" or gives life to the "dead" body of Abraham and Sarah. What does this have to do with us today? Can we call into existence a son and cause a lady an hundred years old to produce a child? No, and neither could Abraham, but Abraham's faith was in God Who could and did. At least Capps admits the novelty of this view in church history when he states: "Now, up until a few years ago, the Church knew very little about this biblical principle."[67] He seems to think he is restoring the gospel. (See paragraph beginning with "Consequently when anyone brags" on page 32.)

Hebrews 1:14

There is another verse that they frequently use: "Are they not all ministering spirits sent forth to minister for those who will inherit salvation?" (Heb. 1:14). The theory is that "Confessing God's Word puts the angels to work for you. Many

---

[65]Russell, *God Works Through Faith*, p. 90.

[66]Charles Capps, *Believers Voice of Victory* magazine, September, 1992, p. 12; see also Cho, *The Fourth Dimension*, p. 14.

[67]Ibid.

Verbally Directing Reality

have never realized that the angels are listening to the words you speak."[68] So when you speak positive words the right way, angels jump to attention and accomplish what you spoke. If you speak correctly, you will be blessed by the angels; but if you speak wrongly, demons, who are also listening, will bring a curse on you. Welcome to the world of the occult with all its magic, mysticism, and continual battle between the good gods and the bad gods, with each winning and losing in accordance with man's magical words!

Capps says that we call angels "off the job" and even our children may get run over by a car while the angel watches if we make a negative confession.[69] Our angels must do all that we say, for if they do not we will be able to judge them.[70] Or, "A few wrong words of unbelief can destroy what their angel has been putting together for months."[71]

The context is concerning Jesus as better than the angels since He is the same essence as the Father (vv. 1-5), worshipped by the angels (vv. 6, 7), referred to as God by the Father (vv. 8, 9), and eternal (vv. 10-12). Then in verses 13 and 14 Paul reveals that the angels minister for those who will inherit salvation. What the angels specifically do in Hebrews 1:14 is not stated. In all probability, though, the Greek word translated "for"[72] ("minister *for* those") means to minister *to* them, not *in the place of* them.[73] The English translation *for* is accurate enough if is remembered that *for* can mean doing something *to* them, as in the example: "Will you cut my hair *for* me?" Though it could mean to do something on their behalf, a different Greek preposition would be more likely.[74] Even if it did mean to minister on their behalf, there is nothing in the context that even remotely suggests that these

---

[68] Capps, *Dynamics of Faith & Confession*, p. 256.

[69] Capps, *Angels*, p. 122ff.

[70] Ibid., p. 129ff.

[71] Ibid., p. 110.

[72] δια with the accusative.

[73] A. T. Robertson, *Word Pictures in the New Testament* (Nashville: Broadman Press, 1932), 5:341; F. Blass & A. DeBrunner, *A Greek Grammar of the New Testament* (Chicago: The University of Chicago Press, 1970), #222.

[74] υπερ.

angels are listening to their words to carry out their wishes. Rather they are carrying out God's wishes for us. This is consonant with the Scripture where we see angels ministering *to* the saints, not carrying out their verbal decrees (Ps. 103:20f; 91:11; 2 Kings 6:15-17; Matt. 4:11).

Proverbs 6:2

The positive confession teachers often use Proverbs 6:2 without verse 1: "(1) My son, if you become surety for your friend, if you have shaken hands in pledge for a stranger, (2) you are snared by the words of your own mouth; you are taken by the words of your mouth." The verses speak against co-signing, but the positive confession people take the second verse to mean that if you speak wrong words that you will not get what you want. Obviously the context militates against this.

Matthew 18:18

Fred Price uses this verse to say that God is bound by our words: "Assuredly, I say to you, whatever you bind on earth will be bound in heaven, and whatever you loose on earth will be loosed in heaven" (Matt. 18:18). First, this is speaking of church discipline (see previous verses), not everything that we say. If His church properly excommunicates someone, then it is as though Christ did so, for to do so properly is to follow His written Word.

Secondly, it may be better to translate the unusual Greek verbs this way: "Whatever you bind on earth *shall have been bound* in heaven, and whatever you loose on earth *shall have been loosed* in heaven" (NASV translation). This would demonstrate that we do what had already been done in heaven, that we are following heaven, not heaven following us.

Thirdly, in this passage and in the similar passage in Matthew 16:19, the Lord was using the rabbinic form of "binding" and "loosing" which pointed to doing this of someone's doctrine, not to any and every event on earth.[75] Heaven does not dance to the tune that earth plays, even if the players are Christians.

The Balance

Some who read these refutations may think that we do not

---

[75] Robertson, *Word Pictures in the New Testament*, 1:133-135.

believe that verbally confessing God's written Word is profitable. Quite the contrary: it is very profitable. God's Word never returns void (Isa. 55:11), and God honors His Word either for blessing or for cursing every time it goes out (2 Cor. 2:16; Isa. 55:11). But the Scriptures do not teach that there is magic in the verbal pronouncing of Bible words or any other words that causes some metaphysical spiritual law to grant us our wish. Let us confess His Word to men, not to manipulate the forces for our own ends, but to honor Christ (Matt. 10:32). The results are in His hands. Let us not engage in magic by speaking to houses and cars that they are sold, but let us pray to the Lord and humbly ask Him for our requests. Whatever happens is His answer.

Can We Do What God Does?

Are We God-Like? (Pantheism)

Pantheism is the belief that man is like God, partaking of His being, or merged with Him in some way. Several years ago there was a movie entitled *The Boy Who Could Fly*. All through the movie the audience was made to wonder if the boy would every fly, whether he could really do it, and at the end he did. In one of the last scenes the daughter asks her mother how her boyfriend could fly, and the answer was that if one wanted to do something badly enough, he could do just about anything. This is what the modern human potential movement would like us to believe. There are limitations, however, to what we can accomplish; we are not God. There is a line of demarcation between the Creator and His creatures. We have our limits; He does not. *The reason the Word of Faith leaders hold to positive confession is pantheism; they believe they are like God, able to create.* This section demonstrates the real essence of the movement and why they believe that man is so powerful. This part, as much as any of this book, reveals their heretical beliefs. Indeed, there would be no positive confession if they did not hold that man is like God.

Pat Robertson says: "In short, Jesus told His disciples that if they truly had faith in God, . . . they would become participants in the same energy and power that prevailed at the creation. They would work as God works. . . ."[76] Again, "We speak to money, and it comes. We speak to storms, and they

---

[76]Pat Robertson, *The Secret Kingdom*, p. 38.

cease. We speak to crops, and they flourish."[77] Apparently, man can do anything.

God and man are merged: "We are to be one with the Father as Jesus was one with Him."[78] "When you were born again, the Bible says you became bone of His bone." "God has been reproduced on the inside of you."[79] Was Jesus the Son of God? Then so are we with no distinction between Him and us.[80] Hagin says, "This eternal life He came to give us is the nature of God."[81] We have "God imparting His very nature, substance, and being into our human spirits,"[82] which he probably got from Kenyon: "We are of His own substance."[83] Again, Hagin says: "He made us the same class of being that He is Himself" and "man belonged to the realm of God."[84]

Hagin misconstrues Psalm 8:5: "You have made him a little lower than the angels, and You have crowned him with glory and honor." He says the Hebrew word for "angels" really means "God" so that God made humans a little lower than Himself. The Hebrew word for "angels" in Psalm 8:5 is *elohim*, often translated "God" in the Old Testament, but contrary to Hagin should be rendered "angels" in this text for several reasons. First, Hebrews 2:7, the inspired interpretation of Psalm 8:5, uses the Greek word for "angel." This alone should settle the matter. Secondly, the Targum and Jewish commentators also interpret the word as angels.[85] Finally, this Hebrew word has many meanings such as rulers, judges, and angels (see Ps. 82:1, 6; 97:7; 138:1).[86]

---

[77] Ibid., p. 74.

[78] Kenneth Copeland, *The Force of Righteousness* (Forth Worth: KCP Publications, 1990), p. 9.

[79] Ibid., pp. 11, 12.

[80] Ibid., p. 18.

[81] Kenneth Hagin, *ZOE: The God-Kind of Life* (Tulsa: Faith Library, 1989), p. 1.

[82] Ibid., p. 2.

[83] E. W. Kenyon, *What Happened from the Cross to the Throne* (1969, fourth edition), p. 64.

[84] Hagin, *ZOE*, p. 36.

[85] Philip Edgcumbe Hughes, *A Commentary on the Epistle to the Hebrews*, p. 85.

[86] Brown, Driver, Briggs, *Hebrew and English Lexicon of the Old Testament*, p.

Verbally Directing Reality

Take serious note of the following passages and ask whether these men are just mixed up a little, or if they have departed from the evangelical faith. Notice especially the quotes by Kenneth Hagin.

> The Universal Man has craved Incarnation.[87]

> Even many in the great body of Full Gospel people do not know that the new birth is a real incarnation. They do not know they are as much sons and daughters of God as Jesus. . . . *Jesus was first divine, and then He was human. So He was in the flesh a divine-human being. I was first human, and so were you, but I was born of God, and so I became a human-divine being!* [emphasis his][88]

> Every man who has been born again is an incarnation and Christianity is a miracle. The believer is as much an incarnation as was Jesus of Nazareth.[89]

> You are . . . a God kind of creature.[90]

> When God looks in the mirror, He sees me! When I look in the mirror, I see God![91]

> You don't have a god living in you; you are one!

> You know, sometimes people say to me, . . . "You just think you're a little god!" Thank you! Hallelujah! You got that right! "Who d'you think you are, Jesus?" Yep![92]

> God created man on His level, in His image and likeness. . . .[93] Likeness indicates a "duplication of kind". . . .[94] By praying one prayer, Jesus could have summoned 72,000 angels! . . . You

---

43.

[87] Essek William Kenyon, *The Father and His Family: A Restatement of the Plan of Redemption* (Seattle: E. W. Kenyon, 1937), p. 127.

[88] Hagin, *ZOE*, p. 40.

[89] Kenneth Copeland as quoted in Michael Scott Horton, *The Agony of Deceit* (Chicago: Moody Press, 1990), p. 44.

[90] Robert Tilton as quoted in Ibid., p. 91.

[91] Casey Treat as quoted in Ibid., p. 91.

[92] Kenneth Copeland as quoted in Michael Scott Horton, *Made in America* (Grand Rapids: Baker Book House, 1991), p. 82.

[93] Charles & Annette Capps, *Angels*, p. 16.

[94] Ibid., p. 18.

might say, "Yeah, but He was the Son of God!" . . . Well, who do you think you are? "Beloved now are we the sons of God" (1 John 3:2).[95]

We are the Word made flesh, just as Jesus was.[96]

When you learn to walk as Jesus walked, without any consciousness of inferiority to God or Satan, you will have faith that will absolutely stagger the world![97]

So apparently, what He [Jesus] does, He opens up that union of the very godhead, and brings us into it. . . .[98] [God] doesn't even draw a distinction between Himself and us.[99]

When Jesus was on earth, the Bible says that first He disrobed Himself of the divine form. He, the limitless God, became a man, that we men, may become as He is.[100]

We know that he [man] was created to be the companion of the Creator; he was not to fill the place of a servant to a Master . . . but was to be a son and fellow companion, an associate of the Eternal Father throughout Eternity.[101]

In other words, when man was created he was made as near like Deity as it was possible for Deity to create him. He [man] ruled not only the animal creation but he also ruled the laws of Creation.[102]

. . . man . . . had an intellect of such calibre as to be the companion of Deity, and . . . he had in his hands the joy or sorrow of God. . . .[103]

---

[95] Ibid., p. 62.

[96] Gloria Copeland, *Walk in the Spirit* (Forth Worth: KCP Publications, 1984), p. 9.

[97] E. W. Kenyon, *The Blood Covenant* (Lynnwood, WA: Kenyon's Gospel Pub. Society, 1969), p. 53.

[98] Paul Crouch as quoted in John F. MacArthur, *Charismatic Chaos* (Grand Rapids: Zondervan Pub. House, 1991), p. 273.

[99] Paul Crouch, Ibid., p. 272.

[100] Benny Hinn, Ibid., p. 274.

[101] E. W. Kenyon, *The Father and His Family*, p. 36.

[102] Ibid., p. 39.

[103] Ibid., pp. 43, 44.

He [man] could not have been a son of God and a partaker of His nature unless he was like God, and being like God he would be eternal and in God's class.[104]

God breathed into Adam the life that was inside Himself; and **Adam became an exact duplication of God's kind** [emphasis his]. . . .[105] Actually, man is supposed to be god over the earth. . . . Where did Satan get the title of being god of this world? He got it from Adam. . . . We were created to be gods over the earth, but remember to spell it with a little "g" . . . The fulness of the Godhead dwells in the Body of Christ.[106]

Your words are not just changing images; they become creative power. When you speak, you will speak to affect things. Your words will change the order of things.[107] . . . Once that happens, you can hardly tell where you quit and the Holy Ghost begins. . . .[108]

Adam was the god of this world.[109]

The statement by Kenneth Copeland seems to be plagiarized from E. W. Kenyon word for word: "The believer is as much an Incarnation as was Jesus of Nazareth."[110] *This is rank heresy, as much so as the Jehovah's Witnesses, and it is time we treat this as heresy. It is time that we stop thinking of these men as slightly off center — they are not in the realm of scriptural orthodoxy at all.*[111] Capps's comment that we are not *the* God but little gods is still pantheistic, although he tries to qualify his heresy.

Kenyon's assertion that we are "as near like Deity as it was

---

[104]Ibid., p. 235.

[105]Charles Capps, *God's Image of You* (Tulsa: Harrison House, 1985), p. 27.

[106]Ibid., pp. 33-34, 38.

[107]Ibid., p. 55.

[108]Ibid., p. 64.

[109]Kenneth E. Hagin, *The Believer's Authority* (Tulsa: Faith Library Publications, 1992), p. 19.

[110]Kenyon, *The Father and His Family*, p. 129.

[111]In America we have devolved into tolerating everything. The only heinous sin is to condemn someone for something, and Phil Donahue dares anyone to condemn the deviants he constantly parades across the TV screen. Christians in America have lost sight of a holy God Who will judge the secrets of men's heart at the Last Day.

possible for Deity to create" us is ludicrous. Either man is infinite or finite. If man is not infinite like God, then there is an infinite distance between us and Him, between the finite and the infinite. If we are infinite, then we are gods. It is not possible for one to be almost infinite just as it is not possible for one to be almost infallible.

Similarly, Paul Cho proclaims that we can control Jesus with our words:

> You create the presence of Jesus with your mouth. If you speak about salvation, the saving Jesus appears. If you speak about divine healing, then you will have the healing Christ in your congregation. If you speak the miracle performing Jesus, then the presence of the miracle performing Jesus is released. He is bound by your lips and by your words. He is depending on you.[112]

We see the pantheistic beliefs of the movement very clearly, but God created man to be His creature, not to be His equal.

Is God Human?

Not only do the Word of Faith leaders deify man, but God is made human. The Father supposedly has needs like us. As Copeland says: "The Father's heart was hungry for a family, and Jesus freely gave Himself for this desire,"[113] and Copeland got this from Kenyon.[114]

It gets even worse, for we read in the metaphysical literature that God created by faith. This would assume a law above God to which He is subject: "God had sent forth His Word, and by faith had created what we call matter...."[115] Like God, man can also create by faith.[116]

The Word of Faith leaders agree with these metaphysical writers. God and man are subject to the same spiritual laws so that what God can do we can do: "*God releases sufficient faith in every word He speaks to cause it to come to pass*" [emphasis

---

[112] Cho, *The Fourth Dimension*, p. 83.

[113] Copeland, *The Force of Righteousness*, p. 10.

[114] Kenyon, *The Father and His Family*, p. 10.

[115] Sanford, *The Healing Power of the Bible*, p. 152.

[116] Ibid., p. 30; see also Russell, *God Works Through Faith*, p. 87.

his].[117] "As partakers of God's nature, *you* are capable of operating on the same level of faith with God." "God used His faith when He created." Even Adam "was created to operate on the same level of faith with God,"[118] and "any person who is born of the Spirit of God . . . is capable of operating on the same level of faith with God."[119] Kenneth Copeland will not be outdone: "The world and the physical forces governing it were created by the power of faith — a spiritual force. God, a Spirit, created all matter, and He created it with the force of faith."[120] Again, "God has used the words written in the Bible to release His faith."[121] God had to use His faith to create, which means there is a law above Him!

On Mark 11:22, which reads, "Jesus answered and said to them, 'Have faith *in* God,'" Hagin says this literally reads: "Have the faith *of* God." He further interprets this to mean the "God kind of faith" or the same kind of faith that God uses. He says, "This is the kind of faith that spoke the world into existence" and "God believed that what He said would come to pass. He spoke the word and there was an earth."[122]

However, it is a well established idiom of Greek to use "faith *of* God"[123] to mean "faith *in* God." Furthermore, in whom would God have faith? "When God speaks something [by our mouths], it is decreed in heaven. It is impregnated into the spirit of the person receiving the word of the Lord, and God's word carries with it the creative, life-giving power of self-fulfillment."[124] Capps says, "God's Word conceived in the heart, then formed with the tongue and spoken out of the mouth becomes a spiritual force releasing the ability of

---

[117] Capps, *Dynamics of Faith & Confession*, p. 36.

[118] Charles Capps, *Authority in Three Worlds* (Tulsa: Harrison House, 1982), p. 10; p. 24; p. 40.

[119] Ibib., p. 225; see also Capps, *Dynamics of Faith & Confession*, pp. 15-30.

[120] Copeland, *The Laws of Prosperity*, p. 15.

[121] Ibid., p. 84.

[122] Hagin, *Faith Edition Bible*, pp. lxxiv, lxxv.

[123] This is called the objective genitive.

[124] Bill Hamon, *Prophets and Personal Prophecy* (Shippensburg, PA: Destiny Image, 1987), p. 65.

God."[125] No doubt these men are regurgitating E. W. Kenyon: "God . . . believed the universe into being."[126]

And faith itself is a spiritual force that produces power. They get this partially from Hebrews 11:1: "Now faith is the substance of things hoped for, the evidence of things not seen." "Substance" is the key word for them, which they interpret to mean a spiritual force. In other words, this is like the law of magnetism. You cannot see, hear, smell, taste, or feel magnetism, but it is real nevertheless. If you put faith to work, like magnetism, the results are just as guaranteed, just as perfunctory. It's that simple, both for God and for man. There is only one minor problem: No two Word of Faith leaders or metaphysicians can agree on the laws that govern this spiritual force called faith. There is even a faith in our faith to produce our own little worlds.[127]

Negative Confessions in the Bible

Psalm 73 is a negative confession, as many of the Psalms are. God does not rebuke us for sharing our hearts with Him. Indeed, it is not sin to pour out our souls to Him, even if it involves negative things. They are a part of life. In Exodus 4:11 we have a negative confession by the Lord: "So the LORD said to him, 'Who has made man's mouth? Or who makes the mute, the deaf, the seeing, or the blind? Have not I, the LORD?'"

The Lord will do more than we confess: "Now to Him who is able to do exceedingly abundantly above all that we *ask* or think, according to the power that works in us" (Eph. 3:20). Or remember the man who said "Lord, I believe; help my unbelief" (Mark 9:24). Perfect faith is not always needed and not possible this side of eternity.

In John 16:1ff the Lord stated that His disciples would be thrown out of the synagogue and be killed.

In Matthew 23 the Lord spent not a few words "confessing" very negative things about people, calling the religious leaders of His day "hypocrites," "fools," "blind guides," "whitewashed tombs," "serpents," "brood of vipers," and

---

[125] Capps, *Dynamics of Faith & Confession*, p. 33.

[126] Kenyon, *The Blood Covenant*, p. 68.

[127] Kenneth Hagin, *Having Faith in Your Faith* (Tulsa: Faith Library, 1980).

many other indictments.

The Lord also lamented to His disciples in the garden before His crucifixion: "My soul is exceedingly sorrowful, even to death. Stay here and watch with Me" (Matt. 26:38). Without committing any sin, He was honestly stating His negative emotional condition. The Apostle Paul spoke of his coming death in 2 Timothy 4:6-16 and of other "bad" things in 1 Timothy 4 and 2 Timothy 3.

Then there are cases where the opposite of one's confession occurs in Scripture. In Acts chapter 12 the disciples were praying for Peter's release from prison, and when they were told that he was outside their door at the gate, they said to Rhoda, the servant girl: "'You are beside yourself!' Yet she kept insisting that it was so. So they said, 'It is his angel'" (Acts 12:15). They did not believe their own prayers nor did they confess rightly, yet God still had mercy on them and delivered Peter.

The Apostle Paul gave "negative" confessions:

> For to you it has been granted on behalf of Christ, not only to believe in Him, but also to suffer for His sake, having the same conflict which you saw in me and now hear is in me (Phil 1:29, 30).

> In fact, we told you before when we were with you that we would suffer tribulation, just as it happened, and you know (1 Thess. 3:4).

> So that we ourselves boast of you among the churches of God for your patience and faith in all your persecutions and tribulations that you endure, which is manifest evidence of the righteous judgment of God, that you may be counted worthy of the kingdom of God, for which you also suffer (2 Thess. 1:4, 5).

> Yes, and all who desire to live godly in Christ Jesus will suffer persecution (2 Tim. 3:12).

It is possible to confess one thing and do another (Matt. 21:28-31), which we all do many times.

Conclusion

Positive confession is designed to get something from God. If only we confess long and loudly enough, God will recognize us and "abracadabra," we would obtain our wish.

The assumption is that God is holding out on us, but Paul says: "He who did not spare His own Son, but delivered Him up for us all, how shall He not with Him also freely give us all things?" (Rom. 8:32). If God has given us the greatest gift of all, His only begotten Son, then why wouldn't He give us all lesser things? He will, and without any manipulation on our part.

"When one has declared that man's good rather than God's glory is the goal of salvation . . . it is not a large step from that to incipient hedonism."[128] Such is what these men have done, having replaced God as the center of their theology with man. When George Burns played God in *Oh God!*, he said to his creature: "If you think it hard to believe in me, it might help you to know that I believe in you." The Word of Faith leaders are saying the same blasphemous thing. God must believe in us because nothing will ever be done unless we confess rightly and invoke the spiritual laws that both God and we are subject to.

The emphasis on confessing the written Word is a good one, but that hollow and vain repetitions will make God do whatever the creature wants is ludicrous. This puts people under an artificial strain and leads to brutal discouragement and bitterness when things do not turn out as promised. Sometimes God gets the blame, and people think that God does not hear or that they cannot perform perfectly enough to merit God's response.

One assumption of positive confession is that for things to be "right" the circumstances must be what we desire instead of the biblical doctrine that our characters must be Christ-like. They insist that God make the circumstances conform to their thoughts instead of making their own thinking conform to the circumstances. Victory in the Christian life is learning to live by faith in humble submission to God through His Word and in submission to providence, not in manipulating circumstances.

Barron sums up well the practical problems with positive confession:

> The picture I get is that as a Christian, I am supposed to be victorious all the time. I may be in pain, physically or mentally,

---

[128] Michael Horton, *Made in America*, p. 75.

but I must keep up my positive confession at all costs. This leads to superficial people with pious masks who cannot disclose to each other who they really are, and therefore cannot experience the grace of God where they hurt. They present their ideal rather than their real self. It's . . . phony.[129]

It is, in fact, rank heresy to claim to be like God, to be an incarnation of God, to have the same power He does. This is a merging of man and God; it is transcendentalism; it is Christian Science, Unity School of Christianity, New Age, and Word of Faith. And all of it is pantheism, which is the age old heresy of man wanting to be God, and the lie Satan told to Eve that she could be like God.

---

[129] Bruce Barron, *The Health and Wealth Gospel* (Downers Grove: InterVarsity Press, 1987), p. 131.

9

Is the Bible Enough?

The Sufficiency of Scripture

. . . that you may learn in us not to think beyond what is written (1 Cor. 4:6).

For I testify to everyone who hears the words of the prophecy of this book: If anyone adds to these things, God will add to him the plagues that are written in this book (Rev. 22:18).

There is one Lawgiver, who is able to save and to destroy (James 4:12).

Is the Bible enough or do we need more? There are two ways that the Bible can be destroyed: adding to it and subtracting from it. One can add human traditions to the Bible or other so-called Scriptures, or he can subtract from its trustworthiness by claiming that it has errors. Either way the Bible is seemingly destroyed.

Since the latter 1800's, Protestant liberals have been using *subtraction* to destroy the Bible. They attempt to reduce God's Word to just another book by saying it is full of errors.

Neo-evangelicals, who want Jesus as Savior but do not believe all the Bible, proclaim that it is infallible in theology but not in science, history, astronomy, and other areas. There was a crucial controversy in the Southern Baptist Convention over whether Scripture is infallible in all things or just in theological matters. A divided infallibility would be idolatry: placing the God of the Bible over sacred things and another god over secular matters. This assumes that there are some things in life that are not theological, that life has "secular" matters *and* "spiritual" matters. This is patently false. All of life is theological or religious since God is the Creator.

In this late twentieth century, the Bible is suffering by *addition* at the hands of both its friends and its foes. Its evangelical "friends" claim that to find God's will for your life you need more than Scripture. The Spirit must speak to you inside your "heart." The implication is that the Bible is not enough. We shall notice throughout this chapter how addition and subtraction are used to attack the Bible, whether done consciously or not.

Mysticism and the Bible

The Unity School of Christianity teaches that the Bible has its place but that we must learn to contact "God" within ourselves and communicate with Him there.[1] This communication from God is apart from the human mind and from one's intuition, often below the conscious level, given directly from God to the "listener" without the means of the written Word. The reader should notice the similarity of the metaphysical cults and the Word of Faith from these quotes:

> Committing your ways unto the Lord seems very difficult to most people. It means, of course, to follow intuition, for intuition is the magic path, the beeline to your demonstration [bringing to pass what you want]. Intuition is a Spiritual faculty above the intellect.[2] . . . So many people are leading such complicated lives because they are trying to think things out instead of 'intuitin'' the way out.[3] . . . Never submit a hunch to someone on the reasoning plane.[4] . . . When we ask for guidance and lay aside the reasoning mind we are tapping the Universal supply of all knowledge. . . .[5]

> Do not try to reason through your mental pictures of fulfillment, or to understand how they are to come about.[6]

> The human spirit has a voice. We call that voice conscience. Sometimes it is called intuition. We call it an inner voice of guidance. It is our spirit talking to us. Every man's spirit has a

---

[1] Agnes Sanford, *The Healing Power of the Bible* (San Francisco: Harper and Row, 1984), pp. 33-34; Emmet Fox, *The Seven Main Aspects of God* (Marina del Rey, CA: DeVorss & Co., 1942, 1970), p. 16.

[2] Florence Scovel Shinn, *The Power of the Spoken Word* (Marina del Rey, CA: DeVorss & Co., 1945), p. 10.

[3] Ibid., p. 15.

[4] Ibid., p. 60.

[5] Ibid., p. 63.

[6] Catherine Ponder, *Dare To Prosper* (Marina del Rey, CA: DeVorss & Co., 1983), p. 11.

voice, whether he is saved or unsaved. But the new birth is a rebirth of the human spirit.

We don't understand the Bible with our mind.[7]

The Church . . . has failed because for the most part it has endeavored to carry on the work of God with only one kind of praying: mental praying.[8]

Again Kenneth Hagin says we are to be tuned "to the inner voice of faith, not the outer voice of human reasoning,"[9] or "God communicates with the spirit and not with our reasoning faculties."[10] Obviously this rules out a reasonable understanding of the Bible.

By-passing the mind is like the occult's spirit guides, like the New Age's higher consciousness, like modern psychologist's inner child, like the human potential ideas we hear so much on TV from the news media stating that we have all the power we need inside us to do anything, and like the metaphysical cults who say that we are one with "God" and thus must learn to contact "Him/It" in ourselves. The Word of Faith leaders are simply a product of our times and refuse to recognize it.[11]

Likewise, the new charismatics in by-passing the mind and following intuition are not concerned with being logical. When they are challenged that their interpretation does not coincide with Scripture, they say, "My spirit man told me this interpretation was correct," or "Jesus gave me this," or "It

---

[7] Kenneth Hagin, *Kenneth E. Hagin Faith Edition Bible* (Tulsa, OK: Kenneth Hagin Ministries, 1972), p. xciii.; p. xxxiv.

[8] Kenneth E. Hagin, *The Interceding Christian* (Tulsa: Faith Publication Library, 1991), p. 19.

[9] Hagin, *Kenneth E. Hagin Faith Edition Bible*, p. lxxxiv.

[10] Ibid., p. xci.

[11] Such negating of reason and wanting to by-pass the mind is the influence not only of the metaphysical cults but also of the Eastern mentality. The reason the Eastern countries have not advanced as the Western ones is that they eschew logical thinking, being fuzzy in their thought patterns, by-passing the mind in "listening" to their spirits. When one challenges them that what they have said is not logical, their response is that it is not supposed to be. One wonders how they logically know that logic is irrelevant. Consequently, they have not done much in the sciences. It took redemption by Jesus to free man to subdue the earth by math and logic, which is what the Western world has done.

feels right." They have bought into the irrationally of the metaphysical cults and of the Eastern religions, especially of the New Age (see Appendix One). To think as these Word of Faith leaders do is to predicate irrationality to the Triune God. As one reads their books, he has the distinct impression that if something is planned, rational, and thought out that God is not in it. God, however, is always rational, and something or someone is always infallible.

Infallibility Inescapable

Infallibility is an inescapable concept.[12] Infallibility, like heavy stones in a wash, will deposit itself somewhere. It is not a question *if* something is infallible; it is only a question of *what* is infallible. Atheists promote reason as infallible, New Agers have inner light and intuition through meditation, the Roman Catholic Church espouses itself as infallible, relegating tradition and the Bible to the background, and new charismatics claim visions and "Jesus told me." In contrast to all these, Reformation Protestantism has claimed *sola Scriptura*, *only Scripture* is infallible, which is what the Bible and the Savior say (Matt. 5:17, 18; John 10:35).

How do the Word of Faith leaders keep their followers from testing their "truths" with Scripture? They do so by "poisoning the wells": they prejudice their hearers in advance with statements like Hagin's, in which he says that a seminary professor is "a fellow with a big education but knowing nothing about the Bible."[13] When Charles Capps explains something unusual, feeling the force of his aberration, he says: "This is quite different from most of our religious ideas."[14] He says: "Many have managed to avoid it through their religious tradition."[15] This is constant in their writings. Again, "Without the knowledge of God, you will believe the things you have heard through religious circles. . . ."[16] In-

---

[12]R. J. Rushdoony, *Infallibility: An Inescapable Concept* (Vallecito, CA: Ross House Books, 1978).

[13]Kenneth Hagin, *Seven Things You Should Know About Divine Healing* (Tulsa: Faith Library Publications, 1987), p. 25.

[14]Charles Capps, *Authority in Three Worlds* ((Tulsa: Harrison House, 1982), p. 55.

[15]Ibid., p. 258.

[16]Charles Capps, *How You Can Avoid Tragedy* (Tulsa: Harrison House, 1980),

Is the Bible Enough?

deed, he has an entire book dedicated to so-called religious traditions that need to be discarded:

> But if you are not careful, religious tradition and man's ideas will make it of none effect, even to the point of holding you in bondage.[17] . . . Several years ago, the Lord said to me, "You need to forget every comment you have heard about the scripture and go back and read the Bible like you never heard it before."[18] . . . ***It's religion that burdens you down*** [emphasis his].[19]

Another Word of Faith writer, John Osteen, says, "If you hold tightly to your church doctrines and rules, and never read the Bible, you will find that you are blind to the truth of God." Again he says, "I am against wicked, evil sectarianism that robs the people of the power of God and lies to them about these things."[20] In the back of *Receive the Holy Spirit*, he contrasts traditions with the Word of God, all having to do with speaking in tongues. Kenneth Copeland cavils: "Very rarely has the whole gospel been preached — only pieces of it!"[21] Oral Roberts says, "God told me in this prophecy that the typical believer has no idea how 'brainwashed' he has become. . . ."[22] They tend to be puffed up by this special knowledge that they allegedly have, and this egotistical posture draws others to them to hear the new knowledge that is supposedly not weighed down with tradition. Infallibility lies with them and their new revelations, not with the Bible, and those who do not listen to them are laden with religious tradition.

There is no end to the disingenuous prejudices they instill

---

p. 14.

[17] Charles Capps, *Kicking Over Sacred Cows* (England, AR: Charles Capps, 1983), p. 100.

[18] Ibid., p. 104.

[19] Ibid., p. 112.

[20] John Osteen, *Receive the Holy Spirit* (Houston: John Osteen Ministries, 1980), pp. 17, 18.

[21] Kenneth Copeland, *The Force of Righteousness* (Forth Worth: KCP Publications, 1990), p. 3.

[22] Oral Roberts, *11 Major Prophecies for You in 1992* (Tulsa: Oral Roberts, 1992), p. 35.

in their followers. Like the politician who appeals to the prejudices of the people for votes, they do the same. And like the politician, there is no logic or coherence to what they say, only fluff in the form of negative emotions. It is very difficult to extricate such false notions from them.

Contrasted with such statements from the new charismatics, Protestants have claimed that the Bible *alone* is the rule of faith.[23] Though infallibility will be attached to something, we recognize only the Bible as infallible, not man, intuition, reason, or anything else.

Bible *Is, Contains,* or *Becomes* God's Word?

We must understand what is called *inspiration* in order to see the root of the error in new charismatic theology. Inspiration and its implications are being denied by the new charismatics, but it means that the Bible in its original languages (Hebrew, Aramaic, and Greek) *is* the Word of God. The health and wealth leaders teach that the Bible *becomes* the Word of God when we *let* it.

Capps says, "The Bible itself is not the sword of the Spirit; but when you get this Word in your spirit and speak it out your mouth, it *becomes* [emphasis added] the sword of the *human* [emphasis his] spirit."[24] They often claim that the Bible is the Word of God, but what they give with one hand they take back with the other. Their forerunner, E. W. Kenyon, said: "You will never enjoy the riches of grace until you confess them."[25] "The word *becomes* [emphasis added] real only as we confess its reality."[26]

Oral Roberts is blatant: "There have been many big misunderstandings and divisions caused when *only* [emphasis added] the written Word, the Bible, is believed to be self-revelational. . . ."[27] Again he says, "However, the problem

---

[23] The reader is referred to Philip Schaff, *Creeds of Christendom,* Vol. III (Grand Rapids: Baker Book House, originally published 1877, reprinted 1977) for quotes from the Protestant Confessions that say the Bible alone is sufficient for life.

[24] Capps, *Authority,* p. 215; see Capps, *Kicking Over Sacred Cows,* p. 76ff.

[25] E. W. Kenyon, *What Happened from the Cross to the Throne* (1969, 4th ed.), p. 156.

[26] Ibid., p. 157.

[27] Roberts, *11 Major Prophecies,* pp. 44, 45.

Is the Bible Enough?

through the generations has been the belief that the written Word is all there is...."[28]

Oral Roberts says a "rhema word" is when "the Bible *becomes* a living, personal word from God directly to us." Otherwise the Bible is just a "Logos word," written but not living.[29] Kenneth Hagin, Jr. agrees that a *"rhema* comes out of our mouth" and a *logos* word is found in the Bible.[30] A *rhema* word, therefore, is personal and verbal and a logos word is unapplied, lying latent in the Bible.[31]

Similarly, those who say that a Bible promise must be claimed before it *becomes* the Word of God specifically for them are denying that the Bible *is* the Word of God. For example, Hagin says, "A promise from God's Word must be confessed as a reality before it ever becomes so. According to the Word, it is already so. But to be made real in your life, *you* must confess it to be so" [emphasis his].[32] Paul Cho says: "All the promises are potentially — not literally — yours."[33] He means that man makes them true in his life, not the Holy Spirit.

The spirit of our age is evident in this theology: All things are relative to private interpretations, God and His Word are meaningful only when men make them so. Neo-orthodoxy teaches that truth must be internalized before it is really truth; it is only potential truth until a fallible sinful creature gives it his imprimatur — then it *becomes* infallible. Personal experience validates the Word of God instead of the Word of God validating experience. In this view, God's revelation is subjective, not objective, and it is true for *me* when I accept it.[34] One must do things, however, because they are *right*, not because

---

[28] Ibid., p. 48.

[29] Ibid., p. 44.

[30] Kenneth Hagin, Jr., *Because of Jesus* (Tulsa: Faith Library Pub., 1989), p. 13.

[31] Likewise, see Paul Yonggi Cho, *The Fourth Dimension* (South Palinfield, NJ: Bridge Publishing, Inc, 1979), p. 90ff.

[32] Kenneth Hagin, *Right and Wrong Thinking* (Tulsa: Faith Library Pub., 1986), p. 10.

[33] Cho, *The Fourth Dimension*, p. 100.

[34] See *Discussions of Theological Questions* by John L. Girardeau, 1905, 1986 (Sprinkle Publications), p. 84ff, for an excellent discussion of this view of revelation, i. e. Schleiermacher and intuition and especially mysticism on p. 125ff. The reader may order the book from Footstool Pub.

he *thinks* they are right.

Similarly, Norvel Hayes states of a vision he had of Kenneth Hagin's ministry, which came to be true: "*That experience was proof* to me that God still speaks to His people through open visions" [emphasis added].[35] His experience was his proof; the Word was secondary. And how does Mr. Hayes know that the vision was of God and not of Satan? "If a vision helps you or others, it's from God."[36] This is nonsense, for there are many "healers" who do miracles, helping others physically but enslaving them spiritually.[37]

We see this same relative error in more subtle fashion in a well-known radio talk-show host. This man is a fine evangelical Christian, but he speaks of the Bible as giving us "guidelines." He says the economic "principles" in the Bible are only general guidelines: "They are not infallible laws." He also says, "This is what the passage says to me; you pray about it and see what God says to you from the passage." By this he means that the Bible conforms to each interpreter; however, there is only one valid interpretation of any passage in the Bible, though there can be many applications.

For example, the Bible says that we are not to be "unequally yoked together with unbelievers" (2 Cor. 6:14). The interpretation in the context is that Christians are God's covenant people and that we are not to be in a covenant relationship with unbelievers. There can be many applications of this "principle," this infallible rule, such as that believers should not marry unbelievers, be business partners with unbelievers, nor be members of a church where unbelievers control the church, such as a liberal church. Interpretation must come first, followed by applications consistent with the interpretation. We must never ignore the context to see what God is saying to us privately, thinking He may say something different to each reader. God says the same thing to everyone from the same passage. His Word does not change to accommodate each reader.

---

[35] Norvel Hayes, *Visions: The Window to the Supernatural* (Tulsa: Harrison House, 1992), p. 27.

[36] Ibid., p. 67.

[37] For confirmation of this, see Matt. 7:22; Gary North, *Unholy Spirit*; and Shirley MacLaine, *Going Within*.

There is a more subtle error in denying Scripture. Sometimes we see the bumper sticker that says: "God said it, I believe it, that settles it." Why does the person have to believe the message for it to be settled? What is settled? Does this mean that the truth of God's Word must wait for someone to believe it before it is settled? It does not matter who believes it, for God's Word is true whether man believes it or not. God's Word is objectively true because God exists independent of us. The Bible *is* God's Word.

Who Can Understand the Bible?

Another part of inspiration is the *clarity*[38] of Scripture. God wrote the Bible to be understood by all, not by an *elite*. The Word of Faith leaders use a form of so-called infallible interpretation. Rather than the normal, grammatical, historical interpretation, they rely on the "Jesus told me" mentality. For example, Capps, commenting on Mark 11:29-33, announces that the Lord told him what would have happened if the religious leaders had answered His question about the baptism of John.[39] He also alleges that the Lord told him that the rich man of Isaiah 53:9 who buried Jesus was not Joseph of Arimathea (as all the Gospels state: Matt. 27:57-60; Mark 15:42-47; Luke 23:50-56; John 19:38-42) but the rich man in Luke 16 who went to hell.[40] For someone to avow that God told him something which is not in Scripture is to take God's name in vain, especially when it is *contrary* to Scripture.

Similarly, Kenneth Hagin says Jesus gave him the true interpretation of why the Apostle Paul did not deal with the evil spirit the first day in Acts 16:18: "He had to wait for the manifestation of the Spirit; he had to wait until the Spirit of God gave him discerning of spirits."[41]

In a letter, Charles Capps said that the Holy Spirit told him something through a Hebrew word in a verse. When Mr. Capps was shown that the Hebrew word he had relied on was not even in the verse, he still maintained that the Holy Spirit

---

[38] Theologians call this *perspicuity*.

[39] Capps, *Authority in Three Worlds*, p. 121.

[40] Ibid., p. 142.

[41] Kenneth E. Hagin, *The Believer's Authority* (Tulsa: Faith Library Publications, 1992), p. 58.

had revealed it to him, thereby indicating that meanings do not come from the grammar and context but directly to the elite. (See "Deuteronomy 28:1" on page 193.)

This is Roman Catholic theology, in which the average parishioner cannot interpret the Bible himself, he must have some esoteric person who has a special "in" with God. This is a denial of the priesthood of all believers. From a Roman Catholic catechism, we read the following question and answer: "How can you get the true meaning of the Bible? You can get it *only* from God's official interpreter, the Catholic Church" [emphasis added].[42] Now we see why so many flock to the new charismatics; they are trained to rely on "God's official" interpreters, those who have visions from God. If they read the Bible themselves and relied on their own knowledge, they would never derive the weird interpretations that characterize new charismatics. They distrust their own minds in reading Scripture, especially when Hagin says that you do not understand the Bible with your mind.

In Roman Catholicism the priests and others are the official interpreters of the Bible. So where is infallibility located in the Roman church? It is in the church itself, not in the Bible. The Reformers understood this, and so did the Roman Catholic Church, but those in the Word of Faith movement, who neglect church history, do not understand how they have compromised what the Reformers fought and died for. John Eck, the Roman Catholic scholar who opposed Martin Luther, stated to Luther: "Scripture is not authentic without the Church's authority: for the canonical writers are members of the Church."[43] At the Council of Trent in 1546, which was called to oppose the Reformers, the Roman Catholic Church decreed that "no one relying on his own judgment shall . . . presume to interpret them [the Scriptures] contrary to that sense which holy mother Church . . . has held. . . ."[44] Apparently the Spirit of God only illuminates the minds of

---

[42] Rev. William J. Cogan, *A Catechism for Adults* (Chicago: ACTA Publications, 1958), p. 10.

[43] John Eck, *Enchiridion of Commonplaces: Against Luther and Other Enemies of the Church* (Grand Rapids: Baker Book House, 1979), p. 13.

[44] Translated by Rev. H. J. Schroeder, *The Canons and Decrees of the Council of Trent* (Rockford, IL: Tan Books and Publishers, 1978), pp. 18, 19.

the hierarchy in the Roman church, not the minds of the laymen. This is precisely the same kind of mental slavery we see in the Word of Faith movement.

Scripture, however, interprets itself, and if the plain sense of the Bible is contrary to what the new charismatics promulgate, guess who is askew? One of the most precious truths that the Reformers touted was the right of each individual to read and reckon with the Bible himself. William Tyndale proclaimed that by translating the Bible into English, the plowman would have more knowledge of Scripture than most clergymen; Tyndale was burned at the stake for this. We hope it was not in vain.

It has been the Protestant and biblical doctrine that God's Word is sufficiently clear for all to read and that Scripture interprets Scripture. One passage sheds light on another, the clearer passages interpreting the more obscure ones. We can see this principle from the way God has given so many passages parallel to one another.[45]

God's Word is so clear that even the Apostle Paul was scrutinized by laymen using Scripture: "These were more fair minded than those in Thessalonica, in that they received the word with all readiness, and searched the Scriptures daily [to find out] whether these things were so" (Acts 17:11). On many occasions Paul and others *reasoned* with people from the Scripture (Acts 17:2, 17; 18:4, 19; 19:8, 9), the assumption being that the average person was thoroughly acquainted with the written Word and would validate Paul's beliefs. That is not to say that the clergy have no place in helping citizens of the kingdom to comprehend the Word; they do (Neh. 8:7, 8). But ultimately God holds each person accountable for his understanding and use of Scripture (James 2:8-12).

---

[45] First and Second Chronicles are parallel to 1 Samuel-2 Kings. The books of Moses parallel one another. The Gospels interpret one another, and 2 Peter 2 and Jude are parallel. Paul's letters have many similar things in them. For example, Ephesians and Colossians are closely related, as are 1 & 2 Timothy and Titus, Galatians and Romans, 1 & 2 Corinthians, 1 & 2 Thessalonians, 1 & 2 Peter, 1-3 John. Old and New Testament books interpret one another: Daniel and Revelation, Leviticus and Hebrews, and so forth. The New Testament interprets the Old Testament and the Old the New.

Is the Bible Enough?

The Sufficiency of Scripture

The third aspect of inspiration is that the Bible is *complete*, containing all God intended us to comprehend this side of eternity. As a friend of mine says, "The Bible is infallible in everything of which it speaks, and it speaks about everything."[46] There is no area of life that the Bible does not address, not one.[47] We do not need *any* additions to the Bible. *If anything is contrary to Scripture, it is wrong. If anything is the same as Scripture, it is not needed. If anything goes beyond Scripture, it has no authority.*[48] Someone may object that the Bible itself repeats things, so are these not needed? God does so for emphasis and can do what He pleases, but we are speaking of saying the same regarding a *completed* Bible.

Can we defend this doctrine of the sufficiency of the Scripture from the Bible? Yes, and the Reformers did. As we saw at the beginning of this chapter in 1 Corinthians 4:6, Paul legislates that we must learn "not to think beyond what is written." The Bible is so clear here that it would take a very sophisticated theologian to make it confusing. Paul uses the normal Greek verb for referring to the Scripture when he says "written," used literally dozens of times in the Greek New Testament to introduce Scripture (see these in 1 Cor. alone: 1:19, 31; 2:9; 3:19; 9:9, 10; 10:7, 11; 14:21; 15:45, 54). Thus it is not debatable that "what is written" refers to the Bible. Furthermore, the Greek dictates that the expression "not to think beyond what it written" was a well known proverb that Paul expected the Corinthians not to take exception to.[49] It

---

[46] Joe Morecraft, pastor of Chalcedon Presbyterian Church, Atlanta, GA.

[47] Occasionally I say this to audiences and watch their response. Once a man said that the Bible did not speak to nuclear physics, to which it was pointed out, "Not so. God created it, which means it is mathematical, understandable, consistent, controllable, subject to economics, capable of being used for good or for evil, and many other things." He got the point.

[48] By *additions*, I mean revelation from God. The local church, suffering, prayer, the ministry of the Holy Spirit in us are all part of the Christian walk and necessary, but they are not revelations to us of God's will.

[49] "The article (to) is in the accusative case as the object of the verb [*mathete*: learn] and points at the words 'Not to go beyond what is written,' apparently a proverb or rule. . . ." A. T. Robertson, *Word Pictures in the New Testament* (Nashville: Broadman Press, 1931), 4:105.

was a very common and acceptable saying among the people, therefore, that we are "not to go beyond what is written."

But someone may object that more Scripture was written by the apostles after Paul wrote 1 Corinthians. That is true, but 1 Corinthians is also "what is written" and so is the balance of the New Testament. Even the new charismatics admit that the Bible was completed two thousand years ago; if so, then their "prophecies" definitely go beyond "what is written."

Another proof that prophecy has ceased is that God has not continuously given prophecy, as in the four hundred silent years between the Old and New Testaments when no prophet spoke. Since God does not unceasingly give prophecy, why should He be doing so today after two thousand years of silence?

Another argument for the sufficiency of Scripture is from 2 Timothy 3:16, 17: "All Scripture is given by inspiration of God, and is profitable for doctrine, for reproof, for correction, for instruction in righteousness, that the man of God may be complete, thoroughly equipped for every good work." Thus the Bible itself says very succinctly that it is sufficient to equip us for *every* good work. Thus we do not need the traditions of the Roman Catholic Church, *Science and Health* by Mary Baker Eddy, the *Book of Mormon* by the Mormons, nor the so-called prophecies of the Word of Faith leaders.

Someone may object that Paul had primarily the Old Testament in mind when he penned these two verses and yet other books were added to the Scripture after Paul wrote this. We must consider, however, that the Holy Spirit had in mind the whole New Testament. The New Testament writers knew they were writing Scripture and sometimes referred to one another's writings as Scripture (2 Peter 3:15, 16 referring to Paul's letters; 1 Tim. 5:18 quoting Luke). Therefore, it may have been that Paul *did* have in mind the New Testament writings, most of which had been written by the time he penned 2 Timothy, but at least the Holy Spirit included the whole of Scripture.

God expressly forbids adding to or taking away from the Bible (Deut. 4:2; Gal. 1:8; Rev. 22:18, 19). If anyone, even an angel, does so, he is accursed. To add to the Gospel of grace for salvation is to add to the Scripture, for the Gospel is now complete. Likewise, to add to the Bible is to add to the completed Gospel. We must not add new doctrines by which a person may be damned if he denies them as Pope Pius IX did in 1854 to the Roman Catholic Church with the doctrine of the Immaculate Conception, pontificating that Mary was born without sin.[50]

Another argument for the cessation of revelation is from Jude 3: "Beloved, while I was very diligent to write to you concerning our common salvation, I found it necessary to write to you exhorting you to contend earnestly for the faith which was *once for all delivered* to the saints." The word translated "once for all" ($\alpha\pi\alpha\xi$) is the same basic[51] word used in Hebrews 10:10 to say that "we have been sanctified through the offering of the body of Jesus Christ *once for all*." Just as the atonement cannot be repeated without denying the sufficiency of what Christ did, so no more revelation can be given without denying the sufficiency of Scripture. There is a finality to Scripture and to its doctrines; they are *once for all* delivered. We are to expect no more.

Furthermore, it was prophesied in Daniel 9 that the canon of Scripture would be closed, that God would add no more books after a certain date. God said that "seventy weeks" (490 years) were determined for the Jewish people "to finish the transgression, to make an end of sins, to make reconciliation for iniquity, to bring in everlasting righteousness, *to seal up vision and prophecy*, and to anoint the Most Holy" (v. 24). Most scholars agree that these things were accomplished by Christ

---

[50] Now Roman Catholics must believe this to go to heaven. Likewise in 1950 Pope Pius XII pontificated that Mary's body was raised from the dead and that she was enthroned as the Queen of Heaven. What happened to those Roman Catholics who did not believe these for 1400 and 1500 years respectively? (Contrary to the Catholics, their church did not begin with Peter but about four to five hundred years later. Thus for *1400* years they did not believe the Immaculate Conception theory.) Over the centuries they have added purgatory, papal infallibility, prayers for and to the dead, works of supererogation (more works than you need to get to heaven!). Where does it end? There is no objective way to limit novel ideas and enslavements. They have a church government by men instead of a government ruled by a document — Scripture. This is why we have a Constitution in the USA, namely, to have government by law, not by fickle and tyrannical men. Because we are under the judgment of God (and getting worse every day), we have not had a Constitutional Republic for about 80 years. The Supreme Court now makes laws by its rulings instead of interpreting the Constitution. The lower courts follow its rulings.

[51] There is a slight difference of form in Hebrews 10:10.

"who made an end of sins," reconciled the people, and sealed up "the vision and prophecy."

We must clearly understand that Christ sealed up "vision and prophecy" in two ways. (1) Being Almighty God and perfect humanity in One Person, He, by Himself, cleansed our sins as the final and sufficient high *priest*. By the same token, He, as the final *prophet*, perfectly revealed the Father so that whoever saw Him had seen the Father (John 14:9). He was also the final *King* (John 1:49), the King of kings and Lord of lords.

To have more offerings for sin or priests after Him would be an abomination, for He was the final high priest (Heb. 2:17; 4:14; 7:25-28; 10:12-14). To promote the idea that there would be more prophets after Him is to say that He revealed God and His will incompletely and thus imperfectly, so that we need more. This disparages Him. Hebrews 1:1, 2 tells us that in times past God spoke through various prophets, but now He has spoken personally, permanently, and sufficiently in His Son, the implication being that no more is needed or possible. A few verses later in Hebrews 2:2-4 we see that miracles and prophecy were already being excluded from some as the book was being written.

There will be no more human kings over God's people, for the ever living King now rules from the Father's right hand (John 1:49; Acts 2:30, 31; Luke 1:32, 33). Now we can understand how Daniel could say that Jesus would end both sacrifice and prophecy. Once the canon of Scripture revealing Jesus was completed, no more was necessary. He is sufficient in what He did, and Scripture is complete in pointing to Him. The finality of the canon of Scripture and the Person and work of Christ are inextricably bound together, one implying the other.

As the great theologian B. B. Warfield so beautifully encapsulated it:

> Because Christ is all in all, and all revelation and redemption alike are summed up in Him, it would be inconceivable that either revelation or its accompanying signs should continue after the completion of that great revelation with its accrediting works, by which Christ has been established in His rightful place as the culmination and climax and all-inclusive summary of the saving revelation of God, the sole and sufficient

redeemer of His people.⁵²

If the work of Christ is complete, then there cannot be any more revelation or shedding of blood.

(2) The second way Jesus "sealed up the vision and prophecy" was in 70 A.D. when He, as the King of kings ruling over the earth from His heavenly throne, sent the Roman general Titus to Jerusalem. He demolished Judaism by destroying the temple and the City, thereby making offerings, sacrifices, the temple, prophecy, and kings over Israel all cease permanently — and they have not been seen again from that day to ours!

Another argument for the sufficiency of the Bible is from Isaiah 8:19, 20:

> And when they say to you, "Seek those who are mediums and wizards, who whisper and mutter," should not a people seek their God? Should they seek the dead on behalf of the living? To the law and to the testimony! If they do not speak according to this word, it is because there is no light in them.

God demands that anyone and everyone must speak according to the law and the testimony and according to nothing else. To go beyond this is to incur His wrath and judgment. In context Isaiah 8:19, 20 seems to be a prophecy of the A. D. 70 destruction of Jerusalem, at least typically.⁵³ If Isaiah 8:19, 20 points to A. D. 70, then after this date nothing could be added to the canon of Scripture. Even if this is not a prophecy, the passage still limits us to the *written* Word, regardless if the written Word is the Old Testament, New Testament, or both.

What is the indication that this may be A. D. 70? Isaiah 8:14, 15 is applied to Christ as the Stone who was rejected by Israel (Luke 2:34; Rom. 9:32, 33; 1 Peter 2:8). Verses 21-22 speak of Israel, who went to wizards and mediums for her knowledge of God. When did they do this? In A. D. 70 when Titus sacked Jerusalem, Josephus speaks of the demonic activity in the city and how the people consulted wizards when they had left their covenant God.⁵⁴ If verses 14 & 15 apply to

---

⁵²B. B. Warfield, *Counterfeit Miracles* (London: Banner of Truth, 1918, 1972), p. 28.

⁵³I am indebted to Phil Kayser, that great scholar and pastor of Trinity Presbyterian Church, Omaha, NE, for this argument.

⁵⁴David Chilton, *Paradise Restored* (Tyler, TX: Reconstruction Press, 1985), p.

Christ as the rejected Stone and verses 21-22 speak of Israel's A. D. 70 destruction, it would seem that verses 19 & 20 would also apply to A. D. 70. Isaiah 8:16 says at the time of Titus' invasion that the *testimony* and *law* (both are words for Scripture) would be cut off.

Another prophecy is Joel 2:28-32 as fulfilled in Acts 2:14-21. Men and women, Peter proclaims in his famous Pentecost sermon, would prophesy in the "last days." "The last days" (Acts 2:17) is an expression that refers to the "last days" of the Old Covenant.[55] In the transition from Old to New Covenant, some would prophesy, and not afterwards, for the "last days" did not extend after the Old Covenant was permanently terminated in A. D. 70 with the destruction of Jerusalem.

First Corinthians 13:8-13 also declares that the sign gifts will cease, mentioning these three: prophecy, tongues, and knowledge. Knowledge has to be special revelation knowledge, for there will never be a time that we will not learn. Paul says only love continues.[56] Why did Paul choose these three miracle gifts out of all the gifts he mentioned in chapter twelve and say only these would cease? It would seem that he is saying that these would cease prior to the others.[57]

There is a final argument for the sufficiency of Scripture: All dogmatic traditions outside Scripture are to be rejected.

237ff.

[55] Heb. 1:1; Acts 2:16, 17; 1 Peter 1:20; James 5:3; Gen. 49:1; Num. 24:14; Deut. 31:29; Ez. 38:14-16; Dan. 2:28; 1 Tim. 4:1; 2 Tim. 3:1; 2 Peter 3:3.

[56] See Robert Glenn Gromacki, *The Modern Tongues Movement* (Philadelphia: Presbyterian and Reformed Pub. Co., 1967), p. 109ff., for a good discussion of 1 Cor. 13:8-13.

[57] Interestingly, Bill Hamon explains that the expression "prophecies shall fail" in 1 Cor. 13:8 means that some did not come to pass as stated. (Bill Hamon, *Prophets and Personal Prophecy* [Shippensburg, PA: Destiny Image, 1987], p. 32.) Apparently God could not pass the test of a prophet! This indicates how little they understand the Greek, and how much they bend passages to promote their errors. The same verb is used in the same verse of knowledge: "Knowledge will vanish away." Obviously the idea is not that knowledge "fails" but that it will "vanish away" or "cease," and not all knowledge (or we would be like rocks, unable to think) but only special revelation knowledge. In verse eleven, using the same Greek verb, Paul says he "put away" childish things. Hamon wants to have fallible prophecies to cover for the many times that his prophecies are wrong (Hamon, *Prophets*, p. 39ff.).

"In vain do they worship Me, teaching doctrines and precepts of men" (Matt. 15:9; Isa. 29:13).[58] The only way to validate a prophecy is to correlate it with Scripture, the assumption being that Scripture is sufficient and complete. If something were prophesied that Scripture could not evaluate, and that supposedly did not contradict Scripture but went beyond it, then the Lord's statement is in vain. The new charismatics have many traditions based on assumed "prophecies," which they claim do not contradict the Bible, but which are additional to the Scripture. This is not good enough, for now there is something that Scripture is not sufficient to evaluate. According to this theory, if something blatantly contradicts the Bible it is wrong; but if the Bible does not speak to the prophecy, then we must use other criteria to evaluate its validity. The Lord, though, in the statement above assumes that there is nothing that the Bible cannot evaluate, for Scripture is sufficient to evaluate *every* proclamation of any prophet.

New Charismatics Deny Scripture's Sufficiency

We have seen that the Bible declares itself to be *infallible*, that it *is* the Word of God, that it is *sufficient* for all of life, and that it is *complete*. Now let us observe what the new charismatics say.

One new charismatic writer, Bill Hamon, states that the "Scripture is sufficient to give us knowledge" about salvation,[59] but there are "particular matters for which the Bible cannot give us specific guidance,"[60] an obvious denial of what 2 Timothy 3:16 and 17 say. Hamon says that God "has now established the prophetic ministry as a voice of revelation and illumination which will reveal the mind of Christ to the human race."[61] Put simply, he is saying that the Bible is not enough, that God is now speaking to us through this new generation of prophets. What is implicit in this quote is explicit later: ". . . the Bible *cannot by itself* provide specific

---

[58] This argument from Francis Turretin (1623-1687), *The Doctrine of Scripture* (Grand Rapids: Baker Book House, 1981), p. 175.

[59] Hamon, *Prophets*, p. 12.

[60] Ibid., p. 71.

[61] Ibid., p. 13.

directions and reveal the Will of God concerning all personal matters" [emphasis added].[62]

Likewise, Kenneth Hagin says, "God's Word" provides direction for *"many* of the affairs of life" [emphasis added].[63] Hagin also places the human spirit above written revelation in some cases. For example, he was trying to decide whether he should stay home with his wife and small children or be in the field preaching and traveling. Hagin says one preacher after another told him to stay home, but Hagin listened to the inner voice over the Bible and over a "multitude of counselors" (Prov. 11:14) and left his family to go preach in other cities.[64] God's Word is clear: a preacher must be "one who rules his own house well, having his children in submission with all reverence (for if a man does not know how to rule his own house, how will he take care of the church of God?)" (1 Tim. 3:4, 5). How can he bring up his children in the discipline and instruction of the Lord (Eph. 6:1ff) if he is not at home?[65]

New Charismatics and the New "Prophets"

Many of the new charismatics promote themselves as prophets. Often Robert Tilton says on TV that he is a prophet giving out the Word of God like a "living, waking Bible." Oral Roberts, in *11 Major Prophecies for You in 1992*, is frightfully audacious: "I believe the Lord manifested the gift of prophecy through me...."[66] He elaborates that these eleven "prophecies ... did not come out of my mind, but by the Holy Spirit revealing them to be in harmony with the inspired and

---

[62] Ibid., p. 92.

[63] Kenneth Hagin, *The Human Spirit* (Tulsa: Faith Library Publications, 1985), p. 24.

[64] Ibid., p. 24.

[65] John L. Girardeau declares that the Quakers in his day (last century), who had changed from the Quakers of Cotton's day, also held the view that the Bible was necessary and inspired but not sufficient: "... there is an "inner light," to be discriminated from the dictates of natural conscience, consisting in new and supernatural revelations made by the Holy Spirit to individuals, which are complementary to the Scriptures as a rule of faith and duty. The Scriptures are confessed to be a revelation from God; but they are not a complete rule of faith and directory of duty. The defect is supplied by the Spirit, who, apart from the Scriptures, communicates new views of faith and duty." Girardeau, *Discussion*, p. 148.

[66] Oral Roberts, *11 Major Prophecies*, Introduction.

infallible Word of God."⁶⁷ But in fact if these "prophecies" came from the Holy Spirit directly to his mind, then it is special revelation, infallible, inerrant, and for all people. If they are in harmony with the Word of God, they are not needed. If they go beyond the Bible, they have no authority, for Oral Roberts needs to be tested first to see if he is genuine prophet.⁶⁸

There is also a unique characteristic of the modern prophets: Prophecy seems to be inherited, especially appearing in families with large ministries. Kenneth Hagin's son, Kenneth Hagin, Jr., is the heir apparent for his father's ministry and role as a "prophet." Likewise, Richard Roberts will assume Oral Roberts's ministry, and is already being groomed for it. It is more like nepotism than biblical prophets, for in Scripture prophets were chosen by God and rarely — if ever — were a father and a son.

There are two ways to test prophets. We must first question whether they carry us to false gods, even though they may perform miracles:

> If there arises among you a prophet or a dreamer of dreams, and he gives you a sign or a wonder, and the sign or the wonder of which he spoke to you comes to pass, saying, "Let us go after other gods which you have not known, and let us serve them," you shall not listen to the words of that prophet or that dreamer of dreams, for the Lord your God is testing you to know whether you love the Lord your God with all your heart and with all your soul. You shall walk after the Lord your God and fear Him, and keep His commandments and obey His voice, and you shall serve Him and hold fast to Him (Deut. 13:1-4; see also 1 John 4:1-6).

Even if the prophet performs a miracle, God may be testing us to see if we will follow His Word. It appears that many of the followers of the Word of Faith leaders have "itching ears."

The second way to test a prophet is to see whether he *ever* prophesies wrongly:

And if you say in your heart, "How shall we know the word

---

⁶⁷Ibid.

⁶⁸The index lists many statements by Roberts that contradict Scripture, revealing that he cannot qualify as a prophet.

Is the Bible Enough?

which the Lord has not spoken?" — when a prophet speaks in the name of the Lord, if the thing does not happen or come to pass, that is the thing which the Lord has not spoken; the prophet has spoken it presumptuously; you shall not be afraid of him (Deut. 18:21, 22).

To be able to test all prophets by Scripture means that the Scripture is a complete and worthy guide to all matters for life and doctrine (2 Tim. 3:16, 17; 1 John 4:1-6). If the prophet promotes idolatry, then he is ungodly, even if he does miracles. If the prophet prophesies error, then he is likewise not of God.

These modern "prophets" have often prophesied wrongly. Edward Irving taught that the Second Coming was very near, within a few years, and the "prophets" associated with him had predicted His near return.[69] Other wrong prophecies by Irving's prophets included the notion that American Indians were the ten lost tribes of Israel,[70] and that Christ's Second Coming would be in 1835.[71] (Another time it was 1864; see paragraph beginning with "In a long discourse" on page 50).

The Bible has not a little to say about false prophets, and the reader is encourage to peruse Jeremiah 23 and Ezekiel 13 and 14 to see how God characterizes these counterfeits. When you scrutinize these chapters, think of the modern day "prophets" — you will avow that these chapters were penned yesterday. They cause God's people to err (Jer. 23:13); they commit adultery and walk in lies (v. 14); they prophesy peace and safety when the people are in sin (v. 17);[72] the Lord did not send these prophets or give them words to speak (v. 21). The Lord says they "try to make My people forget My name by their dreams which everyone tells his neighbor" (v. 27). When people come to such prophets for a word from the Lord, *He* answers them according to their folly and confirms

---

[69] Arnold Dallimore, *Forerunner of the Charismatic Movement, The Life of Edward Irving* (Chicago: Moody Press, 1983), p. 73ff.

[70] Ibid., p. 110.

[71] Ibid., p. 151.

[72] Charles Capps on the radio stated that God would not judge America because we do so much for God, like sending missionaries. This seems to be an example of the prophets who say "peace and safety" when there is none.

them in their wickedness (Ez. 14:4-9).

New Charismatics and the New "Prophecy"

Of course, as with twentieth century "prophets," the alleged reason the prophecies (some forty-six) of Irving's prophets failed was because of lack of faith on the part of the recipients.[73] If healing fails, it is the sick person's fault. If prophecies fail, it is because the recipient did something wrong. Such reasons give the prophet a convenient place to put the blame.

The leaders in the Word of Faith movement give out "prophecies" that are the Word of God for all the people of God for all time, not just "personal" prophecy for one person for a specific time. For example, Gloria Copeland quotes a "prophecy" of Kenneth Hagin in her book as though it had the same authority and assurance as Scripture. She introduces his "prophecy" by saying: "We have to learn to walk in the spirit[74] to fulfill God's plan for this hour," stating that his "prophecy" is for the "end times." She then boldly asserts that because of the prediction in his "prophecy" that we are in the "last hour," there will come a time when "we will flow in the supernatural" in the last hour. This outpouring of the Spirit will be so profuse that "We will not even be conscious of using our faith."[75] She confidently speaks of this future outpouring because of Hagin's "prophecy."

In another part of her book, she asserts: "I heard Kenneth Hagin give this *prophecy* at Camp-meeting, 1977. This *word form* [sic] *the Lord* corrected me, instructed me, chastened me (2 Tim. 3:16, 17; Heb. 12). *By the Holy Spirit* he began to talk about the great and might [sic] army of the Lord. . . . *The prophet of God* said at the end of the prophecy. . . ."[emphasis added].[76] Observe the divine authority she attributes to Hagin's so-called prophecies. Several pages later she declares of Hagin's "prophecy": "If I had not listened to the Holy Spirit when the Word of God came from the prophet and allowed

---

[73] Dallimore, *Forerunner*, p. 155; Hamon, *Prophets*.

[74] Without a capital "S," it seems that she does not mean the Holy Spirit but our spirits.

[75] Gloria Copeland, *Walk in the Spirit* (Forth Worth: KCP Publications, 1984), p. 8.

[76] Ibid., p. 80.

that Word to correct me, I would have continued getting colder and colder and colder."[77] She speaks of Russian believers who did not have Bibles, but who could "listen" to their humans spirits and receive the Word of God.[78] Furthermore, God is raising up a "glorious church" which shall be able to "hear the voice of His Spirit and obey Him in whatever we are told to do."[79] Of course, Kenneth Hagin encourages this by claiming to be a prophet.[80]

Mrs. Copeland states, "As you learn by experience to walk in the spirit [human spirit], remember that God's Word comes to us in two ways. We have the written Word *and* we have the Holy Spirit speaking in our spirits" [emphasis added].[81] Like the Roman Catholics against the Reformers, God's Word is from the Holy Spirit through Scripture *and* from the Holy Spirit apart from Scripture. The Word and tradition are equally infallible sources, but they (the new charismatic leaders) are the infallible interpreters. They have added to the Scripture and thus to the Gospel. Again Gloria Copeland avows: *"We are no longer under obedience to written revelation, but we are still to serve in obedience. We are now to serve by obeying the prompting of the newborn spirit controlled by the Holy Spirit"* [emphasis added].[82]

All of this is wickedness, exalting a standard for righteousness outside Scripture, making the traditions of men binding on others, denying the sufficiency of Scripture and uniqueness of the final prophet, the Lord Jesus. Once we allow new revelations, there is no limit, no objective restraint, to the heresies that Satan can introduce. The only limit is the unsanctified imagination of the "prophets."

There are three things that "prophet" John Osteen considers equal: "I call myself exactly what God shows me, either by the *Bible*, by *vision*, or by *revelation*" [emphasis added].[83]

---

[77]Ibid., p. 84.

[78]Ibid., p. 89.

[79]Ibid., p. 90.

[80]Hagin, *Faith Edition Bible*, p. xciii.

[81]Gloria Copeland, *Walk in the Spirit*, p. 56.

[82]Ibid., p. 52.

[83]John Osteen, *Four Principles in Receiving from God* (Houston: John Osteen,

Notice that "vision" and "revelation" are looked upon as different from but equal to the Bible.

Others refer to their writings as being inspired. Oral Roberts announces about his booklet: "I take every word I have written here as a prophecy for God's people, you and me, for 1992."[84] Charles Capps gives several "prophecies" that came to him; several are pages long.[85]

Other prophecies for all people abound. In *How To Write Your Own Ticket With God*, Hagin says Jesus told him, "*If anybody, anywhere, will take these four steps or put these four principles into operation, he will always receive whatever he wants from Me or God the Father*" [emphasis his].[86] Of course Hagin contends that Jesus showed him how to prove these "four steps" from the Bible, but this is only trying to justify his unbiblical revelations. At the very least, Hagin was given an infallible interpretation that could be inserted into our Bibles as an infallible footnote, giving the true meaning of Scripture. This would be a study Bible with inspired explanatory notes.

Another "infallible" interpretation is promoted by Charles and Annette Capps: "As I was praying one day, the Spirit of God began to speak to my spirit. He shared [!] some things with me about angels and how they operate in our behalf. He said...."[87] Capps cannot find his twisted doctrines about angels in the Bible so he has Jesus tell him directly.

Furthermore, the leaders may indeed publish another "Bible" or at least their infallible interpretations. Hamon says, "Those ["prophecies"] that were recorded have all been typed and placed in a five inch ring notebook, which contains over 600 pages of... text. They amount to over 150,000 prophetic words...."[88] Collecting the manuscripts is the first step to canonizing them as Scripture! Likewise, Richard Eby was supposedly told by the Lord to write down his experiences

---

no date), p. 27.

[84] Roberts, *11 Major Prophecies*, p. 3.

[85] Capps, *Authority*, pp. 191, 199.

[86] Kenneth E. Hagin, *How To Write Your Own Ticket with God* (Tulsa: Faith Library Publications, 1985), p. 5.

[87] Charles & Annette Capps, *Angels* (Tulsa, OK: Harrison House, 1984), p. 75.

[88] Hamon, *Prophets*, p. 8.

with the Lord for the blessing of others.[89]

The men who circulate this word are on the horns of a dilemma: Since these "prophecies" are for all the people of God, this is new Scripture; if it is not Scripture, then it cannot be for all people. I predict they will issue their prophecies as new Scripture to solve this dilemma, but I may be wrong as I am no prophet.

The Lord apparently erred in some "prophecies" given to these men. For Bill Hamon receives "prophecies" from the Spirit in King James English, and some of them did not come to pass.[90] Capps says the Lord told him that there was evil creative power released for the enemy to use against us when we speak wrongly.[91] Hagin assures us that he has had a tour of hell, having left his body by his spirit through his mouth.[92]

Is the Bible enough? Absolutely, for the Holy Spirit works *only* through the written Word. The Bible, therefore, is not only necessary but also sufficient for all of life and godliness. God forgot nothing that we need to know to live righteously, and if something is not revealed then we do not need it.

The Holy Spirit and the Written Word

Separating the Spirit of God from the Word of God is a very grave error that most in our day have not considered. The Protestant Reformers understood this. If the Holy Spirit speaks to people apart from the Word (as the Roman Catholic Church teaches), that is special revelation. In other words, the way the Bible was primarily written was that the prophets and apostles received revelation in the form of visions, dreams, verbal communications, non-verbal communications, or the Holy Spirit moving directly on them — usually apart from the written Word. This was legitimate and necessary when the

---

[89] Richard E. Eby, *Didn't You Read My Book?* (Shippensburg, PA: Companion Press, 1991), p. 102.

[90] Hamon, *Prophets*, p. 5. Wayne Grudem has written *The Gift of Prophecy in the New Testament* (Westchester, IL: Crossway Books, 1988) in which he takes the position that New Testament prophecy may be wrong. For a refutation of this, order *The Charismatic Gift of Prophecy* by Dr. Kenneth L. Gentry, Jr. from Footstool Pub., whose address is in the front of this book.

[91] Capps, *Dynamics of Faith & Confession*, p. 66.

[92] Bruce Barron, *The Health & Wealth Gospel* (Downers Grove, IL: InterVarsity Press, 1987), p. 123ff.

Bible was being written.

The battle in the Reformation over the connection of the Spirit and the Word was tenacious. The Reformers proclaimed that *only* the Bible was infallible. The Roman Catholic Church could not support all their doctrines from the Bible so they taught that tradition, which had been handed down verbally and in the writings of the early church fathers, was equally valid with the Bible. How did anyone know what was legitimate tradition? The Roman Catholic Church was the custodian of these traditions and the official interpreter of both tradition and the Bible. No one else was allowed to interpret either.

By this maneuver, the church had located the Holy Spirit in the officials of the church and separated Him from Scripture. It was the church that was infallible, the Spirit of God guarding the church, speaking directly to it and through it. This is how a new doctrine such as the Immaculate Conception originated.

The Reformers rightly saw that this would lead to enormous subjectivity, to endless new doctrines, and to continued enslavement of the lay people to the hierarchy of the church. They argued that though the Holy Spirit was a person and the Bible a book, nevertheless He always spoke through Scripture alone. To separate the Holy Spirit from the written Word was the very essence of Roman Catholicism, locating infallibility in those who could "hear" Him and essentially placing the Bible in the background.

In March, 1539, Roman Catholic Church leader Jacopo Sadoleto wrote an open letter to the good citizens of Geneva, where John Calvin was laboring.[93] Sadoleto challenged the Genevans that we receive the word of the Gospel on the authority of our ancestors "as truly dictated and enjoined by the Holy Spirit."[94] In several such statements, it was obvious to Calvin that Sadoleto had made the church leaders the custodian of the truth and the elite of the church the official interpreter of the Bible, thereby separating the Holy Spirit from the Bible. With devastating logic and classic insight,

---

[93] John Calvin, *A Reformation Debate* (Grand Rapids: Baker Book House, 1966, translated by John C. Olin), p. 7.

[94] Ibid., p. 37.

Calvin gave his reply.

> For seeing how dangerous it would be to boast of the Spirit without the Word, He declared that the Church is indeed governed by the Holy Spirit. But in order that government might not be vague and unstable, He annexed it to the Word. For this reason Christ exclaims that those who are of God hear the Word of God — that His sheep are those which recognize His voice as that of their Shepherd, and any other voice as that of a stranger (John 10:27).[95]

> ... the principle weapon with which they [the Pope and the Anabaptists] assail us is the same. For when they boast extravagantly of the Spirit, the tendency certainly is to sink and bury the Word of God, that they may make room for their own falsehoods. And you, Sadoleto, by stumbling ... have paid the penalty of that affront which you offered to the Holy Spirit when you separated Him from the Word.

> Learn, then, by your own experience, that it is no less unreasonable to boast of the Spirit without the Word than it would be absurd to bring forward the Word itself without the Spirit.[96]

Calvin argued in his *Institutes of the Christian Religion* that the Spirit points us only to Christ, not speaking of anything else but Him (John 16:13-15).[97] We are to "search the Scriptures, for in them you think you have eternal life; and these are they which testify of" Jesus (John 5:39), and the Spirit of God takes this written testimony to speak of Christ — not of Himself (John 16:8-11).[98] The Holy Spirit enables His people to understand and accept the things given to us in Holy Scripture, which the natural man would not accept (1 Cor. 2:12-16). In other words, the Spirit illuminates our minds *to the written Word*, not to intuition, as Luke wrote:

> Then He said to them, "These are the words which I spoke to you while I was still with you, that all things must be fulfilled which were written in the Law of Moses and the Prophets

---

[95] Ibid., p. 60.

[96] Ibid., p. 61.

[97] John Calvin, *Institutes of the Christian Religion* (Philadelphia: Westminster Press, 1975, translated by Ford Lewis Battles), 1:9:1.

[98] Ibid., 1:7:1.

and the Psalms concerning Me." ***And He opened their understanding, that they might comprehend the Scriptures*** (Luke 24:44, 45).

Jesus always based His works and doctrines on the Scriptures. Why would God go through so much effort to give us the Bible and keep it preserved for thousands of years, only to supplant it with something else?[99] Again Calvin, quoting Chrysostom (347-407), cannot be improved:

> Many boast of the Holy Spirit, but those who speak their own thoughts claim him falsely. As Christ testified that he spoke not from himself [John 12:49; 14:10], because he spoke from the Law and the Prophets [John 12:50], so let us not believe anything that is thrust in under the title of the Spirit apart from the gospel. For just as Christ is the fulfillment of the Law [Rom. 10:4] and the prophets, so is the Spirit the fulfillment of the gospel.[100]

Therefore, we see that the Reformers, reflecting the Savior and the Holy Spirit, did not separate the Holy Spirit from the written Word.

New Charismatics and the Guidance of the Spirit

Hagin says if we would listen to "inward intuition," we could avoid problems in our lives.[101] Tal Brooke, who was a New Age mystic and the main American disciple of Sai Baba, an Indian maharishi, said that intuition is one of the two pillars of the New Age. (See paragraph beginning "As Tal Brooke says" on page 381.) Preachers especially have to learn to listen to their spirits, they maintain. "It is your spirit that picks up these things [guidance] from the Holy Spirit and then passes them on to your mind by an inward intuition, or inward witness."[102]

How does one know if the intuition is from the Holy Spirit or the devil? Jesus allegedly told Hagin: "You had a *velvety-like*

---

[99] By the way, notice that Jesus opened their minds, and He did this before His Ascension, demonstrating that He was functioning as God while on earth (see Chapter Twelve).

[100] Ibid., 4:8:13.

[101] Hagin, *How To Be Led*, p. 53.

[102] Ibid.

feeling in your spirit. That's the *green light*. That's the go-ahead signal. That's the witness of the Spirit to go" [emphasis his].[103] Hagin says, "We must learn to let our spirits dominate our minds if we are going to be successful Christians."[104]

Norvel Hayes gives a slight twist to Hagin's "feeling," saying of the "inward witness": "You'll feel so good down in your spirit, you'll know that your call and ministry have been confirmed by the Lord."[105] To make matters even more complicated, Hagin manufactures a distinction between the "inward voice" and the "inward witness."[106] He is not able to articulate the distinction though he is sure it exists. Tilton also plays down the mind: "The gift of tongues enables you to communicate with God in your spirit without the interference of your human reasoning" [emphasis added].[107] As John MacArthur rightly observes: "In other words, ignore your mind, forget your beliefs, disregard your theology and common sense; the sensation in your upper abdominal area will let you know how much weight a 'prophecy' really has."[108]

Then there is the so-called "word of knowledge," which, interestingly, is only mentioned in 1 Corinthians 12:8. Whatever the gift was, new charismatics have typically developed a whole theology from this one phrase, making majors of minors. For them this "gift" is knowledge about persons and events that one would not normally know, revealed directly by the Holy Spirit.[109] If we consider the prophets of both Old and New Testaments as being the recipients of special revelation or a "word of knowledge," we must recognize that their prophecies were specific. For example, the prophet would tell

---

[103] Ibid., p. 25.

[104] Kenneth E. Hagin, *Man on Three Dimensions* (Tulsa: Faith Library Publications, 1991), p. 23.

[105] Hayes, *Visions: The Window to the Supernatural*, p. 97.

[106] Kenneth E. Hagin, *How You Can Know the Will of God* (Tulsa: Faith Library Publications, 1983), pp. 13ff.

[107] From a tract entitled "New Creation Truths." Of course there is a color picture of Tilton in the tract and an ad for his book, *God's Miracle Plan for Man*.

[108] John F. MacArthur, *Charismatic Chaos* (Grand Rapids: Zondervan Pub. House, 1992), p. 72.

[109] Hagin, *How To Be Led*, p. 77; see also Pat Robertson, *The Secret Kingdom*, large print, p. 287.

the people or the king that they would win a war with a specific enemy at a specific time and place. They did not say — like those today: "God just told me *someone, somewhere* was being healed of cancer" — vague things. There is a legal and logical principle called "void for vagueness." If a clause in a contract or a law is so vague that it could mean anything or nothing, then it is thrown out. This would apply to the so-called "word of knowledge" as practiced today. Something that is so vague that it cannot be verified must also be voided; it states nothing.[110]

Often they use 1 Kings 19:11, 12 to promote their subjective view of God speaking directly to us:[111] ". . . the Lord was not in the wind; and after the wind an earthquake, but the Lord was not in the earthquake; and after the earthquake a fire, but the Lord was not in the fire; and after the fire a still small voice." Even if "still small voice" were the correct translation, it does not indicate that the voice was inside Elijah but outside him as the wind and earthquake were. Most commentators, however, favor a different translation, such as "a low whisper,"[112] or the "sound of a gentle blowing."[113] Both the context and the language, therefore, are not in favor of those who say that a still, small voice is the Holy Spirit speaking to the heart.

Another abused verse is Proverbs 20:27: "The spirit of a man is the lamp of the Lord, searching all the inner depths of his heart." The typical Word of Faith interpretation is: "God uses our spirit to enlighten us, to guide and direct us. He speaks to our spirit by an inward witness."[114] Human intelligence allegedly has no part in it. But the verse is not saying that God talks to our human spirit although it is often interpreted that way. Nowhere in the Bible does God by-pass the mind and communicate below the conscious level. The Hebrew word for "spirit" does not mean the human spirit as

---

[110] Vagueness is especially true of the so-called prophecies of Nostradamus whereas the Bible gives names, places, dates, etc.

[111] Hamon, *Prophets*, pp. 93, 94.

[112] Brown, Driver, Briggs, *Hebrew English Lexicon of the Old Testament*, p. 201.

[113] *New American Standard Bible*; Keil and Delitzsch, *Old Testament Commentaries* (Grand Rapids: Associated Publishers and Authors), 2:719.

[114] Hagin, *Man on Three Dimensions*, p. 22.

separate from the human soul, as Hagin assumes, but refers to the essence of the person, the human personality.[115] "Man becomes known to himself according to his moral as well as his natural condition";[116] his spirit functioning as the conscience enlightened by the Spirit of God through the written Word enables him to know his moral strengths and weaknesses.[117]

In 1 Corinthians 2:11 the "spirit of the man" that knows the "things of a man" refers to inward personality, not to the human spirit as distinct from the human soul. (Similarly, when the King James Version speaks of "searching the belly" the idea is not the literal belly but the personality.[118])

Another misused passage is Colossians 3:15. Hamon asserts, "He also instructed us to let the peace of Christ rule — that is, govern and direct — our hearts (Col. 3:15)."[119] According to Hamon, the presence of peace in our hearts indicates whether something is God's will or not. The verb for "rule"[120] means to decide,[121] being used in the papyri in the sense of "administering."[122] The verb refers to a decision being made and is used of umpires ruling.[123] What, then, is the meaning within the context? Observe that in the verses before and after we are commanded to be loving, forgiving, letting the Word of Christ dwell in our hearts richly — all of which mean that

> nothing is more fatal to such "peace" than the indulgence of

---

[115] Brown, Driver, Briggs, *Hebrew & English Lexicon of the Old Testament*, p. 675; see also Franz Delitzsch, *A System of Biblical Psychology* (Grand Rapids: Baker Book House, 1899, 1977), p. 98.

[116] Ibid.

[117] Charles Bridges, *Proverbs* (Carlisle, PA: The Banner of Truth Trust, 1846, 1979), p. 361.

[118] Keil and Delitzsch, *Old Testament Commentaries*, 4:704.

[119] Hamon, *Prophets*, p. 96.

[120] Greek is βραβευω.

[121] Arndt and Gingrich Greek lexicon, second edition, p. 146.

[122] Moulton and Milligan, *The Vocabulary of the Greek New Testament* (Grand Rapids: Wm. B. Eerdmans Pub. Co., 1930, 1972), p. 116.

[123] J. B. Lightfoot, *Saint Paul's Epistles to the Colossians and to Philemon* (Grand Rapids: Zondervan Pub. House, 1879, 1974), p. 223.

those foul and angry passions which the apostle warns them to abandon in the preceding verses (5-9), and . . . nothing so conducive to its purity and permanence as the cultivation of those serene and genial graces which are enjoined in verses 12, 13, and 14.[124]

Nothing in the context remotely indicates that Paul is presenting principles that tell us *how* to make decisions. Rather Paul declares how *to live* before God and man, which character qualities are acceptable, and that one of these qualities is the peace of Christ, which is to rule our hearts. Look especially at the parallel between verses fifteen and sixteen: "Let the peace of God rule in your hearts" (15) and "Let the word of Christ dwell in you richly" (16). This parallelism indicates that we gain peace by having the word of Christ in us, which is the Gospel and the written Word, the doctrine of Christ. The Lord Jesus is both the giver of His Word and the theme, being exalted both ways.

Romans 8:16 is also terribly misused: "The Spirit Himself bears witness with our spirit that we are children of God." Hamon alleges, "To know and follow God's will for our lives, then, we must be very sensitive to the checks and restraints of the Holy Spirit. He will also 'bear witness with our spirit' (Rom. 8:16) to help us know His mind."[125] But John Murray has written an exceptionally pungent and insightful article entitled "The Guidance of the Holy Spirit."[126] Murray declares there are two witnesses in the verse: the Spirit and the Christian. Paul uses the verb ("bear witness") two other times, and they also indicate that two witnesses are involved. In Romans 2:15 the two witnesses are written revelation and the conscience of man, and in Romans 9:1 the two witnesses are Paul's conscience and the Holy Spirit. In this verse the Holy Spirit bears witness along *with* us (two witnesses), not directly *to* us (only the Spirit would then be bearing witness). Murray concludes: "We are not to construe this witness of the Spirit as consisting in a direct propositional revelation to the effect,

---

[124] John Eadie, *Colossians* (Minneapolis: James and Klock Pub. Co., 1856, 1977), pp. 247, 248.

[125] Hamon, *Prophets*, p. 97.

[126] John Murray, *Collected Writings of John Murray, 1: The Claims of Truth*, Volume 1 (Edinburgh: Banner of Truth Trust, 1976), p. 186ff.

'Thou art a child of God.'"[127] Murray's insight conforms well to the whole Bible, as Scripture itself always calls for two witnesses to confirm any fact (Deut. 17:6; 19:15; Matt. 18:16; 1 Cor. 13:11).

To summarize, the witness is indirect: the Holy Spirit and the Christian use the Word and the moral progress in one's life to draw the common conclusion that one is a child of God. To be more explicit, the believer bears witness by his own conscience (v. 15), but he does so by the power of the Spirit of adoption. The Spirit Himself bears witness (v. 16), not by direct revelation in speaking to the believer's heart, but by enabling the Christian to put to death the deeds of the body (v. 13 and preceding). Therefore, with the Christian's conscience and the Spirit's enabling, we conclude that we belong to Him because of the moral progress in our lives. The passage has absolutely nothing to do with daily guidance.

Similarly, 2 Corinthians 13:5 says: "Examine yourselves as to whether you are in the faith. Prove yourselves. Do you not know yourselves, that Jesus Christ is in you? — unless indeed you are disqualified." Through perseverance we arrive at the conclusion that we belong to Him (see also 2 Peter 1:10, 11; 1 John 2:3, 4).

Kenneth Copeland asserts: "Believers are not to be led by logic." We can miss what the Spirit is saying if we try "to figure it out mentally."[128] Hagin agrees: "But nowhere does the Bible say God will guide us through our mentality."[129] Bill Hamon goes further: "Human reasoning and the five natural senses are normally the greatest hindrances to fulfilling personal prophecies."[130] Irving strongly encouraged distrusting the mind as something that will hinder the working of the Spirit.[131] Similarly, Pat Robertson states that we must learn to

---

[127] John Murray, *The New International Commentary on the New Testament: Epistle to the Romans* (Grand Rapids: Wm. B. Eerdmans Pub. Co., 1957, 1975), 1:297; see also C. E. B. Cranfield, *The International and Exegetical Commentary, The Epistle to the Romans* (Edinburgh: T. & T. Clark, 1977), 1:402, 403.

[128] Copeland, *The Force of Faith*, p. 6.

[129] Hagin, *How To Be Led*, p. 1.

[130] Hamon, *Prophets*, p. 111.

[131] Dallimore, *Forerunner*, p. 138ff.

hear "the voice of God" in our spirits.[132] Or Kenneth Hagin boldly asserts: *"Instantly obey the voice of your spirit.* Remember, God speaks to our spirit; He doesn't speak to our head or reasoning faculties" [emphasis his].[133]

By contrast, God forbids short-circuiting the mind, stating that it is sin not to do things decently and in order, for the spirits of the prophets are subject to the prophets (1 Cor. 14:23ff). There is not to be "slaying in the Spirit" where people lose consciousness. God considers the human intellect to be the primary means of learning about Him and of communicating with Him through His written Word.

How is this different from those in the New Age who are told to keep their minds out of the way and follow their intuitions? What is the standard to keep one from having spirit guides (that is, demons) to direct him? In Irving's group, they even practiced automatic writing.[134] Such mindless Christianity is not only dangerous in that it opens one to demons, it is a contradiction to Scripture and thus sin: "Jesus said to him, 'You shall love the Lord your God with all your heart, with all your soul, *and with all your mind*'" (Matt. 22:37).

Hagin also speaks of the "leading" of the Spirit in Romans 8:14 as something all Christians *ought* to have,[135] as something subjective, a speaking to the heart. The passage does not say, however, that God's sons *ought* to be led, but that they *are*: "For as many as are led by the Spirit of God, these are sons of God." If you are not His it is because you are not led; thus *all* His sons are led.

The great theologian B. B. Warfield has written the definitive exposition of Romans 8:14.[136] Warfield observes that the leading of the Spirit is "not to enable us to escape the difficulties, dangers, trials or sufferings of this life, but specifically to enable us to conquer sin." And is not this the context? Many terms in Romans 8 are virtually synonymous: "walking according to the Spirit" (vv. 1, 4), "in the Spirit" (v.

---

[132] Robertson, *The Secret Kingdom*, p. 249.

[133] Hagin, *The Human Spirit*, p. 26.

[134] Dallimore, *Forerunner*, p. 121.

[135] Hagin, *How To Be Led*, p. 53.

[136] B. B. Warfield, *Biblical and Theological Writings* (Philadelphia: The Presbyterian and Reformed Pub. Co., 1952), p. 543ff. A "must read."

9), "being led by the Spirit" (v. 14), and especially the previous verse, "putting to death the deeds of the body" (v. 13). As Warfield rightly says, "the leading of the Spirit" is a synonym for sanctification,[137] for that working of the Spirit in our lives to conform us to the moral image of Christ. In the parallel passage in Galatians 5:16-26, the "leading of the Spirit" (v. 18) is the same as the fruit of the Spirit (v. 22) and walking in the Spirit (v. 16); the opposite of the works of the flesh (vv. 19-22).

The Greek verb for "leading" in the Romans passage is present tense, passive voice, and these combined with its usage lead Warfield to four conclusions: (1) The passive voice indicates someone else is doing the controlling or leading (the Holy Spirit), (2) the verb indicates the completeness of the control over the subjects (Christians), (3) the present tense indicates that this is a continual process,[138] and (4) the context reveals the pathway over which resultant progress is made (holiness of life in putting to death the works of the flesh).[139]

How to Have Guidance

Obey Scripture and do what you like. The end.

More should be added lest someone misunderstands. In biblical guidance, we emphatically use our minds, and we use them in understanding Holy Scripture in its context — not to find some personal *"rhema"* or a verse the Lord supposedly gave us that is yanked out of context. We *never* rely on impressions, dreams, visions, personal words from God, or any such thing. Scripture is so clear, so comprehensive, so sufficient, so infallible that there is nothing God has not addressed either directly or indirectly. Even most evangelicals have not understood the guidance of the Spirit because they have been guilty of separating the Holy Spirit from the Bible, making Him reveal things directly to them. They are not even aware of their error.[140]

---

[137] Ibid., p. 546

[138] The present tense is not always durative, but in this context it is, for the Christian at any time can tell he is His by the fact that he is putting to death the deeds of the body.

[139] Ibid., p. 548. In Matthew 4:1 the leading of the Spirit is done by providence (see Deut. 8:1ff from which this New Testament passage is drawn). Calvin's commentary on Matthew 4:1ff is very good.

[140] Even in the well-researched book by Gary Friesen (a fellow student in

There is no need to "claim" verses, since all God's Word is true whether we claim it, believe it, apply it or deny it. It is objectively true for all, believers and unbelievers, and subjectively and irresistibly applied by the Holy Spirit to Christians. (This is not to say that Christians do not use means to grow in the Christian life; we do. We use means such as church attendance, the sacraments, Bible study, prayer, suffering, and many other things.)

We must use our minds to apply verses understood contextually to "find God's will for our lives," and having done this, we are free to choose what we like. In other words, God gives us principles (laws) to obey, and we are to be satisfied with them. Observe these passages where the mind was used:[141]

> Therefore, when we could no longer endure it, **we thought it good** to be left in Athens alone, and sent Timothy, our brother and minister of God, and our fellow laborer in the gospel of Christ, to establish you and encourage you concerning your faith, that no one should be shaken by these afflictions; for you yourselves know that we are appointed to this (1 Thess. 3:1-3).

> Yet **I considered it necessary** to send to you Epaphroditus, my brother, fellow worker, and fellow soldier, but your messenger and the one who ministered to my need; since he was longing for you all, and was distressed because you had heard that he was sick (Phil. 2:25, 26).

> And when I come, **whomever you approve** by your letters, I will send to bear your gift to Jerusalem. But if it is fitting that I go also, they will go with me (1 Cor. 16:3, 4).

> Then the twelve summoned the multitude of the disciples and said, "**It is not desirable** that we should leave the word of God and serve tables. Therefore, brethren, **seek out from among you** seven men of good reputation, full of the Holy

---

seminary), *Decision Making and the Will of God* (Multnomah Press, 1980), he does not seem to be aware of the theological error of believing that the Spirit reveals things apart from the Word. His analysis of what he calls the "traditional approach" (traditional to his dispensational circles, not to Reformed circles) is very good, but his presentation of what he calls the "wisdom approach" is weak and confusing.

[141] Most of these were researched by Gary Friesen (see previous footnote).

Spirit and wisdom, whom we may appoint over this business; but we will give ourselves continually to prayer and to the ministry of the word" (Acts 6:2-4).

For it seemed good to the Holy Spirit, and to us, to lay upon you no greater burden than these necessary things: that you abstain from things offered to idols, from blood, from things strangled, and from sexual immorality. If you keep yourselves from these, you will do well. Farewell (Acts 15:28, 29).

Do you not know that *we shall judge angels? How much more, things that pertain to this life*? If then you have judgments concerning things pertaining to this life, do you appoint those who are least esteemed by the church to judge? I say this to your shame. Is it so, that *there is not a wise man among you, not even one, who will be able to judge between his brethren*? (1 Cor. 6:3-5).

These verses demonstrate that we are to use our minds in making decisions and to do so in conjunction with Holy Scripture. Let us not be so naive as to think that we can discern His will without thinking. How do the new charismatics know when not to think?

In our most important decisions, we use our minds and the Bible. In the "call" to the ministry, Paul says two things are necessary: a male must *desire* the ministry (1 Tim. 3:1) and then *meet the qualifications* (1 Tim. 3:2-7). He knows if he desires the ministry, and a body of ordained men discern whether he is qualified. By this method we have checks, balances, and accountability: the person who presents himself and those who determine if he is called. There is nothing mystical.[142]

---

[142] No one was more biblical and practical in this than Charles Spurgeon. "You may think it odd, but still I feel very well assured, that when a man has a contracted chest, with no distance between his shoulders, the all-wise Creator did not intend him habitually to preach . . . When the Lord means a creature to run, he gives it nimble legs, and if he means another creature to preach, he gives it suitable lungs." Charles H. Spurgeon, *Lectures to My Students* (Grand Rapids: Baker Book House, 1875, 1980), pp. 34, 35. This would be too rational and biblical for today's mystical existentialists. Spurgeon regularly turned down candidates for various reasons, one for having a "rotary action of his jaw the most painful sort to the beholder. I could not have looked at him while preaching without laughter if all the gold of Tarshish had been my reward. . . ."

Another momentous decision is whether we should marry and if so to whom. We should marry if we have no sexual control, for "it is better to marry than to burn" (1 Cor. 7:9). As to whom, Paul's divine instruction to widows was this: "A wife is bound by law as long as her husband lives; but if her husband dies, she is at liberty to be married *to whom she wishes, only in the Lord*" (1 Cor. 7:39). Notice the twofold instruction: to whom she wishes (use the mind to choose) but only a Christian (obey Scripture). There is freedom within bounds. If a person has two Christian candidates from which to choose, he may marry either without sin. God has given him a choice. If he chooses "Mary" over "Linda," has he violated Scripture? No. Then he has not sinned, for *only* what is contrary to Scripture is sin (1 John 3:4; Isa. 8:19, 20; James 4:11, 12). Anything else is just human opinion.

People fear they will miss God's best for them if they do not divine every decision by some mystical method. God's best, however, is given in Scripture. We are to live by these principles (laws); and if Scripture does not address such specifics as time, place, and person, then we should remember that God has given us a mind and if we are in obedience to the Bible, any choice we make is legitimate. It is just that simple. Obey Scripture and do what you like. If it is revealed in the Bible, it is for us; if not revealed, we don't need it.

If we lack wisdom, we should pray and God grants wisdom (James 1:5). *How* He grants wisdom is not stated in James 1:5, but we know from Proverbs that wisdom is skill in applying the Bible to our lives. Proverbs tells us to dig and study (presumably the Bible) deeply in our pursuit of wisdom (Prov. 2:1ff). There are times when a multitude of counselors is good, assuming that the men are godly (Prov. 11:14).

Finally, the new charismatics have no understanding of how God's providence is to be applied to decision-making. If they can create their own "providence," their own reality, then what need do they have of a God whose works in our every day lives are *His* (not ours) "most holy, wise, and powerful preserving and governing all his creatures, and all their actions" (Shorter Catechism)? We know God's will from

---

Ibid., p. 35. Another was turned down for a thick tongue who could not speak clearly, another without teeth, another who did not know the alphabet (today we place a premium on ignorance) — would that we had more Spurgeons!

two sources: Scripture and what happens (providence). We are obligated to obey Scripture; God brings about "what happens" for our good and His glory. Man proposes; God disposes: "A man's heart plans his way, but the Lord directs his steps" (Prov. 16:9). We earnestly pray to God for whatever is according to His will, and *all* our prayers are answered by providence. Whatever happens is our answer. If these errant men understood providence, they would not be afraid of fouling up God's program if they did not receive special "guidance" for every little thing. We must obey Scripture; we cannot foul up His program (Eph. 1:11; see Chapter Ten on sovereignty).

The practical problem with the subjective approach to guidance is that one becomes hopelessly enslaved to his feelings. When I asked my pastor how I could know when God was speaking to me, he said: "When you get mature enough, you just know." Dallimore says of Edward Irving: "The attitude he developed was one of almost constant introspection, an unrelenting concern about impulses and impressions."[143] When I held to a similar view of guidance some twenty years ago, I was continually frustrated, not knowing how to interpret my feelings. It was very liberating to realize that only the Bible was my guide. John Murray has grasped the idea well:

> [It is] contrary to the situation in which God has cast our lot, contrary to the rule under which he has placed us, contrary to the perfection and sufficiency of the Scripture with which he has provided us, and dishonoring to the Holy Spirit, for us to expect or require special revelations to direct us in the affairs of life.
>
> . . . we may still fall into the error of thinking that while the Holy Spirit does not provide us with special revelations in the form of words or visions or dreams, yet he may and does provide us with some **direct** feeling or impression or conviction which we are to regard as the Holy Spirit's intimation to us of what his mind and will is in a particular situation [emphasis his].[144]

Notions of leading by feelings, impressions, or whatever, is separating the Spirit of God from the Word of God, and it is

---

[143] Dallimore, *Forerunner*, p. 149.

[144] Murray, *Collected Writings of John Murray*, pp. 186, 187.

sin. The Spirit without the Word is special revelation, and the Word without the Spirit is a dead book.

The Restoration Movement

The Restoration movement is part of the Word of Faith movement and teaches that Jesus will return very soon, usually within our generation, and that to prepare for this coming He has restored prophets, apostles, and all the supernatural gifts of the first generation Christians. Claiming a restoration of the prophetic gifts, the Word of Faith leaders indicate that the Bible is not enough for this "last" generation.

Remember from Chapter Two that it has been characteristic for these so-called prophets to justify their excesses with the excuse that we are living in the last days just prior to the Second Coming.[145] Gloria Copeland predicts that "we are the generation which will usher in the coming of the Lord Jesus Christ. Before He comes, God will manifest Himself more intensely than He did in the time of Moses."[146]

On the front cover of the January 1993 edition of the *Believer's Voice of Victory*, published by the Copelands, there is an alleged prophecy from the Lord to Kenneth Copeland:

> And 1992 was the year for you. And 1993, saith[147] the Lord, is the year for Me. 1993, men will go free. For the glory of the Lord shall be made manifest more than in any time in the history of the human race. You are going to see more in the next few months and the next few years, than has ever been exposed to humankind in its history. You are the chosen, privileged generation. You are the blessed of God. For you are the end-time. . . . You're My last generation, saith the Lord. We're going to do it together. . . . Nothing left now but the clean up and the Resurrection. The ages have been fulfilled.

What blasphemy for one to claim the Lord's Name on such prophecies! The Lord Jesus said that no one knew the time of His coming (Matt. 24:36), but apparently the Copelands

---

[145] Smith Wigglesworth, *Faith That Prevails* (Springfield, MO: Radiant Books, 1938, 1989), p. 28; Edward Irving in Dallimore, *Forerunner*, p. 73.

[146] Gloria Copeland, *Walk in the Spirit*, p. 3.

[147] Notice that the Lord uses King James English!

Is the Bible Enough?

are the exception. And what will happen to all those who believe these date-setters? They will fall away like many have from the Jehovah's Witnesses who set dates.

Oral Roberts is not to be outdone. In his booklet he says the "Body of Christ is to get a *world view* . . . for what we believe will be the soon return of Christ. . . ." [emphasis his][148] We have, according to him, an "end-time Holy Spirit visitation."[149] Once again, they seem to need something more than the Bible.

Oral Roberts proclaims:

> The Lord told me in this prophecy that confining the work of the Christian ministry only to pastors, teachers and evangelists, and openly leaving out the apostles and prophets God has raised up for these last days, MUST CHANGE. The apostlic [sic] and prophetic covering over pastors, teachers and evangelists will continue in 1992. ***But the beginning of the restoration of apostles and prophets will bring new and powerful outpourings of God's Spirit upon His people*** [emphasis his].
>
> The Bible reveals that this single restoration and recognition of apostles and prophets is indispensable to the ability of the members of the Body of Christ to finally fulfill Jesus' prayer that we may be one, even as He and the Father are one.[150]

In this Roberts reveals that another purpose of the Restoration is to unite the body of Christ into one fellowship, a desire that the charismatics have had for some time.

Here is the Lord's response: "For false christs and false prophets will arise and show great signs and wonders, so as to deceive, if possible, even the elect" (Matt. 24:24). If ever there were a time when this is true, it is today. False prophets are working miracles and are promoting another Gospel and another authority in addition to or in lieu of the Bible. Everywhere someone is proclaiming that some truth was lost for hundreds of years and is now being restored through him/her. It is time for the elect to tell them to stop.

---

[148] Roberts, *11 Major Prophecies*, p. 18.

[149] Ibid., p. 41.

[150] Ibid., pp. 42, 43.

Unity Versus Doctrine

The Word of Faith movement, and charismatics in general, want unity at any price, building unity around a common experience even though there are blatant doctrinal differences. For example, the charismatic movement has entered the Roman Catholic Church, and the Word of Faith movement is making inroads as well, seeking unity based on a common experience but which embraces heretical doctrine. New charismatics in Romanism do not mind embracing transubstantiation (the elements in the Lord's Supper become the literal body and blood of Christ), relics, and human works to merit heaven.[151] Charles Capps says of the so-called unity movement in the last day that God "didn't mention *the unity of the doctrine*" [emphasis his].[152]

The Word of Faith movement especially wants to be considered evangelical, even though that they do not teach orthodoxy. *Unity is not to be gained around a common experience at the expense of the doctrines of Scripture but unity is gained because of communality of belief based on the Bible.* Experience is never to be the basis of unity but only doctrine, for doctrine gives us the Gospel, the Trinity, the deity and humanity of Christ, the forgiveness of sins by faith alone in Christ alone. This and this *only* is the basis of unity. Of course, one can have doctrine and not be a Christian, but he cannot be a Christian without correct doctrine.

Conclusion

In doing Bible conferences on the major cults, I have given this definition of a cult: any group who, on the basis of another authority, preaches another Gospel and/or another Jesus thereby denying the Trinity. Two components are true of all cults and one can be true of many. The two always true are another authority and another Gospel, the two being Siamese twins. If a cult did not preach another Gospel, they would not be a cult. This places them under the anathema of Galatians 1:8, 9. Most cults, though not all (Roman Catholicism being one exception), teach another Jesus, denying either His full humanity (Christian Science), His full deity

---

[151] MacArthur, *Charismatic Chaos*, p. 16ff.

[152] Charles Capps, *God's Image of You* (Tulsa: Harrison House, 1985), p. 76.

(Jehovah's Witnesses), His One personhood (Christian Science), or all the above.

The new charismatics do not explain books of Scripture expositionally, verse by verse. I have never seen this in their books, on their TV shows, or heard it on their radio programs. If they stay in a passage very long, their theology gets snagged by the context. They especially neglect Paul's epistles. They quote isolated verses from the epistles, but they prefer the narrative sections of the Bible, such as the Gospels and Acts. The reason is obvious: They cannot support their errant theology by contextual, consistent exegesis, especially of doctrinal portions like Paul's letters. The same characteristic is true of cults in general. The hop, jump, and skip method lends itself naturally to twisting since one context is not considered long enough to comprehend the flow of the argument. Sometimes they mock those who do verse by verse exegesis.[153]

The Bible is so sufficient, so well-planned, so comprehensive that there will never be a problem that we encounter that God did not anticipate. God is omniscient, thus He wrote His Word to be our *only* infallible standard for life and godliness, having considered every possible problem that we humans could have. The fathers who wrote the Constitution of the United States were brilliant and anticipated most of the problems of government, but they were not omniscient. Some things they did not consider. God, however, is infinitely wiser, having thought out every conceivable thing we would need to know, which He placed in His Bible.

The new charismatics promote a Bible that is infallible in what it says but ineffectual for all of life, competent but not complete, efficient but not enough, tested, tried, and true but truncated. The Spirit allegedly speaks to people apart from Scripture, something the Bible itself denies. Though they usually deny that their prophecies are actual Scripture, the result of this "revelation" is that new Scripture is being written and quoted by others in the movement as such. And the teaching that one cannot trust his mind, that revelations are still coming from God, and that the elite in the Word of Faith movement receive the revelations, leads inevitably to enslave-

---

[153] Michael G. Moriarty, *The New Charismatics* (Grand Rapids: Zondervan Publishing House, 1992), p. 137.

ment of the masses to these "insiders" with God. Something the leaders have not left unexploited. But God says,

> Forever, O Lord, Your word is settled in heaven (Ps. 119:89).

> Every word of God is pure; He is a shield to those who put their trust in Him. Do not add to His words, lest He reprove you, and you be found a liar (Prov. 30:5, 6).

10

What is God like?

The Absolute Sovereignty and Nature of God

In whom also we have obtained an inheritance, being predestined according to the purpose of Him who works all things according to the counsel of His will (Eph. 1:11).

All the inhabitants of the earth are reputed as nothing; He does according to His will in the army of heaven and among the inhabitants of the earth. No one can restrain His hand or say to Him, "What have You done?" (Dan. 4:35).

What is God like? All heresies stem from a defective view of God. In Scripture there is only one God who eternally exists as three equal Persons, who are the same in essence, equal in power and glory. He does not have a body, has no needs, and has infinite knowledge and power. There is nothing and no one above Him, being absolutely sovereign. He is unique in every way possible, to the infinite degree.

But the Word of Faith leaders promote a different God. Benny Hinn has stated that the Father, the Son, and the Holy Spirit each has a body, soul, and spirit.[1] Kenneth Copeland stated that since Adam was created in God's image that he (Adam) was God in the flesh.[2] When Adam sinned, he lost this divinity to Satan, who is now called the "god of this world." Thus redeemed man is restored to his original divinity as seen in Adam, the first man.

The sin of Satan was wanting to be like God, to have creative power and make all things serve him, and the essence of the New Age movement is the pursuit of personal divinity. The Word of Faith leaders now proclaim the same. Their god

---

[1] West Coast Believers Convention as quoted in *Word Faith: The Cancer Within* (Adonai Productions, 1991), a video.

[2] Copeland tapes, #01-3001, as quoted in ibid.

is limited in nature, having a body, and limited in power, relying on man to accomplish His purpose. One can try to be like God by bringing God down to himself or by lifting himself up to God, and the Word of Faith leaders do both. In this chapter we shall concentrate on the nature and especially the sovereignty of God.

All Christians claim to believe in the sovereignty of God; in reality very few do. When asked if God is in control of all things, they enthusiastically respond Yes! But then come the qualifications, one after the other, like waves pounding a beach. By the time the myriad qualifications have rolled in, God is sovereign only when the devil or humans *let* Him be. They might say that God is *ultimately* in control *somehow*, but the plain fact is that the Bible teaches that God *absolutely* governs.[3]

The Word of Faith leaders have an elaborate theory regarding sovereignty. Apparently, once God delegated His authority to Adam, He did not retain ultimate authority over the earth, and Adam had complete freedom to use his authority as he wished. When he (Adam) sinned, he gave all authority to Satan. Redeemed man can take up this authority again if he learns how to use the spiritual laws that both he and Satan are subject to. God teaches man how to use these laws, but He does not intervene unless man gives Him permission. If God intervened without permission, it would not be fair to Satan.

Most of the errors of the Word of Faith leaders would be solved if they only understood the absolute sovereignty of God. In fact, most of the problems of modern Christendom could be solved by dethroning man and enthroning God. Twentieth century Christianity is unquestionably man-centered. *We* worship God in our own way, not His. *We* demand that He give us what *we* want, when *we* want it. All our efforts are aimed at helping man, not glorifying God. *We* speak of how important the self-image is, how *we* can be loved, how *we* can adjust; in short, man is hub and all else the spokes.

Since the Word of Faith leaders consider man to be in control, God must wait for man to believe in Him for man to be saved. Miracles are possible *if* man has enough faith. Man

---

[3] See Appendix Four for the sovereignty of God in salvation.

can be healthy *if* he can fulfill the conditions. Man can be rich *if* he confesses verbally and gives his money. Man can control his circumstances *if* he can realize his identity with God by confessing his "mantra" to bring to pass what he has visualized. In each case, God has done all He can, and now it is "up to man" to finalize the transaction with his will. On the other hand, if God is sovereign, then He saves whom He will (Rom. 9:11-23), grants miracles only when He wishes, allows some to be sick for His purposes, supplies riches to only a few, and controls our circumstances as seems best to Him.

There are only four possibilities: (1) the devil is sovereign; (2) chance is the boss; (3) man is in control; or (4) God is the potentate. If the devil is sovereign, this world belongs to him and we are all demarcated for hell. If chance is the boss (the Greeks called this fate), then there is no design for our lives; God could not predict the future in prophecy, much less control it. If man is the boss, that makes you and me mortal enemies, for you may hinder my will. Might makes right: if I have more might than you, I am god over you. But if God is sovereign, we have security, the devil is defeated, all that happens is for our good (Rom. 8:28), there is no chance, and we can love one another, not having to compete to control one another. This, of course, is what Christians have believed for centuries and what the Bible teaches.

If God Were Not Sovereign . . .

If God were not sovereign, the universe would be chaotic; each being, whether demon or human, would be at war with other beings for the control of the world. Our world would be a hundred times worse than today.

Charles Capps obscures any distinction between man and God when he blunders, "Anything man can imagine or conceive in his heart, he can perform."[4] If man or Satan were sovereign, there would be no distinction between the creature and the Creator, the creature would have the very nature of God. If man is the boss, then he stands alongside God. Man's obedience would make God his debtor; in assuming this sovereignty, man has assumed the prerogative of God.

If God were not sovereign, man and Satan would engage

---

[4] Charles Capps, *Authority in Three Worlds* (Tulsa: Harrison House, 1982), p. 54.

in every sort of magic imaginable to control nature and others. Incantations, long lists of formulas, white and black magic, would dominate our lives. Instead, though, we have loving providence, the doctrine that a loving God is in control of this world. There is no chance. Even the dice thrown by gamblers is ordained by Him (Prov. 16:33).

If God were sovereign, the health and wealth gospel would be unnecessary and eschewed, for it would be God — not man by magical incantations — who determined who would be rich, who would be well or sick, and even who would be saved. There would be no desire for further revelation, since God has sovereignly decreed that completed revelation lies in the Bible. Such sovereignty does not sit well with these Christian humanists, so they have invented a whole theology that is man-centered.

The very nature of faith is submission to God in humble trust and obedience; it is not a force directed at God to control Him. God does not exist to serve us, but we were created to serve Him. As John MacArthur accurately states: "Word of Faith theology has turned Christianity into a system no different from the lowest human religions — a form of voodoo where God can be coerced, cajoled, manipulated, controlled, and exploited for the Christian's own ends."[5] This is a turning of faith on its head; indeed, *it is not to have faith at all*. A "faith" without submission to the sovereignty of God is self-deception, for the "believer" is serving himself not God. Likewise, MacArthur says, ". . . the believer uses God, whereas the truth of biblical Christianity is just the opposite: God uses the believer."[6]

Compare the following passages:

> I began to change my attention. I became more diligent. I knew I had to change my heart if I wanted to be a part of the army. Jesus knocked at the door of my heart that night and I heard His voice and opened the door. . . . I enlisted! I volunteered! I am so glad I did. I offered my body a living sacrifice.[7]

---

[5] John F. MacArthur, *Charismatic Chaos* (Grand Rapids: Zondervan Pub. House, 1992), p. 265.

[6] Ibid., p. 266.

[7] Gloria Copeland, *Walk in the Spirit* (Ft. Worth: KCP Publications, 1984), pp. 84, 85.

> The Pharisee stood and prayed thus with himself, "God, I thank You that I am not like other men — extortioners, unjust, adulterers, or even as this tax collector. I fast twice a week; I give tithes of all that I possess (Luke 18:11, 12).

Notice that Mrs. Copeland uses the pronoun "I" fourteen times. The Pharisee thanks God that he is not like others, which is pseudo-piety, an excuse to praise himself. Mrs. Copeland speaks similarly, "*I* am so glad *I* did." According to both speakers, God should be glad that the sinner did Him the favor of giving himself to Him. In both paragraphs the sovereignty and pretended autonomy of man are assumed. Mrs. Copeland says of *herself*, "Gloria is a faithful and wise servant,"[8] just like the Pharisee, and exactly opposite of Luke 17:10: "So likewise you, when you have done all those things which you are commanded, say, 'We are unprofitable servants. We have only done what was our duty to do.'" Humble recognition of one's sin is the heart of a true believer.[9]

William Ernest Henley (1849-1903) wrote a famous poem called *Invictus*:

> Out of the night that covers me,
> > Black as the pit from pole to pole,
> I thank whatever gods may be,
> > For my unconquerable soul.
> In the fell clutch of circumstance
> > I have not winced nor cried aloud.
> Under the bludgeonings of chance
> > My head is bloody, but unbowed.
> Beyond this place of wrath and tears
> > Looms but the Horror of the shade,
> And yet the menace of the years
> > Finds and shall find me unafraid.
> It matters not how strait the gate,
> > How charged with punishments the scroll,
> I am the master of my fate:
> > I am the captain of my soul.[10]

---

[8] Ibid., p. 10.

[9] Friedrich Nietzsche, a philosopher at the end of the 1800's, stated that man had finally become his own god. See *Joyful Wisdom* (New York: Frederick Ungar Pub. Co., 1975), pp. 275, 276.

[10] Burton Egbert Stevenson, *The Home Book of Verse* (New York: Holt, Rinehart

This poem, so dearly loved and oft-quoted in our day, summarizes that element of man-centeredness that we see in the Word of Faith movement.

God Has Dominion Over All — NOW!

To say that God is sovereign only when we *let* Him is a contradiction, a *non sequitur*. To say that God is sovereign is to say that He is the highest authority and rules over all. God by definition is sovereign. It is His name. The Hebrew *el shaddai* and the Greek *pantokrator* are the names of God used when speaking of His sovereignty.[11]

There is no evidence whatsoever in Scripture that God has ever surrendered His dominion. Neither Genesis 1:28 nor subsequent biblical statements suggest that God is less sovereign for having given dominion to Adam. Delegating authority to another does not mean that one has relinquished it himself; the person is still accountable to the one who delegated it. Our elected officials are still accountable to the people who delegate authority to them. Likewise God delegated dominion to Adam, but He did not relinquish it. Nothing in the Bible indicates that God's dominion is subordinated to the dominion given to man (and from man, to some extent, to Satan). Man still has dominion after the Fall, especially redeemed man, and God retains dominion over all.

The verses which speak of God's power and dominion we believe to their fullest expression. Psalm 22:28 says: "For *dominion* belongs to the Lord and he rules [has dominion] over the nations." The Psalmist makes clear two things: God has dominion and that dominion includes the various nations of humanity *after* the Fall. Psalm 145:13 records: "Your kingdom is an everlasting kingdom, and your *dominion* endures through all generations." There is no suggestion of an interruption or reduction in God's dominion in history.

Daniel says much about God's dominion. "How great are His signs, and how mighty His wonders! *His kingdom is an*

& Winston, 1965), pp. 3500-3501.

[11] The next few pages were researched and written by Pete Frye, who graduated from Dallas Theological Seminary in 1978. He is no longer dispensational. I have added some paragraphs regarding new charismatics and changed some of the wording. I have also added the footnotes.

everlasting kingdom, and His dominion is from generation to generation" (Dan. 4:3). "Then to Him [Christ] was given dominion and glory and a kingdom, that all peoples, nations, and languages should serve Him. *His dominion is an everlasting dominion, which shall not pass away, and His kingdom the one which shall not be destroyed"* (Dan. 7:14). Notice this very important truth: The dominion of God is put on the same plane as the essence and existence of God. *His dominion is just as immutable as He Himself is.*

God is the Most High, Lord of heaven *and earth.* "He is subject to none, influenced by none, absolutely independent. God does *as* He pleases, *only* as He pleases, and *always* as He pleases" [emphasis added].[12] So His own Word expressly declares: "Declaring the end from the beginning, and from ancient times things that are not yet done, saying, 'My counsel shall stand, and I will do all My pleasure'" (Isa. 46:10). "But He is unique, and who can make Him change? And whatever His soul desires, that He does" (Job 23:13). "But our God is in heaven; He does whatever He pleases" (Ps. 115:3). "Whatever the Lord pleases He does, in heaven and *in earth*, in the seas and in all deep places" (Ps. 135:6). "The king's heart is in the hand of the Lord, like the rivers of water; He turns it wherever He wishes" (Prov. 21:1). "The Lord has made all things for Himself, Yes, even the wicked for the day of doom" (Prov 16:4). God even refers to Cyrus, the pagan ruler, as His shepherd who "shall perform all My pleasure" (Isa. 44:28). One gets the impression that God does not answer to anyone!

God has a purpose and a plan for all of His creation. Hear the words of Isaiah: "This is the purpose that is purposed *against the whole earth*, and this is the hand that is stretched out over all the nations. For the Lord of hosts has purposed, and who will annul it? His hand is stretched out, and who will turn it back?" (Isa.14:26, 27). It is clear. He has planned and purposed; it includes "all nations." Such thoughts moved Isaiah to praise when he said, "O Lord, You are my God. I will exalt You, I will praise Your name, for You have done wonderful things; Your counsels of old are faithfulness and truth" (Isa. 25:1). Isaiah records the very words of God: "Did you not hear long ago how I made it, from ancient times that

---

[12] Jerry Bridges, *Trusting God* (Navpress: Colorado Springs, 1988), p. 44.

I formed it? Now I have brought it to pass, that you should be for crushing fortified cities into heaps of ruins?" (Isa. 37:26).

Paul built on this idea and uttered words which are problematic for many in the church today, "In whom also we have obtained an inheritance, being predestined according to the purpose of Him who works *all things* according to the counsel of His will" (Eph. 1:11). God's dominion is very much in effect, bringing His eternal plan to pass in history, which was planned before the Fall of man into sin. Psalm 33:10, 11 adds, "The Lord nullifies the counsel of the nations; He frustrates the plans of the peoples. The counsel of the Lord stands forever, *the plans of His heart from generation to generation.*" "From generation to generation" means moving through human history.

Christ was "slain from the foundation of the world." Contrary to E. W. Kenyon, this clause in Revelation 13:8 modifies "slain" so that Christ was *slain* before the world began. Peter said of Christ on the Day of Pentecost, "Him, being delivered by the determined counsel and foreknowledge of God, you have taken by lawless hands, have crucified, and put to death" (Acts. 2:23).[13] Or as the disciples said in Acts 4:27, 28 that Jesus had been crucified by Pilate, the Jews, and the Gentiles according to what God's hand and purpose had "predestined to occur." God had purposed from eternity past that Jesus would die on the cross. God delights in using the desires and wicked schemes of men and Satan to accomplish His purpose. The ungodly do precisely what they want to do, not knowing that they are accomplishing the secret purposes of God. What a wonderful God! Instead of being left to work out our own security, Christians have a God who has sovereignly planned their security.

There would be no typology in Scripture if God did not have a plan that He was executing in history. For there to be

---

[13]"Foreknowledge" is not simply knowledge in advance. It is that, but we must ask on what basis the knowledge is gained. If God looked down through history and approved what was already going to happen, then men and events would be sovereign, dictating to God what must occur. God, then, would simply be rubber stamping someone else's plans. "Foreknowledge" when used of God in Scripture means knowledge in advance based on His sovereign decree. He knows what will happen because He planned it. So in this verse "foreknowledge" is "the determined counsel."

typology, He had to order the events of the Old Testament so that they became examples of New Testament truth.

God's Dominion and Creation

God did not leave the world once He created it. The ten plagues against Egypt were effected by the decree of God in which "natural" forces were under His control. God caused the earth to open up and swallow the rebellious Israelites at the foot of Sinai. In the book of Jonah, everything instantly obeys God except Jonah. God causes the storm to come, He causes the fish to swallow Jonah and later to regurgitate him, and the gourd to grow and die as a result of a God-caused east wind.

God's dominion continued over His creation so that *He sent famine*: "Now Elisha had said to the woman whose son he had restored to life, 'Go away with your family and stay for a while wherever you can, because *the LORD has decreed* a famine in the land that will last seven years'" (2 Kings 8:1). Elijah was not a false prophet when he said the LORD decreed the famine.

The Scripture says that God feeds the birds of the air and that He clothes the lilies of the fields. His dominion over creation continues. He even continues to send rain on the just and the unjust. The rain is not a consequence of natural processes set in motion by creation, but it is also superintended by God's providence, moment by moment.

This brings us to a deeper aspect of God's dominion. He did not create the world or the things in the world to be self-sustaining. The Son is the radiance of God's glory and the exact representation of his being, *"sustaining all things by his powerful word"* (Heb. 1:3). Or as the King James puts it, "He upholds all things by the word of His power." In the Greek, the verb (upholding) is present tense and in this case durative in meaning. *Upholding* is something that God (Christ) does continually. He created all things and He keeps all things in existence; He sustains. If all things were self-sustaining, there would be no need for upholding. Similarly, Paul describes Christ's dominion in Colossians 1:15, 16 when he says, "He is the image of the invisible God, the firstborn over all creation. For by Him all things were created; things in heaven and on earth, visible and invisible, whether thrones or powers or rulers or authorities; all things were created by him and for him. He is before all things, *and in him all things hold together.*" Christ, so to speak, is the "glue" of creation.

Only God has self-existence: "For as the Father has life in Himself, so He has granted the Son to have life in Himself" (John 5:26). Never are these words spoken of men. Paul was speaking to the unregenerate men of Athens, and what he says applies to both saved and unsaved men: "So that they should seek the Lord, in the hope that they might grope for Him and find Him, though He is not far from each one of us; *for in him we live and move and have our being*" (Acts 17:27, 28). Our being, our existence, is not independent of God; it is *in* God. Consequently, if God were to cease to exist, all *creation* would cease to exist because it is no longer being upheld. *Since creation is continually and totally dependent upon the sustaining work of God, it is impossible to conceive that God has given up any dominion over it.*

God's Dominion and the Nations

The Scriptures teach that every single nation is under the sovereign power of God. No nation will ever exist apart from God's sovereign will. When Daniel received from God the interpretation of Nebuchadnezzar's dream, he exclaimed in praise, "*He removes kings and raises up kings*; He gives wisdom to the wise and knowledge to those who have understanding" (Dan. 2:21). Nebuchadnezzar's rule was divinely appointed and initiated (Dan. 2:36). Later Nebuchadnezzar himself declares, "The Most High rules in the kingdom of men, *gives it to whomever He will*, and sets over it the lowest of men" (Dan. 4:17). No clearer words could be uttered to indicate that God is active in human history to the point that He "raises up kings." But listen to the words of Paul:

> God, who made the world and everything in it, since He is Lord of heaven **and earth**, does not dwell in temples made with hands. Nor is He worshiped with men's hands, as though He needed anything, since He gives to all life, breath, and all things. And He has made from one blood every nation of men to dwell on all the face of the earth, **and has determined their preappointed times and the boundaries of their habitation** (Acts 17:24-26).

Nations can trace their origins to God. Observe also that God is still "Lord of heaven *and earth*."

Is God or Satan lord of the nations? "For the kingdom is the Lord's, and He rules over the nations" (Ps. 22:28). It was God who ended the reign of Belshazzar. It was God who sent the evil spirit to King Saul (1 Sam. 18:10). It was God who raised up Cyrus to free His people from the Babylonian captivity (Isa. 45:1). With great effectiveness He deposed King Herod (Acts 12:23). In the story of Abimelech, the LORD said to him about Abraham's wife Sarah: "Yes, I know that you did this in the integrity of your heart. For *I also withheld you from sinning against Me*; therefore I did not let you touch her" (Gen. 20:6). It was God Who hardened Pharoah's heart (Ex. 4:21; 7:3; 14:4, etc). And why did Joshua win all the wars against the Canaanites? "For it was of the Lord to harden their hearts, that they should come against Israel in battle, that He might utterly destroy them, and *that they might receive no mercy, but that He might destroy them*, as the Lord had commanded Moses" (Joshua 11:20).

The examples are endless, but one more will have to suffice. The LORD wanted to destroy the wicked king Ahab so we read:

> And the Lord said, "Who will persuade Ahab to go up, that he may fall at Ramoth Gilead?" So one spoke in this manner, and another spoke in that manner. Then a spirit came forward and stood before the Lord, and said, "I will persuade him." The Lord said to him, "In what way?" So he said, "I will go out and be a lying spirit in the mouth of all his prophets." And He said, "You shall persuade [him], and also prevail. Go out and do so." Now therefore, look! **The Lord has put a lying spirit in the mouth of all these prophets of yours**, and the Lord has declared disaster against you (1 Kings 22:20-23).

And this is the LORD speaking, not a prophet who may have mistakenly thought the LORD said this (as new charismatics often assume).

God's Dominion and Evil

We do not intend to discuss where evil came from and why God has allowed it. We may, however, study God's *use* of evil. In doing so we must remember two things: (1) God is not the author sin, and (2) man, the devil, and all sin are controlled by God.[14] To restate these two things in different ways, though God irresistibly controls all things, God does not make sinful beings do what they do not wish. We cannot totally comprehend how God controls sin and yet remains free from culpability "so that the problem of God's relation to sin remains a mystery."[15]

Theologians have divided evil into two categories: natural and moral. Natural evil is an earthquake or hurricane and leprosy or cancer. Moral evil describes murder, rape, theft, covetousness, and so forth. All evil is traceable to the devil though we do not mean that the devil personally causes all evil. It may be that some particular evil is traceable to him in the sense that he introduced evil into the world. We do not wish to be so naive to say every time we sin, "The devil made me do it." God does not personally cause men to sin (James 1:13), but He controls evil in some way, as He did the worst sin of all: the crucifixion of Christ.

In 1 Kings 22 we have already seen how the LORD used an evil spirit to accomplish His purpose in causing Ahab's evil prophets to prophesy wrongly. Of course Ahab's prophets did precisely what they desired, just as Pilate, Judas, the Gentiles, and the Jews did what they wished in crucifying Messiah. God did not personally grab them by the throat and force them to do what they did; they freely did what they wanted to do and what was in their hearts. But in both cases they also did what God had planned.

There is a parallel incident which will take place at the Second Coming. Paul records in 2 Thessalonians 2:9-12 the following:

> The coming of the [lawless one] is according to the working of Satan, with all power, signs, and lying wonders, and with all unrighteous deception among those who perish, because they did not receive the love of the truth, that they might be saved. And for this reason **God will send them strong delusion**, that they should believe the lie, that they all may be condemned who did not believe the truth but had pleasure

---

[14]For a good study of this, see L. Berkhof, *Systematic Theology* (Grand Rapids: Wm. B. Eerdmans Publishing Co., 10th ed., February 1968), p. 171ff. Berkhof refers to this under Providence as the doctrine of "divine concurrence."

[15]Ibid., p. 175.

in unrighteousness.

Again it is said that God uses lying.

God cannot sin, nor should we sin so that good may come (Rom. 6:1). Somehow, though, God uses deception by means of His sovereign power without being the liar. We are not attempting to reconcile the obvious problem of God and evil but observing that the biblical text records God's *use* of evil; the author is Satan.

The new charismatic understanding of God and Satan implies that there are two gods: one who is good and one who is evil. This is gnostic dualism at its worst, the Manichaean brand: "In the Manichaean system there are powers of darkness, which seize by force some parts of the kingdom of light."[16] The good god, because of his disassociation with evil, must constantly be inventing expedients to work around what is done by the evil god. Gnostics taught that "God is the source only of good. As evil exists it must have its origin not only outside of Him, but independently of Him."[17] The health and wealth understanding of the relationship between God and the devil and good and evil has God making adjustments in His plan to work around the acts of the devil. The God of the universe would be in the ambulance business, regularly sending His emergency squads to correct what He could not control nor anticipate. In this case Jesus would die *hoping* that some would believe in Him but not being able to determine that any would. In gnostic dualism, neither god has ultimate authority, the triune God cannot use evil, cannot have anything to do with it, must often yield to the devil, being often thwarted in His plans. Welcome to new charismatic doctrine.

If God has to work around the devil or man in any sense, that necessarily means that the influence of Satan or man over God's purposes is real and effective. To the extent that God must make adjustments for Satanic or human activity means that God is controlled by external events. We must reject that notion thoroughly because in it God cannot do as He pleased. *If God is not Lord of all, He is not Lord at all.* It is undeniable that God controls the births of all people, the time, the place,

---

[16]Philip Schaff, *History of the Christian Church* (Grand Rapids: Wm. B. Eerdmans Pub. Co., 1910, 1979), 2:454.

[17]Charles Hodge, *Systematic Theology* (Wm. B. Eerdmans Pub. Co., 1964), 2:399.

whether rich or poor, what country and to which parents. If He controls the births, would He not likewise control the deaths? To give the power of life and death to man or to the devil is to consider him divine.

There is a common statement in new charismatic teaching: "God could not associate with sin and unrighteousness." If this means that God can never be personally involved in committing some sin, such as adultery or lying, we fully agree. Beyond that we cannot agree. I am a justified sinner. In other words, I am redeemed; I am regenerated, but I still sin. I still have a "principle warring in my members" (Rom. 7:5); I am still in a corruptible, sinful state. At the same time, however, my body is His temple of the Holy Spirit. Somehow the Holy God "associates" with the sinful me. They might respond that He touches my human spirit. There are two problems with that. First, if my spirit is perfectly holy so that God associates with me, how do I sin? First Corinthians 6:19 does not say that my "spirit" is the temple of the Holy Spirit but "my body," the one that will perish in corruptibility, which is the temple.

Secondly, Christ — God manifest in the flesh — associated with sinners of the worst type. He was even labelled a winebibber because of this association. So the Holy God in the flesh associated with sinners in some sense. The most revealing is that Christ "became sin" for us. He bore the guilt and punishment of these sins. If it were not for this association, there would have been no redemption.[18]

Who is Lord of the Earth?

The new charismatics believe that Satan is lord of the earth, that Adam gave the "earth lease" to Satan when he sinned, and that God or Christ has little if any authority on earth.

However, Jesus is Lord of lords and King of kings. He triumphed over Satan in His death and resurrection, though this was only confirmatory, as He was Lord before the resurrection. Earlier in this chapter we saw that God has dominion over the nations and the whole world. Jesus is God; thus He has had dominion from day one — even before there were days.

---

[18]This ends the section written by Pete Frye.

Furthermore, not only was Jesus Lord because He was (is) God but also because He was Messiah. In Isaiah. 9:6, 7 we read that He would be governor from His birth and that His kingdom would continually increase from the time of His birth:

> For unto us a Child is born, unto us a Son is given; and the government will be upon His shoulder. And His name will be called Wonderful Counselor, Mighty God, Everlasting Father, Prince of Peace. ***Of the increase*** of His government and peace there will be no end, upon the throne of David and over His kingdom, to order it and establish it with judgment and justice from that time forward, even forever. The zeal of the Lord of hosts will perform this.

Again of Christ we read: "Then to Him [Messiah] was given dominion and glory and a kingdom, that all peoples, nations, and languages should serve Him. His dominion is an everlasting dominion, which shall not pass away, and His kingdom the one which shall not be destroyed" (Dan. 7:14).

If the Lord is to spread His Gospel throughout the world, it is necessary for Him to have the authority to do so. In other words, if nations had authority over Him or Satan's authority were greater than His, then either the Gospel could not be preached in a nation whose leaders outlawed the Gospel or the Lord would be in rebellion. Yet the Lord Himself said after His resurrection, "All authority has been given to Me in heaven and *on earth*" (Matt. 28:18), which includes the authority over the nations to preach the Gospel. "Go therefore and make disciples of all the *nations*."

By virtue of His resurrection, Jesus was enthroned as both Lord and Messiah (Acts 2:36). He is not waiting for some future date to *become* Lord of lords, He is *now*. Indeed, "He must reign till He has put all enemies under His feet" (1 Cor. 15:25), and at the end of this current reign He will deliver to the Father a conquered kingdom (1 Cor. 15:24). He is political King as well as King of the church. All nations are accountable to Him — now. Though His dominion is now, He has not yet finished conquering (Heb. 2:7-9).

Someone may object that the Lord said that His kingdom was "not *of* this world" (John 18:36). He did not mean that His kingdom would have nothing to do with this world but that His kingdom did not *originate* from this world and was not of the moral character of this world.[19]

The new charismatics, however, promote Satan as lord now. Satan is "the Being who is today ruling the earth, who sits as the Prince of the Nations, who has the Authority to rule the hearts and lives of men" and who has the "Authority to cast into Hell."[20] "As the Prince he is the political head of the nations."[21] It is difficult to imagine anything more ludicrous than Satan as the king of kings.

Capps quotes Psalm 115:16 ("The heaven, even the heavens, are the Lord's: but the earth hath he given to the children of men") and concludes: "Adam could do what he would with the earth, and he did. He sold the earth lease to Satan and left God on the outside."[22] There is apparently nothing God can do as the earth now belongs to Satan. The verse, however, does not say God does not still have dominion over man.

But consider what else the Bible says: "The kingdoms of this world *have become* the kingdoms of our Lord and of His Christ, and He shall reign forever and ever!" (Rev. 11:15). The Apostle John did not say the nations would some day be His, but that they "have become" His, and he said this before Revelation 20.[23] We read in Psalm 2 that the Father says to the Son: "Ask of Me, and I will give You the nations for Your inheritance, and the ends of the earth for Your possession. You shall break them with a rod of iron; You shall dash them in pieces like a potter's vessel'" (vv. 8, 9), which is quoted five times in the New Testament (Acts 4:25; 8:33; Heb. 1:5; 5:5;

---

[19] If one will study John's technical use of the prepositions *of* and *in*, (Greek is εκ, εν.) which the grammars speak of (Nigel Turner, *A Grammar of New Testament Greek* [Edinburgh: T. & T. Clark, 1963], vol. 3, pp. 260-263; Vol. 4, p. 76; Maximillan Zerwick, *Biblical Greek* [Rome: Biblical Institute Press, 1963], #134-5; Nigel Turner, *Grammatical Insights Into the New Testament* [Edinburgh: T. & T. Clark, 1965], p. 120; A. T. Robertson, *Word Pictures in the New Testament* [Nashville: Broadman Press, 1932], vol. 5, p. 57), he will find this to be true. For example, we are to be spatially *in* the world (John 17:11, 15) but not morally *of* the world (John 17:14, 16; 1 John 4:5).

[20] E. W. Kenyon, *The Father and His Family: A Restatement of the Plan of Redemption* (Seattle: E. W. Kenyon, 1937), p. 73.

[21] Ibid., p. 77.

[22] Charles & Annette Capps, *Angels* (Tulsa, OK: Harrison House, 1984), p. 21.

[23] Premillennialists believe that Rev. 20 is when Jesus becomes Lord of the world.

What Is God Like?

Rev. 2:27), emphasizing its present fulfillment. Rev. Alexander McLeod (1774-1833) cites several other passages demonstrating that Jesus is presently political Lord over the nations as well as spiritual Lord over the church:[24]

> Jesus Christ, the faithful witness, the firstborn from the dead, and the ruler over the kings of the earth (Rev. 1:5).
>
> Jesus spoke these words, lifted up His eyes to heaven, and said: "Father, the hour has come. Glorify Your Son, that Your Son also may glorify You, as You have given Him authority over all flesh. . . ." (John 17:1, 2).
>
> The Lord is at Your right hand; He shall execute kings in the day of His wrath. He shall judge among the nations, He shall fill the places with dead bodies, He shall execute the heads of many countries (Ps. 110:5, 6. This Messianic Psalm is quoted more than any other Old Testament passage in the New Testament).
>
> And what is the exceeding greatness of His power toward us who believe, according to the working of His mighty power which He worked in Christ when He raised Him from the dead and seated [Him] at His right hand in the heavenly places, far above all principality and power and might and dominion, and every name that is named, **not only in this age** but also in that which is to come (Eph. 1:19-21).
>
> Therefore God also has highly exalted Him and given Him the name which is above every name, that at the name of Jesus every knee should bow, of those in heaven, and of those on earth, and of those under the earth, and that every tongue should confess that Jesus Christ is Lord, to the glory of God the Father (Phil. 2:9-11).

When did God give Jesus this exalted Name and dominion? It was both before the resurrection (John 17:1, 2) and after the resurrection (Matt. 28:18-20), indicating that He always has had this dominion but also received it in renewed form at His Ascension.

But does Satan have the authority to cast into hell? Kenyon uses Luke 12:4, 5 (see also Matt. 10:28) to support this notion:

---

[24] Alexander McLeod, *Messiah: Governor of the Nations of the Earth* (Elwood Park, NJ: Reformed Presbyterian Press, 1803, 1992).

"And I say to you, My friends, do not be afraid of those who kill the body, and after that have no more that they can do. But I will show you whom you should fear: Fear Him who, after He has killed, has power to cast into hell; yes, I say to you, fear Him!" Is Jesus here speaking of Satan? The very idea is ridiculous. *God* casts into hell, and it is the "fear of the LORD that is the beginning of wisdom" (Prov. 1:7), not the fear of Satan.

If Satan determines who goes to hell, who casts him in? Matthew 25:31-46 says it is the Lord Jesus Who casts into hell, for He proclaims to those on His left hand: "the King will answer and say to them, 'Assuredly, I say to you, inasmuch as you did it to one of the least of these My brethren, you did it to Me.' Then He will say to those on the left hand, 'Depart from Me, you cursed, into the everlasting fire prepared for the devil and his angels'" (vv. 40, 41). In James 4:12 it is the Lord who "is able to save and to destroy," using the same word for "destroy" that Matthew uses in 10:28. Furthermore, the normal understanding of the word in Matthew 10:28 is that God is the subject of the verb "cast."[25] Finally, the word "fear" used in this Matthew 10:28 passage is often used of respect by Christians toward *God* (Luke 1:50; Acts 10:35; 1 Peter 2:17). No reputable commentator understands the verse to mean Satan casts into hell nor is there *any* mention in Scripture of Satan doing so.

The health and wealth leaders believe that Satan is currently lord of this world. Jesus allegedly said to Kenneth Hagin: "Adam originally was the god of this world," but he gave over his dominion to Satan when he sinned.[26] To add further to his unbiblical notion, Hagin asserts that the Lord had a confession to make concerning the lack of food and clothing of some of His children: "I'm not withholding adequate food and clothing from your children — that's not Me! It's the devil. He's the god of this world."[27] What this amounts to is that Jesus' hands are tied; this is the devil's world.

---

[25] Arndt & Gingrich, *A Greek-English Lexicon of the New Testament and Other Early Christian Literature*, 2nd ed., p. 863a.

[26] Kenneth Hagin, *How God Taught Me About Prosperity* (Tulsa: Faith Library Publications, 1988), p. 15.

[27] Ibid., p. 16.

According to Hagin, Jesus confesses Satan as lord! Again Hagin says, "The world is presided over by Satan. . . ."[28] Hagin's idea came from Kenyon who stated that "the whole human race lives today under the cruel Emperor Satan,"[29] and not this world only but Satan is "Emperor of the Universe."[30] To posit two gods, one good who is incapable of even using evil, and one evil, is the gnostic dualism we spoke of in Chapter One. Here we have the eternal conflict between good and evil with each one winning and losing.

Yet how simple it is to see the error in such misguidedness. The expression that Satan is the "god of this world" does not mean he is lord of lords, but that he is the god of this world in the sense that *many worship him* — not that he is almighty. His work is primarily in blinding the minds of people to the Gospel (2 Cor. 4:4; John 12:31; 14:30; 16:11; Eph. 2:2; 1 John 5:19), but even that blindness is stripped away when the mighty grace of Jesus brings one to belief in Himself (Matt. 11:27; Acts 13:48; 16:14; Phil. 1:29).

Furthermore, that Satan is called by the Lord Jesus "the ruler of this world" (John 14:30) does not mean that there is not a Ruler above him, Who is Ruler of the universe and the Ruler of all rulers. Because there is a governor of Tennessee, do we conclude that there is not also a President of the United States who has greater authority than the governor? Besides, the Lord also stated: *"Now is the judgment of this world; now the ruler of this world will be cast out"* (John 12:31). What else does the expression "Lord of lords" mean except that Jesus is the *ultimate* Ruler? And was it not true that when Jesus commanded Satan to leave Him in Matthew 4:10, 11 that Satan did so without a word? Did not the demons obey the Lord every time He commanded them and without hesitation?

Where do the health and wealth people get the idea that Satan owns this world? Here is how Frederick K. C. Price reasons.[31] God gave Adam dominion over the earth. This dominion was a legal dominion, much like we would deed

---

[28] Kenneth Hagin, *The Real Faith* (Tulsa: Faith Library Pub., 1985), p. 28.

[29] Kenyon, *The Father and His Family*, p. 61.

[30] Ibid., p. 62.

[31] 04/27/92 broadcast, WPTY-TV Memphis, TN, 12 p. m.

someone property. The earth was deeded to Adam by God; it was his to do with as he pleased. This dominion included not only the animals but also the mineral rights so that he owned all the gold, silver, diamonds, oil, and so forth. When Adam sinned, he gave his property to Satan, and God no longer had a legal right to the earth. Now the planet is Satan's, and even God must honor this agreement. Redeemed man can reclaim his rights and be rich. Capps agrees: "It's illegal for God to come to earth and destroy the work of the devil with His divine Godhead powers."[32]

Yet the truth is that though Adam came under Satan's dominion to some extent, primarily Adam was under *God's* curse for sinning. Kenneth Hagin says: "If God is running everything, He does have things in a mess."[33] Fred Price is even more blatant: "God can't legally do anything in this earth realm except what we allow Him to do."[34] He also says, "God does not have physical possession of the earth, Satan does," and "If God came here, He would be arrested as a trespasser." Price goes on to condition his audience to accept these blasphemies with such statements as these: "Evangelicals consider this heresy, and they would never say this." "Tradition and theology reject this." "I hope you don't think God is running this world, evangelicals think that." "If this is an example of how God runs things, I don't want to go to heaven." They distance themselves from the evangelical community with such statements ("we" versus the "evangelicals"), thereby separating themselves from the body of Christ, and establishing themselves as a cult.

Price uses two other passages to promote the idea that the world is Satan's: Luke 4:1-8 and Matthew 9:35-38. The major passage for Price is: "And the devil said to Him, 'All this authority I will give You, and their glory; for this has been delivered to me, and I give it to whomever I wish'" (Luke 4:6).

Our first response must be that *Satan is a liar* (John 8:44). Price says that Satan is telling the truth since Jesus did not rebuke him. But it is an argument from silence that leads Price

---

[32] Charles Capps, *God's Image of You* (Tulsa: Harrison House, 1985), p. 50.

[33] Kenneth E. Hagin, *The Interceding Christian* (Tulsa: Faith Publication Library, 1991), p. 13.

[34] Frederick Price, TBN Network, 05/04/92, 12:00 to 1:00 A.M., Memphis, TN.

to the deafening conclusion that Satan was for once telling the truth. Even if the Lord had not answered the devil, the inference is not valid. In the most elementary logic class one learns that he can conclude anything or nothing from what is *not* stated.[35] But the Lord did answer Satan: "Get behind Me, Satan! For it is written, 'You shall worship the Lord your God, and Him only you shall serve'" (v. 8). The Lord answered the real point behind Satan's pseudo-offer: worship reveals Who the real God is, and we are to worship the Triune God only. If the Lord had said the kingdoms did not belong to Satan, He would not have been confronting the point of the offer. Observe also that Satan instantly obeyed the Lord when He commanded him to leave, which showed Who was really in authority.

Secondly, *God the Father made the same offer to Christ.* Psalm 2 is a Messianic Psalm, using the name "Messiah" in verse two (sometimes translated "anointed") and the word "Son" in verse twelve. In verse seven the Son quotes the Father: "I will declare the decree: The Lord has said to Me, 'You are My Son, today I have begotten You.'" This verse is quoted several times in the New Testament of the resurrection of Jesus. The Father raised Him from the dead, and, to the consternation of the nations (vv. 1-3), He made Jesus King of kings. In other words, even though the nations did not want Him ruling over them, and even though they sought to cast off His "bonds" (vv. 1-3; bonds=His law, see Jer. 2:20; 5:5), the Father laughed and made Him King over them anyway. In light of this, the Father says to His only Son: "Ask of Me, and I will give You the nations for Your inheritance, and the ends of the earth for Your possession" (v. 8).

Now who has made the genuine offer of the world to Jesus, God or Satan? Who is the liar, God the Father or the devil? Who really owns the world and could offer it to Jesus, the Father or Satan? In the verses that follow the Father's offer, it is obvious that the Son did ask and the Father gave Him the nations, for He shall rule them with a rod of iron (v. 9), and the rulers must repent (vv. 10, 11) or perish under the Son's wrath (v. 12). The Lord Jesus emphatically stated that "all

---

[35] It is evident that the Word of Faith leaders have not studied logic, which is part of God's truth. It is not possible to communicate without logic, and the Bible is full of examples. See Gordon Clark, *Logic*, published by the Trinity Foundation.

authority has been given to Me in heaven and *on earth*" at the resurrection (Matt. 28:18; see also Dan. 7:14). (Most commentators agree with this interpretation.[36])

To support his misguided views of Satan's authority, Price also uses Matthew 9:38: "Therefore pray the Lord of the harvest to send out laborers into His harvest." Price reasons that if the harvest is God's, why does He not do anything until we pray? One is startled by such a ludicrous notion. God commands us to pray (Matt. 6:9), and also gives us the grace to do so (Rom. 8:26ff). And God would not be God if He had to be *allowed* anything by men.

Does God Have Needs?

If God is God, by definition He is self-sufficient, independent, self-sustaining, and absolutely without any needs. Within the Trinity there is perfect fellowship, harmony, love, and everything necessary — all perfected to infinite capacity. Once one denies the absolute sovereignty of God, there is no limit to the subjective theories regarding His nature.

One of the strangest aberrations in the Word of Faith movement is that God has needs. E. W. Kenyon said with all solemnity, "The entire Plan of Redemption is a revelation of the heart-hunger and loneliness of the Great Father God; the first step in this stupendous drama of Creation was God's dream and His blueprints of Man's beautiful Home."[37] Apparently God was lonely; the other *infinite* Members of the Trinity were not enough — He needed *finite* man! Again Kenyon dares to say:

> Before the Morning Stars sang their first anthem to the heart of the lonely Father God, before the foundations of the earth were laid, before the first rays of light ever passed through the dark expanse, the heart of the great Creator God had a yearning, deep, mighty, eternal. It was the primordial passion for children.

---

[36] See William Hendriksen, *New Testament Commentary: Luke* (Grand Rapids: Baker Book House, 1978), p. 236; Norval Geldenhuys, *Commentary of the Gospel of Luke* (Grand Rapids: Wm. B. Eerdmans Pub. Co., p. 1975), p. 160; I. Howard Marshall, *The Gospel of Luke: A Commentary of the Greek Text* (Grand Rapids: Wm. B. Eerdmans Pub. Co., 1978), p. 172; Frederick Louis Godet, *Commentary on the Gospel of Luke* (Grand Rapids: Zondervan Pub. House, 1887), p. 214ff.

[37] Kenyon, *The Father and His Family*, p. 10.

The Father heart of the Creator God longed for sons and daughters.[38]

If the Earth is the reason for the heavens, and Man is the reason for the Earth, what is the reason for Man? There is only one answer, and it is very simple: the lonely heart of the great Father God.[39]

The idea of a Father God who wanted children sounds ominously like Mormonism with its "Father God" having children. Current Word of Faith leaders parrot Kenyon's ideas: "The Father's heart was hungry for a family, and Jesus freely gave Himself for this desire."[40] Rather, God is infinitely self-sufficient, needing nothing, having perfect love within the Members of the Trinity, and there is no verse anywhere in the Bible that indicates that He needed fellowship. How could fellowship with a creature compare with fellowship with another infinite Person?

Another blasphemous idea is that God is limited in power, taking long ages to create, being unable to do so instantaneously: "He took ages on ages to build an earth-home, to store it with treasures that only His mind could conceive and His power create." "Ages and ages He worked storing up treasures of all kinds of wealth for His Man."[41] (One wonders if He reported to work each "morning" much as we do until the "job" was completed.) "God so wanted Man and so loved Man that He spent millions of years in preparation for him...."[42] One wonders why He did not create someone for His fellowship many ages ago. Apparently He just did not think of it.

It seems that God had to think things out, not being omniscient: "This yearning passion [for a family] *took form*, and God planned a universe for His Man, and in the heart of that universe He purposed a Home" [emphasis added].[43] If it took God a long time to devise a plan, then He must have had

---

[38] Ibid., p. 28.

[39] Ibid., p. 32.

[40] Kenneth Copeland, *The Force of Righteousness* (Forth Worth: KCP Publications, 1990), p. 10.

[41] Kenyon, *The Father and His Family*, p. 32; p. 29.

[42] Ibid., p. 33.

[43] Ibid, p. 28.

to learn something, which means He is not omniscient, which means He is not God.

Hagin is very confident when he says, "He [God] can't get along without you any more than you can get along without Him."[44] God apparently needs man to fulfill Him by relieving His loneliness and by allowing Him to work through us to fulfill His purpose. Such an idea cuts at the very heart of Godness, revealing that these men are not familiar with the way the Bible presents God, twisting the Bible and engaging in crass blasphemy.

Is God Accountable to Man?

One would think this question absurd, but not so to these "thinkers":

> Man is ever accusing God of injustice in His dealings with the human race, and has declared that He had no right to create man in the face of the fact that He knew man would fall.

> Man questions God's right to judge the human race and to execute sentence commensurate with the crime. Can God justify Himself in the face of these age-old accusations?[45]

> If God should assume the liabilities of man's fall and pay man's penalty independently of man, then God will have answered the criticism of man against His justice.[46]

> God stands acquitted before the tribunal of universal human consciousness in that He did not leave man after his treason without means of salvation.[47]

> God is just to the devil; nowhere does God take advantage of the devil, but God's eternal justice to frail man and to mighty Satan is manifest. Not only is He just to man and to the devil, but He is just to Himself.[48]

This work to restore man must not take advantage of Satan,

---

[44] Kenneth E. Hagin, *The Believer's Authority* (Tulsa: Faith Library Publications, 1992), pp. 27-28.

[45] Kenyon, *The Father and His Family*, p. 139.

[46] Ibid., p. 143.

[47] Ibid., p. 144.

[48] Ibid., pp. 144, 145.

because God is stronger than he.[49]

God is so enslaved to man, Satan, and to so-called spiritual laws that He must stand before the bar of their justice and be judged. Only a few Scriptures will be sufficient to refute such outlandish statements. Does God render a reason to man for what He does? "But God is the Judge: He puts down one, and exalts another" (Ps. 75:7). "Moreover the Lord answered Job, and said: 'Shall the one who contends with the Almighty correct Him? He who rebukes God, let him answer it'" (Job 40:1, 2). "Woe to him who strives with his Maker! Let the potsherd [strive] with the potsherds of the earth. Shall the clay say to him who forms it, 'What are you making?' Or shall your handiwork say, 'He has no hands'?" (Isa. 45:9).

Does man judge God for finding fault when God *knew* (read: planned) of his Fall into sin?

> You will say to me then, "Why does He **still** find fault? For who has resisted His will?" But indeed, O man, who are you to reply against God? Will the thing formed say to him who formed it, "Why have you made me like this?" Does not the potter have power over the clay, from the same lump to make one vessel for honor and another for dishonor? (Rom. 9:19-21).

Hagin disagrees with Paul: "If God demands that we have faith when it is impossible for us to have faith, then we have a right to challenge His justice."[50] Mrs. Eddy agrees with Hagin: "Does divine Love commit a fraud on humanity by making man inclined to sin, and then punishing him for it?"[51]

God is not accountable to man but man to God. God does not exist to serve man but man God. Indeed, God Himself is man's worse enemy, the One who opposes sin and judges all who practice wickedness. We are His enemies until we are reconciled to Him through the merits of Jesus (Rom. 5:10; 8:7; 2 Cor. 5:18-21; Col. 1:20, 21), whom He Himself gra-

---

[49] Ibid., p. 147.

[50] Hagin, *Faith Edition Bible* (Tulsa: Kenneth Hagin Ministries, 1972), p. ix.

[51] Eddy, *Science and Health*, p. 356. Charles Finney may be the source of man's pretended autonomy, for he denied man's total sinfulness and maintained man's moral ability. See *Finney's Systematic Theology*, Bethany Fellowship, 1976, Chapters 1-7.

ciously gave for our sins. Until we are justified by faith in Jesus, we are in infinite trouble, and there is no being powerful enough to deliver us from His hand. Only He is infinite. Man and Satan can only make us miserable for a few years, but God casts into hell forever. Pharaoh has been in hell for several thousand years, and he has no less time to suffer under the wrath of God than when he first entered the realm of the damned. The *only* escape is through Jesus.

Who Is Lord of Natural Disasters?

Charles Capps says, "When you hear of a tornado destroying a city, invariably newspaper headlines describe it as 'an act of God.' Don't blame God! It was the devil who visited that town!"[52] The "act of God," contrary to Capps, is exactly what we see in Scripture:

> He who strikes a man so that he dies shall surely be put to death. But if he did not lie in wait, **but God delivered [him]** into his hand, then I will appoint for you a place where he may flee. But if a man acts with premeditation against his neighbor, to kill him by treachery, you shall take him from My altar, that he may die (Ex. 21:12-14).

The assumption is that God is in control of all events. Thus if someone accidently kills another, "God delivered him into his hand" and the person is not guilty of murder. On the other hand, if the person hated his neighbor and killed "him by treachery," then he was to forfeit his own life.

According to E. W. Kenyon, when man was created he ruled the laws of creation, including "the very stars in their courses."[53] Since the Fall into sin, occasionally a great man arises who can still exercise this kind of dominion. Kenyon says, "Moses had the dominion over the laws of nature when he spoke to the Red Sea." Later he points to Joshua speaking to the Jordan and to the sun and moon, commanding that they remain still. Jesus, he says, also exercised this authority.[54] Man had "the legal authority to rule the universe."[55]

---

[52]Capps, *Authority in Three Worlds*, p. 30.

[53]E. W. Kenyon, *The Father and His Family*, p. 39.

[54]Ibid., p. 40.

[55]Ibid., p. 44.

Of course no Scripture is ever cited for such a preposterous view. God gave Adam dominion over the living animals of the earth (Gen. 1:26, 28), not over the universe or over physical laws to command them at will. Man is not above physical law, only God is. Man is not above moral law, only God is. If these men think they can defy physical laws, then one of them should walk off a twenty story building.

Who Controls Our Trials?

The prosperity preacher tells us that God does not control our trials, for we know better than He does what we need, how much we need, and when we need it. If we only knew how to use our faith correctly, we would be rich, healthy, and live until *we* decided to die. The only trials we have are those *we* allow, and they *always* come from the devil, never from God.

Norvel Hayes confidently proclaims: "If we're not going to bind up anything on earth, God will have to sit there from the beginning of our life until the end of it and not be able do [sic] anything about what happens to us."[56] Consider how much guilt this would place on a person who is sick or disabled. He is obviously not living by faith, or these trials would not be his.

Oral Roberts says, "When disaster strikes . . . there are those who say, 'This is the will of God.' Not so with Jesus."[57] Hagin is typically more forceful: "You cannot find anywhere in the Bible where God causes these things to happen to teach His people something,"[58] but read Psalm 119:71: "It is good for me that I have been afflicted, that I may learn Your statutes."

Kenneth Copeland, in response to the statement that "we are made stronger by the trials and tribulations of this life," says, "The Bible does not say that at all!"[59] Again, Copeland

---

[56] Norvel Hayes, *Visions: The Window to the Supernatural* (Tulsa: Harrison House, 1992), p. 68.

[57] Oral Roberts, *Miracle of Seed-Faith* (Tulsa: Oral Roberts, 1972), pp. 37, 102, 142.

[58] Kenneth Hagin, *How You Can Be Led by the Spirit of God* (Tulsa: Faith Library Publications, 1989), p. 91.

[59] Kenneth Copeland, *The Force of Faith* (Tulsa: KCP Publications, 1989), p. 24.

complains, "There are those in the church who think we are to glory in tribulations."[60] Yes, like the Apostle Paul: "I will boast . . . in my infirmities" (2 Cor. 12:5). "And not only that, but we also glory in tribulations" (Rom. 5:3). Copeland responds, "There is no glory in knuckling down and enduring a trial."[61] The Apostle James disagrees: "Blessed is the man who perseveres under trial; for when he has been proved, he will receive the crown of life which the Lord has promised to those who love Him" (James 1:12).

Even further, the scripture declares of Jesus that "for the joy that was set before Him endured the cross" (Heb. 12:2), which emphatically states that suffering was planned by God for Jesus and that he endured it with joy. Indeed, without His suffering, we would all go to hell.[62] The Lord suffered because it was God's will for Him (Rom. 8:3), and He suffered unjustly as He had never sinned. Did Christ die because he did not have enough faith when He prayed in the garden for His Father to remove the "cup"? From the greatest suffering came the greatest good.

God Controls Our Trials

The Scripture is clear that God controls our trials.

> And you shall remember that the Lord your God led you all the way these forty years in the wilderness, to humble you and test you, to know what was in your heart, whether you would keep His commandments or not. So He humbled you, allowed you to hunger, and fed you with manna which you did not know nor did your fathers know, that He might make you know that man shall not live by bread alone; but man lives by every [word] that proceeds from the mouth of the Lord (Deut. 8:2, 3).

This passage is quoted in the New Testament of Christ, Who also was "led" into the wilderness by the Spirit of God for the express purpose of being tempted by the devil (Matt. 4:1). Consider other passages:

> And do not lead us into temptation, but deliver us from the evil

---

[60] Ibid., p. 25.

[61] Ibid.

[62] The arguments in this paragraph are again from Pete Frye.

one. For Yours is the kingdom and the power and the glory forever. Amen (Matt. 6:13).

And what more shall I say? For the time would fail me to tell of Gideon and Barak and Samson and Jephthah, also of David and Samuel and the prophets: who through faith subdued kingdoms, worked righteousness, obtained promises, stopped the mouths of lions, quenched the violence of fire, escaped the edge of the sword, out of weakness were made strong, became valiant in battle, turned to flight the armies of the aliens . . . of whom the world was not worthy. They wandered in deserts and mountains, in dens and caves of the earth. And all these, having obtained a good testimony through faith, did not receive the promise, God having provided something better for us, that they should not be made perfect apart from us (Heb. 11:32-34, 38-40).

For the Lord will not cast off forever. Though He causes grief, yet He will show compassion according to the multitude of His mercies. For He does not afflict willingly, nor grieve the children of men (Lam. 3:31-33).

No temptation has overtaken you except such as is common to man; but God is faithful, **who will not allow you to be tempted** beyond what you are able, but with the temptation will also make the way of escape, that you may be able to bear it (1 Cor. 10:13).

So they departed from the presence of the council, rejoicing that they were counted worthy to suffer shame for His name (Acts 5:41).

For I will show him how many things he must suffer for My name's sake (Acts 9:16).

That no one should be shaken by these afflictions; for you yourselves know that we are appointed to this. For, in fact, we told you before when we were with you that we would suffer tribulation, just as it happened, and you know (1 Thess. 3:3, 4).

My brethren, count it all joy when [not if] you fall into various trials, knowing that the testing of your faith produces patience (James 1:2, 3).

In this you greatly rejoice, though now for a little while, if need be, you have been grieved by various trials, that the genuineness of your faith, being much more precious than gold that perishes, though it is tested by fire, may be found to praise, honor, and glory at the revelation of Jesus Christ, whom having not seen you love. Though now you do not see [Him], yet believing, you rejoice with joy inexpressible and full of glory, receiving the end of your faith — the salvation of [your] souls (1 Peter 1:6-9).

Capps says of the martyrs in Hebrews 11 that if they had had the Holy Spirit and someone to intercede for them then all those things would not have happened to them.[63] In verse 39, however, Paul says, "all these obtained a good testimony through faith." So much for Capps.

The last two passages from James and 1 Peter demonstrate that God uses trials to increase and strengthen our faith. Naturally the health and wealth people deprecate this idea, saying that no trial ever made someone better. They may be wrong or right. No one believes that the trial itself makes one stronger, any more than one believes that a broken arm itself makes the arm stronger. The trial is the occasion for strengthening one's faith, but how one responds is vitally important. For once we quote Charles Capps approvingly: "You may come out of a trial stronger. But if you do, it is because you acted on the Word of God. It is not a direct result of the trial. The trial just gave you an opportunity to put God's Word to work in your life."[64] Did any Christian ever say differently?

The Case of Job

If ever there were a book in the Bible that clearly teaches that God is sovereign over our afflictions, it is the book of Job. One of the main points that prosperity preachers miss is that it was not Satan but the Lord who began the contest over Job.

> Now there was a day when the sons of God came to present themselves before the Lord, and Satan also came among them. And the Lord said to Satan, "From where do you come?" So Satan answered the Lord and said, "From going to and fro on the earth, and from walking back and forth on it." Then the Lord said to Satan, "Have you considered My

---

[63] Charles Capps, *Kicking Over Sacred Cows* (England, AR: Charles Capps, 1983), p. 63ff.

[64] Ibid., p. 88.

servant Job, that there is none like him on the earth, a blameless and upright man, one who fears God and shuns evil?" (Job 1:6-8).

Satan's response was that the only reason Job loved God was for the things God gave him, which sounds ominously like the prosperity preachers. Satan said that God — not Job — had placed a hedge around Job. God gave Satan permission to take all his possessions but could not touch Job. The scenario is repeated, and once again the Lord begins the contest by asking Satan what he thought of Job now. Again God gives him permission to touch Job but not to take his life. God Himself specifically states: "In all this Job did not sin nor charge God with wrong" (v. 22).

How did Job react? Did he jump with joy and confess that all his possessions were not really gone? Did he claim his healing? Contrary to the modern prosperity men, he sat in ashes, tore his clothes, confessed that all things were gone, and did not sin! Similarly, the Lord of glory, Jesus, cried out to the Father in the Garden of Gethsemane, sweating drops of blood, feeling the effects of the trial just prior to the crucifixion, yet He never sinned. *It is not wrong to feel downcast when a trial comes*; it only becomes sin when we stop trusting God, avoid using the means of grace, or cease using the means to remove the trial.

In all this did Job curse God? No, his response is classic: "Naked I came from my mother's womb, and naked shall I return there. The Lord gave, and the Lord has taken away; blessed be the name of the Lord" (Job 1:21).

What do the prosperity people do with something so clear? First, they allege that Job's statement was in error. They do not mean the Bible is wrong; Job is quoted accurately and Job really believed that. But, they say, Job erred; the Lord gave but it was the devil who took away.[65] They cannot conceive that *both* the Lord *and* the devil took away. It was the Lord who had given to Job, and it was the same Lord who also had the prerogative to take away. Their interpretation is clearly contrary to the context.

Secondly, like the metaphysical cults, they say that it was Job's fear that caused the hedge around himself to be re-

---

[65]Ibid., p. 29.

moved.66 They quote Job 3:5: "For the thing I [Job] greatly feared has come upon me, and what I dreaded has happened to me." There is no mention of fear as the reason for his trials but only that the Lord tried him as gold, refining him, proving that Job loved Him not for "the abundance of things which a man possesses" (Luke 12:15) but for Who He is. Job was merely referring to a natural human fear he had experienced.

That the Lord was the One controlling things is further seen in that it was "the fire *of God*" that fell on Job's servant and sheep (Job 1:16) and from Job's family who comforted him "for all the adversity that *the LORD* had brought upon him" (Job 42:11). And what does the Lord *Himself* say to Satan when he came before Him after he had taken all his possessions? "Then the Lord said to Satan, 'Have you considered My servant Job, that there is none like him on the earth, a blameless and upright man, one who fears God and shuns evil? And still he holds fast to his integrity, *although you incited Me against him, to destroy him without cause*'" (Job 2:3). The Bible does not get any clearer than that.

It is interesting to note that the two areas that the Word of Faith movement are most concerned with are the two areas Satan wanted to test Job in: wealth and health. Satan thought that Job would hate God if He took all his possessions. Then Satan said that a man will do anything to stay alive. In other words, take his health, and Job will curse God. Again the health and wealth leaders clearly promote Satan's idea that God does owe us health. Job, however, so loved the Lord for Who He was that he said, "Though He slay me, yet will I trust Him" (Job 13:15).67

The sorry comforters that visited Job bear an uncanny resemblance to the health and wealth preachers, who would say to Job that the calamity came because he had sinned. If Job had enough faith, these things would not have occurred, and not having enough faith is sin (Rom. 14:23). At the very least, according to them, he feared and let his own hedge down. But the Lord said he had *not* sinned. What does the

---

66 Ibid., p. 33.

67 The Massoretic text probably has the better reading: "He will slay me, I will have no hope." This becomes a statement of despair, which fits the rest of the verse better though the verse which follows would agree with the traditional rendering.

What Is God Like?

Lord say to these sorry comforters? "And so it was, after the LORD had spoken these words to Job, that the LORD said to Eliphaz the Temanite, 'My wrath is aroused against you and your two friends, for you have not spoken of Me what is right, *as My servant Job has*'" (Job 42:7). Job had spoken correctly, especially when he said that the Lord had given and had taken away, blessed be His Name, but these "friends" — the health and wealth preachers — had *not* spoken accurately. "My wrath is aroused against" such preachers, says the Lord!

Romans 8:28

This verse ("And we know that all things work together for good to those who love God, to those who are the called according to [His] purpose") has been one of the most precious verses to Christians for centuries. The Word of Faith leaders, however, try to rob us of its meaning. Capps says:

> All things don't work for good. . . . The context of verse 28 is this: after you have prayed according to God, **then** you know that all things you have prayed about will work together for good [v. 27; emphasis his]. . . . You see, the apostle Paul is the one who wrote this verse, and he didn't even believe that everything which happened worked together for good. If it were true that all things did work together for good, then you would have to say, "Adam sinned, and it worked together for good; so I guess my sin will work together for good."[68]

It seems unnecessary to have to comment at all on such ridiculous thought, but in the interest of completeness, we must. First, Capps has not studied the entire context. Paul is giving encouragements to the people of God for the sufferings they endure in this life (Rom. 8:18-39), and these encouragements are four: (1) the Christian will be resurrected (vv. 18-25); (2) when we need to pray in our trials and are not sure what to pray for, the Spirit intercedes on our behalf (vv. 26, 27); (3) all things work together for good; (4) we are secure in the Lord, nothing being able to separate us from Him (vv. 31-39). Therefore, Romans 8:28 fits the context beautifully. To qualify verse 28 with verse 27 is nonsense. Also, Capps directly contradicts Paul by stating the exact opposite: "All things don't work for good." Finally, Capps seems unable to

---

[68]Capps, *Kicking Over Sacred Cows*, pp. 120, 121.

understand the biblical truth that God uses sin to work things out for good. Paul does not say that all circumstances in themselves are good or that *everything* is good, but he does say that God causes everything to work out ultimately for good. Scripture is replete with such examples.

Hebrews 12:5-16

How do the health preachers respond to such a clear passage as God's loving discipline in Hebrews 12? Capps says, "*Chasten* [in v. 6] *means to child train*" [emphasis his].[69] It is God training you as you would a child, he says, not God sending you some calamity.[70] You wouldn't send your child some calamity to train him, would you? Neither does God, he argues.

Our response must be that we may not send calamities to our children, but in obedience to Scripture we do discipline them, verbally and corporeally. In fact, our children probably think of discipline as a calamity. As the passage says, God deals the same way with us, and while we may consider our chastenings "calamities," He does not.

In addition, Capps's understanding of the Greek word for "chastening" is incorrect. Even though it means "child training" in Ephesians 6:4,[71] which is the passage he uses to support his definition, it does not mean it has the same meaning here. In fact, the Arndt and Gingrich Greek lexicon gives the word the meaning of "training" in Ephesians 6:4 (noun) and of "discipline with punishment" in Hebrews 12:6 (verb).

Moreover, Capps does not mention the word "scourges" which is used in the same verse, and means to "whip, flog" or "punish, chastise" (same lexicon). "For whom the Lord loves He chastens and *scourges*." Apparently, he has no misconstruing for this word so he omits any discussion.

Furthermore, the context says, "no chastening seems to be joyful for the present, but *painful*," indicating that it is not a pleasant experience. This is true for our own children when we discipline them and for us when our heavenly Father

---

[69] Ibid., p. 10.

[70] Ibid.

[71] Ibid., p. 11.

disciplines us. If the discipline is *painful*, it must involve "chastening" *and* "scourging." Also, the purpose of discipline is that we may grow in personal holiness: "that we may be partakers of His holiness" (v. 10) and that we may have "the peaceable fruit of righteousness" (v. 11), "without which no one will see the Lord" (v. 14). From this last verse we see why God disciplines *all* His children. Without discipline there is no personal holiness, and without holiness we go to hell.[72] Again, God is sovereign, not allowing us to go our own way, but disciplines us with or without our permission so that we may not be condemned with the world.

Lastly, we must notice God's motive: "For whom the Lord *loves* He chastens." We discipline our own children because we love them, caring how they turn out, instructing them to leave sin alone. God does no less with us.

God's Providence Versus Spiritual Laws

To understand fully the nature of our trials, we must understand God's providence and how it affects us. What are God's works of providence? They are "His most holy, wise, and powerful preserving and governing all His creatures and all their actions."[73]

Deism, which is often remembered as the faith of Thomas Jefferson, is the belief that "God wound up the clock of the world once and for all at the beginning, so that it now proceeds as world history without the need for his further involvement."[74] "Deism teaches that the universe is ruled by natural law rather than divine providence. Whereas deism proper refers only to the *physical* laws governing the universe, the metaphysical cults (and Kenyon) maintain that there are *spiritual* laws as well" [emphasis his].[75] New charismatics give lip service to a personal God, but since everything is determined by spiritual law, God can do nothing personally for us except applaud on the sidelines.

---

[72] We do not merit our salvation, but perseverance is the necessary evidence that we belong to Him. We persevere by His irresistible grace. Trials are one way that God makes us endure; see James 1:12.

[73] *Shorter Catechism*, Question Eleven.

[74] M. H. MacDonald, *Evangelical Dictionary of Theology* (Grand Rapids: Baker Book House, 1984), p. 304.

[75] D. R. McConnell, *A Different Gospel* (Peabody, MA: Hendrickson, 1988), p. 146.

In the Bible, however, we have a personal God who is not only transcendent (infinitely above His creation) but Who is also immanent (personally involved with His creation). As we have seen, He upholds all things by the word of His power, and He does this every day, moment by moment. He, by His loving providence, has foreordained all things for our good and His own glory. Each day His mercies are new (Lam. 3:23), and each day reveals a Father who cares for His people on a personal level. We often forget parts of His Bible, and we err and sin. Yet He still blesses us because we are in a personal relationship, not an impersonal one governed by myriad "neutral" laws. If we fail, He still helps us. He does not watch us lie on the ground and say, "There is nothing I can do. My child must use the laws I have established; it is up to him."

The Apostle Paul recognized that God providentially controls all things when he said that He "works all things according to the counsel of His will" (Eph. 1:11). Unlike some today who think they can determine their future, Paul conditioned his daily life and daily affairs according to the will of God:

> But took leave of them, saying, "I must by all means keep this coming feast in Jerusalem; but I will return again to you, **God willing**." And he sailed from Ephesus (Acts 18:21).

> That I may come to you with joy **by the will of God**, and may be refreshed together with you (Rom. 15:32).

> But I will come to you shortly, **if the Lord wills**, and I will know, not the word of those who are puffed up, but the power (1 Cor. 4:19).

> For I do not wish to see you now on the way; but I hope to stay a while with you, **if the Lord permits** (1 Cor. 16:7).

Even in the area of spiritual growth we are subject to His will:

> Therefore, leaving the discussion of the elementary [principles] of Christ, let us go on to perfection, not laying again the foundation of repentance from dead works and of faith toward God, of the doctrine of baptisms, of laying on of hands, of resurrection of the dead, and of eternal judgment. And this we will do **if God permits** (Heb. 6:1-3).

God's loving providence controls all things and not us. In our more sober moments, we would not want it otherwise.

Conclusion

In reading thousands of pages of Word of Faith material, I never saw a single presentation of the sovereignty of God over the believer, over Satan, over the world, over anything. Yet many exhausting pages covered the sovereignty of man over God, over Satan, over the world, over everything. Not only is this blasphemous, one can only imagine the lives that are being wrecked by this teaching. They ignore the truth that man's chief end is to glorify God, and how man must do this, but repeatedly man is instructed in how he can obtain what he wants from God, making God his debtor. Such a religion is man-centered from beginning to end.

Dave Hunt accurately summarizes:

> And to whatever extent we seek our own will, seek to use God to bring about our will, pander to our self-centered desires, or in any way are afraid or unwilling to surrender wholly to God's will — to that extent we are exalting ourselves to the position of gods, whether we call it that or not.[76]

The Apostle Paul said, referring to those who would promulgate such ideas: "Who exchanged the truth of God for the lie, and worshiped and served the creature rather than the Creator, who is blessed forever. Amen" (Rom. 1:25). They have not given glory to God but have assumed it for themselves by arrogating sovereignty to themselves.

It is a great encouragement for the Christian to know that everything that happens to him must first be filtered through God's sovereign will, for "God is faithful, Who will *not allow* you to be tempted beyond what you are able" (1 Cor. 10:13). God Almighty will not allow anything into our lives without His prior approval. What a comfort! It is like the small boy fishing with his father in a boat, and when the boat began to rock violently, he was fearful. When he turned around, however, and saw that it was his father doing the rocking, all fear left him. We see the underside of the embroidered material, but our heavenly Father sees the top. We see only isolated threads and no pattern to our lives; He sees the beauty of the finished product. We see the outward man decaying, but He

---

[76] Dave Hunt & T. A. McMahon, *The Seduction of Christianity* (Eugene, OR: Harvest House, 1985), p. 90.

sees the inward man being renewed day by day.

How easy and comforting it is to rest and relax in the arms of One who loves us and will keep us from falling (Jude 24), who will keep us from the evil one (John 17:15; 2 Thess. 3:3), and who will not allow us to permanently injure ourselves because of our mistakes.

11

Can We Make It Alone?

Local Church versus Individualism

And I also say to you that you are Peter, and on this rock I will build My church, and the gates of Hades shall not prevail against it (Matt. 16:18).

Which is more important, the individual or the community? Over the centuries people have held to both extremes. Anarchism centers on the individual while totalitarianism makes a god of the community. Christianity, however, with its understanding of unity and distinct Persons in the Trinity, says that both the individual and the community are equally ultimate and important. This balance is what we must achieve in society and in our churches. The health and wealth people, however, do not see any importance in community or churches. They may deny it, but when we observe what they *do* — not what they say — we are forced to such a conclusion. Many of their assemblies do not even have the word "church" in the title. They prefer names like "tabernacle" or something apart from "church."

You can build a large congregation quickly by catering to people's covetous desires, being man-centered, and teaching the sovereignty of man. To build a church based on God and His Word, though, takes much preaching and long, hard work. It is not that the Word of Faith leaders do not have churches; some do. But the churches like that of Fred Price are basically institutions centered on teaching, not on worshiping God. The attention is on the preacher, his message, and how the people can get what they want from God, not on the Triune God.

You will never see a minister make the front cover of a

national magazine because he preaches the truth but because he has a lot of followers. Who cares what the people believe as long as there are lots of them?[1]

The church has fallen on bad times in this late twentieth century. While we cannot cover everything regarding the local church, we can show the major weaknesses of the health and wealth movement in this area. Only one book of the many read about the Word of Faith authors mentioned anything about the local church,[2] which shows the lack of importance in most peoples' minds. None of the numerous books by the health and wealth leaders speak of the church and its importance. Since each person can "contact" God within his human spirit, why attend church? Such a belief indicates that God is not concerned with His people corporately. Furthermore, narcissism, hedonism, and just plain selfishness are the order of the day. Simply put, it is me, me, me. We do not think we need anyone; we live in America where each person is his own boss. We think we can take or leave the church, sort of a smorgasbord approach, choosing only the church activities that we like. If something displeases us at one church, we will leave without proper protocol, attend another church, daring anyone to question us.

In the early 1800's, a new theology arose that emphasized the individual over the church, especially during the Second Great Awakening. Though many were apparently converted, the preaching and the emphasis was on the individual. "Revival" preaching sprang up, in which the preacher and the response of the people were the emphases, and this was especially true under Charles Finney's preaching. In place of the sacraments of baptism and the Lord's Supper, another "sacrament" arose: walking the aisle. Until this time, the practice was unknown in church history. Gradually worship services in which the Triune God and His Word were the focus gave way to people's response and to theatrical preaching. Thus the focus became the "decision," and the preacher who could manipulate the most "decisions" was the successful one. Christian worship moved from God to man, from the

---

[1] This observation is from Rev. Douglas Mills.

[2] Michael Scott Horton, *Made in America* (Grand Rapids: Baker Book House, 1991), p. 165ff.

church to the individual, and from quoting His written Word back to Him to the eloquence and teaching of the preacher.[3]

Is There Salvation Outside the Church?

"There is no other way to enter into life unless this mother [the church] conceive us in her womb, give us birth, nourish us at her breast, and lastly, unless she keep us under her care and guidance until, putting off mortal flesh, we become like the angels (Matt. 22:30)."[4] Calvin did not teach that the church died for us and that we go to heaven by believing in the church. What he meant, and what the Scriptures teach, is that the church is an avenue of grace that nurtures us. Just as our natural mothers did not give us life but nurtured us to maturity, so the church does not give us life but nurtures us until we go home. Jesus is the Christian's source of eternal life, but Christians in the New Testament were never mentioned outside of local churches.

What would we conclude about one who said that he loved his wife but didn't live with her, who claimed he loved his job but never went to work? Likewise, anyone who says he loves God and yet does not worship Him is a hypocrite. It was the church that Jesus redeemed (Eph. 5:25ff); not a TV audience. It was the Bride Jesus came for, not the Lion's Club. Those who are redeemed are plainly called by the Bible *the church*.

The Call to the Ministry and the Purity of the Church

In both Testaments God *calls* His ministers, and His people confirm or *ordain* them. The man called is responsible to use his gifts for the edification of God's people, and the people are accountable to avail themselves of his gifts. Of course, the process can break down. We have already seen how new charismatics were obligated to ordain themselves since they were not preaching the Gospel. (See heading "Directly Called by God" on page 37 and paragraph begin-

---

[3] These observations are from the Right Reverand Royal U. Grote who is writing a book about these things. May he finish this much needed work quickly!

[4] John Calvin, *Institutes of the Christian Religion* (Philadelphia: The Westminster Press, seventh printing, 1975), 4:1:4.

ning with "In our most important decisions" on page 247.) Both calling and ordination are necessary to keep the Gospel pure. If we had a purer church in America, most of these health and wealth preachers would not have been allowed to preach; the churches would have stopped them.

Paul used the laying on of hands in ordination by the presbytery (1 Tim. 4:14) and also instructed that one not be ordained too soon: "Do not lay hands on anyone hastily, nor share in other people's sins; keep yourself pure" (1 Tim. 5:22). Ordaining people to the ministry at age fourteen and allowing them to minister in churches (Capps's daughter; see paragraph beginning with "Likewise, women in the modern movement" on page 34) is a direct violation of this verse. Mature men need to carefully examine a person who presents himself for the ministry to be sure he understands the Gospel and can communicate it, "not a novice, lest being puffed up with pride he fall into the same condemnation as the devil" (1 Tim. 3:6).

The candidate must be a male; otherwise, how can he be the *"husband* of one wife" (1 Tim. 3:2) and rule *his* house well (1 Tim. 3:5)? If the "minister" is a woman, is she the boss of her husband at church (Heb. 13:7), but he is the boss at home (Eph. 5:24)? Paul said he did "not permit a woman to teach or to have authority over a man, but to be in silence" (1 Tim. 2:12). Paul's commands were divine instructions for the church of God (1 Tim. 3:5, 15). The health and wealth people have women as pastors, which is directly contrary to the Bible.

Norvel Hayes speaks of a seventeen year old girl suddenly being called to the ministry by a vision.[5] The suddenness of these "calls" to the ministry should indicate to us their fallacy, for God allegedly speaks directly to their hearts, by-passing the regular process of ordination. But the pattern all through Scripture is males called and ordained and takes considerable time. Even the Old Testament prophets were confirmed when the people judged if they spoke wrongly or tried to lead them astray. (See paragraph beginning with "There are two ways to test prophets" on page 230, two ways to test prophets.) Unfortunately, the proof of one's ministry today is grounded in pragmatism: a girl's ministry was believed to be of God

---

[5] Norvel Hayes, *Visions: The Window to the Supernatural* (Tulsa: Harrison House, 1992), p. 98.

since Jimmy Swaggart was converted under her preaching.[6]

The Worship of God

The most important duty and privilege of God's people is corporate worship, but it is virtually dead in the USA. Almost no one worships God. Many come together to have a good time, to watch a play, and to do whatever is pleasing in their own sight. Some tell jokes, sing whatever crosses their minds, yell out at one another, all pray out loud simultaneously, and in general create chaos. Paul saw this problem, and he gave divine instructions that women are not to speak in the churches (1 Cor. 14:34), that only one person at a time speak (1 Cor. 14:23ff), and other things concerning proper order in the church.

One aspect of worship is especially emphasized in Scripture: it is to be done corporately. Repeatedly in 1 Corinthians 11-14 Paul speaks of the people "coming together." Likewise, in the Old Testament the people came together for the offerings and sacrifices. Often people say they can worship God at home, in their car, or while watching TV. While there is a sense in which all of life is to be done in worship of God, the formal worship of God is to be done corporately, together, and in a specific location.

To demonstrate how selfish we are and how worship is virtually non-existent, notice most people's response to the Sunday morning service: "I really enjoyed that," "I loved the music," "We need more testimonies," or "I got nothing out of that." All of these statements are irrelevant. We are there to give to God, to give Him ourselves by singing His praise, proclaiming His Word back to Him, confessing our sins, confessing our faith, and many other things. Whether we enjoy it or receive anything is a lesser importance. The focus is God, simply put; when we put Him as the supreme center of our worship experience, the blessing will inevitably follow.

The Word and the Sacraments

There are means that we use for nurturing in the Christian life. Just as one could not sustain his physical life without using

---

[6]Ibid., p. 101.

the means of eating, drinking, and sleeping, so we cannot sustain our spiritual life without the means that God has ordained in His church. These means are the Word and the sacraments.

The Word is both the preached word and the Scripture read. God attends the preaching of His Word in worship very powerfully. Television and radio may be used for God's glory, especially in evangelism. But a pastor needs to be free to meet the specific needs of his people; his primary duty is not to reach a radio audience with a generic message that may be irrelevant for his church members.

The sacraments of baptism and the Lord's Supper are suffering even at the hands of ministers, much less lay people who think they do not need them. Baptism is the sign and seal of our entrance into Christ (Rom. 6; 4:11), which gives us our entrance into the body of Christ and into the local church.[7] In the New Testament, it took the place of Old Testament circumcision (Col. 2:11, 12). This can only be done once.

The Lord's Supper took the place of the Old Testament Passover. Baptism initiates us into His body and the Supper sustains us. Baptism points to justification and the Lord's Supper to sanctification; baptism is for union and the Supper for communion. Both are vitally important.

I am not saying that one will go to hell if he does not partake of these, but he might. The thief on the cross was saved and went to heaven without baptism or the Lord's Supper, but he was the exception and not the rule. In the New Testament one was baptized when he was converted or when his parents were converted.[8] The assumption in Scripture is that if one is baptized then he is a Christian.

The Word and sacraments, that is, the means of grace, are available only in a local church. I recall seeing Paul and Cheryl Crouch having a communion service and inviting their TV audience to join with them. This is not what Christ had in mind! When His people assemble to worship and to partake

---

[7] We do not mean that baptism in itself saves or that the Holy Spirit does not engraft us into the body of Christ; He does. It is possible that one may be baptized and not be a Christian.

[8] This is not the place to argue for infant baptism. I refer the reader to the theologies for this.

of the means of grace, He is present in a powerful way with them to bless the means to their growth and spiritual maturity.

> Therefore if the whole church comes together **in one place**, and all speak with tongues, and there come in those who are uninformed or unbelievers, will they not say that you are out of your mind? But if all prophesy, and an unbeliever or an uninformed person comes in, **he is convinced by all, he is judged by all**. And thus the secrets of his heart are revealed; and so, falling down on his face, he will worship God and report that God is truly among you (1 Cor. 14:23-25).

There is a powerful ministry of the Spirit in the midst of His people when they do what is right in His sight. A person can partake of this blessing *only* when he is *there* in the physical place of corporate worship.

Many today think that the sacraments mean nothing, being only empty symbols or remembrances of a by-gone era. Baptism and the Lord's Supper are not seen as a means of grace; the individual and his private knowledge are considered sufficient for growth in grace. There is no concept of a corporate sanctification, of the people in the church being a means of grace to one another, while mutually supporting one another. According to the Word of Faith movement, the individual will need no support, either emotionally, spiritually, or financially, for if he has the right knowledge and the right faith, he will have no emotional or spiritual problems, no financial needs, and no trials in his life. Narcissism is complete.

In new charismatic circles, there is no concept of corporate responsibility, of one person being judged or blessed for another's obedience. Though God does bless us individually, He also does so corporately. If the father of a home sins by not working or by gambling away all the money he earns, the whole family suffers. If the leaders of a nation violate God's economic laws by removing the gold standard, by printing inflationary paper money, by taking money from one family to give to another family, and by condoning homosexuality, then the whole nation will suffer inflation and financial problems. No amount of "naming it and claiming it" will overcome this judgment until the whole nation repents. Poverty will come on the nation as a whole. If a nation refuses to eat what God has allowed (many in India refuse to eat cows), then many will starve, often children. Deuteronomy 8 and 28 clearly reveal how God functions corporately (or covenantally) with people.

Accountability

The local church gives us accountability and discipline, or it should. Gnostics did not believe in church discipline.[9] Most churches do neither. No human should ever be without accountability: "A man who isolates himself seeks his own desire; he rages against all wise judgment" (Prov. 18:1). If one is without accountability, he tends to become a law unto himself. Sometimes pastors fall into sin because they violated this principle. In one case, every time a pastor was confronted either with his own sin or with the sins of his people, he would get angry or say it was none of the inquirer's business. He would not hold anyone accountable for his sins, and he refused to be held accountable. Consequently he fell into serious sin and to this day has not repented. The church did the biblical thing; they excommunicated him. They did not do so to punish him so much as to lovingly regain him.

Furthermore, accountability affords protection. There is safety in numbers. When buffalos are attacked, they form a circle with the females and calves in the middle, leaving the wolves unable to attack. The wolves seek to isolate a lone buffalo, especially a calf. Likewise, Satan can easily attack and defeat the lone Christian, but if he is in a covenant community, in a local church that is faithful to God, there is tremendous protection, not only from Satan, but from our own tendency to sin.

God has given us many covenants for protection, such as the local church, employment, government, and family. Each one has a sphere of authority that holds us accountable and each one also presents us with an umbrella of protection. If we neglect these, we are subject to great judgment.

One who shuns accountability to God's appointed elders

---

[9] Philip Schaff, *History of the Christian Church* (Grand Rapids: Wm. B. Eerdmans Publishing Co., 1910), 2:459.

is shunning accountability to Christ Himself. How can that person say he loves Jesus when he hates — by his actions — His church officers and His people (1 John 4:20)? He is literally playing with fire. The health and wealth people virtually never speak of these things in their writings. Their neglect of these important truths shows not only ignorance of the Word of God, but a disdain for His clear precepts.

"No Man Is an Island"

A Christian cannot grow in grace apart from other Christians, for Christ does not put Christians out to pasture as isolated believers, but He places them in a flock, a Body (singular), a Bride (singular), a church (singular). We all grow together. There is not only an individual sanctification and growth, but primarily there is a corporate sanctification.

> In whom **the whole building**, being joined together, grows into a holy temple in the Lord, in whom you also are **being built together** for a habitation of God in the Spirit (Eph. 2:21, 22).

> And He Himself gave some to be apostles, some prophets, some evangelists, and some pastors and teachers, **for the equipping of the saints for the work of ministry**, for the edifying of the body of Christ, till we all come to the unity of the faith and the knowledge of the Son of God, to a perfect man, to the measure of the stature of the fullness of Christ; that we should no longer be children, tossed to and fro and carried about with every wind of doctrine, by the trickery of men, in the cunning craftiness by which they lie in wait to deceive, but, speaking the truth in love, may grow up in all things into Him who is the head — Christ — from whom **the whole body**, joined and knit together by what every joint supplies, according to the effective working by which every part does its share, causes **growth of the body** for the edifying of itself in love (Eph. 4:11-16).

The latter passage especially emphasizes the ministry of gifted men to build up Christians so that they can be discerning and not fall prey to every wind of doctrine. This is the ministry of the local church. Where else can one be known by name and by face, be supported even though his sins are known, be loved when he is down and disciplined when he needs it, except by the local church?

Conclusion

Unfortunately, some churches have become so large that most of the members are simply faces in a sea of anonymity. The people are not ministered to personally, and they very often do not want to be. They want little accountability; indeed, what they seek is anonymity. They can go to a large church, pick what activities they want, not attend worship, and no one will say anything. Or they can leave when they choose with impunity, even if they have offended someone.

The health and wealth teachers are primarily concerned with how people can receive from God rather than how they can give to Him in worship. The complete disregard for worship is a by-product of self-centeredness. Only when the redeemed people of God see Him in His glory and see their own insufficiency can they fall down in true worship, adoration, and dependence.

12

Another Jesus

Jesus: His Person and Work

Then — when He said to them, "I AM," — they drew back and fell to the ground (John 18:6).

For even the Son of Man did not come to be served, but to serve, and to give His life a ransom for many (Mark 10:45).

What is the health and wealth view of the Person and work of Christ? We come now to the second most important chapter or truth in this book, the next chapter being the most important. *The Person of Christ is the heart of the Gospel. If they are wrong here, they are a cult and preach no Gospel.* We see in this chapter and the next the elements of their theology coming together and forming something of a consistent though unbiblical position.

Person of Christ

There are many ways to deny the Person of Christ. One is to deny that He is God; another is to deny that He is fully Man; or one can deny that He is one Person, calling Him two separate persons. Some deny that He was sinless. The Word of Faith leaders sometimes deny that He was God while on earth. Another but very subtle heresy in the Word of Faith movement is that He was God while on earth but did not function as God. Many of the leaders boldly proclaim that He *only* functioned as a Man during His incarnation.

The Orthodox Teaching

The orthodox position on the Person of Christ has been settled since the Council of Nicea in A.D. 325, which is that Jesus (1) is Almighty God, equal with the Father in every way conceivable; (2) after His incarnation was thoroughly human while still continuing to be God, yet without sin, (3) was one

Person, not two; (4) was no mixture of the natures of God and man, being neither something less than God nor something more than man. We may summarize this as follows: Jesus is 100% God, 100% man, one Person, and no mixture of the natures of deity and humanity. This fourth point is not mentioned much today. Jesus was so human that He felt the pain of the Cross and so much God that He could do anything while on earth. Such has been the universal confession of the church, Roman Catholic, Eastern Orthodox, and Protestant. Let any departure from this be called heresy.[1]

The Scripture is so replete with the proof of these four points that not much documentation is required. While on earth, Jesus, contrary to Kenyon's belief,[2] claimed to be equal with the Father. In John 5:18 He "said that God was His Father, making Himself equal with God"; He claimed to be the I AM (John 8:24, 28, 58), and said that if one rejected Him as I AM that he "will die in his sins" (John 8:24);[3] He was omnipresent, being simultaneously on earth and in heaven as the King James version states (John 3:13; see also John 1:48);[4] omniscient (John 2:24; 16:30); and omnipotent as seen by the miracles He did.

He did "spiritual" miracles that no one but God could do, and He did them in His own name. He forgave sins, which more than anything demonstrated that He was functioning as God while on earth, for Who but God can forgive sins (Matt. 9:1ff)? The assumption in His forgiving sins is that He was the One offended, which was, of course, true.

He said that *He* — not the Holy Spirit — had seen

---

[1] It is not my purpose to discuss the Lutheran view of the deified human nature of Christ. Hodge has a good discussion in his *Theology*, 2:407ff. For a Lutheran view, read Martin Chemnitz, *The Two Natures in Christ*, translated by J. A. L. Preus and published by Concordia Publishing House.

[2] Kenyon, *What Happened From the Cross to the Throne* (1969, 4th ed.), p. 36.

[3] Greek indicates *I AM*, not simply *I am (He)*, identifying Him with the I AM of the Old Testament in Ex. 4:11.

[4] I know the modern versions leave out the italics, The Son of Man *who is in heaven*. The majority text has the expression, and even if one does not hold to the majority text the manuscript evidence is overwhelming for its genuineness. See Metzger's Commentary on the critical apparatus to see why they did not think it was genuine: "This reflected later Christological development." In other words, John could not have had a doctrine of Christ that developed. How subjective can one be?

Nathanael "under the fig tree," which had been physically impossible, and this led Nathanael to confess His deity (John 1:47-51). The Lord commended him for this confession.

He claimed to be able to call men to spiritual life, which is the prerogative of God: "Most assuredly, I say to you, the hour is coming, *and now is*, when the dead will hear the voice of the Son of God; and those who hear will live" (John 5:25). "All things have been delivered to Me by My Father, and no one knows the Son except the Father. Nor does anyone know the Father except the Son, *and he to whom the Son wills to reveal Him*" (Matt. 11:27).

The Lord asserted that He gave people eternal life even as He spoke: "My sheep hear My voice, and I know them, and they follow Me. And *I give* [present tense] them eternal life, and they shall never perish; neither shall anyone snatch them out of My hand" (John 10:27, 28).

He claimed to be one with the Father in giving eternal life to His sheep and that no one could snatch His sheep from the Father: "I and My Father are one" (John 10:30). The Jews understood this to be a claim to deity and picked up stones to kill Him for blasphemy (vv. 31-33).

Unfortunately, some have misunderstood the Lord's response to the Jews, who wanted to stone Him:

> The Jews answered Him, saying, "For a good work we do not stone You, but for blasphemy, and because You, being a Man, make Yourself God." Jesus answered them, "Is it not written in your law, 'I said, "You are gods"'? If He called them gods, to whom the word of God came (and the Scripture cannot be broken), (36) do you say of Him whom the Father sanctified and sent into the world, 'You are blaspheming,' **because I said, 'I am the Son of God'**? If I do not do the works of My Father, do not believe Me; but if I do, though you do not believe Me, believe the works, that you may know and believe that the Father is in Me, and I in Him." Therefore **they sought again to seize Him**, but He escaped out of their hand (John 10:33-39).

The Jehovah's Witnesses claim that Jesus qualified the statement that He and the Father were one by asserting that He was only a god in the sense that God called the Old Testament judges gods, who applied the word of God (see Ex.

22:9, 28). By contrast, though, consider that His answer is "I am the Son of God" and that the Jews *still* wanted to stone Him ("they sought *again* to seize Him"). So whatever interpretation we understand, it is obvious that He was very pointedly claiming to be God in His explanation. The best understanding seems to be that the word of God came to the judges and they were called gods in the sense of having divine authority for their proclamations and judgments. Jesus was the Word of God incarnate who came to earth, the Son of God, literally God; how much more should it be true that He would claim such! Apparently such was the Jews' understanding, or they would not have *still* wanted to stone Him.[5]

John often presents the understanding of the Jews and the Jewish leaders to teach the reader what Jesus was claiming. Even today a good novelist will instruct his readers about his main character by the reactions of other characters in the story. The Jews did *not* comprehend His spiritual message of salvation (2:19ff; 3:1ff; 8:22ff, etc), but they did understand His claims to deity (5:18; 10:31ff; 19:7).

When the early church fathers stated that Jesus was fully God, they certainly did not mean that though such was true yet He did not function this way while on earth, for that would be to deny with one statement what they maintained with another. The early church and Scripture meant that He was God while on earth and that He *functioned as God* while on earth.

It is true that Jesus lived by the power of the Holy Spirit, and did not do miracles except after the Holy Spirit came on Him at His baptism. But this emphatically does not imply that He was not God nor that He was not functioning as God. Because the Holy Spirit performed a certain act, does this mean that Jesus in His deity could not do so also? How in the name of all that is biblical and rational could Jesus be God and not function as God? Such thought is ludicrous beyond comprehension. Could we be human and not function humanly? Could an elephant not function as an elephant? Jesus did indeed live as a man by the power of the Holy Spirit as the Substitute for His people, for He had to perfectly obey

---

[5] Jesus quoted Ps. 82:6. The next verse stated of the human judges that they shall die like men.

the law of God for them. But this in no way precludes that He was not God or not functioning as God. *To maintain that He did not function as both God and man denies the Person of Christ by maintaining that He did not have two natures (God and man), that if He used one of the natures meant that the other nature was voided in some way.* Jesus was both God and man, functioning both as God and man.

If He were not God or not functioning as God, the atonement means nothing, for it was necessary for Him to be functioning as an infinite One in order to satisfy the infinite righteousness of the Father. If these men had studied their Bibles and church history, they would have known that they had joined the ranks of the heretics and that these issues had been settled in A. D. 325 at the Council of Nicaea and especially in A. D. 451 at the Council of Chalcedon. In this latter Council, the biblical position of the two natures of Christ was stated to be "without mixture, without change, without division, and without separation." In 1600 years we have not improved this statement, nor can we.

Martin Chemnitz (1522-1586) has summed up quite well the cooperation of the two natures in Christ while He was on earth:

> Antiquity was very careful to note in the case of Christ's miracles how each nature in the incarnate Christ operated in communion with the other. In the cleansings and resurrections of the dead He used either the tangible or the bodily Word, as for example in Matt. 8:3 in the case of the leper; or in Luke 14:4 the man with the dropsy; or in John 9:6, where He healed the blind man with a touch; or in Mark 7:33, where He put His finger into the ears, touched the tongue, and healed the deaf and dumb man; and in Luke 7:14, where He touched the coffin and raised the dead man; . . . or in John 11:43, where, as He was about to raise Lazarus, He calls upon him with His bodily voice; or John 20:22, where, as He was in the process of bestowing the Holy Spirit, He uses the corporeal breath. Obviously He could have performed all of these miracles without bodily touch or voice, by a simple nod and the force of His divine power, without bodily touch or voice; but by deliberate counsel He willed to show also His flesh as an organ of deity, so that in these outward and visible miracles He might show us the use of the assumed humanity,

so that no one could argue that in these highest works of the Messiah, such as our redemption, reconciliation, justification, vivification, mediation, and salvation, He had no use for His creaturely human nature, since these are things which might seem to us to be more easily and properly accomplished by the power and strength of the deity alone.[6]

What a magnificent statement! The whole church throughout the centuries has ascertained that Jesus was both God and man and that He functioned both ways while on earth, but these new prosperity men have other ideas. Who is right, the whole church for two thousand years or these neophytes? Which is right, the Scripture or their "prophecies"?

Ancient Heresies

The early church fought many heresies regarding the Person of Jesus. The Arians denied that He was fully God, Apollinaris denied that He was fully man, Nestorius maintained that He was two persons, and Eutyches said He only had one nature.[7]

In an interesting twist, Apollinaris taught the Platonic idea that man was a trichotomy, composed of body, soul, and spirit. The divine Word indwelt, according to him, the human spirit of the man Jesus. Thus Jesus was less than human since His human spirit did not exist. Again, the modern health and wealth preachers teach that humans are composed of body, soul, and spirit, and they also teach that we "contact" God with our human spirits, that God dwells in our human spirits.

The Nestorians taught that the divine Word indwelt the human Jesus, much as the Holy Spirit indwells Christians, with the result that Jesus was two persons: the human Jesus and the divine Word. Once more, the Word of Faith people teach that we are also an incarnation of God like Jesus since we have God dwelling in us. (See Capps's letter on page 325

---

[6] Martin Chemnitz, translated by J. A. O. Preus, *The Two Natures in Christ* (Saint Louis: Concordia Publishing House, 1578, 1971), p. 219.

[7] G. C. Berkouwer, *The Person of Christ* (Grand Rapids: Wm. B. Eerdmans Pub. Co., 1954, 1977), p. 59ff. See also the most excellent discussion of the heresies in Charles Hodge's *Systematic Theology*, vol. 2, p. 378ff. If you read nothing else on the Person of Christ, at least read Hodge. B. B. Warfield's classic, *Christology and Criticism* (reprinted by Baker Book House); and John Walvoord in *Jesus Christ Our Lord* (Moody Press) is also helpful.

which begins "James 1:13 says.") Nestorius, therefore, taught that Jesus performed His miracles by the Holy Spirit and not by His own power. It is this position that most accurately represents the Word of Faith leaders. The early church fathers recognized that such a position took away the deity of Christ and that He was one person in two natures, which in turn took away our salvation. Therefore, in 431 the Council of Ephesus, representing the whole, undivided orthodox church, said in one voice:

> If anyone shall say that Jesus as man [humanity] is only energized by the Word of God [His deity], and that the glory of the Only-begotten is attributed to Him as something not properly His: let him be anathema.
>
> If any man shall say that the one Lord Jesus Christ was glorified by the Holy Spirit, so that He used through Him a power not His own and from Him received power against unclean spirits and power to work miracles before men and shall not rather confess that it was His own Spirit through which He worked these divine signs; let him be anathema.[8]

The later Council of Constantinople II in A. D. 553 reaffirmed the same:

> If anyone shall say that . . . His miracles . . . in the flesh were not of the same Person: let him be anathema.[9]

Later an attempt was made to lessen His humanity by saying that the human nature of Jesus did not have a will but that the divine nature functioned as His only will. This the church strenuously rejected as lessening His humanity as well as taking away from the temptations that He suffered. God cannot be tempted but a man can. Jesus had a human will.

Against all these for two thousand years the church, on the authority of Scripture, has taught the full humanity and the full deity of Jesus: "For in Him dwells all the fullness of the Godhead bodily" (Col. 2:9). Here we see one Person ("Him"), fully God and yet in a body. It was not that God dwelt in Jesus as He does in us, but that the second Person of the

---

[8] Henry R. Percival, *The Seven Ecumenical Councils of the Undivided Church* (Grand Rapids: Wm. B. Eerdmans Pub. Co., 1979), pp. 213-214.

[9] Ibid., p. 312.

Trinity, God the Son, added to Himself a perfect human nature, yet one without sin. He did not cease to be God, but continued as He had always existed, for He is "the same yesterday, today, and forever" (Heb. 13:8). The gnostics have said that Jesus was something less than God or that He did not have a true body or both. The gnostics have always had a defective view of the Person of Jesus from the Second Century to our day (Col. 2:9). The Greek word for "Godhead" means the full essence of deity. It does *not* mean *like* God but God in very essence. Also Paul stated that Jesus was this *bodily*; that is, while He was on earth. Of course, He was also God from all eternity (John 1:1 Micah 5:2). Jesus was God before He came to the earth physically, God after the incarnation, and God today. In other words, "Jesus Christ is the same yesterday, today, and forever" (Heb. 13:8), which is the way in which this verse should be understood (of His essence).

He did not transform Himself into only a man and then become God again later, if such a monstrous thing were even possible. Nor is it true that He was still God while on earth but only functioned as a man, if that were possible. The eternal Son *added* to an already eternally existing Person a human nature. Thus the Son had no beginning but the human nature did. "It was a divine person, not merely a divine nature, that assumed humanity, or became incarnate. Hence it follows that the human nature of Christ, separately considered, is impersonal."[10] "The Son of God did not unite Himself with a human person but with a human nature."[11] The incarnation, therefore, is not God dwelling in Jesus, but Jesus as God becoming man so that He was both God and man.

The health and wealth leaders promote a Jesus who either gave up His deity or who suppressed His deity. They say that Jesus did not unite Himself with a human nature, for that is all He was — human. If that is true and He suppressed His deity, then the logical consequence is that He was not God.

Whatever can be said of either nature can be said of the one Person of Jesus but not of the other nature. For example, Jesus said "I thirst." Was His deity thirsty? Of course not, but it could be said of the Person Jesus that He was thirsty. When

---

[10] Charles Hodge, *Systematic Theology*, 2:391.

[11] Ibid.

Jesus said "I AM," was this true of His humanity? Of course not but it was true of His deity and of the Person Jesus. It is true to say of the Person Jesus that He had limited intelligence, for He was human; but it is also true to say that He had unlimited intelligence, for He was God. At the same time that Mary was holding the Babe in her arms and nursing Him, Jesus was also "upholding all things by the word of His power." Such is the mystery of the incarnation, man and God in one glorious Person. Anything less than this is to have no mediator, no Messiah, no Savior.

Contemplated as both God and man, Jesus is our Redeemer, our Prophet, Priest, and King, who was made to us righteousness, sanctification and redemption (1 Cor. 1:30). It was God who shed His blood for us (Acts 20:28). In some things it was His human nature which worked, in others His deity, and in yet another class the God-man works, as in redemption.

Other passages that maintain that He was fully God and fully man *while on earth* are important:

> Concerning His Son Jesus Christ our Lord, who was born of the seed of David according to the flesh, and declared to be the **Son of God** with power, according to the Spirit of holiness, by the resurrection from the dead (Rom. 1:3, 4).

> In the beginning was the Word, and the Word was with God, and the **Word was God**. And the Word became flesh and dwelt among us, and we beheld His glory, the glory as of the only begotten of the Father, full of grace and truth (John 1:1, 14).

> Behold, a virgin shall be with child, and bear a Son, and they shall call His name Immanuel, which is translated, "**God with us**" (Matt. 1:23).

> Of whom are the fathers and from whom, according to the flesh, Christ came, who is over all, **the eternally blessed God**. Amen (Rom. 9:5).

To use a loose but helpful analogy, we are body and soul. Someone may have part of the body severed and we may say of the person, "He had his arm cut off." Was part of his soul cut off? No, but it was true of the person. We may say *he* was converted. Was this true of the body? No, it was true of the soul, though certainly his body will be raised and glorified, yet the statement is true of the person. We are not a spirit with a soul living in a body; the real person *is* body and soul. Whatever can be said of either body or soul can be stated of the person but not necessarily of the other "nature." Thus the church has confessed Christ to be God and man in One Person and that He functioned that way while on earth.

The Virgin Birth

The Word of Faith leaders have a warped view of the Virgin Birth, which is another bedrock truth of Christianity. Mary Eddy said:

> The Virgin's mother conceived this idea of God, and gave to her ideal the name of Jesus — that is, Joshua, or Saviour.... The illumination of Mary's spiritual sense put to silence material law and its order of generation, and brought her child by the revelation of Truth, demonstrating God as the Father of men.[12]

Kenyon said, "You see, Jesus did not partake of the mother's nature, she simply clothed Him with sinless flesh."[13] Kenyon is right and wrong. Of course Jesus was sinless, but He most certainly partook of her human nature. Capps said:

> It was the Word that was made flesh. Mary conceived the Word of God in her heart.... Here is what the Spirit of God said to me about the situation [Virgin Birth]: "Mary conceived the Word sent to her by the angel (God's Word) and conceived it in the womb of her spirit. Once it was conceived in her spirit, it manifested itself in her physical body. ***She received and conceived the Word of God in her spirit***" [emphasis his].... The embryo in Mary's womb was nothing but the pure Word of God — and it took flesh upon itself.[14] ... Mary conceived the Word in her spirit. It manifested itself in her physical body.[15]

---

[12] Mary Baker Eddy, *Science and Health*, p. 29.

[13] Kenyon, *What Happened*, p. 21.

[14] Charles Capps, *Authority in Three Worlds* (Tulsa: Harrison House, 1982), pp. 81-83.

[15] Charles Capps, *Dynamics of Faith & Confession* (Tulsa: Harrison House, 1987), p. 87.

Eddy and Capps both err in believing that Jesus was not simply born by the power of the Holy Spirit but that He was conceived by the cooperation of Mary's mind and belief. When the Word was spoken to Her, they say, she confessed it, took it in, and Jesus was conceived. Such nonsense is the ultimate in visualization, in which Mary brings to pass with her mind what she "sees." If this were possible for Mary, why could this not happen again? (See paragraph beginning with "Not only knowledge and faith" on page 74.) Here again we see metaphysical law and utter nonsense. Jesus was conceived by the Holy Spirit in Mary's womb (Matt. 1:18-23), but the *mechanics* are not revealed.[16]

Derek Prince continues the idea:

> The angel had brought to Mary a **rhema** — a direct personal word from God to her. That **rhema** contained in it the power to fulfill what it promised. The outcome depended on Mary's response. "Behold, the bondslave of the Lord," she replied; "be it done to me according to your word" (Luke 1:38). By these words Mary unlocked the supernatural power of God in the **rhema** and opened herself to its fulfillment in her physical body. As a result, there occurred the greatest miracle of human history: the birth of God's eternal Son from the womb of a virgin.[17]

There is danger in denying the humanity of Jesus and His lineage. If Christ were not of Mary's nature, sin excepted, then He was not human; and if He were not human, then there is no redemption (Heb. 2:14-17). Another way to state the same idea is that Jesus had to be of the lineage of Abraham and David, as the genealogy in Matthew chapter one establishes. Indeed, Jesus had to be of the *seed* of the woman (Gen. 3:15), whose seed and lineage went through Abraham (Gal. 3:16, 19, 29) and David (Matt. 9:27; 12:23; 15:22; 20:30; 21:9, 15; 22:42; 2 Tim. 2:8, etc). If Jesus were somehow born of Mary's thoughts, how could He have been the promised seed, the

---

[16] Some have guessed — and it is a poor guess — that since the baby does not receive the mother's blood, that Jesus was kept pure from sin this way. They surmise that sin is transmitted through the male semen or through the male blood. Such guesses do more harm than good. It is better to say with Calvin that what God has not revealed is better left alone.

[17] Derek Prince, *Faith To Live By* (Ann Arbor: Servant Books, 1977), pp. 87, 88.

One Who would crush Satan's head in Genesis 3:15, the Messiah of the Old Testament? The very truths of God are violated by such teaching.

Did Jesus Have Sin?

Transcendentalism evolved into Christian Science and the Unity School and taught that Jesus was just a man. Edward Irving was apparently influenced greatly by Coleridge the transcendentalist concerning the Lord's nature. At least we know that Irving was deposed from the ministry for teaching the sinful nature of Christ. (See paragraph beginning with "It was Coleridge's mysticism" on page 47.) Irving agreed to the following in a meeting of Presbyterian ministers:

> Christ did no sin; but His human nature was sinful and corrupt; and His striving against these corruptions was the main part of His conflict. . . . I admit imputation to its fullest extent, but that does not go far enough for me. Paul says, "He hath made Him to be sin for us, who knew no sin."[18]

This last quote indicates that Irving believed that Jesus actually became a sinner for us. Other points of Irving's view of Jesus and His ministry are cited:

> [Christ's] victory was not the result of any special strength in Himself, but it came from the baptism with the Holy Spirit, which He received at the beginning of His ministry.
>
> Accordingly, Christ is the supreme example to all mankind. [Thus salvation means] to walk in Christ's steps.
>
> The Holy Spirit, by whom Christ obtained victory, is equally available to all of us, and we may experience the same baptism with the Spirit and be endued with the same power as that exercised in Christ.
>
> [At the close of His ministry Christ] was able to present to God a perfect human nature. . . . In turn, that acceptance, that coming together of God with man, Irving terms **reconciliation** and "at-one-ment," and that great work was accomplished by Christ not in His death, but in His life.[19]

---

[18] Arnold Dallimore, *Forerunner of the Charismatic Movement: The Life of Edward Irving* (Chicago: Moody Press, 1983), p. 94.

[19] Ibid., p. 96.

Another Jesus?

Transcendentalism taught, and hence the beliefs of the prosperity movement, that each man has a spark of the divine within. "Salvation" is what each man must do to overcome his limitations. If Jesus were unique, then our salvation would lie totally in Him and not ourselves, which was not acceptable to man-centered believers. Thus Jesus had to be just a man like us, with the same problems as us (sinful nature), but He overcame these problems by knowing that He could contact the "divine" within. The same metaphysical spiritual laws that He used are available to us today. Thus the works He did, we can do and even greater. Therefore, we do not need the substitutionary death of Christ, but we need to learn to do what He did, to imitate Jesus. The essence of salvation, according to them, is to learn to overcome our sin and our trials like Jesus did by the same Holy Spirit He had. The imitation of Jesus, not the substitution by Jesus, is how we are saved. The Bible may have some good things in it (Unity School), it may even be the Word of God (Word of Faith), but it does not have everything in it, and thus it *alone* was not sufficient for life and godliness. Intuition (transcendentalism) or prophecy (Irving and Word of Faith movement) was also necessary for the Christian life. So goes the "theology" of Edward Irving and of the health and wealth leaders.

Surely every true Christian would confess that Jesus, the Man, was born without sin of any kind. But some, not understanding Romans 8:3 ("God did by sending His own Son in the likeness of sinful flesh"), have stated that He was a sinner. The great theologian and exegete of last century, William G. T. Shedd, explains the truth of this verse in his commentary on Romans:

> ... the human nature spoken of is a sinful and corrupt human nature, if contemplated *in itself* and *apart from* the miraculous conception by the Holy Ghost. The qualifying epithet "sin" describes human nature simply as it descends from Adam. As such, it is a sinful nature. St. Paul is contemplating it from *this point of view*, only, when he employs this epithet. It does not follow that when a portion of this sinful and corrupt human nature is *assumed into union* with the Eternal Logos, it is still sinful and corrupt. In and by the miraculous conception, it is perfectly sanctified. . . .[20]

---

[20]William G. T. Shedd, *A Critical and Doctrinal Commentary . . . on Romans*

Christ's humanity, therefore, was not sinful.

Dallimore states that Coleridge had a view of Christ as something less than deity and that Irving adopted this view shortly thereafter.[21] The modern health and wealth preachers have, however, slightly altered Irving's view, now saying that Jesus was born without sin but that He became a sinner in His atoning work, actually assuming the nature of Satan! Kenyon claims of Jesus when He died, that

> The moment that He became sin, His body became mortal, only then could He die. . . .When this happened, spiritual death, the nature of Satan, took possession of His Spirit.[22]

> 1 Timothy 3:16 reveals that Christ Himself was made righteous in spirit. He had been made sin, and when the penalty was paid He, Himself, had to be made righteous. . . . It was Christ's having our spiritual death laid upon Him that made Him sin, as unrighteous as we were.[23]

But notice that Gloria Copeland and Hagin believe what Irving taught:

> Jesus kept His flesh under submission by praying, spending time with the Father.[24]

> He took upon Himself our sin nature.[25]

Because he does not understand Scripture's use of legal language to describe Christ's work, Kenyon has completely missed the point. First, he says that Jesus morally became a sinner for us, whereas Scripture says He legally became sin for us. (If this sounds picky, see heading "The Essence of the Atonement" on page 129ff.) Secondly, 1 Timothy 3:16 most emphatically does *not* say Jesus was *made* righteous but that

---

(1879; rpt. 1978 Klock and Klock), p. 230.

[21]Arnold Dallimore, *Forerunner of the Charismatic Movement*, p. 61.

[22]Kenyon, *What Happened*, p. 20.

[23]E. W. Kenyon, *The Father and His Family: A Restatement of the Plan of Redemption* (Seattle: E. W. Kenyon, 1937), pp. 284-285.

[24]Gloria Copeland, *Walk in the Spirit* (Ft. Worth: KCP Publications, 1984), p. 32.

[25]Kenneth E. Hagin, *Redeemed from Poverty, Sickness, and Spiritual Death* (Tulsa: Faith Library Publications, 1983), p. 28.

Another Jesus?

He was *vindicated*. Consider the verse: "And without controversy great is the mystery of godliness: God was manifested in the flesh, *justified* in the Spirit, seen by angels, preached among the Gentiles, believed on in the world, received up in glory." The Greek word translated "justified" does not mean to *make* righteous but to *declare* that one is righteous. Arndt and Gingrich say of the Greek word in this passage: "God is *proved* to be right."[26] The idea is *vindicated*, or as William Hendriksen rightly observes: "By his enemies his claims were denied, and he himself was cast out (Heb. 13:12). But by the Spirit he was vindicated: his own perfect righteousness and the validity of his claims were fully established."[27]

Furthermore, as Hendriksen points out, the word "Spirit" should be capitalized since it refers to the Holy Spirit: "It was especially by means of *his resurrection from the dead* that the Spirit *fully* vindicated the claim of Jesus that he was the Son of God (Rom. 1:4)."[28]

Therefore, we see that the health and wealth people, following in the wake of transcendentalism and Irving, believe that Jesus was a sinner. The only difference is the point in time when this occurred, Irving saying He was born with a sin nature and the modern leaders maintaining that He became a sinner at death.

The Bible, however, unequivocally states that Jesus offered Himself to God without sin of any kind, either Personal sin or Satan's nature imparted to him (see next chapter):

> How much more shall the blood of Christ, who through the eternal Spirit **offered Himself without spot** to God, purge your conscience from dead works to serve the living God? (Heb. 9:14).

> For Christ also suffered once for sins, **the just for the unjust**, that He might bring us to God, being put to death in the flesh but made alive by the Spirit (1 Peter 3:18).

Was Jesus Born Again?

It is difficult to believe that anyone would claim that Jesus

---

[26] Arndt & Gingrich, 2nd ed., p. 198a.

[27] William Hendriksen, *New Testament Commentary: 1-2 Timothy, Titus* (Grand Rapids: Baker Book House, 6th ed., 1974), p. 140.

[28] Ibid.

was born again since such an act is necessary only for sinners. But to be consistent with the belief that Jesus was a sinner or at least made a sinner for us when He went to hell, then His being born again would make sense. *This is, however, blatant heresy and beyond belief.* They teach that when Jesus died, he received the nature of Satan, went to hell to pay off Satan; and when He was raised from the dead, it was thus necessary for Him as a *sinner* to be *made* righteous, to be born again by receiving the very nature of God. It is necessary to reprint these blasphemies from Kenyon:

> God made Jesus sin. Sin was not only reckoned to Him, but His spirit actually became sin. . . . When was Jesus justified? When He was made alive in spirit. . . . Jesus was the first person ever Born Again.[29] . . . Jesus was made sin with our sins. He was made weak with our weaknesses. He was made a failure with our failures. He was made sick with our sicknesses. He was made unrighteous with our unrighteousness.[30]
>
> His spirit absolutely became impregnated with the sin nature of the world. . . . He is the first born out of spiritual death, the first person who was ever born again.[31]

And the modern Word of Faith people, as usual, parrot Kenyon:

> The third and most important area of Jesus' triumph over Satan is His victory in the new birth.[32]
>
> God sent mercy and not judgment to us in the form of Jesus. He was born into the world, died on the cross, and was reborn from the dead by the mercy of God.[33]
>
> When Jesus was raised from the dead, He was born again of the Spirit of God.[34] . . . Because He suffered and died spiritually

---

[29] E. W. Kenyon, *Two Kinds of Righteousness* (Lynwood, WA: Kenyon's Gospel Pub. Society, Inc., 1965), p. 23.

[30] Ibid., p. 60.

[31] Kenyon, *What Happened*, p. 63.

[32] Kenneth Copeland, *The Force of Righteousness* (Ft. Worth: KCP Publications, 1984), p. 19.

[33] Kenneth Copeland, *The Mercy of God* (Ft. Worth: KCP Pub., 1986), p. 34.

[34] Capps, *Authority in Three Worlds*, p. 188.

for us, He was born again and called ***the firstborn from the dead*** (Col. 1:18); ***the firstborn among many brethren*** (Rom. 8:29); and ***the first begotten from the dead*** (Rev. 1:5). Jesus was born again, and He has become the door [emphasis his].[35]

Upon first reading these ideas, one is stunned at how heretical these men are. But to answer Capps's charge that Jesus is the *firstborn*, we must point out that the Greek word translated *firstborn* seldom means the first person literally born.[36] The Greek word is composed of two words: *first* and *born*. The idea of *birth* has dropped out of the word and the emphasis is on *first* or *preeminence*. In other words, the word means that Jesus is preeminent over all persons and things. It is emphatically not the Greek word that means a sinner is born again (which is *gennao*, used in John 3).

Capps in fact uses the same passages that Jehovah's Witnesses use to deny the deity of Jesus. The Greek word *firstborn*, however, expresses two basic ideas: *priority* or *preeminent* to all creation, and *sovereignty* over all creation. In another place (Col. 1:15), Paul proclaims of Messiah that "by Him all things were created" (sovereignty) and that "He is before all things" (priority).[37] If Capps and the Jehovah's Witnesses were correct, Paul would have said that He was the "first created," "before all *other* things," or He "created all *other* things"[38] but Paul's words admit no exceptions. The Word is *absolutely* before all things, not in the same class as creatures because He is the Creator, without beginning and without end.

The term *firstborn* is very similar to the word "only begotten" (one word in Greek, though composed of two words), emphasizing the eternality of the Son, His preeminence over all creation, and His one-of-a-kind, distinct-from-all-creation, the originator-of-creation.[39] In the New Testament "first-

---

[35] Ibid., pp. 218-19.

[36] See John Eadie, *Colossians* (Minneapolis: James & Klock Christian Pub. Co., 1856, 1977), p. 49ff.

[37] For an excellent discussion of the Greek word, see J. B. Lightfoot in his commentary on Colossians, p. 146ff.

[38] The Jehovah's Witnesses add the word *other* in their *New World Translation* where I have inserted it but it is not in the Greek.

[39] Lightfoot, p. 147. In the translation of the Old Testament (Septuagint) done

born," when used of Christ, with only one exception (Luke 2:7), always emphasizes the *first* in *firstborn*, and the *born* has dropped out. The meaning, therefore, is that Jesus is the *first*, the preeminent One, the special One who has sovereignty over all others, which is the way the Old Testament often used the word and the way that writers contemporary with the New Testament would have understood the term[40] (and also the way the early church fathers understood the word).

We have hinted that the word "only begotten" (*monogenes*), though coming from a different Greek word, has a similar meaning to "firstborn." Indeed, this word comes from a root word that means "class" or "kind" (*genos*), and the usage supports this. The "class" from which Jesus came is Godhood; thus He is one of a kind. As the standard lexicon says of "only begotten" when used of Jesus in John: "The meanings *only, unique* may be adequate for all its occurrences here."[41] The lexicon goes on to say that "it would be analogous to 'firstborn.'" As "firstborn" can refer to the literal first born son, so "only begotten" can refer to an "only" child (Luke 7:12; 8:42), but we must not think that such a usage precludes the exalted usage that John gives the term. God indeed has many sons that are born again in the ethical sense (all sinners who enter the kingdom of God) but only one "unique, only begotten" Son who is of His essence.

---

around 200 B. C., the term "firstborn" came to mean first in importance [See *Theological Dictionary of the New Testament*, Edited by Gerhard Friedrich, 10 vols (Grand Rapids: Wm. B. Eerdmans Pub. Co., 1971), 6:872-6]. It could be used in Psalm 89:26-28 (LXX = Ps. 88:26-28) of David as God's "firstborn" in the sense that David was the most important of the kings of the earth, not literally the first born. We know that David had seven older brothers (1 Sam. 16:10, 11). Likewise in Exodus 4:22 Israel is called God's "firstborn," but we know that Israel or Jacob was born after Esau, the point being that Israel was chosen by God and occupied a special place in God's eyes. The "firstborn" in the Old Testament had a special relation with his father and received the double inheritance. This meaning occurs not only in the Old Testament but also in writings outside the Old Testament. The pseudopigrapha, Philo, Josephus, and the Rabbis often used the word "firstborn" in the sense of the most important or occupying a special relation to someone. See above, Friedrich, *TDNT*.

[40] *Theological Dictionary of the New Testament*, 6:878. FIRSTborn is a homonym to firstBORN, the latter perhaps not used in the Old Testament or the New. The former word means *preeminent* while the latter means the *first one born*. Ibid., 6:874.

[41] Arndt and Gingrich, 2nd edition, p. 527.

Another Jesus?

We have seen that "only begotten" (*monogenes*) is the "unique, one of a kind" Son and that "firstborn" (*prototokos*) is the one who is "preeminent" over the universe. The expression, "Thou are My Son, *Today I have begotten Thee*" comes from Psalm 2:7, and has yet a different word for "begotten" (*gennao*). It is used several times in the New Testament (Acts 13:33; Heb. 1:5; 5:5). The early church fathers understood the term "begotten" to mean "eternally begotten by the Father," that there was no time in which He did not exist as the second Person of the Trinity. Thus in the Nicene Creed we read of Jesus: "Begotten of His Father before all worlds; God of God, Light of Light, very God of very God; Begotten, not made." They emphasized the word "today," saying that it was not "yesterday" or "tomorrow" but the "eternal day" of existence, like Jesus as the I AM. The doctrine has come down to us as "the eternal generation of the Son."[42]

While this certainly maintains orthodoxy and while doctrinally we have no quarrel with the fathers, modern scholarship tends to understand "Today I have begotten you" in a different sense.[43] From Psalm 2 Keil and Delitzsch say that the Old Testament understanding is "a setting up in the kingship," an enthronement of Jesus as King.[44] The whole Psalm is speaking of the enthronement of Jesus as King over the world even though the rulers object and want to "cast away" His cords or law. When a king wanted to establish another in kingship, he would pronounce that the new ruler was his son and had a right to the throne, and then he was anointed as king. Jesus is called the Anointed in verse 2. Jesus was both God and Man, both of the essence of His Father and of His mother. He was King by divine right and also by human birth.[45] How was He exalted? The New Testament tells us.

---

[42] See J. C. Philpot, *The Eternal Sonship of the Lord Jesus Christ* (Harpendon, England: Gospel Standard Baptist Trust, 1861), especially pp. 85ff.

[43] Some have suggested that we drop the expression "the eternal generation of the Son." See J. Oliver Buswell, *A Systematic Theology of the Christian Religion* (Grand Rapids: Zondervan Publishing House, 1973), 1:111ff. Buswell does not mean that we should drop the essential truth that Jesus is the great I AM and thus eternal, without beginning and without end.

[44] Keil and Delitzsch, *Old Testament Commentaries* (Grand Rapids: Associated Publishers and Authors, no date), 3:900.

[45] See also Philip Edgcumge Hughes, *A Commentary on the Epistle to the*

In the New Testament the "Today I have begotten You" is used of the bodily resurrection of Jesus (Acts 13:33ff), emphasizing that He is the exalted King and Ruler. It was not that He suddenly became the King of the world at His resurrection but that He was recognized as such. In the words of Romans 1:4, He was *declared* to be the Son of God by the resurrection from the dead, but not *made* to be such. Therefore, though Jesus was God, yet this exaltation was confirmed at His bodily resurrection, emphasizing again His deity and His humanity. There is nothing in the context that even remotely suggests that He was a sinner in need of regeneration but that He was "begotten" to the resurrection, enthroned on high, confirmed as King of kings. The "today" is His resurrection and the "begotten" is the formula used by a king to enthrone another one.

In Hebrews 5:5ff He is the priest who cannot die, who was chosen by God to be a priest according to the order of Melchizedek, and who, though a Son, yet learned obedience by the things He suffered (v. 8). Again He was declared to be High Priest by His enthronement, not made to be such. "Melchizedek" means "king of righteousness" so that Jesus as the king of righteousness is "begotten" to this exalted position. Similar to Acts 13:33, the "today" is His exaltation to His priesthood at His resurrection and the "begotten" is the formula of installation. Nothing in the context suggests that He was morally born again.

In Hebrews 1:5 His deity comes to the forefront as He is presented as the exalted Son whom the angels are to worship. He is exalted in that He came into the world as the "firstborn," the preeminent one. Jesus is "begotten" to this relationship with the Father; that is, recognized. The Father is not making Him God or giving Him something new regarding His deity but only recognizing what He is: Son, begotten, firstborn, and God. Indeed, in verse 8 the Father says of the Son: "But to the Son He says, 'Your throne, O God, is forever and ever; a septer of righteousness is the scepter of Your kingdom.'" Jesus is *recognized* as God, the King of righteousness who rules His kingdom well. He is not made God by the Father or begotten into something He never was. The "today" has no

---

Hebrews (Grand Rapids: Wm. B. Eerdmans Publishing Co., 1977), p. 54ff.

particular reference and the "begotten" is simply recognition that Jesus is the "Son, the begotten, the firstborn, and God" (Heb. 1:5-8). Again the context militates against the idea that He was morally born again.

Though the term "begotten" is used of those who are ethically born again as sinners (John 3:1ff), yet in no case and in no sense is Jesus ever spoken of being "begotten" in this manner. Though we may disagree with how the early church fathers understood "Today I have begotten you," we emphatically agree with their theology.

Was He Only a Man while on Earth?

The Christian Science people say that Jesus is one Person and that the Christ is another, the "Christ" having come on Jesus at His baptism.[46] Unfortunately, the theology of the Word of Faith movement is that Jesus was *only* a man or only functioned as a man on earth. Repeatedly in the Word of Faith literature concerning Jesus we read:

> He was recreated so that God said of Him, "Thou art my Son, this day have I begotten thee."[47]

> Of course, Jesus stands in a class by Himself, personally, and as Deity. But when it comes to **ministry**, Jesus does not stand in a class by Himself. . . . Even though Jesus was the Son of God, and divine blood flowed through His veins, yet **He was ministering on the earth as a human being** — a prophet anointed with the Holy Spirit [emphasis his].[48]

> Jesus did not minister with His divine attributes while He was on earth. He ministered as **a man** anointed by the Holy Spirit [emphasis his].[49] . . . The Bible says that Jesus voluntarily laid aside His power and glory as the Son of God (Phil. 2:6-8), and ministered as a man **filled and anointed with the Holy Spirit** — the same way **we** are to minister [emphasis his].[50]

---

[46] Mary Baker Eddy, *Science and Health*, pp. 26, 29, etc.

[47] E. W. Kenyon, *Two Kinds of Righteousness*, p. 19.

[48] Kenneth Hagin, *Hear and Be Healed* (Tulsa: Faith Library Publications, 1987), p. 8; pp. 13-14.

[49] Kenneth Hagin, Jr., *God's Irresistible Word* (Tulsa: Faith Library Publications, 1989), p. 36.

[50] Ibid., p. 35.

> ... Jesus always operated as a man while on earth. He operated by faith in God like you and I have to do.[51]

> God wants us to walk in the same dominion and anointing that Jesus Himself experienced on this earth![52] ... Jesus kept His flesh under submission by praying, spending time with the Father.[53]

The metaphysical cults agree. Emmet Fox, a former leader of Unity School Christianity, stated that we can do what Jesus did.[54]

We have already stated that the Word of Faith leaders do not uphold the deity of Christ by either denying that He was fully God while on earth or that He did not function as God in His incarnation. In Capps's books the expression that Jesus was "*back* in His Godhead powers" after His resurrection appears.[55] The statement implies that Jesus was not God while on earth, which is no different than what the Jehovah's Witnesses believe.

I called his office (12/28/90), but Mr. Capps was not in. I asked the lady who answered what this expression "*back* in His Godhead powers" meant. She explained that according to Mr. Capps Jesus was only a man while on earth — not God. I said, "Then Mr. Capps does not hold to the Trinity." She stated that he did. I queried: "How could there be a Trinity if one member — God the Son — were only a man while on earth?" She did not know; apparently she had not thought about it. She could not answer one of the most basic orthodox questions. A letter was written to Capps asking what he meant. Here is his answer:

> Concerning your letter ... and your question about Jesus being back in His Godhead powers after He arose from the dead — You see, the Bible teaches that Jesus laid down His divine power and glory when He came to this earth. (Phil. 2:6-7) The Greek

---

[51] Bob Buess, *The Laws of the Spirit* (Van, TX: Bob Buess, 1968), p. 36.

[52] Gloria Copeland, *Walk in the Spirit*, p. 31.

[53] Ibid., p. 32.

[54] Emmet Fox, *The Seven Main Aspects of God*, (Marina del Rey, CA: DeVorss & Co, 1942), p. 18.

[55] Charles Capps, *Kicking Over Sacred Cows* (England, AR: Charles Capps, 1983), p. 76.

says it this way — that He stripped Himself of His divine power and glory. So Jesus came to the earth as a man. He was the Son of God alright, but He was a man. Read Hebrews 2:14-18 and Hebrews 4:15. This tells us that Jesus was a man, that He was tempted in all points like as we are, yet without sin. He was tempted to do evil just like every man.

James 1:13 says, "let no man say when he is tempted, I am tempted of God, for God cannot be tempted with evil, neither tempteth He any man." If Jesus kept all His Godhead powers while He was here on earth, He could not have been tempted with evil. It would have been impossible, yet I know the scripture says "God was manifest in the flesh." What that is saying is that God was manifest in Jesus' flesh. He is also manifest in your flesh if you have been born-again, for He dwells within you.

The punctuation is the same as in the letter with the exception that the quotation marks he omitted are balanced. The letter is hopelessly confused. If Capps literally means that Jesus laid down His divine power, then He was not omnipotent and not God, and we have a non-Christian writing this letter. He uses the passage (Phil. 2:6, 7) that the liberals in Germany abused last century to try to establish that Jesus gave up His deity when He came to the earth (see *kenosis* below). He said Jesus was the Son of God, but what does he mean by this? There is a clue when he said that we are "God manifested in the flesh" like Jesus because we have God within us, making us and Jesus the same.

To say that Jesus must have been man because He was tempted is to say that He is human. Capps, however, seems to mean by this that He never functioned as God or that He was not God. Neither is acceptable. Of course God cannot be tempted, but Jesus was human. Though He was tempted in all points like us, He was incapable of sin.[56]

---

[56] Capps would reject an impeccable, human Jesus, though the Scriptures clearly teach this. To say that Jesus could not have been functioning as God because He was tempted begs the question, for then we must ask what he means by "tempted." One of the determining questions is what the word "tempt" means. To some it means the possibility of falling into sin. All admit that Jesus *did* not sin, but we confess that He *could* not sin. Good men have been on both sides of this particular issue but the question is whether Jesus was God as well as man and the Person Jesus, consequently, *could not* sin. The great theologian Charles Hodge opted for peccability, *Systematic Theology*, 2:457, while most

Whatever view one adopts of Jesus' temptations, it is nevertheless true that He was both God and man on earth and functioned through both natures. Another letter was written to Capps to ask for clarification regarding the deity of Christ *while on earth*. Here is his answer:

> No, you did not understand me correctly. I did not say that Jesus was only a man. I said that Jesus was a man. . . . Jesus was also the Son of God, yet He was not operating as God while he was here on earth. . . . He came to the earth as a man. He was the divine Son of God. Yet He came to the earth as a man because it [sic] had to be a man to redemn [sic] man, but he also had to be sinless. . . . He was equal with the [sic] God the Father in unity and purpose. that [sic] is why He said "if you have seen me, you have seen the Father" because the Father dwelled in Him and did the works of God the way God works through us today. . . . Concerning the Trinity being temporarily voided during His life on the earth — The Bible does not say, so I have no idea.

Again the punctuation and spelling are his. At best the man is hopelessly confused, and at worst he is no better than the Jehovah's Witnesses who deny His deity and who also maintain that Jesus was one with the Father in unity and purpose but not in essence. That he does deny His deity is obvious, for according to him we are the same as Jesus since we have God *indwelling us*. This is *not* the incarnation. Jesus did not simply have God dwelling *in* Him, He was God in very essence. If He only had God indwelling Him and we have the same, then obviously Jesus was not uniquely God.

The conclusive point is his comment on the Trinity, for the Bible is completely clear that God cannot cease to be Himself, that Jesus never gave up His deity, that the Trinity has always been just that, one God *eternally* existing in three equal Persons, Who are the same in substance, equal in power and glory. Therefore, he is not evangelical. (See heading "What Is Evangelicalism?" on page 7 and following.) Lest someone thinks we are being unkind, remember that this is

---

have disagreed with him. In theology class, the question is often asked this way: Was Jesus not able to sin or able not to sin? But what does it mean to be "tempted" if Jesus could not sin? "Is it possible to attempt the impossible?" John F. Walvoord, *Jesus Christ Our Lord*, (Chicago: Moody Press, 1969), p. 147.

the heart of the Gospel. Remember what Paul said in Galatians 1:8. There can be no compromise here.

In another place, Capps denies that Jesus was unique:

> This points out that we should see ourselves as Jesus was. We should walk in the same authority, power, and dominion that Jesus exercised when He walked this earth.[57]

Kenneth Hagin, Jr. agrees that Jesus was not unique, for ". . . we have the same power available to us today that was available when Jesus walked on the earth."[58] Did Jesus do all those miracles because He was God? Again Hagin, Jr. says: "No, He did not. It was because He was anointed with the Holy Spirit that He was able to do all the miraculous things He did."[59] All through the booklet, *Because of Jesus*, Hagin, Jr. spoke of the majesty of Jesus and called Him Man numerous times, but not once did he say that Jesus was equal with the Father.

Are We One with the Father?

In the claim that we are one with the Father, we see the pantheism of the movement surfacing. Russell of the Unity School states: "As we accept Jesus' statement, 'I and the Father are one,' we pass from belief in God to realization of God."[60] Again, "The primary purpose of spiritual therapy is to establish the Consciousness of Oneness with this Allness."[61] To the normal mind, these statements are confusing, but Russell means that we and "God" are one.

Emilie Cady of Unity School Christianity stated that we are one with the Father,[62] and "The ultimate aim of every man should be to come into the consciousness of an indwelling God."[63] Mary Baker Eddy of Christian Science affirmed: "Jesus of Nazareth [they love the expression 'Jesus of Naz-

---

[57] Charles Capps, *God's Image of You* (Tulsa: Harrison House, 1985), p. 32.

[58] Kenneth Hagin, Jr., *Because of Jesus* (Tulsa: Faith Library Publications, 1989), p. 3.

[59] Ibid., p. 4.

[60] Russell, *God Works*, p. 141.

[61] Ibid., p. 142.

[62] H. Emilie Cady, *Lessons in Truth* (Unity Village, MO: Unity Books, no date), p. 7.

[63] Ibid., p. 15.

areth'] taught and demonstrated man's oneness with the Father...."[64]

Kenyon, promoting the same idea, stated: "We are of His own substance."[65] Again he said: "We are become partakers of His own nature."[66] Likewise Kenneth Copeland says: "We are to become one with the Father as Jesus was one with Him."[67] The truth, however, is that Jesus and the Father are one in essence; we are only creatures. The Bible is clear that a great chasm exists in terms of the creature being qualitatively and immensely different from the Creator, and any mixing of man with God is pantheism.

Did Jesus Empty Himself of His Deity?

Again the Word of Faith movement's ignorance of theology and of history has led them into heresy. Last century there was a new theory about the Person of Christ. From a twisting of Philippians 2:7, German liberal theologians concluded that Jesus *emptied* (from the Greek word *kenoô* and thus termed the *kenosis* theory)[68] Himself of His deity and that He was changed into a man entirely, and increased in wisdom and power until He again resumed His deity after the resurrection.[69] Other liberal theologians maintained that He emptied Himself of His eternal attributes (omniscience, omnipresence, omnipotence) while retaining His internal ones (love, compassion, etc.).

In a similar vein, Kenyon says of Philippians 2: "Here is a being with whom God performs a miracle: first by taking Him out of the Godhead or from the Godhead in heaven and placing Him in the womb of a Virgin to be unioned with flesh by a unique conception."[70] Of course, "taking Him out of the

---

[64] Mary Baker Eddy, *Science and Health*, p. 18.

[65] E. W. Kenyon, *From the Cross to the Throne*, p. 64.

[66] Ibid.

[67] Kenneth Copeland, *The Force of Righteousness*, p. 9.

[68] See Warfield's comments in *Christology and Criticism*, p. 375ff.

[69] Louis Berkhof, *The History of Christian Doctrines* (Carlisle, PA: Banner of Truth, 1937), p. 120; see also G. C. Berkouwer, *The Person of Christ* (Grand Rapids: Wm. B. Eerdmans Pub. Co., 1977), p. 27ff. This is similar to the heresy of adoptionism that the early fathers condemned.

[70] Kenyon, *The Father and His Family*, p. 135.

Godhead" would mean that the Trinity would be suspended, at least temporarily, while God the Son was on earth, a most horrendous concept. Such terrible teaching is in fact "incarnation by divine suicide."[71]

There are some things unthinkable and impossible for God, such as that He could sin or cease to be God. A few biblical citations should suffice to demonstrate that God cannot cease to be God: "Before the mountains were brought forth, or ever You had formed the earth and the world, even from everlasting to everlasting, You are God" (Ps. 90:2). In Hebrews 1:11, 12; 13:8, God declares that Jesus is the same forever; He has not changed. The heavens may change but Jesus will not. If He gave up His deity, not only did the Triune God change, but Jesus changed. Furthermore, if Jesus gave up His deity, then how could we understand the passages that say He upholds all things by the word of His power (Col. 1:17; Heb. 1:3)? Who was doing this while He was on earth? If we rightly understand that He was fully God while on earth, as the church has for two thousand years, then Jesus was upholding all things even while He was also a Man.

On his television show, Pat Robertson answered a question from a lady who said: "When did Jesus become aware of Who He was and what His mission was?" I was dumbfounded at the question, thinking that Pat would quickly set her straight. He did not. Instead, he spoke of Jesus slowly coming into consciousness of His mission as He matured, apparently thinking that Jesus had "ceased from His cosmic functions and His eternal consciousness, and reduced Himself absolutely to the conditions and limits of human nature."[72] This is the *kenosis* theory of Jesus, patently unbiblical. Even when He was twelve years old, He instructed His human parents that He must be about His Father's business (Luke 2:49). Certainly on the human level He developed (Luke 2:52), but on the divine level He was infinite in every capacity conceivable.

To think of Jesus born simply as a man and gradually realizing His God-consciousness and finally becoming God at the resurrection, is to posit two persons in Christ, the human

---

[71] Berkhof, *History*, p. 121.

[72] Ibid., p. 121.

Jesus and the divine Christ, which is what gnosticism does. And it is logically impossible for a finite being to make the leap to being infinite.

The Christian Science leaders readily proclaim that Jesus and Christ are two persons, adding that all of us can partake of the same "Christ" that Jesus partook of. We can and should, they say, imitate His life by the power of the same "Christ life" that came on Him at His baptism. The Word of Faith people call this the baptism in the Holy Spirit and Christian Science people refer to it as the "Christ" descending on Him. Though the terms are different, the substance is the same. (Not all charismatics who hold to the baptism in the Holy Spirit are this far off base; they are in error but not heresy.)

Let us look at the whole passage:

> (6) Who, being in the form of God, did not consider it robbery to be equal with God, (7) but made Himself of no reputation, taking the form of a servant, and coming in the likeness of men (Phil. 2:6, 7).

Verse six definitely states that He existed as God. The word "form" "means the essential attributes."[73] When Paul says: "did not consider it robbery," he means "a prize to be held on to rather than something to be won."[74] Paul emphatically states that Jesus was equal with God. There is a subtle difference between the words "being" and "coming." The former is the present participle emphasizing continual existence as God, while the latter is the aorist participle emphasizing a new thing, "coming" in the likeness of men. The "new thing" was His human nature.

His Deity	His Humanity
Present ptcp: "being" in form of God	Aorist ptcp: "became" in likeness of men
Eternal existence	Added humanity
Form or *morphe* is essential nature	Form or *schema* is external or appearance
Preincarnate as God	Incarnate as God-man

---

[73] A. T. Robertson, *Word Pictures in the New Testament* (Nashville: Broadman Press, 1933), 4:444.

[74] Ibid.

In regard to Philippians 2:7, the Greek word for "emptied" usually means "to make void" (Rom. 4:14; 1 Cor. 9:15; 2 Cor. 9:3). Its only other occurrence in the New Testament is Philippians 2:7, and its meaning is debated. Most consider it to mean that He emptied Himself, but the question is, what does "empty" mean? The words before it (v. 6) indicate that Paul does not mean that He gave up His deity, for Paul emphasizes that He continues (present participle) in the form of God. The participles after "empty" in verse seven, however, give us some clues: He took (aorist participle) on the form of a servant, and became (aorist participle) a man. We have the same contrast in John 1 with Jesus eternally existing as God: "Word *was* God," (v. 1, imperfect tense) and yet He *became* (aorist tense) flesh (v. 14). The aorist tenses indicate the *beginning* of His humanity while the present and imperfect tenses emphasize the *continuing* of His deity.

What did Jesus give up then? First, He gave up the outward display of His glory which He had eternally with the Father, for He was found as a man, as any other man, with no beauty that we should desire Him (Isa. 53:3). He had this glory with the Father in eternity (John 17:5); He veiled it in His human flesh as the tabernacle outwardly did not look beautiful but inwardly was full of precious jewels;[75] He displayed it at His transfiguration (Matt. 17:1ff).

After His Ascension He is only seen in His glory. When Paul saw Him, he was blinded. When John saw Him, he fell at His feet as dead. Steven only saw a vision then died from the stones. (Those in our day who claim to talk with Jesus as one would with a friend are liars. They would be consumed with His glory.)

The second aspect of His "emptying" Himself is that He gave up His absolute authority and became a servant, for "though He was a Son, yet He learned obedience by the things which He suffered" (Heb. 5:8). Though His power continued after His incarnation as seen in that He "upholds all things by the word of His power" (Heb. 1:3), yet His authority as a man was subject to the Father. As a man He obeyed God's law, and as the substitute for His elect He obeyed God

---

[75] In John 1:14 the Greek says He tabernacled among us, and John said by faith he saw that He was really the Son of God, the only begotten of the Father!

perfectly.

Thirdly, He gave up His favorable relation to divine law, "having redeemed us from the curse of the law" (Gal. 3:13), having been made sin for us that we might receive righteousness (2 Cor. 5:21). As God, He is above the law and is the final Judge, but as man He took our curse of God's law in our place.

It is interesting to notice the prosperity reaction. Fred Price said that the curse was poverty and lack.[76] His reasoning is that there are only two blessings from God: material and spiritual (notice again the gnostic dualism). Abraham, of whom Paul is speaking in this Galatians 3:13, could not have been born again, as no Old Testament person was born again or a Christian. He reasons such because Jesus was supposedly the first Person born again, and He had not come yet. Thus Paul could not have been speaking of salvation regarding Abraham, implying that Paul must be speaking of a material curse. Yet when we look at the context, we see that such is not the case:

> Just as Abraham believed God, and it was accounted to him for righteousness. Therefore know that [only] those who are of faith are sons of Abraham. And the Scripture, foreseeing that God would justify the nations by faith, preached the gospel to Abraham beforehand, saying, "In you all the nations shall be blessed" (Gal. 3:6-8).
>
> For you are all sons of God through faith in Christ Jesus (Gal. 3:26).
>
> And if you are Christ's, then you are Abraham's seed, and heirs according to the promise (Gal. 3:29).

The curse is eternal destruction. Poverty *is* part of the curse of the law, but like sickness it is the result of the curse. Just as Jesus took our sicknesses by taking our sins, so He took our poverty by taking our spiritual curse. There is no separation between physical and spiritual as these modern gnostics assume. And of course, there is no guarantee that we shall be wealthy in this life anymore than we shall be without sickness in this life.

Another passage they use to say that Jesus was not God while He was on earth is 2 Corinthians 8:9: "You know the

---

[76]TBN, 12 midnight, WPTY, Memphis, TN, 05/11/92.

grace of our Lord Jesus Christ, that though He was rich, yet for your sakes He became poor, that you through His poverty might become rich." That He gave up riches says nothing of giving up His deity. As Warren Wiersbe so accurately states it:

> Jesus shed His blood to satisfy the holy law of God so that lost sinners might be forgiven and reconciled to God. Jesus didn't die to make us healthy, wealthy, and happy; He died to make us holy. To turn Calvary into a sanctified credit card that gives us the privilege of a hedonistic shopping spree is to cheapen the most costly thing God ever did.[77]

The Work of Christ

The Orthodox Teaching

It was necessary that Jesus *function* as both God and man in order to be the Redeemer, not simply as man or simply as God. As Charles Hodge rightly summarizes:

> ... it follows that although the divine nature is immutable and impassable, and therefore neither the obedience nor the suffering of Christ was the obedience or suffering of the divine nature, yet they were none the less the obedience and suffering of a divine person. The soul of man cannot be wounded or burnt, but when the body is injured it is the man who suffers. In like manner the obedience of Christ was the righteousness of God, and the blood of Christ was the blood of God. It is to this fact that the infinite merit and efficiency of his work are due. This is distinctly asserted in the Scriptures. It is impossible, says the Apostle, that the blood of bulls and goats could take away sin. It was because Christ was possessed of an eternal Spirit that He by the one offering of Himself hath perfected forever them who are sanctified (Heb. 9:14; 10:10, 12, 14). This is the main idea insisted upon in the Epistle to the Hebrews.[78]

It was the God-man who shed His blood (Acts 20:28), and the God-man Who had His hands and side pierced so that Thomas confessed Him as God (John 20:28). The Father sent

---

[77] Michael G. Moriarty, *The New Charismatics* (Grand Rapids: Zondervan Publishing House, 1992), p. 316.

[78] Hodge, *Systematic Theology*, 2:395.

the eternal Son to be the savior (Matt. 1:23; John 3:16, 17). To merge His deity into His humanity by suppression (He only functioned as a man) or to eradicate it by saying He laid it aside, denies the Gospel. *We are not speaking of minor differences but of the very essence of the Gospel.*

He had to be God to satisfy infinite righteousness, and He had to man to be like His brethren (Heb. 2:14, 15). What He accomplished as the divine-human Savior is what is called penal substitution. (See paragraph beginning with "Jesus took our guilt" on page 130ff for the biblical presentation of this.) The very heart and essence of Christianity is the God-man Who was perfectly obedient to the law of God in our place, and Who took the penalty of God's law and the wrath of God in our place. By functioning as man He obeyed and died in our place, and by functioning as God His obedience and death receives infinite merit. Anything less than this is not the Gospel.

How did Christ accomplish this? How was He our personal substitute? "We do not dream of a . . . transfer of personal acts, or of the personal attributes expressed in such acts."[79] In other words, Jesus was our substitute officially, as the legal head, but not personally. To elaborate, Jesus did not become a sinner for us, and He personally was never a sinner nor did He ever assume any of our personal sins. To believe such is heresy.[80]

If the Lord's penal satisfaction is denied, logical consistency leads people to deny other biblical doctrines. One of these is God's immutable attribute of righteousness, which demands justice and judgment. God is now seen only as love (the curse of our age!), not as One who is infinitely holy. "They give us a God of expediency, instead of a God of righteous and eternal principles."[81] They promote a God of compromise, instead of a God who upholds His righteous standard

---

[79] R. L. Dabney, *Christ Our Penal Substitute* (Harrisonburg, VA: Sprinkle Publications, 1978), p. 11.

[80] George Smeaton in *The Doctrine of the Atonement According to Christ* (1871, rpt. 1979, Winona Lake, IN: Alpha Publications) explains this as the difference between "the personal and official capacity of our Lord," p. 158. Dabney uses different words, potential and actual guilt (ibid., pp. 10-11), but arrives at the same conclusion.

[81] Dabney, *Christ Our Penal Substitute*, p. 93.

without compromise. The God of the Bible requires justice so He sends His Son to uphold it and to take the punishment of His people. The "God" that these compromisers promote needs to offer satisfaction to Satan!

If Jesus was not subjected to all He went through by divine plan but by Satan, then we are at the mercy, not of a loving God who directs providence, but of the god of this world. The only way we can defeat him is by learning to use spiritual law. But as Dabney rightly said, they have made redemption depend on what man does, making God's love the main point in salvation rather than His righteousness.[82] According to them, God in His love has done all He can, and now it is "up to man" to keep His plan from being a failure by learning to use spiritual laws, by allowing God to save him.

The whole plan of redemption, according to the prosperity teachers, is turned on its head: God gave Adam the earth. Adam in turn lost it to Satan so that ever since the world has *legally* belonged to Satan. From then on man is born with Satan's nature (whatever that is). God has no legal authority on earth. In the words of Fred Price, "If God came here He would be trespassing, for He has no legal right here."[83] There was no new birth in the Old Testament; there could not be such until Jesus came. When Jesus came, He "operated" only as a man by the "anointing" of the Holy Spirit. The miracles He did we can do by the same Holy Spirit. When He died, He had not finished the plan of redemption but had to go to hell to compensate Satan. While in hell, He received Satan's nature and literally became a sinner. Satan and the demons tortured Him for three days and nights. Since Jesus had never personally sinned, legally Satan could not hold Him. But Jesus still had Satan's nature so God made Jesus righteous, justified Him, and caused Him to be the first one ever to be born again. Then the Father raised Him from the dead to exercise dominion. When we are justified, we receive the Father's very nature, which is also the new birth. It is not possible to blaspheme more than this.

---

[82] Ibid., p. 94.

[83] TBN, 12 midnight, Memphis, TN in May/June, 1992.

Did Jesus Descend to Hell to Pay Off Satan?

Not only are the health and wealth preachers wrong about the Person of Christ, but they are also heretical about His work. They have resurrected the heretical doctrine of early church history regarding the atonement that the fathers rejected: the ransom to Satan theory, which is explained by Hodge:

> The [theory] appeals to the old principle of the rights of war, according to which the conquered became the slaves of the conqueror. Satan conquered Adam, and thus became the rightful owner of him and his posterity. Hence he is called the god and prince of this world. To deliver men from this dreadful bondage, Christ offered Himself as a ransom to Satan. Satan accepted the offer, and renounced his right to retain mankind as his slaves.
>
> In answer to the question, How Satan could accept Christ as the ransom for men, if he knew Him to be a divine person? It was said that he did know Him to be divine, because His divinity was veiled by His humanity.[84]

The following statements by the Word of Faith leaders validate what Hodge has summarized, revealing that the Word of Faith leaders have revived this ancient heresy:

> He [Jesus] must be born out of spiritual death into life, that Paul may say that "He is the first-born from the dead, the Head of the Church."
>
> Then when He is Made Alive in that dark domain of Hell, He must meet Satan, the strong, and conquer him, binding him in his own house and taking away the arms in which he is trusting: Paul graphically puts it, "He put off from Himself the principalities and powers, and made a show of them openly, triumphing over them." This is a vivid picture of Jesus in Hell with all the hosts of demons upon Him seeking to keep Him prisoner in their dark kingdom.[85]
>
> If the physical death of Jesus paid the penalty of man's transgressions, then sin is but a physical fact.

---

[84]Hodge, *Systematic Theology*, 2:564; see also Philip Schaff, *History of the Christian Church* (Grand Rapids: Wm. B. Eerdmans Pub., Co., 1910), 2:585ff.

[85]Kenyon, *The Father and His Family*, pp. 149-50.

But we hold that the physical death of Jesus did not touch the sin issue at all; it was only a means to an end, and the real suffering of Jesus, the Substitute, must be spiritual as well as physical [notice the gnostic and metaphysical dualism].[86]

Can God demand spiritual suffering from the human race, that is, suffering in Hell, if His Substitute only suffered physically? . . . Can God justly send the human race to Hell, and finally into the Lake of Fire, the great Federal Prison of Eternity, unless His Son went to Hell and suffered there for the human race? . . . If He [Jesus] goes to Hell and suffers for the human race, then God stands vindicated and man is silent. Man no longer has a case against God for He has sent out of Heaven His own Son who has come to the earth and has paid the penalty of man's guilt without asking man to have any part in the awful transaction.[87]

Why has God not disposed of the Devil if He has the power to do it; why has He permitted Satan to rule the earth and cause so much misery, if He is God Almighty. . . . Adam evidently had a legal right to transfer this dominion and authority into the hands of the enemy. God has been obliged through the long period of human history to recognize Satan's legal standing, and legal right and authority, and on this ground, and this only, can we understand the legal side of the Plan of Redemption. . . . He is Almighty, but He has never taken advantage of Satan.[88]

Man at the dawn of human history became a partaker of Satanic nature. That nature was breathed into his spirit by the Devil, and man became a subject of Satan.[89]

The very moment the sin problem was settled, that moment Jesus Christ was legally justified, was made alive in spirit once more, and assumed His wonderful dominion, authority, and power. Hurling back the hosts of demons, He became the Master of Hell; putting them off from Himself, He hurled them hopeless and powerless back into the dark abyss.[90]

---

[86] Ibid., p. 151.
[87] Ibid., pp. 151-52.
[88] Ibid., pp. 47-48.
[89] Ibid., p. 51.
[90] Ibid., p. 172.

We understand that God created man, placing him here on the earth, and that He conferred upon him certain legal rights. Legal rights that are conferred are more easily forfeited than those that come by nature. These rights man transferred to Satan, God's enemy.

That brings the Devil into the plan so that he must be dealt with, and the whole scheme of Redemption is God's seeking to redeem the human race from Adam's sin, and doing it upon such an equitable basis that it will perfectly satisfy the claims of Justice, meet the needs of man, and defeat Satan on legal grounds. . . . He must do it in such a way as not to be unjust to Satan, nor unjust to man. . . . Satan has Legal Rights over the sinner that God cannot dispute or challenge.[91]

When Jesus died, His spirit was taken by the Adversary, and carried to the place where the sinner's spirit goes when he dies.[92] . . . The eighty-eighth Psalm gives us a foreview of the substitutionary sacrifice of Jesus in Hades.[93] . . . Colossians 2:15 gives a description of a battle that took place in Hades before Jesus arose from the dead.[94] . . . On the cross, Satan believed he had that Man [Jesus] at his mercy. For three days and three nights he caused that Man to suffer beyond anything that the human imagination can dream.[95]

Satan had conquered Jesus on the Cross.[96] . . . I was asked, "Do you think Satan knew about all this before? Didn't he know what Christ was doing on the Cross? Didn't he know that if Christ went to Hell He would conquer him?" . . . Satan knew nothing of it.[97] . . . For three days and three nights He had gone through the agonies of the Eternities to redeem man and justify God. . . . It is the beginning of the New Redemption, a Spiritual Redemption. It is Redemption from Satan.[98]

---

[91] Ibid., pp. 247, 248, 251.

[92] Kenyon, *What Happened*, p. 47.

[93] Ibid., p. 59.

[94] Ibid., p. 65.

[95] Ibid., p. 88.

[96] Ibid., p. 89.

[97] Ibid., pp. 90-91.

[98] Ibid., pp. 93, 141.

Jesus primary purpose in coming to earth was to destroy the Devil's works.[99]

Very little refutation is needed. First, man by sin became subject to the penalty of God's law and so did Satan.[100] When man sinned, the woman blamed the man, the man accused Satan, but God judged all three. Satan did not have much dominion then, but God exercised His dominion over all. There is not even a hint that God gave up dominion or that Satan then came to own the earth. The penalty of sin is death (Rom. 6:23), a death imposed by the righteous judgment of God (Gal. 3:10; see also Rom. 1:18, 32; 2:3).

Secondly, it is true that Satan afflicts us and that Christ destroyed him and his works (1 John 3:8), but the primary reason Christ came, contrary to Capps, is to uphold the righteousness of God, to satisfy the judgment of God, *"to demonstrate at the present time His righteousness, that He might be just* and the justifier of the one who has faith in Jesus" (Rom. 3:26). There are many benefits to Christ's death: the defeat of Satan, the restoring of the world from the curse (Rom. 8:20-22), one day being completely made holy and free from all sickness, and many other things. These are not, however, the essence of the atonement but the fruits. The essence is being justified, having God's wrath removed.

Thirdly, when Kenyon quoted Colossians 2:15 above, saying that those events happened when Jesus was in hell, he conveniently omitted the rest of the verse: "Having disarmed principalities and powers, He made a public spectacle of them, triumphing over them *in it.*" He left out the italicized words *in it.* To what do these refer? The Greek word for *it* is a relative pronoun that refers back to the word *cross* in the previous verse.[101] Notice the context, again conveniently omitted by Kenyon: "Having wiped out the handwriting of requirements that was against us, which was contrary to us. And He has taken it out of the way, having nailed it to the *cross.*" Christ did not go to hell to pay off Satan, but Christ *on*

---

[99] Capps, *Authority in Three Worlds*, p. 125.

[100] I am indebted to Hodge for most of these insights, *Systematic Theology*, 2:565ff.

[101] A relative pronoun agrees with its antecedent in gender and number, and the *it* so agrees with *cross* in v. 14.

the Cross satisfied *God's* moral law (the "handwriting of requirements"). (See Appendix 5: Did Jesus Go to Hell?)

"It Is Finished"

According to the prosperity gospel men, the atonement was not finished when Jesus said these final words. According to them, the Lord still had to descend to hell to satisfy Satan.

> He cried, "It is finished," and yields up His Spirit. . . . He does not mean that His substitutionary work is finished, for that could not be until He rose from the dead and carried the tokens of His victory into the Heaven's Holy of Holies, laying them down before the Father. . . . Now He must go into the dreaded regions and pay the penalty of our sinful nature. . . . The real suffering of Gethsemane was this: He [Jesus] saw that as a sin-substitute He must be separated from His Father and must become a subject of Satan, and more than that, that He must become sin.[102]

> Many have thought that when Jesus said on the cross, "It is finished" He was talking about our salvation. No! No! No! Our salvation wasn't finished when Jesus died. Remember He said to Mary, "Touch me not; for I am not yet ascended to my Father. . . ." (John 20:17). Soon afterwards He appeared to the disciples . . . He said, "Why are ye troubled? and why do thoughts arise in your hearts? Behold my hands and my feet, that it is I myself: handle me, and see. . . ." (Luke 24:38, 39) Why did Jesus tell Mary not to touch Him, and the disciples to touch Him? . . . So salvation wasn't complete until He ascended into the heavenly Holy of Holies to obtain eternal redemption for us.[103]

> As Jesus hung on the cross, He said, **It is finished** (John 19:30) . . . He didn't mean God's plan for redemption was finished. He was saying that **the last sacrifice to be offered under the Old Covenant was finished** [emphasis his].[104]

> The cross is actually a place of defeat. . . .[105]

---

[102] Kenyon, *The Father and His Family*, pp. 173-75.

[103] Kenneth Hagin, *ZOE: The God-Kind of Life* (Tulsa: Faith Library Publications, 1989), p. 43.

[104] Capps, *Authority in Three Worlds*, p. 141.

[105] Kenneth E. Hagin, *The Believer's Authority* (Tulsa: Faith Library

Another Jesus? 341

There are several objections to these quotes. First, the statement by Hagin that Jesus said not to touch Him (John 20:17) and then to touch Him is based on the King James Version, whereas the Greek actually says, "Stop clinging to Me."[106]

Secondly, Jesus meant precisely that redemption was completed. That the Lord Jesus was made a curse for us while He hung on the Cross is abundantly clear, as Paul stated: "Christ has redeemed us from the curse of the law, having become a curse for us (for it is written, *'Cursed is everyone who hangs on a tree'*)" (Gal. 3:13). The plan of redemption was coming to a climax. The Lord of glory demonstrated that He had been numbered with the transgressors by the following: His arrest as if He were a criminal, His ecclesiastical trial where He was accused of blasphemy, the mockery and shame of the people, His secular trial where He was condemned to die after being found innocent by Pilate, and His crucifixion. All these indicate that He was engaged in atonement, and Hebrews says it was "once for all" (Heb. 10:10, 12, 14).

Furthermore, notice how Smeaton beautifully explains "it is finished."

> After these hours of inconceivable sorrow and desertion on the cross, under a darkness which just resembled the blackness awaiting the lost, the Lord felt that His work was accomplished; and He gave utterance to that saying which has brought light, rest, and liberty to so many minds: "It is finished" (John 19:30).[107] He meant that the expiatory sufferings had reached their climax, and were sufficient; that the guilt of mankind was fully atoned for; that there was nothing left undone; that God and man were reunited and reconciled;

Publications, 1992), p. 16.

[106] It is a negative present imperative, which often, though not always, means to stop doing what one is now in the act of doing. Most modern translations agree with this rendering. The Amplified Bible, which the new charismatics prefer, translates "Do not cling to Me," which correctly implies that she was touching Him. (Some have correctly referred to the Amplified as the "multiple choice Bible.") The New American Standard Bible also renders it as I have. Jesus did not make two Ascensions, a secret one after His conversation with Mary and a public one in the presence of His disciples.

[107] As Smeaton explains, this did not refer to all prophecies finished but to His vicarious suffering as finished.

and now He had but to resign His spirit into His Father's hands. As Priest and victim, He had now only one act to perform — to lay down His life by the priestly act of commending His spirit to God. Nature was not exhausted, nor did life ooze away; for He still had power over His life, and no man took it from Him (John 10:18). After having done all and endured all, He deemed it fitting, without more delay, to resign His life or spirit into His Father's hand as an acceptable sacrifice. It was the High Priest offering up His soul to God that said, "Father, into Thy hands I commend my spirit." And He uttered it with a loud voice, to show that strength still remained in Him, and that, by His own authority, He released the spirit from the lacerated and wounded body.[108]

Let us summarize the events around John 19:30. Darkness indicated the wrath of God and the outer darkness of the lost. The hyssop (v. 29) was used in the Passover offering (Ex. 12:22; Num. 19:6, 18), and the whole proceedings here were done at the time of the Passover (v. 31). Passover was the yearly sacrifice of the lamb. Jesus was very conscious of fulfilling Scripture and of His mission (v. 28; Mark 10:45). Furthermore, most significantly the veil of the temple was torn in two from the top to the bottom (Matt. 27:51; Mark 15:38; Luke 23:45),[109] which separated the people from the very presence of God. Only the high priest was allowed to enter the holy of holies and only once a year, but when Jesus died and said "it is finished" God revealed in the most clear manner possible that redemption was now completed. No more would the high priest enter the holiest once a year, for now the *final* High Priest, even Jesus, had entered with His own blood making the perfect and once for all sacrifice (Heb. 9:7-8, 24-27). In light of all this, surely "Christ, our Passover, was sacrificed for us" (1 Cor. 5:7), and this statement ("It is finished") indicated that redemption was completed. Virtually all commentators on John 19:30 agree with our interpretation, which has been the church's view for hundreds of years.

---

[108] Smeaton, *Doctrine of the Atonement*, pp. 181-2.

[109] "Top to bottom" probably indicated that salvation was from God to man, not something man offers to God.

And what about His resurrection? Was it a part of the atonement? Yes and no.[110] It certainly was the Father's "Amen" to the Son's "It is finished." Without the bodily resurrection of Jesus we are still in our sins (1 Cor. 15:17), but "The resurrection of the Lord does not enter into the meritorious part of the Redeemer's work. . . ."[111] Rather, "The atonement and resurrection stand to each other in the relation of service and reward, of cause and effect."[112]

Conclusion

If we give the Word of Faith leaders the best construction in their view of Christ, that Jesus was God and man but only functioned as a man, they are still guilty of great heresy, which the Church has opposed for 2,000 years. It may sound innocuous to say that Jesus did not function as God while on earth, but such a concept rips out the very heart of the Gospel. The early Church was known by its uncompromising stand for orthodoxy while the late twentieth century Church is known by its refusal to oppose anything. "Tolerance" and "love" are the buzz-words of today, which is idolatry if the Gospel is compromised. It is idolatry because we give deference to man before we do to God, His Word, and His truth. If we are unwilling to condemn — and condemn clearly, forcefully, and consistently — the ancient heresies that the early Church gave its life for, we are good for nothing but to be spewed out of the mouth of Christ.[113] The Word of Faith movement is such a heresy. The most basic doctrine of the Church universal has been the Trinity and the two natures of God and man in the one person, Jesus, with both natures fully functioning. *Any* compromise here rings the death knell for the late twentieth century church, bringing us under His judgment.

The whole Christian church, Roman Catholic, Greek Orthodox, and Protestant, has with one voice maintained *both* that the Person of Christ was God and man in one Person *and*

---

[110] For the exposition of Rom. 4:25, see John Murray's commentary on Romans.

[111] Smeaton, *The Doctrine of the Atonement*, p. 183.

[112] Ibid.

[113] See R. J. Rushdoony, *The Foundations of Social Order* (Fairfax, VA: Thoburn Press, 1968), pp. 100ff.

functioned with both natures on earth, *and* that His work was a substitution and penal satisfaction rendered to God for the breaking of His law by us. One must not take lightly the universal voice of Christendom.[114] But these self-proclaimed Word of Faith "scholars" have denied these things. They may seem to affirm some things; but when one evaluates their definitions of evangelical terms, they actually deny them.

If Christ received the nature of Satan in His person, was a sinner needing to be born again, either was not God or did not function as God, offered a payment to Satan in hell, then what is left of the Gospel? What more could possibly be distorted? The words of God through Paul could not be more appropriate:

> But I fear, lest somehow, as the serpent deceived Eve by his craftiness, so your minds may be corrupted from the simplicity that is in Christ. For if he who comes preaches another Jesus whom we have not preached, or if you receive a different spirit which you have not received, or a different gospel which you have not accepted, you may well put up with it. For such are false apostles, deceitful workers, transforming themselves into apostles of Christ. And no wonder! For Satan himself transforms himself into an angel of light. Therefore it is no great thing if his ministers also transform themselves into ministers of righteousness, whose end will be according to their works (2 Cor. 11:3, 4, 13-15).

---

[114]Dabney, op. cit., p. 99ff. Lest we are misunderstood, we are not saying that the Roman Catholic church or the Greek church preaches a pure Gospel. When the Roman church teaches that Mary is co-savior and co-redeemer with Christ, when both teach that our human works merit forgiveness of sins and meritoriously determine our final acceptance with God, then they come under the anathema of Galatians 1:8, 9. They rightly confess the Trinity and preach the same Jesus as Paul did regarding His person, but they preach another gospel when they add human works to obtain justification.

13

Another Gospel

New Charismatics and the Gospel

> But even if we, or an angel from heaven, preach any other gospel to you than what we have preached to you, let him be accursed. As we have said before, so now I say again, if anyone preaches any other gospel to you than what you have received, let him be accursed (Gal. 1:8, 9).

As previously stated, there are two ways to destroy the Gospel: by addition and by subtraction. If we add works to the Gospel, as the Roman Catholics do, we are left with no Gospel. If we take away the deity of Christ or His substitutionary work, we are again left with no Gospel. The health and wealth preachers do both. In order to see how they have changed the Gospel, we begin with a discussion of their view of man, which determines to a great extent their view of salvation. Then we will look at their understanding of God, the new birth, faith and works, and other issues in the Gospel.

New Birth

Do We Partake of the Essence of God?

What is the new birth according to new charismatic teaching? What is righteousness? They think that the new birth and righteousness are the same. The new birth is when "God recreated your spirit and gave you His life."[1] They conceive of regeneration as man's spirit impregnated by the nature of God, adding something new to man, and lifting man to the level of deity.

> Yes, Sir! He absolutely makes man a New Creation, imparts His own nature to man, and drives out that cringing fear nature, sin

---

[1] Kenneth Copeland, *The Force of Righteousness* (Ft. Worth: KCP Publications, 1990), p. 12.

nature, Satan nature.²

> When I understood that one could receive Eternal Life — the very nature of God, then I knew that this thing you have been telling us about Righteousness was real.³

> ... we receive God's nature and we become the Righteousness of God in Christ. ... It is the nature of the Father imparted to us.⁴

> We become partakers of the Divine Nature, so that we are righteous by nature and righteous by faith.⁵

This latter quote from Kenyon gives evidence that he does not adhere to a legal righteousness, which is the essence of the Gospel. He confirms this a few pages later:

> When He said my righteous ones shall live by Faith, He is describing a New Creation that has been made righteous with His own nature. ... This is **not** a legal righteousness, **nor a reckoned** righteousness, but the actual impartation of God's own righteous nature [emphasis added].⁶

Kenyon holds to the Roman Catholic concept of justification, that it is practical righteousness. Another way to say this is that Kenyon's justification is the Bible's sanctification. The Bible does not say that we become partaker's of God's essential nature, which would be pantheism.

There are two aspects of righteousness in Scripture for the believer. The first is justification. It is a legal term that means the person is found not guilty and even more is given Christ's righteousness as a free gift. This righteousness does not affect the person himself. The other aspect of righteousness is sanctification, which is moral, not legal. This changes the person into the moral image of Christ on a daily basis. While justification cannot be improved, sanctification is con-

---

²E. W. Kenyon, *The Blood Covenant* (Lynwood, WA: Kenyon's Gospel Publishing Society, 1969), p. 59.

³E. W. Kenyon, *Two Kinds of Righteousness* ((Lynwood, WA: Kenyon's Gospel Publishing Society, 1965), p. 4.

⁴Ibid., p. 10.

⁵Ibid., p. 17.

⁶Ibid., p. 27.

stantly being improved in the believer's life. Both are granted simultaneously so that one either has both or neither. Though we can analyze these two concepts separately, we are not to think of them as two graces. They are one.

Notice the contrast between justification and sanctification:

Justification	Sanctification
A *legal act* by which the righteous Judge acquits me and accepts my person as righteous, though I am still sinful (Rom. 4:1-13; 8:32-34)	An *ethical process* by which the Holy Spirit makes me righteous, conforming me to the moral image of Jesus (Phil. 3:21; Col. 3:10; Rom. 6:1-14; 8:1-16)
Objective: A declaration that the sinner is righteous, which does not affect the sinner's personal pollution within (Gal. 2:16). He is *outwardly* clothed with Christ's righteousness (Phil. 3:9).	*Subjective*: The Spirit works within me to produce faith and Christ-like-ness (Phil. 2:12, 13). I am *inwardly* being made like Jesus (1 John 3:3).
Substitutionary: Based on the death of Christ in my place (1 Peter 2:24; Matt 10:45).	*Not substitutionary*: The Spirit irresistibly enables the sinner himself to do good works (Phil. 2:12, 13; 1 John 3:9; 5:18).
Justification is the *ground* for sanctification, for God cannot conform one to Christ until the sin question of that sinner has been settled (Rom. 5:21-6:2).	Sanctification is justification *in action*, for God will surely continue what He has begun (Phil. 1:6).
Not a process but a once for all completed act (Rom. 5:1).	*A process* that is not completed in this life (1 John 1:6-10; 3:2, 3).
God's work *for* us in Christ two thousand years ago (Rom. 5:8).	God's work *in* us now by the Holy Spirit (2 Thess. 2:13).
Once for all saved from the penalty of the sin of transgressing God's law (Rom. 6:23; 1 John 3:4).	*Being continually saved from the power* of indwelling sin (Eph. 4:20; 1 John 3:9; Rom. 8:11).
Imputed righteousness, which is like a coat worn on the outside.	*Imparted* righteousness, which is being made holy on the inside.
Imputed righteousness gives the sinner eternal and *irrevocable standing* with God.	Imparted righteousness *displays to man* that the sinner belongs to God (Heb. 12:14).

We are not denying that the new birth is necessary or that

we receive righteousness in conversion, but we are saying that in the Gospel we trust only in Jesus and that as a consequence He justifies us, accepts us as His child. If we make our conformity to Christ, our inherent righteousness, the condition to be accepted by God, then we are like Roman Catholics and have denied not only the whole Reformation but also Scripture. If we are accepted only after we are made righteous enough, then we must ask, in light of the fact that we are still sinners, when will we be perfectly righteous? The answer is not in this life, which means that our final acceptance is conditioned on our being good. This is, of course, a human works salvation.

On the other hand, if we believe the Gospel, we understand that God will accept us for what Jesus has done, and then He will make us holy as a consequence. Our acceptance by God is settled, based solely on the merits of Christ. We are accepted by God while still sinners.

If Kenyon and the new charismatics are right, then we receive only the essence of God's nature, which *makes* us righteous, not the legal righteousness of Christ, which either means that we work our way to heaven or that we are perfectly holy and incapable of ever sinning again. Both are wrong.

Someone may object: What about the "divine nature" in 2 Peter 1:4? "By which have been given to us exceedingly great and precious promises, that through these you may be partakers of the divine nature, having escaped the corruption that is in the world through lust." The context indicates that this is not the divine nature in the sense of His substance and essence but in the sense of sanctification. In other words, we partake of His *moral* nature by being conformed to the moral image of Christ. Our characters are being made like Jesus' character, but we will never be the same in essence as Jesus. Consider that Peter says it is through the "precious promises" that we become partakers of the divine nature — not through participating in the Godhead. In the context Peter says "grace and peace" are multiplied to us and that we add "virtues" to our characters, which are "escaping the corruption in the world," and "faith, knowledge, self-control, perseverance, godliness, kindness, and love." Obviously, these are moral qualities, not the essence of God's divine nature.

Kenyon gets even more bizarre: "You see, it is very evident

that the life that is imparted to a man in the new birth enters his blood stream."[7] He even maintained that one could tell if another were born again by chemically analyzing his blood. This is too ridiculous to need refutation. Is this impartation of God's nature to us unique to Kenyon? Sadly, no:

> It is, in reality, God imparting His very **nature, substance,** and **being** into our human spirits [emphasis added].[8]

> Then eternal life is the nature of God. It is the being or substance of God.[9]

Do they realize that they have departed from the basic message of the church? Yes:

> The fact that in the new birth we actually receive the nature of God has not been majored by the Church.[10]

We so partake of His nature that we are Jesus:

> Even many in the great body of Full Gospel people do not know that the new birth is a real incarnation. They do not know they are as much sons and daughters of God as Jesus.
>
> ***Jesus was first divine, and then He was human. So He was in the flesh a divine-human being. I was first human, and so were you, but I was born of God, and so I became a human-divine being!*** [emphasis his].[11]

The new birth does not make us Jesus, nor does it cause us to partake of His very essence, or receive God's nature into our human spirits. These things are stated without biblical support because none is available. If God dwells in man's spirit or man's spirit is lifted to the level of deity, then the new birth is not so much a moral renovation as a metaphysical change, changing fallen man into deified man. It is not man's nature that is changed in the new birth but man's moral

---

[7] Kenyon, *What Happened from the Cross to the Throne*, p. 20.

[8] Kenneth E. Hagin, *ZOE: The God-Kind of Life* (Tulsa: Faith Library Publications, 1989), pp. 2.

[9] Ibid., p. 27.

[10] E. W. Kenyon, *The Father and His Family*, p. 205.

[11] Hagin, *ZOE*, p. 40.

depravity or inclinations that are changed. Regeneration is ethical, not metaphysical.

What Is the New Birth?

The new birth is a sovereign act of God whereby (1) He immediately (apart from any human means) imparts new life to us and (2) changes the governing disposition of the soul (the immaterial part of man) from sin to holiness.[12] (For the sovereignty of God and moral aspects, see Appendix Three.) Justification is a legal change of standing from being condemned to being accepted by God. Regeneration is a moral change, the receiving of a new heart. The wicked "heart" of man is renovated so that what he once hated (God and righteousness) he now loves.

Regeneration is a comprehensive work, extending to every part of the soul. In short, regeneration does two things: (1) it is the change, the permanent renovation, of the moral disposition of the soul from an orientation to sin to an orientation to holiness, in addition to the (2) introduction of spiritual life. To put it another way, the person is given eternal life and is made holy so that the power of sin in his life is broken.

The Scriptural proof of this is extensive. In Hebrews 8:10, which quotes Jeremiah 31:33, God states that He shall write His laws on the hearts of His people. If this is not a moral change, one does not exist. In Ezekiel 36:26, 27 it is further stated that the regenerate will have the old heart taken away. Second Corinthians 5:17 says that all things have become new and that the old things have passed away, speaking of the moral renovation that has taken place.

First John was my nemesis for years until I understood regeneration. How could God say that the one who was born again would not love sin and would not practice it any more? I had thought that the regenerate had a choice to live a life of sin or a life of holiness, but John disagreed. I thought we had two natures and that we could function through either one; it was up to us. John does not say this, but I was reading something into his little book. For example, observe how John describes the nature of those born again: they practice right-

---

[12] L. Berkhof, *Systematic Theology* (Grand Rapids: Wm. B. Eerdmans Pub. Co. 1968), p. 469.

eousness (2:29), they cannot practice sin (3:9), they love the brethren (4:7), they overcome the world (5:4), and they believe in Jesus (5:1). To be able to love, obey God, overcome, and believe in Jesus is a total renovation of the *moral* character of the person, not becoming a god.

If the new birth is man becoming God by having His nature become a part of ours, then we do not have New Testament Christianity. In such an idea, salvation is becoming a god, not simply having new life and the ability to live morally. Salvation is metaphysical rather than moral, a pantheistic union of man and deity in lieu of changing man's sinful heart. These ideas are not biblical and not evangelical.

Faith and Works

Are we justified — having our sins forgiven and being given the legal righteousness of Jesus our Substitute — by faith alone or by faith and works? What is the Word of Faith view? They believe that the Old Testament saints were not born again, and that they were justified by works while the New Testament saints are justified by a faith that does not work. Let us begin by examining their views of justification in the Old Testament, and then we shall examine their view of New Testament justification:

Old Testament Justification: Works Without Faith

> [Speaking of Abraham and Old Testament saints] No one on earth had yet received the benefit of His substitutionary sacrifice. No one had yet been born again. No one knew anything about it.[13]

> Under the Old Covenant . . . what you would call laity did not have the Spirit of God upon them or in them.[14]

> I remember something important Jesus said to me once when He appeared to me in a vision. . . . He said, "Israel were not sons of God."

> They never had been born again. They just had a promissory note on redemption.[15]

---

[13] Kenyon, *What Happened*, p. 75.

[14] Kenneth E. Hagin, *How You Can Be Led*, p. 23; see also p. 32.

[15] Kenneth E. Hagin, *Seven Things You Should Know About Divine Healing*

> There were no New Creations, no one was Born Again until the day of Pentecost.[16]
>
> John [the Baptist] was not a born again man, and the people he baptized were not born again.[17]
>
> They weren't born again. They were operating under the Old Covenant.[18]
>
> Under the old covenant there was what we call the old law. People had a limited righteousness under the old law. It was through the law of works.[19]
>
> Under the law, their works made them righteous. But under the New Covenant, righteousness is not by works but by faith.[20]
>
> Gideon was not a reborn man; consequently, he was forced to rely on physical evidence. He had no knowledge of God whatsoever because his entire family were followers of Baal.[21]

How, in the name of all that is biblical, did the Old Testament saints live a godly life? Apparently it was by their works. If they were not born again, did not have the Holy Spirit, and saved themselves by their works, then man saved himself. Is this true? Let's see what the Bible says:

> Jesus answered and said to him [Nicodemus], "Most assuredly, I say to you, unless one is born again, he cannot see the kingdom of God." Nicodemus said to Him, "How can a man be born when he is old? Can he enter a second time into his mother's womb and be born?" Jesus answered and said to him, **"Are you the teacher of Israel, and do not know these things"?** (John 3:3, 4, 10).

What then shall we say that Abraham our father has found

(Tulsa: Faith Library Publications, 1987), p. 20.

[16] Ibid., p. 136.

[17] Charles Capps, *Authority in Three Worlds* ((Tulsa: Harrison House, 1982), p. 122.

[18] Ibid., p. 229.

[19] Charles Capps, *Kicking Over Sacred Cows* (England, AR: Charles Capps, 1983), p. 3.

[20] Charles Capps, *Dynamics of Faith and Confession* (Tulsa: Harrison House, 1987), p. 16.

[21] Kenneth Copeland, *The Force of Righteousness*, pp. 15-16.

Another Gospel?

according to the flesh? For if Abraham was justified by works, he has something of which to boast, but not before God. For what does the Scripture say? "Abraham believed God, and it was accounted to him for righteousness." Now to him who works, the wages are not counted as grace but as debt (Rom. 4:1-4).

And the Scripture, foreseeing that God would justify the nations by faith, **preached the gospel to Abraham beforehand**, saying, "In you all the nations shall be blessed." So then those who are of faith are blessed with believing Abraham. For as many as are of the works of the law are under the curse; for it is written, "Cursed is everyone who does not continue in all things which are written in the book of the law, to do them." For you are all sons of God through faith in Christ Jesus. And if you are Christ's, then you are Abraham's seed, and heirs according to the promise (Gal. 3:8-10, 26, 29).

Isn't it refreshing to see how clear and directly contradictory Scripture is to their theories? Jesus was aghast that Nicodemus did not understand the new birth and was a teacher of Israel. The new birth had "been around" in the Old Testament thus indicating that they were saved men just like us. Furthermore, Paul argues that we are justified just like Abraham: by faith apart from the works of the law. In Galatians Paul says the Gospel was preached to Abraham, "foreseeing that God would justify the nations by faith." In other words, we are justified the same way Abraham was: by faith in Messiah.

The Apostles declare Old Testament salvation to be by faith alone in Messiah:

> Of Him all the prophets bear witness that through His name every one who believes in Him has received forgiveness of sins (Acts 10:43).

> By faith Moses, when he had grown up, refused to be called the son of Pharaoh's daughter; choosing rather to endure ill-treatment with the people of God, than to enjoy the passing pleasures of sin; considering the reproaches of **Christ greater riches than the treasures of Egypt** (Heb. 11:24-26). [Obviously Moses was a believer in Christ.]

> Seeking to know what person or time the Spirit of Christ within

them was indicating as He predicted the sufferings of Christ and the glories to follow (1 Peter 1:11).

All were baptized into Moses in the cloud and in the sea; and all ate the same spiritual food; and all drank the same drink, for they were drinking from a spiritual rock which followed them; and the rock was **Christ** (1 Cor. 10:2-4).

Paul . . . set apart for the gospel of God, which He promised beforehand through His prophets in the holy Scriptures, **concerning His Son** (Rom. 1:1-3).

Behold, I lay in Zion a stone of stumbling and a rock of offense, and he who **believes in Him** will not be put to shame (Rom. 9:33 quoting Isa. 28:16).

Remember that you were at that time [Old Testament] separate from **Christ**, excluded from the citizenship of Israel, and strangers to the covenants of promise, having no hope and without God in the world (Eph. 2:12; if the Gentiles had been without Christ, then the implication is that the Old Testament Jews had not been without Him! On several occasions Paul states that the Prophets and Moses spoke of the death and resurrection of Messiah: Acts 26:22, 23; 28:23, 24; Rom. 1:1-3; 2 Tim. 3:14, 15).

Christ Witnesses to Himself from the Old Testament:

And He said to them, "O foolish men and slow of heart to believe all that the prophets have spoken. Was it not necessary for the **Christ** to suffer these things and to enter His glory?" And beginning with Moses and the prophets, He explained to them the things **concerning Himself in all the scriptures** (Luke 24:25-27; also verses 44-47).

You search the Scriptures, because you think that in them you have eternal life; **and it is these that bare witness of Me** (John 5:39).

Your father Abraham rejoiced to see My day; and he saw it, and was glad (John 8:56).

Many at the time of Jesus' incarnation were looking for Messiah:

He found first his own brother Simon, and said to him, "We have found the Messiah" (John 1:41).

Philip found Nathanael, and said to him, "We have found Him, of ***Whom Moses in the law and also the prophets wrote***, Jesus of Nazareth" (John 1:46).

The woman said to Him, "***I know that Messiah is coming*** (He who is called Christ); when that One comes, He will declare all things to us" (John 4:25).

And behold, there was a man in Jerusalem whose name was Simeon; and this man was righteous and devout, ***looking for*** the consolation of Israel; and the Holy Spirit was upon him. And it had been revealed to him by the Holy Spirit that he would not see the death ***before He had seen the Lord's Christ*** (Luke 2:25, 26).

And at that very moment she came up and began giving thanks to God, and continued to speak ***of Him [Christ]*** to all those who were ***looking for the redemption*** of Jerusalem (Luke 2:38).

Even from the oldest Book of the Bible:

I know that my Redeemer lives, and at the last day He will take His stand on the earth (Job 19:25).

Even now, behold, my witness is in heaven, and my Advocate is on high (Job 16:19).

This evidence is overwhelming; let all the earth keep silence.

New Testament Justification: Faith Without Works

There are two extremes concerning justification. Some hold that we are justified by faith plus works (Roman Catholics) and others that we are justified by a faith that never works (the carnal Christian theory). Both are heresies, and the Word of Faith preachers say that the Old Testament saints were justified by works without faith and the New Testament saints by faith without works.

Most Christians get born again but will not allow Jesus to be Lord in their lives.[22]

Many things have happened to Christians because they didn't let Jesus be Lord.[23]

---

[22] Gloria Copeland, *Walk in the Spirit* (Ft. Worth: KCP Publications, 1984), p. 67.

[23] Hagin, *ZOE*, p. 30.

There are many fine, understanding people — born again, filled with the Spirit of God — who are absolutely defeated in every area of their lives.[24]

What did James mean when he said we were to be doers of the Word? Did he mean we were to Keep the Ten Commandments? . . . No, that isn't what he was talking about. Actually, the Ten Commandments were given for spiritually dead people; they are not for spiritually alive people.[25]

The Reformers used to say that though we are justified by faith alone, the kind of faith that saves is not alone. In other words, true faith is not alone but is always accompanied by good works. We are not justified because of the good works. Faith is only the hand that receives the gift, but once the gift is received it manifests itself in a changed life. An example the Puritans used is the human eye. It is the only instrument that sees, but it does not exist by itself, being supported by the body. Several Bible verses that help are the following:

> Now by this we know that we know Him, if we keep His commandments. He who says, "I know Him," and does not keep His commandments, is a liar, and the truth is not in him (1 John 2:3, 4).

> They profess to know God, but in works they deny Him, being abominable, disobedient, and disqualified for every good work (Titus 1:16).

> Thus also faith by itself, if it does not have works, is dead (James 2:17).

These verses from Ephesians show us the balance, that we are saved by faith alone but a faith that produces obedience:

> For by grace you have been saved through faith, and that not of yourselves; it is the gift of God, not of works, lest anyone should boast. For we are His workmanship, created in Christ Jesus **for good works**, which God prepared beforehand that we should walk in them (Eph. 2:8-10).

Someone may object that the Bible never says we are saved

---

[24] Kenneth Copeland, *The Laws of Prosperity* (Ft. Worth: KCP Publications, 1989), p. 34; see pp. 41, 43.

[25] Kenneth E. Hagin, *The Human Spirit*, pp. 16-17.

by faith *alone,* which is true if one means that these exact words are not printed in the Bible. God does say, however, that we are justified by faith minus all human effort (Rom. 4:1-9; Gal. 2:16; Eph. 2:8, 9), which is equivalent to faith *alone*.

Not only do the Word of Faith leaders promote a faith without works, but they also have a New Testament faith with human effort added so that we may go on to greater things in the Christian life. The nature of faith they espouse, in other words, is not biblical. First it is devoid of the reflex action of obedience as necessarily contained in faith. Then works as a separate category are added.[26]

How Many Mediators?

If a Christian needs Robert Tilton, Oral Roberts or any other person in order to receive God's blessings, then there is another mediator besides Jesus, which is blatantly contrary to 1 Timothy 2:5: "For there is one God and *one Mediator* between God and men, the Man Christ Jesus." This is a major point that no one seems to address. Repeatedly these men tell people to come to *them*, to send *them* money, to contact *them* for prayer, and *then* they will receive God's blessing. The obvious point is that no blessings are received without the intercession of the Word of Faith leaders. It is blasphemous for any man to make himself the conduit for God's blessings, and it is a denial of the most basic element in the Gospel, namely, that Jesus is the *only* mediator between God and men (1 Tim. 2:5), that He is the *only* way to God (John 14:6). Such false preaching is no better than the Roman Catholic heresy that people must go through Mary and other saints to get to God.

Metaphysical writer Morton Kelsey says: "The shaman [guru, witch doctor] is the mediator between the individual and spiritual reality, both good and evil, and because of this the healer of diseases of mind and body."[27] In other words,

---

[26]"The dangerous 'and' . . . in contrast to the evangelical *sola* [only], causes sin (Gal. 2:18, 19; 3:19; Rom. 7:7-25) and places those who employ it under the curse accruing to those who wish to live before God and men on the basis of their obediences (Gal. 3:10)." Frederick Dale Bruner, *A Theology of the Holy Spirit* (Grand Rapids: Wm. B. Eerdmans, 1974), p. 247.

[27]Dave Hunt & T. A. McMahon, *The Seduction of Christianity* (Eugene, OR:

the sick person goes to the "expert," the one who has God's power to heal. This is why we see so many people writing to Oral Roberts, Robert Tilton, and others for their healing or prayer requests. They do not seem to understand that true Christians have direct access to God themselves; they do not need to approach Him through the "expert" or through any mediator except Christ.

What Comes After the Gospel?

Since they say the Gospel alone does not guarantee success in the Christian life, then what does? The answer is our works: "Just because we are born again does not necessarily mean that he is a successful Christian."[28] "The higher life, the life that is lived in the spirit [human spirit] is where the Joy is! Only the faithful will find it."[29] What comes after the Gospel is something greater than the Gospel, according to these writers. In fact, we must quickly leave the Gospel and go on to prosperity, wealth, the "baptism in the Holy Spirit," tongues, and the "higher" life — whatever that is.

The assumption is that there is something greater than the Gospel and that there are other ways besides the grace given to us in conversion to attain these "benefits." Apparently God does not give us everything we need at conversion; there is still more, and it takes our works to attain it. We must, by ourselves, master any sins in our lives to get the "baptism in the Holy Spirit," (which means that we do not need Him if we can do it ourselves). According to this teaching, God has *not* given us the greatest gift in His Son (contrary to Rom. 8:32) but is holding out on us. There is no better refutation than that of Bruner:

> Grace itself, or the forgiveness of sins, appears in Pentecostalism to play a role only in the Christian's conversion, rarely appears in other discussions, and thus ceases for all practical purposes to be the center, accompaniment, and determinant of the whole Christian life. The reversal of the apostolic sequence of grace-

---

Harvest House Publishers, 1985), p. 133.

[28]Kenneth E. Hagin, *Faith Edition Bible* (Tulsa: Kenneth Hagin Ministries, 1972), p. xlvi.

[29]Gloria Copeland, *Walk*, p. 13.

then-obedience lies at the bottom of the Pentecostal error.[30]

> Forgiveness must inevitably appear insufficient and preliminary if beyond it a still higher benefit is posited. Wherever forgiveness is mere there will be passion for more. Where forgiveness and the sonship it includes are understood as only a part of what God has to give there must be the discovery of means other than forgiveness to attain privileges higher than sonship.[31]

One searches in vain to find discussions of the Gospel in the new charismatics' writings, for the attitude is that we must leave the Gospel of the grace of God and go on to greater things. Consequently their writings are glutted with many rules, regulations, supposed visions, steps to get what you want, concerning which Paul proclaims: "Let no one defraud you of your reward, taking delight in [false] humility and worship of angels, *intruding into those things which he has not seen,* vainly puffed up by his fleshly mind, and *not holding fast to the Head,* from whom all the body, nourished and knit together by joints and ligaments, grows with the increase which is from God" (Col. 2:18, 19). We must hold fast to our Head, Jesus Christ, Whom to know is life eternal.

New charismatics do not deny faith's *necessity*, but they deny its *exclusiveness*. In other words, it is not faith alone that is sufficient for the Christian life but faith plus works. Just as they deny that the Bible *alone* is enough for life and godliness, so they deny that faith *alone* is sufficient for the Christian life: ". . . faith is never prefixed in Paul by an adjective, nor heightened by an absolute. This cannot be accidental."[32] Where superlatives and absolutes are used, it is of the grace of God. By "canceling the sole necessity of faith" they have cancelled "the sole sufficiency of Christ"[33] by adding human works as necessary to attain to the fulness of His grace. Christ is necessary but not sufficient.

The truth is that God has given us the greatest gift of all — His Son. What could possibly be greater than Him? To speak of more is to disparage Him, to think that Paul was

---

[30] Bruner, *A Theology of the Holy Spirit*, p. 233.

[31] Ibid., p. 234.

[32] Ibid., p. 253.

[33] Ibid., p. 283.

wrong when he stated that since God has given us the greatest He will also give us the lesser things: "He who did not spare His own Son, but delivered Him up for us all, how shall He not with Him also freely give us all things?" (Rom. 8:32). Everything we have or ever will have is a result of forgiveness of sins. This is not the beginning; it is the ultimate, the door to all *lesser* blessings. If we did not have to beg God and fulfill dozens of conditions to receive the ultimate, we shall not have to do this to receive the lesser gifts. (See the appendix on the "Baptism in the Holy Spirit.") The condition for receiving all gifts is to receive Jesus. When we get Him and His righteousness, God throws in all the rest!

Is Man Body, Soul, and Spirit?

Because the Word of Faith leaders promote the platonic and metaphysical idea that man is body, soul, and spirit[34] and because the idea is so prevalent in their writings, it is necessary to look at this. They share the idea that "man *is* a spirit, that he *has* a soul, and that he *lives* in a body" [emphasis added].[35] They maintain that the real person is the spirit man, while the body is only the temporary house in which he lives; the soul is how he relates to the world. In other words, man has to have a body to have authority in this world, a soul to be able to think and have "sense knowledge" through the five senses, and the spirit is what he "contacts God with." "Sometimes we hear a preacher announce that 'souls' were saved. However, it is not the *soul* of man that is saved at that moment; it is the *spirit* of man that is born again" [emphasis his].[36]

Again, they do not know (nor care, evidently) that the origin of such an idea is platonic and metaphysical, which the church has never adopted, and that Scripture does not teach this. Actually the "three-part view" (trichotomy) is not heretical in itself, though very few theologians have held to it, but

---

[34]Kenneth Hagin, Jr., *God's Irresistible Word* (Tulsa: Faith Library Publications, 1989), p. 9; Cady, *Lessons in Truth*, p. 21; Kenneth Copeland, *Force of Faith*, pp. 2-3; Kenneth E. Hagin, *How You Can Be Led* (Tulsa: Faith Library Publications, 1989), pp. 2, 4.

[35]Hagin, *How You Can be Led*, p. 2.

[36]Kenneth E. Hagin, *The Human Spirit* (Tulsa: Faith Library Publications, 1985), p. 5.

the way they use it is heretical. They think that man participates in the being of God through his spirit, that he communicates with God apart from his mind through his spirit, and that the new birth is man's spirit being recreated or renewed in some way. The body is supposedly for the physical world and the soul for the mental world. In the words of Kenneth Hagin, "With our spirit we contact the spiritual world; with our soul we contact the mental world; and with our body we contact the physical world."[37] Again he proclaims: "*Feeling* is the voice of the *body*. *Reason* is the voice of the *soul* or *mind*. *Conscience* is the voice of the *spirit*" [emphasis his].[38]

They have adopted a bizaare application of the trichotomy view of man. In saying that man has a spirit that contacts God, they actually teach a form of pantheism in alleging that man's spirit partakes of the nature of God. This supposedly happens when one is born again: his human spirit is some how replaced with the being of God.[39] By this method a person is divinized, can communicate directly with God by "going within," by mysticism, or by "listening" to his "spirit man." Such communication, they maintain, is below the conscious level, not by the mind. This is their form of intuition and pantheism.

Sometimes they follow Watchman Nee's *The Spiritual Man*, in which he promotes the trichotomy view strongly. Occasionally they argue that since God is three parts that man is also three parts. They are grossly wrong about God, Who is not three parts but three Persons, the same in substance, equal in power and glory. It does not take three parts to make up the One being, God, but three Persons are equally God in all aspects to the infinite degree.

Scriptural Refutation

There are several reasons for saying that man is a monad, a single unit, composed of body and soul. (See paragraph beginning with "Objection:" on page 143.) First, the Greek

---

[37] Kenneth E. Hagin, *How You Can Know the Will of God* (Tulsa: Faith Library Publications, 1983), pp. 3-4.

[38] Ibid., p. 6.

[39] Apollinaris, who was condemned as a heretic (see last chapter), taught that man had three parts and that Christ's human spirit was replaced by His deity. The Word of Faith leaders promote the same concerning every Christian.

lexicons do not make the fine distinctions that the new charismatics do between soul and spirit, and those who write lexicons have made a living studying Greek all their lives. For example, "spirit" can mean wind (John 3:8), breath (Matt. 27:50), man as immaterial (Col. 2:5), state of mind or disposition (1 Cor. 4:21), evil or angelic spirits (Acts 23:8), and many other things. "Soul" can mean life in its physical aspects (Luke 12:20; Acts 2:27), man as immaterial (Matt. 10:28, 39; 11:29), and so forth. Therefore, to make such sharp distinctions between the three is to go beyond what the Bible does.

Secondly, biblical usage is against the distinctions between soul and spirit that they attempt. As John Murray, the late head of the theology department at Westminster Theological Seminary, accurately stated, sometimes the Bible speaks of the whole person as body and soul or body and spirit with no distinction between the two:[40]

> Is not life [soul] more than food and the body more than clothing? (Matt. 6:25).

> And do not fear those who kill the body but cannot kill the soul. But rather fear Him who is able to destroy both soul and body in hell (Matt. 10:28).

> The unmarried woman cares about the things of the Lord, that she may be holy both in body and in spirit. But she who is married cares about the things of the world — how she may please her husband (1 Cor. 7:34).

> Therefore, having these promises, beloved, let us cleanse ourselves from all filthiness of the flesh and spirit, perfecting holiness in the fear of God (2 Cor. 7:1).

These passages describe the complete elements of human personality. "In Matthew 10:28 the completeness of penal destruction is the main lesson, and in 1 Corinthians 7:34 and 2 Corinthians 7:1 it is the completeness of sanctification that is envisioned."[41] In James the "the body without the spirit is dead," but if man has three parts then the body without a spirit is not dead, for according to the Word of Faith leaders,

---

[40] John Murray, *Collected Writings of John Murray: Systematic Theology* (Edinburgh: The Banner of Truth Trust, 1977), 2:24.

[41] Ibid., p. 25.

non-Christians have body and soul but not a spirit. And James does not say this death is only of the saved or the lost but uses language that seems to encompass either.

There are times when Jesus is said to be troubled in His soul (John 12:27; Matt. 26:38) and troubled in His spirit (Mark 8:12; John 13:21) with no distinction discernable. In fact the writer of Hebrews indicates that the psychological suffering He experienced was of the *Person* of Christ, thus indicating that no distinction of soul and spirit in the Gospels was indicated (2:9, 10; 5:7, 8).

Soul and spirit are used synonymously:

> And Hannah answered and said, "No, my lord, I am a woman of sorrowful **spirit**. I have drunk neither wine nor intoxicating drink, but have poured out my **soul** before the Lord" (1 Sam. 1:15).

> Therefore I will not restrain my mouth; I will speak in the anguish of my **spirit**; I will complain in the bitterness of my **soul** (Job 7:11).

> With my **soul** I have desired You in the night, yes, by my **spirit** within me I will seek You early; for when Your judgments are in the earth, the inhabitants of the world will learn righteousness (Isa. 26:9).

In this last verse the soul and spirit seek after God, and the words are used interchangeably. Even God is said to have a soul and surely we would not say He has a spirit separate from His soul (Isa. 42:1; Matt. 12:18). God *is* Spirit (John 4:24).

In the Old Testament, "the highest spiritual exercises are ascribed to the soul as well as to the spirit."[42] Likewise in the New Testament soul and spirit are used of the highest spiritual exercises and without distinction: "And Mary said: 'My *soul* magnifies the Lord, and my *spirit* has rejoiced in God my Savior'" (Luke 1:46, 47). Surely this includes Mary's whole personality in each description. Paul says to the Philippians, "only let your conduct be worthy of the gospel of Christ, so that whether I come and see you or am absent, I may hear of your affairs, that you stand fast in one *spirit*, with one *mind*

---

[42]Ibid., p. 26. For the soul see Ps. 42:1-6; 63:5; 103:1, 2; 116:7; 130:6; Isa. 26:9, and for the spirit see Ps. 32:2; 34:18; 51:10, 12, 17; Prov. 11:13; 16:19; Isa. 57:15; Ez. 11:19; 18:31; 36:26.

[soul] striving together for the faith of the gospel" (1:27). Obviously no distinction between the two is indicated here.

The soul is saved by grace (Acts 14:22; James 1:21; 5:20; 1 Peter 1:9, 22; 2:11, 25) and the spirit is saved by grace (1 Cor. 5:5; 6:17, 20; Gal. 6:18; 2 Tim. 4:22; Philm. 25; Heb. 12:23) without distinction. The whole person is referred to by the word *soul* (1 Peter 3:20; 2 Peter 2:8, 14) or by the word *spirit* (Rom. 1:9; 1 Cor. 6:17, etc.). The spirit in man understands (1 Cor. 2:11; Eph. 4:23), and the soul understands (Matt. 22:37; Mark 12:30, 33; Luke 10:27, etc.). One's spirit goes to heaven (Acts 7:59) or his soul (Rev. 6:9; 20:4).

Objections to the Biblical View

There are common objections that some raise against the view that man is body and soul. They state that 1 Thessalonians 5:23 is an example of man having three parts: "Now may the God of peace Himself sanctify you completely; and may your whole spirit, soul, and body be preserved blameless at the coming of our Lord Jesus Christ." First we must state that this is the *only* verse in the Bible that lists all three together. Secondly, the passage seems to indicate the entire personality of man, but so do many other passages in differing terms:

> For you were bought at a price; therefore glorify God **in your body and in your spirit**, which are God's (1 Cor. 6:20).

> There is a difference between a wife and a virgin. The unmarried woman cares about the things of the Lord, that she may be holy **both in body and in spirit**. But she who is married cares about the things of the world — how she may please her husband (1 Cor. 7:34).

> And you shall love the Lord your God with **all your heart, with all your soul, with all your mind, and with all your strength.** This is the first commandment (Mark 12:30).[43]

---

[43] Some point to the order and say this is progressive: heart, soul equals the mind, and strength. The heart is the spirit or inner self, the soul is the mind, and the strength is the body. The heart is God-related, the soul is man-related, and the strength is the body. This is no indication, however, that the Lord had an order in mind, and the Old Testament verse He quotes (Deut. 6:5) leaves out the word "mind." Anyone who takes the time to study the various Hebrew and Greek words with a concordance will discover that often the words are used synonymously, as they are here in Mark.

In light of these verses and many others, it would be straining at a gnat to think that 1 Thessalonians 5:23 is the definitive verse on the entire personality of man. Why not one of the others? Maybe man has four parts or two. In Mark 12:30 the immaterial substance of man is referred to in four slightly different ways (heart, soul, mind, strength). The fact is that many varying terms are used in Scripture to describe the psychology of man, and I know of no one who has done an exhaustive study on this.[44]

Thirdly, there is the question of translating 1 Thessalonians 5:23.[45] Hendriksen argues for this translation: "And may He, the God of peace, sanctify you through and through, and without flaw may be your spirit, and your soul-and-body without blame at the coming of our Lord Jesus Christ may it be kept." The Greek word he renders "through and through" is an adjective used as an adverb (much like we often use *good* as an adverb).[46]

That is not to say that *soul* and *spirit* can never have a slightly different meaning. Perhaps in 1 Thessalonians 5:23 they do. The difference would be that *spirit* refers to man's relation to God and the *soul* to "the seat of sensations, affections, desires."[47]

The Word of Faith leaders adduce Hebrews 4:12 to say that man has three parts: "For the word of God is living and powerful, and sharper than any two edged sword, piercing even to the division of soul and spirit, and of joints and marrow, and is a discerner of the thoughts and intents of the heart." Our response, first, is that if they wish to state that man is three parts from this verse, they have stated too little.

---

[44] One admiral attempt to do so was by Franz Delitzsch, *A System of Biblical Psychology* (Grand Rapids: Baker Book House, 1899, rpt. 1977), 585 pages of very technical material. Many do not agree with all his fine points.

[45] For a most excellent discussion of the grammar see William Hendriksen, *New Testament Commentary: 1 and 2 Thessalonians* (Grand Rapids: Baker Book House, 1974), p. 141 and especially p. 146ff.

[46] Moulton and Milligan, p. 447. The Greek adjective "without flaw" modifies *spirit* and the Greek adverb "without blame" modifies the verb *kept*. I diagrammed the sentence in Greek and grammatically Henndriksen has a good rendering. There are two main verbs in the sentence, *sanctify* and *kept* (both are aorist optatives) and Hendriksen has made his translation around these verbs.

[47] Hendriksen, op. cit., p. 150.

The verse thus used would divide man into *five* parts: soul, spirit, joints, marrow, and heart.

Secondly, that there is no intention to give a statement concerning the nature of man can also be seen by the division of the verse: The Word of God *pierces* and *discerns* and is the subject of the sentence. Man's nature is not the subject. God's Word *pierces* the inner most part of man's being (joints, marrow, soul, spirit), and as a parallel statement it *discerns* (the heart). Thus Paul[48] states the same thing in two ways, "heart" being parallel to the other four words. Furthermore, there is another parallelism here: joints and marrow are parallel and are of one substance, and soul and spirit are parallel and are of one substance. Thus we have these parallels: joints and marrow, soul and spirit, and heart parallel to all.

Thirdly, the Greek word for "division" (*merismos*) never means to divide things into distinct identities, like dividing eggs from horses, but it does mean to "divide within" a class or to rent asunder one thing, like tearing up a single piece of paper. In other words, it means to distribute *one* substance or to divide up *one* substance, not to separate one substance from a different substance.[49]

Therefore, while Hebrews 4:12 may make some minor distinctions between spirit and soul, it is a distinction of function of the one immaterial substance in man, just as bones and marrow are a distinction of the one material substance in man. The point of the verse is that the Word of

---

[48] I believe, as most of the church has for centuries, that Paul wrote Hebrews.

[49] Murray, *Systematic Theology*, p. 30. Here are the occurrences of *merismos*. In Hebrews 2:4 we have the Holy Spirit "*distributing* gifts of the Holy Spirit, according to His own will." The gifts are all of the same essence. Hebrews contains the only examples of the noun in the New Testament. Likewise the verb (*merizo*): a single kingdom is *divided* against itself (Matt. 12:25, 26; Mark 3:24-26), Christ is not *divided* (1 Cor. 1:13), a wife and virgin are *separate* (1 Cor. 7:34), a single inheritance is *divided* (Luke 12:13), two fish are *divided* (Mark 6:41), God has *distributed* to each Christian a measure of faith (Rom. 12:3) and gifts (1 Cor. 7:17), God has *appointed* or *distributed* to us a sphere of operation (2 Cor. 10:13), and Abraham *distributed* a tenth (Heb. 7:2). These are all the uses of the noun and verb in the New Testament, and not once does the word mean to divide between different kinds of substances. Sometimes it means to distribute one thing or at other times it carries the idea that one substance is divided, but it is never used in dividing two or more completely different substances. Other Greek words (perhaps *aphorizo* in Matt. 13:49; 25:32, separating sheep from goats) may mean to divide substances.

God is able to discern the innermost recesses of a man's "heart" or being, not what kind of being man is. The terms used are a "rhetorical accumulation of terms to express the whole mental nature of man on all its sides" with the "Word of God probing the inmost recesses of our spiritual being."[50] In other words, the Word of God or the Bible is the best psychologist of all!

Man, therefore, *is* body and soul, material and immaterial, combined to make one unified person. Man is not made of parts like a car, he *is* in the image of God, body and soul, or body and spirit, but not body, soul, and spirit. When man is regenerated, there is no spirit part added to him or reborn into existence, but the immaterial "man" is renovated so that he loves God, hates sin, and believes in Jesus.

What Is the True Gospel?

Paul tells us in great detail in Romans what the Gospel is, not only by the words he uses but also the order in which he presents the Gospel. The order is that all men are sinners: Gentiles (1:18-32), Jews (2:1-3:8), and all men (3:9-20). Next is the person and work of Jesus (3:21-26), then justification by faith alone in Christ alone for both Jews and Gentiles (3:27-5:21), and sanctification as a necessary consequence of justification (chs. 6-8).

When man fell into sin in the garden, he lost his righteousness and came under the wrath of God. The Gospel basically is that man is a sinner, totally incapable of earning forgiveness of sins and under the wrath of God, that Jesus is God and Man in one Person who obeyed God's law perfectly and took man's wrath as his Substitute, that God raised Him bodily from the grave, that man must turn from his sins and trust in Jesus alone, and that when man does such God forgives his sins (wrath propitiated) and gives the sinner the righteousness of Jesus.

Sanctification, however, always follows justification automatically. So when the sinner is justified, having righteousness imputed, simultaneously he also receives the practical, imparted righteousness so that Paul can say that one who is

---

[50] F. F. Bruce, *The New International Commentary on the New Testament: The Epistle to the Hebrews* (Grand Rapids: Wm. B. Eerdmans Pub. Co., 1964), p. 82.

saved by grace cannot continue in sin (Rom. 6:1).[51]

Earlier in this chapter we saw that Kenyon said that we do not receive a legal righteousness, a righteousness that is reckoned to us. *Reckoned* is a legal term that means we are now considered His. It means forgiveness of sins and free righteousness. Paul contradicts the statement by Kenyon:

> What then shall we say that Abraham our father has found according to the flesh? For if Abraham was justified by works, he has something of which to boast, but not before God. For what does the Scripture say? "Abraham believed God, and it was **accounted** [Greek = reckoned] to him for righteousness." Now to him who works, the wages are not counted as grace but as debt. But to him who does not work but believes on Him who justifies the ungodly, his faith is **accounted** [reckoned] for righteousness (Rom. 4:1-5).

Righteousness is what the Gospel is all about. We do not have it, Jesus does. If we trust in Him alone, He will grant us as a free gift His righteousness. It is *reckoned* to us, which simply means it is written to our account. God does not leave us at this point, but also begins to make us what He has declared us to be, namely, the righteousness of Christ. What a wonderful Gospel!

Furthermore, the Gospel is not the work of the Holy Spirit in us, as necessary and biblical as His work is. The Holy Spirit works in us as a *consequence* of the Gospel. This point cannot be stated too strongly. The Gospel is not the working of the Spirit *in* us now, but the work Christ did *for* us two thousand years ago. However, the Spirit does work in us because of the Gospel. The Spirit's work is a process, but Christ's work has been completed. The Gospel is objective, outside of us, something done by Jesus. The Spirit's work — and it is a glorious and necessary work — is subjective, something done

---

[51] The logical order (not the temporal order, as all these things happen simultaneously) begins with regeneration, which is the giving of new life and the changing of the soul's orientation from sin to holiness. Then follows belief in Jesus, at which point is given legal righteousness, which means he is a child of God by adoption. As a child, he is also given grace (which began in regeneration) to live a holy, though not a perfect, life. The power of sin is basically broken in his life. What we have is this: regeneration, belief, justification, and sanctification. The work of sanctification is not complete until the person sees the Lord (1 John 3:2). At glorification, sanctifying righteousness will equal justifying righteousness.

in us now. Our faith must be solely in Jesus, in His death and resurrection, in the Triune God.

The *nature* of justification is forensic, which means it is a legal declaration that the sinner is accepted; the *ground* of justification is solely the person and work of God the Son, Jesus, who obeyed the law and bore the wrath of God in our place; the *means* of justification is faith alone in Jesus alone; the *accomplishment* of justification is forgiveness of sins and the free gift of Jesus' righteousness; and the *effect* of justification is good works in the believer's life. This is the Gospel.

How They Present the Gospel

Does Only One Sin Send to Hell?

> There is only one sin for which they will be judged: that is the rejection of the Lord Jesus.[52]

> He will be convicted of only one sin, his rejection of Jesus Christ as his Savior.[53]

> The sinner does not need to think that God is mad at him or that God is against him. *The sin that sends a man to hell is not an act or deed, such as lying, stealing, or cheating; it is rejecting the Lord Jesus Christ!* [emphasis his].[54]

> The *only* sin keeping anyone out of the kingdom of God is the sin of rejecting Jesus and what He has provided (John 16:9) [emphasis added].[55]

Does only one sin send to hell? Yes and no. The one sin of unbelief is the mother sin that gives birth to all other sins. The sin of unbelief cannot be separated from other sins. It is true that the Holy Spirit convicts us of the sin of unbelief (John 16:8-11) and that anyone who dies in unbelief goes to hell (John 3:36). But it is not true that this is the only sin that is judged:

> But the cowardly, unbelieving, abominable, murderers, sexually

---

[52] Kenyon, *What Happened*, p. 135.

[53] Kenyon, *The Father and His Family*, p. 285.

[54] Hagin, *Present Day Ministry* (Tulsa: Faith Library Publications, 1983), p. 30.

[55] Copeland, *Force of Righteousness*, p. 3.

immoral, sorcerers, idolaters, and all liars shall have their part in the lake which burns with fire and brimstone, which is the second death (Rev. 21:8).

But outside are dogs and sorcerers and sexually immoral and murderers and idolaters, and whoever loves and practices a lie (Rev. 22:15).

For this you know, that no fornicator, unclean person, nor covetous man, who is an idolater, has any inheritance in the kingdom of Christ and God (Eph. 5:5).

Do you not know that the unrighteous will not inherit the kingdom of God? Do not be deceived. Neither fornicators, nor idolaters, nor adulterers, nor homosexuals, nor sodomites, nor thieves, nor covetous, nor drunkards, nor revilers, nor extortioners will inherit the kingdom of God (1 Cor. 6:9, 10).

And He said, "What comes out of a man, that defiles a man. For from within, out of the heart of men, proceed evil thoughts, adulteries, fornications, murders, thefts, covetousness, wickedness, deceit, licentiousness, an evil eye, blasphemy, pride, foolishness" (Mark 7:20-22).

People manifest all these sins because of unbelief, and they go to hell for *all* of their sins. Some will be judged more severely than others (Matt. 11:23, 24) and some beaten with many stripes while others only with a few (Luke 12:48), which means that more than one sin will be judged. So such a presentation of the Gospel is not accurate at this point. We should do like the apostles who preached in the book of Acts: Preach Jesus, His resurrection, and the judgment to come. Peter accused the Jews of murdering the Messiah (Acts 2:23; 3:13: 5:30), an act done in unbelief. Peter preached against both their unbelief and their specific sins. At Ephesus Paul preached against magic and the converts burned their books (Acts 19:19). Preaching the Gospel necessitates preaching against the sins of the day, and Paul preached against homosexuality, lying, unthankfulness, and so forth (Rom. 1:18ff).

Examples of Their Gospel

How specifically do the new charismatics present the Gospel? Here are some examples:

The sinner simply needs to say to God, "Dear God, I am a

sinner. I cannot save myself. I know according to your Word that I cannot make myself righteous, but I thank You because You love me, and You sent the Lord Jesus Christ to die for me. And through His righteousness, redemption is made available to me. I believe that Jesus died for my sins according to the Scripture. I believe that He was raised from the dead and is my justification. I confess Jesus now, and I take Him as my Savior."[56]

Jesus Christ is my Lord and Savior. By His shed blood my sins are forgiven and I have been made a new person.[57]

Oral Roberts says it this way.[58] "Here, in four steps, is how you may be saved." 1. Come to Christ just as you are (Matt. 11:28). You can never be good enough to come so remember that the best you can do is filthy rags (Isa. 64:6). 2. Repent (2 Cor. 7:10). We must be sorry for our sins and want to live a new life. 3. Believe (John 1:12). Take God at His Word and simply trust the Person of Christ. 4. Confess (Rom. 10:9, 10) Jesus, His resurrection and do this publicly (Matt. 10:32, 33).

Can one become a Christian by listening to these presentations? Absolutely. Some may object that I said they are a cult and do not preach the Gospel. And I stand by this. Their statements are not wrong in themselves, and a reader or listener could become a Christian, *if and only if*, he understands the terms from the Bible's point of view.

In other words, when one hears that Jesus is his righteousness, does he understand this to mean that he partakes of God's being, becoming like God, or does he understand that this means forgiveness of sins and the imputation of Christ's perfect obedience? When he hears that Jesus is his redemption, does he understand this to mean that Jesus went to hell to pay off Satan, or that God is righteous, that Jesus satisfied God's uncompromising standard, that his well-deserved judgment was taken by Jesus? When he hears that Jesus is his Savior, does he think that Jesus has shown him how to have victory over indwelling sin by overcoming His own sinful

---

[56] Hagin, *Right and Wrong Thinking* (Tulsa: Faith Library Publications, 1986), p. 6.

[57] Oral Roberts, *Miracle of Seed Faith* (Tulsa: Oral Roberts, 1970), p. 74.

[58] Oral Roberts, *A Daily Guide to Miracles* (Tulsa: Pinoak Publications, 1975), p. 163ff.

nature, or does he understand that Jesus took his sins, bearing God's wrath in his place, that Jesus never sinned but took his punishment? Does he think that Jesus was not God while on earth and only functioned as a man, or does he rightly understand that He was God and man, functioning in both natures? When he hears that Jesus is his substitute, does he think that Jesus vicariously became a sinner for us, needing Himself to be born again and justified, receiving the nature of Satan, or does he see that Jesus was sinless and took our punishment, never being a sinner or unrighteous? The former option in each case is not the Gospel but the latter is. If one were to hear the Word of Faith definitions of these terms, he would not hear the Gospel, but if he heard only the summaries I have quoted from their literature, already having evangelical understandings of these things, he would hear the Gospel.

    The point being made cannot be emphasized too strongly: ***The Gospel is not just words; it is words that carry biblical content.*** Do they preach the Gospel? NO! One can, however, *if he already has evangelical understanding*, become a Christian while listening to them. "The difference between various beliefs lies in the objects or propositions believed, not in the nature of belief."[59] Dr. Clark means that faith is only as good as its object, and the object is only as good as its content. Sometimes I hear people, even preachers, say "No creed but Christ." Such carelessness has no place in the Christian faith. It is a matter of life or death, heaven and hell, which Christ one believes in, the Christ of the Jehovah's Witnesses or the Christ of the Bible. The two are not the same. It is true that we trust in a Person for forgiveness of sins; the question is, which person? The Christ of the Jehovah's Witnesses does not exist; the God-man in one Person of the Bible does. Why would Jesus Himself say "If you do not believe that I AM, you will die in your sins" (John 8:24) if it makes no difference? Why did John write the Gospel of John to present Jesus as the Son of God so that we may have life (John 20:30, 31) if we can believe whatever we like?

    There is a vast difference in preaching faith itself and

---

[59] Gordon Clark, *Faith and Saving Faith* (Jefferson, MD: The Trinity Foundation, 1983), p. 15.

preaching the object of faith. Because they are existentialists, the Word of Faith leaders preach faith itself. For the sake of space, we have not documented the many books and booklets that the Word of Faith leaders have written on faith, but the number is staggering. Most of their sermons are centered on faith itself. They think that the way to get what you want is to have faith, and the route to faith is to preach faith itself. In Scripture the pathway to faith is to preach the *object* of faith: Jesus and Him crucified and resurrected. For example, if you approach a rickety bridge, no amount of telling yourself that you need faith in order to cross the bridge safely would help you. You could hear a thousand sermons on positive confession, on how to get faith, but it would avail nothing. The problem is that you do not trust the object. If, however, an engineer were to tell you how the bridge was constructed, that despite its outward appearance it was made of the finest wood that was termite proof, that he himself would drive his fully loaded ten-ton truck over the bridge first, then faith would come. Similarly, the apostles did not preach faith itself in their sermons in the book of Acts, not once — they preached Jesus and His resurrection. The object of faith is what the Spirit of God honors in producing faith in hearers, not how man can allegedly conjure up faith by pumping himself up.

We are not saying that there is never an occasion to teach about faith itself; James does so in the second chapter of his epistle. We are saying, however, that the way to produce faith is to preach the object of faith: the Triune God. The Word of Faith leaders spend most of their time preaching faith itself rather than the object of faith, the Triune God. (As for Oral Roberts preaching the Gospel, see paragraph beginning with "In fact, Patti Roberts" on page 59.)

What Is Grace?

Grace cannot be earned in any sense whatsoever. (For a fuller treatment of this, see Appendix Four: The Sovereignty of God in Salvation. This section assumes the reader has read these pages. You will not understand my discussion of grace unless you read this.) Grace, by its very nature, is irresistible; if it is earned by "free will," then it is not grace. Grace is a gift totally apart from any consideration of man, whether this consideration is concerning his nature, his will, or his desires. Man apart from grace always desires sin; he never desires God. It takes grace to change this.[60]

God gives grace to His elect to do what He commands. Those who do not receive grace only have the command, and consequently they only choose sin and unbelief. To condition grace on something is to nullify grace. Therefore, to assert that we can ever make God our debtor is to imagine that our obedience merits something. It is to miss grace if we think there is something beyond the Gospel that we must obtain by our dedication, our consecration, our prayers, our positive confessions, or any other works: "I do not set aside the grace of God; for if righteousness comes through the law [good works], then Christ died in vain" (Gal. 2:21). God has abundantly shed His grace on His elect in Jesus, and there is nothing we can do to merit it and no good thing that God will keep from us. We can receive nothing unless God has given it (John 3:27); and if He has given it, then it is good. The reason we receive anything is because of the Person and work of God the Son; the reason we make any attempt to keep His commandments is because His grace is already working in us; the reason we are blessed in any area of life is because God has given us the grace to obey. But even when we obey, our obedience is only partial; and when we have done the best we can, "we are unprofitable servants; we have done what was our duty to do" (Luke 17:10). The doctrine of the church for hundreds of years has been unchanged regarding grace, as seen from St. Augustine:

> First, that works done before faith are not good, but evil; secondly, that works done after faith, although good, as being the fruits of grace in the believer, are so imperfect in themselves, and so defiled by remaining sin, that they need to be sprinkled with the blood of Christ, and can only be accepted through His merits. . . .[61]

---

[60] Grace, therefore, is always indicative then imperative; that is, God gives grace (indicative) and then commands (imperative).

[61] James Buchanan, *The Doctrine of Justification* (Grand Rapids: Baker Book House, 1867, 1977), p. 89.

Conclusion

Faith is no better than its object, and the object no better than its content. *Why* does one trust in Jesus, and *in what Jesus* does He believe? In new charismatic doctrine, the "Jesus" is not the Jesus of the Bible. The work that their "Jesus" did was not the redemption that the Jesus of the Bible accomplished. They trust in a Jesus to have power over Satan, health, and wealth, and to create their own realities.

In true Christianity, though, the sinner believes in the God-man Jesus, Who functioned both as God and as man, Who lived perfectly obedient to the law of God, Who died on the cross for our sins in answer to the righteousness of God, Who as our Substitute took our punishment, which was the judgment of God, and Who raised Himself from the dead. We trust in Him for forgiveness of sins, which acquits us of God's wrath, and to receive the free gift of Jesus' righteousness. This Jesus is the true object of faith while theirs is a figment of their blind imaginations. May God be pleased to open their eyes, for except for His grace thus would we all be.

God, not Satan, is the one to fear (Prov. 1:7). God is our enemy (Rom. 5:10), and our lack of righteousness is the problem (Rom. 3:9-20; 10:2-4). Until we obtain righteousness, we are under God's wrath and judgment. This is why the atonement was toward God, not toward Satan. Consider these:

> But if our unrighteousness demonstrates the righteousness of God, what shall we say? Is **God unjust who inflicts wrath?** (I speak as a man.) Certainly not! For then how will God judge the world? (Rom. 3:5, 6).

> Much more then, having now been justified by His blood, we shall be saved **from wrath** through Him (Rom. 5:9)

> What if God, wanting to show **His wrath** and to make His power known, endured with much longsuffering the vessels of wrath prepared for destruction (Rom. 9:22).

> Among whom also we all once conducted ourselves in the lusts of our flesh, fulfilling the desires of the flesh and of the mind, and were by nature **children of wrath,** just as the others (Eph. 2:3).

> Let no one deceive you with empty words, for because of these things **the wrath of God** comes upon the sons of disobedience (Eph. 5:6).

> For they themselves declare concerning us what manner of entry we had to you, and how you turned to God from idols to serve the living and true God, and to wait for His Son from heaven, whom He raised from the dead, **even Jesus who delivers us from the wrath to come** (1 Thess. 1:9, 10).

Our only hope is in the Jesus of the Bible, in His substitutionary death and bodily resurrection. If we are not justified by faith in His blood, we shall face the wrath to come. God, not Satan, is either our worst enemy or our best friend. We stand or fall in relationship to Him, not to Satan. Trust in Jesus alone by faith alone for forgiveness of sins, in Him who was both God and man in one person, who functioned as both God and man. Amen.

14

Conclusion

Nor is there salvation in any other, for there is no other name under heaven given among men by which we must be saved (Acts 4:12).

The health and wealth people add to the Gospel. Only if one assumes evangelical meanings from their terms is the Gospel existent in the movement. The "tree" of the Gospel of life is lost in a "forest" of additions: healing, getting rich, positive confession, and so on. God has made it clear that His power is ethical and is in the Gospel. But these espousers of another gospel believe that real power is in miracles. The Lord's warning is still apropos: "A wicked and adulterous generation seeks after a sign" (Matt. 16:14). Signs and miracles were given to validate the real power: the Gospel that forgives men's sins and transforms lives.

By contrast the Protestant Reformers clearly and truthfully proclaimed the uniqueness of Christ, the uniqueness of His life, death, and resurrection, and the uniqueness of Scripture. They put it this way: we are justified *only* by the blood of Christ, *only* by God's grace, *only* by faith, *only* by Scripture, and *only* to the glory of God. Once again we have to defend the Gospel from additions. Like the Roman Catholics, the prosperity preachers dislike the word *only*. If one can lose his salvation, then he is not justified *only* by the blood of Christ but also by his own works. If we must work to receive God's grace, if we must follow five, six, seven, however many, steps to be healed, to have financial success, to get the baptism of the Holy Spirit, and so on, our salvation is then not by grace *only* and not by faith *only*. In these compromises, all the glory goes to man, for nothing is done in this world or in anyone's life until man does something *first*. Man is the initiator, God the responder, and the glory is to man for initiating. The reason why one person will be in heaven and not another is that he responded and the other did not. He could, like the Pharisee, thank God that he was not like the others because he did something.

The God of the prosperity preachers is not the sovereign God of the Bible who created all things by His power, but a God who has a body, who in order to create must function by faith in laws above Him, and who is dependent on man to run this world since He has no legal authority here. What a pathetic "God."

The Jesus they believe in is some hybrid, neither fully God nor a Man incapable of sinning. He was not unique and did no miracles to demonstrate who He was but only as an example for us to imitate *if* we have enough faith. He did not finish redemption when He said He did ("It is finished"), but He had to go to hell to be tortured by Satan and demons so his (Satan's) justice could be satisfied.

The salvation they espouse is to lift man up to "God," making man on the same level as God. It is pantheism to merge man and God. Man receives the nature of God, His essence, which enables man to do the things of God by using the same spiritual laws and the same faith He does. Salvation is by imitating Jesus, not by trusting in Him as the Substitute who took our sins and took God's wrath for us. Jesus was our example, doing mighty works by the same Holy Spirit we have, which, according to them, means we can do the same things He did. Salvation is metaphysical rather than ethical, man becoming God rather then receiving forgiveness of sins. This is no salvation at all.

To them there are greater things than the Gospel, like healing, money, and creating one's own reality, which things are *earned* by what we do. What we have is the sinner's effort and then God's gift(s), which is exactly the opposite of the Gospel.

They have virtually no concept of worship because they lack an understanding of a God worthy to be worshipped. They are given to theatrics — not to confessing sin, confessing their faith using the ancient creeds or the Psalms. They see nothing wrong with revelation apart from Scripture.

Those who claim to have miracles and yet teach false doctrines invalidate their claim to be genuine. Demons can do miracles though not the unique ones of the Lord, but they cannot preach the truth of the Gospel. Those who claim that Christ died for their literal diseases are in grave danger of completely missing the atonement, its significance and its purpose.

We have a great responsibility to evangelize the people in the movement. I doubt that most are aware how far they have deviated from the Bible and from historic Christianity. I doubt that most of the followers hold to all the bizarre and false doctrines that the preachers do, but in twentieth century America people have itching ears. I'm afraid that many do not want to hear the truth so God is sending them strong delusion.

My friend, if you are in this Word of Faith movement, we do not hate you but love you and desire to share the true, old-fashioned, biblical Gospel with you. The reason I have spent so much time in refuting the false is in the hope that God will open your heart to His Word, that you will see your need as a sinner, and call on the true Jesus, trusting in Him *alone* to forgive your sins and to give you His legal righteousness as a free gift. If God has given you the greatest gift of all as a free gift, do not torture and weary yourself to receive lesser things, because He will freely give you these. He will do so as seems best to Him, not that which seems best to you.

May the sovereign Triune God bless you.

Appendix One

New Age and Word of Faith

So far I have made numerous comparisons between gnosticism, the metaphysical cults, and the Word of Faith movement. I thought it would be helpful to do the same with the New Age and Word of Faith to make the comparisons complete. Since the New Age is a metaphysical cult, the comparison will again demonstrate that the Word of Faith is just another metaphysical cult with a little Christianity sprinkled in the system to make it palatable.

As Tal Brooke says in his book *Lord of the Air*, the great cornerstones of the New Age are intuition and experience.[1] The New Age movement may be characterized by the following: a belief in reincarnation, karma (what you reap in this life is what you sowed in a former life) or the supreme rule of spiritual law, pantheism (all is god), we are "God" and to contact the divine within ourselves we must put all thoughts out of our minds. Contacting the divine within is the key to success, and we must do so according to spiritual law.

Tal Brooke was the primary American disciple of Sai Baba of India for several years. He was in the inner circle of Baba, who was the avatar (an incarnation of God). (Sai Baba's full name is Bhagvan Sri Sathya Sai Baba, which means "God.") The first time Tal met Baba he called Tal by name (without introduction), told him what physical ailment he had, and materialized ash for Tal to eat to cure his intestinal problems. It worked! Baba's miracles have become legendary in India, and because of these he is worshipped by millions in India and the world over as an incarnation of "God." Miracles, as we saw in Chapter 4, do not necessarily convey that one is of God. I doubt that Satan can raise the dead or heal a man born blind as Jesus did, but he can certainly perform some limited miracles as the magicians of Pharoah did with the serpents when Moses turned his staff into a serpent (Ex. 7:9-11).

There are reports that Baba turned water into gasoline for his car.[2] Dr. Thathachari, Professor of Dermatology at Stanford University Medical School, had an incurable carcinoma. When he was in India, Baba "called his name [one in a crowd of thousands], identified why he was there, materialized vibhuti, rubbed it on the doctor's back, and then told him to go back to America." "He electrified his colleagues because no matter how many tests they ran on him, there was no trace of the malignancy at all." Satan can heal. Baba even takes the illnesses of his followers as his own,[3] but he cannot take

---

[1] Tal Brooke, *Lord of the Air* (Eugene, OR: Harvest House Publishers, 1990), p. 39.

[2] Ibid., p. 37.

[3] Ibid., p. 113, p. 226.

their sins!⁴

I'm not going to suggest in this appendix that the Word of Faith leaders are pure New Agers, but there are a lot of common threads to both as well as a common source.

Man is a trichotomy of body, soul, and spirit.

New Age:

> There is body, there is mind, there is soul. They each have their attributes.⁵

Word of Faith: Man is composed of body, soul, and spirit, sometimes referred to as body, soul, and mind.⁶

> We have to understand that man is a spirit, that he has a soul, and that he lives in a body.⁷

We must contact God inside ourselves.

New Age: Shirley MacLaine speaks of "going within" oneself and making "contact with a very personal essence that I can only describe as being connected to the Divine."⁸ "Going within" oneself by meditation is the way to solve personal problems and reduce stress.⁹

> I hold each yoga position for twenty seconds and internally chant, "I am God in light."

> So when we go within and come into alignment with our spiritual power, we come into connection with that spark of Divinity that I have

---

⁴Brooke discovered that Baba was a devilish fraud when he uncovered that Baba was homosexual, and an incarnation was supposed to be above this. Sexual sins are often the giveaway of spiritual fakes; just think of some of the televangelists in the past few years. Another clue about Baba was his great affluence gained by exploiting his followers as contrasted by those who worship him who have virtually nothing. Finally, Baba had no accountability to anyone but himself, being a law unto himself. "There is nothing new under the sun." Sex, money, and despising authority are three prominent characteristics of false prophets right out of 2 Peter 2 (verses 3, 10, 14, the whole chapter).

⁵Mary Ann Woodward, *That Ye May Heal* (Virginia Beach: Edgar Cayce Foundation, 1970), p. 6; Shirley MacLaine, *Going Within* (New York: Bantam Books, 1990), p. xii.

⁶Charles Capps, *Authority in Three Worlds* (Tulsa: Harrison House, 1982), pp. 17, 18; Kenneth Hagin, Jr., *God's Irresistible Word* (Tulsa: Faith Library Pub., 1989), p. 9; Oral Roberts, *The New Testament with Personal Commentary* by Oral Roberts (Tulsa: Oral Roberts Evangelistic Association, Inc., 1969), p. 725; Kenneth Copeland, *The Force of Faith* (Ft. Worth: KCP Pub., 1989), pp. 2, 3; Smith Wigglesworth, *Faith That Prevails* (Springfield, MO: Radiant Books, 1989, originally published 1938), p. 22.

⁷Kenneth Hagin, *How You Can Be Led by the Spirit of God* (Tulsa: Faith Library Pub., 1989), p. 2; Kenneth Hagin, *Kenneth E. Hagin Faith Edition Bible* (Tulsa, OK: Kenneth Hagin Ministries, 1972), p. xxx.

⁸MacLaine, *Going Within*, p. 12.

⁹Ibid.

mentioned before. . . . .[10]

We must contact that great storehouse of Universal Force and Power (God) which can be reached only through meditation and communion.[11]

I am truly God.[12]

Word of Faith:

The intellect and the physical senses will fight him every step of the way. . . . [13]

We are to be tuned "to the inner voice of faith, not the outer voice of human reasoning."[14]

The Holy Spirit is dwelling in your spirit. You cannot contact God with your mind. God is not a mind.

God communicates with the spirit and not with our reasoning faculties.[15]

Guidance comes from within ourselves.

New Age: Ms. MacLaine says we each have "our guides and teachers" to help us better find ourselves and God.[16] She calls these spirit guides, which I strongly suspect are demons.

One had to implicitly obey the inner voice of the atma, or its concretization, the Master.

. . . our ultimate basis for judgment was a private inner experience of intuition. . . .[17]

Each must allow his intuitive self, or Christ Consciousness within, to guide him. . . .[18]

Word of Faith: Sometimes they receive guidance by feeling "a release in" their "spirit."[19]

---

[10] Ibid., p. 83.

[11] Woodward, *That Ye May Heal*, p. 1.

[12] Brooke, *Lord of the Air*, p. 293.

[13] Kenneth E. Hagin, *Faith Bible Edition* (Tulsa, OK: Kenneth Hagin Ministries, 1972), p. xlix.

[14] Ibid., p. lxxxiv.

[15] Ibid., p. xxv; p. xci.

[16] MacLaine, *Going Within*, p. 15.

[17] Brooke, *Lord of the Air*, p. 253, p. 198.

[18] Woodward, *That Ye May Heal*, p. 16.

[19] Oral Roberts, *Miracle of Seed Faith* (Tulsa: Oral Roberts, 1970), p. 31.

> Faith is not the product of reason. . . . They missed what He [Jesus] was saying by trying to figure it out mentally. They were reasoning.[20]

Copeland goes on to say that "Believers are not to be led by logic," and "Common sense will keep you bound when it is time to act in faith on God's Word!" Similarly, Hagin says: "nowhere does the Bible say God will guide us through our mentality."[21] Edward Irving also taught the same things.[22]

All healing is spiritual:
New Age:

> The closer the body will keep to those truths . . . within self through trust in spiritual things, the quicker will be the response in the . . . body.

> Since healing itself is of a spiritual nature, we naturally ask, . . . Are all physical weaknesses and ailments caused primarily from breaking spiritual laws, instead of just physical laws?[23]

> Although it is clear that all healing is spiritual and must come from within, certain treatments from without may be of great aid. . . .[24]

> Disease in the body, as I have learned from experience, begins first with a blockage of energy in the spirit.

> . . . when I go within and literally "ask" my Higher Self why I am manifesting a particular physical problem, I usually get an answer and always it relates to some fear, rejection, or feeling of "nonworthiness." I try to reconnect with spiritual harmony and God. If I'm successful, I get well.[25]

> As you can see, the issue of disease is really a spiritual issue, since the root cause of all your diseases is YOU [emphasis his].[26]

Word of Faith:

There are many who could be quoted, but Hagin, who is the current leader of the movement, says: "When God heals, He heals through the *spirit*. God is not a *mind*. God is not a *man*. God is a *Spirit*."[27] Or, since all sickness

---

[20] Copeland, *The Force of Faith*, p. 6.

[21] Hagin, *How You Can Be Led*, p. 1; see also Bill Hamon, *Prophets and Personal Prophecy* (Shippensburg, PA: Destiny Image, 1987), p. 111.

[22] Arnold Dallimore, *Forerunner of the Charismatic Movement* (Chicago: Moody Press, 1983), pp. 138, 139.

[23] Woodward, *That Ye May Heal*, pp. 2, 3.

[24] Ibid., p. 14.

[25] MacLaine, *Within*, p. 103.

[26] Ric A. Weinman, *Your Hands Can Heal* (New York: E. P. Dutton, 1988), p. 105.

[27] Kenneth Hagin, *Seven Things You Should Know About Divine Healing* (Tulsa: Faith

allegedly comes from the devil, then all healing is spiritual.[28]

Edward Irving taught "that bodily disease was the direct infliction of Satan, and that therefore faith and prayer, and these only, should be employed as the means of deliverance. . . ."[29]

Only the weak need doctors:
New Age:

> As to how soon you may leave off the treatments depends upon how soon you can trust in your spiritual self, your mental self, to direct your physical being.[30]

Word of Faith:

The doctor is a man's best friend if the man does not know how to use his faith.[31]

Smith Wigglesworth viewed those who had to use doctors as weak in faith.[32]

Healing sometimes gradual:
New Age:

Not all of His healings were instantaneous. Not because He did not have sufficient power, but the personality of the seeker had to be considered. Did the person have sufficient faith? Did he want to be healed badly enough to cooperate?[33]

Word of Faith: The healings of the Word of Faith leaders are almost never instantaneous but gradual.[34]

Healing is a substance in the hands:

New Age: There is a book entitled *Your Hands Can Heal: Learn to Channel Healing Energy*, written by Ric A. Weinman (New York: E. P. Dutton, 1988). In this book he states that one can learn to channel energy through his hands and actually heal people. Instead of calling this a substance, he terms it "energy." Shirley MacLaine also speaks of using hands and other things to transfer healing power to others.[35]

Library Pub., 1987), p. 65; see also Smith Wigglesworth, *Faith That Prevails*, p. 28.

[28] Ibid., pp. 13-15.

[29] Dallimore, *Forerunner of the Charismatic Movement*, p. 117.

[30] Woodward, *That Ye May Heal*, p. 14.

[31] Copeland, *The Force of Faith*, p. 7.

[32] Stanley Frodsham, *Smith Wigglesworth: Apostle of Faith*, p. 24.

[33] Woodward, *That Ye May Heal*, p. 17.

[34] Charles Capps, *Dynamics of Faith & Confession* (Tulsa: Harrison House, 1987), p. 236ff.

[35] MacLaine, *Going Within*, p. 259ff.

Word of Faith:

> The Lord said to me, "This is the primary way you are to minister, with the healing anointing. However, the healing anointing will not work unless you tell the people exactly what I told you. That is, you tell them that I appeared to you. Tell them that you saw Me. Tell them that I spoke to you. Tell them that I laid the finger of my right hand in the palm of each of your hands. Tell them that the healing anointing is in your hands."[36]

Hagin goes on to say that God's healing power is "a tangible substance; a heavenly materiality" [sic] and that it is "transferable by the touch, a cloth, or a handkerchief. *And faith gives it action* [emphasis his].[37]

Healing Can Be Lost:

New Age: See chapter eight of MacLaine's book.

Word of Faith: "However, to maintain their healing, these people should continue to feed on God's Word."[38]

Meditation and Communication Directly with God Without Thoughts:

Both New Age and Word of Faith agree that one must contact God within ourselves apart from human thoughts. This is very dangerous as it opens one to spirit guides and demons. Both promote the idea that we receive vital "information" from somewhere inside us below the conscious level. The Word of Faith leaders speak of communicating with God in our human spirits, receiving non-verbal directions from Him there.

New Age:

> Meditation is not something to be taken casually. It is a pathway into the center of self.[39]

> The heart — feelings, emotions — is the seat of the Divine consciousness, not the intellect of the mind.[40]

Both movements seem to relish contradiction. Ms. MacLaine says with glee: "Oriental systems of thought [are] . . . less exact, more diffused and abstract, and therefore more capable of holding many contradictory concepts simultaneously."[41] In regard to meditation and solving problems, Tal Brooke was

---

[36] Kenneth Hagin, *Hear and Be Healed* (Tulsa: Faith Library Pub., 1987), p. 5.

[37] Ibid., p. 32.

[38] Kenneth Hagin, *The Real Faith* (Tulsa: Faith Library Pub., 1989), p. 3; see also Kenneth E. Hagin, *The Believer's Authority* (Tulsa: Faith Library Publications, 1992), p. 63ff.

[39] MacLaine, *Going Within*, p. 69.

[40] Ibid., p. 191.

[41] Ibid., p. 206.

instructed: "Do not think. Do not conceptualize. Trust and relinquish your self totally to the process."[42]

Word of Faith:

Capps speaks of our human spirit, which is the same as our non-literal heart:

> He [Jesus] was referring to your spirit (heart) or the core of your being. When something scares you, you have said, "My heart jumped up into my mouth." But where did you feel something? It was down in the pit of your stomach. That's where your spirit is.[43]

Capps bases this on 1 Cor. 2:11, 12:

> For what man knows the things of a man except the spirit of the man which is in him? Even so no one knows the things of God except the Spirit of God. Now we have received, not the spirit of the world, but the Spirit who is from God, that we might know the things that have been freely given to us by God.

It should be patently obvious that these verses say nothing about *where* the spirit of man is. Nor do these verses say that God communicates directly to us, apart from Scripture, and on a non-verbal level. All these things are Word of Faith imaginations. And in verse ten where the Word says: "the Spirit searches all things, yes, the deep things of God" Capps thinks the word "Spirit" is not the Holy Spirit but the human spirit. What's his proof? He quotes Prov. 20:27: "The spirit of a man is the lamp of the Lord, searching all the inner depths of his heart"! What does this have to do with 1 Cor. 2:10? Who knows? That verse ten is indeed speaking of the Holy Spirit is clear; Who else could search out the deep things of God except God? Verse eleven specifically states that "no one knows the things of God except the *Spirit of God.*" The verse from Proverbs indicates that just as a lamp dispels darkness so the spirit or conscience of a man, when enlightened by the Lord, searches out all his hidden secrets and hidden sins.

Pat Robertson says the same as the Word of Faith leaders. "For miracles to happen through us, God's will must first be transmitted by the Holy Spirit to our spirits."[44]

Both believe in self-love:

Western culture has virtually made a cult out of self-love and the self-image concept. Modern humanistic psychologists and even Christian ones tell us that unless we love ourselves we cannot love others. This has produced a narcissism or extreme selfishness. Modern Christians incessantly want to

---

[42] Brooke, *Lord of the Air*, p. 27.

[43] Charles Capps, *Dynamics*, pp. 47, 48.

[44] Pat Robertson, *The Secret Kingdom* (New York: Walker and Company, 1982, large print edition), p. 270.

know how to adjust, how to love themselves, how to get things from God — in short, how to please themselves.

New Age:

> The *point* is that a great many of the horrors we live among exist precisely because we have neglected to recognize and celebrate and utilize the positive strengths within ourselves — we have neglected self-love.[45]

> If we are not in harmony with ourselves, how can we possibly be in harmony with anyone else, much less the world we inhabit?[46]

Word of Faith:

> Did you know you can't love anybody else until you love yourself? That's what's wrong with the world today. People place no value on their own life. . . .[47]

> The Bible says to love your neighbor as yourself. If we go overboard in judging ourselves, we are not going to be able to love our neighbor because we will not be able to love ourselves.[48]

Both hold to positive confession:

These verbal confessions supposedly speak to the inner man or spirit.
New Age: When chanting "I am God in light," Ms. MacLaine says

> The sound vibrations literally caress certain internal areas of myself that seem to respond to the frequency of the mantra's vibrations.[49]

> Chanting has always been believed to be very effective in experiencing "God."

> All religions seem to agree that the actual naming of the deity in each respective culture gets better results.[50]

> When a body . . . has so attuned or raised its own vibrations sufficiently, it may — by the motion of the spoken word — [eventually bring physical healing].[51]

Quoting Mark 11:24, Edgar Casey, in one of his readings or trances (read possessions), states that we humans can manifest spiritual forces in healing

---

[45] MacLaine, *Going Within*, p. 32.

[46] Ibid., p. 36.

[47] Kenneth Hagin, Jr., *How To Be a Success in Life* (Tulsa: Faith Library Pub., 1983), p. 22.

[48] Kenneth Copeland, *The Mercy of God* (Fort Worth: KCP Publications, 1990), p. 33.

[49] MacLaine, *Going Within*, p. 68.

[50] Ibid., p. 68.

[51] Woodward, *That Ye May Heal*, p. 19.

people.[52] Ms. MacLaine thinks that our confessions or actions come back to us in the form of Karma, "the law of cause and effect — that which we put out comes back to us."[53] Both groups believe in spiritual laws that govern both us and "God" and that what we speak and say invokes these laws to bring us good or bad. This is similar to creating our own reality.

Word of Faith: Charles Capps is so serious about this that in the back of his book he gives numerous verbal confessions written out with instructions for the reader to say these out loud three times a day. God allegedly told him, "Confession is to your faith as the thrust is to that airplane."[54] We must say these confessions "over a period of time for it to really be" effective.[55] How this differs from saying a Rosary over and over is not clear. Even when we pray we must not pray the problem (what we don't want) but pray the solution. I guess Jesus blundered in the garden when He prayed the problem and asked the Father if it was His will to let the cup pass.

We Create Our Own Reality:

Both movements state that we can create our own private worlds by what we say and think.

New Age: "Remember too that we create our own reality." One of the ways we do this, according to Ms. MacLaine, is by meditating.

> The real question is, What do I think of me? All the time, the only true arbiter, the only referee, the only creator of values has to be the very core of our being.[56]

Speaking of her circumstances, Shirley MacLaine plays God and places guilt on her followers: "Why have *I* created this?" Again, "Remember too that we create our own reality."[57]

Word of Faith: "The Word of God is the seed you should sow by saying it — decreeing it — confessing it. It will eventually bring the manifestation of the thing you planted."[58] Continually Capps bellows that we receive what we decree, whether good or evil.[59] According to Capps, God allegedly stated of man: "Anything man can imagine or conceive in his heart, he can perform."[60]

---

[52] Ibid., p. 1.

[53] MacLaine, *Going Within,* p. 55.

[54] Capps, *Dynamics,* p. 307ff.; p. 96.

[55] Ibid., p. 174.

[56] MacLaine, *Going Within,* p. 69; p. 80.

[57] Ibid., p. 47. p. 69.

[58] Capps, *Dynamics,* p. 51.

[59] Ibid., pp. 33, 59-64, 128.

[60] Capps, *Authority in Three Worlds,* p. 54.

Bill Hamon states:

> When the **prophet** lays hands on and prophesies gifts and callings to a person, his words have the Christ-gifted ability to impart, birth, and activate that ministry into the member [emphasis his].[61]

Fear Blocks Our Blessing:
Both believe that fear is what keeps us from receiving the blessings we deserve.

New Age: "Fear blocks access to the God within."[62]

> By manifesting hate, jealousy, contention or things of that nature, we are making our own ills and pains.[63]

Word of Faith: Copeland says that fear activates Satan.[64] "Fear will stop the flow of God's wisdom."[65]

Human Works Lead to Blessing:
New Age:

> Then Baba addressed the whole group to say enlightenment is no easy matter or random gift that one happens to stumble upon. It is difficult. But without grace, Baba assured, it would be impossible to attain.[66]

Word of Faith: "The blood of Jesus is the basis of our victory. But we have to add our testimony, our confession, to it."[67]

We Can Do What Jesus Did:
The way of justification or acceptance with God is to do what Jesus did. He is primarily our example, not our substitute.

New Age:

> We must bear what He bore, because we must travel the same way to perfection that He traveled.[68]

> The only way to overcome evil and sin of any kind is to fill one's life so full of good that there is no room for evil.[69]

---

[61] Bill Hamon, *Prophets and Personal Prophecy*, p. 27.

[62] MacLaine, *Going Within*, p. 69.

[63] Woodward, *That Ye May Heal*, p. 5.

[64] Copeland, *The Force of Faith*, p. 11.

[65] Charles Capps, *How You Can Avoid Tragedy* (Tulsa: Harrison House, 1980), p. 20.

[66] Brooke, *Lord of the Air*, pp. 60, 61.

[67] Hagin, *Faith Edition Bible*, p. lvii.

[68] Woodward, *That Ye May Heal*, p. 8.

[69] Ibid., p. 8.

Word of Faith: This is the doctrine of Edward Irving and many since him. Jesus was not our penal substitute but our example to show us how to overcome. What He did we can do. See the chapter on the Gospel.

Faith is a Force:

New Age: Like the health and wealth people, the spiritual qualities or virtues are all metaphysical forces, not ethical qualities.

> Give then the understanding of self, and add to the surrounding forces first that of understanding, of love, of virtue, of knowledge, of faith, of the forces from within, as directed and guided by that ever-sourceful force that gives and takes away, and present thyself holy and acceptable unto Him who maketh none afraid.[70]

Our thoughts are also forces that create our own reality:

> These, *spiritualized*, are the emanations that may be sent out as thought waves, as a force in the activity of universal or cosmic influence, and thus have their effect upon those to whom by suggestive force they are directed toward.[71]

Word of Faith: Copeland says: "Faith is a power force. It is a tangible force. It is a conductive force. It will move things. Faith will change things. Faith will change the human body."[72] Typically, Capps is even more bizarre. Faith is a force that engages a spiritual law so that even God released faith in His words to create the world:

> Here, essentially, is what God did. God filled His words with faith. He used His words as containers to hold His faith and contain that spiritual force and transport it out there into the vast darkness by saying, "Light, be!"[73]

Likewise, when we use faith, it is *"the divine energy of God* to cause the manifestation of that promise" [emphasis his].[74] There could not be a purer example of New Age mysticism than faith as a force.

We Are Gods:

New Age: This is one of the greatest similarities between the two movements. In all cults either man is made divine or God is made human. Shirley MacLaine glories in man's godhood, even chanting to herself "I am God in light,"[75] further stating that this "is the basic principle of the New

---

[70] Ibid. p. 6.

[71] Ibid., p. 45.

[72] Copeland, *The Force of Faith*, p. 10.

[73] Capps, *Dynamics*, p. 29.

[74] Ibid., p. 151.

[75] MacLaine, *Going Within*, p 68.

Age."[76] "The more we are connected to higher resources, the more infinite we become as human beings," she says, referring to Carl G. Jung for support.[77]

Word of Faith: is similar. They speak of Christians as an incarnation of God as much as Jesus was,[78] that man has "an intellect of such calibre as to be the companion of Deity,"[79] and that "Universal Man has craved Incarnation. Man is an eternal being. He could not have been a son of God and a partaker of His nature unless he was like God, and being like God he would be eternal and in God's class."[80] Mary Eddy in *Science and Health* agrees that man is eternal: "Man: God's spiritual idea, individual, perfect, eternal."[81]

Learning to Contact God is Very Difficult:

In both New Age and Word of Faith, learning to "contact the god within" (New Age) or "walking in the Spirit" is a very difficult process, filled with many rules, involving a tedious and lengthy procedure, which is very difficult to present in words.

New Age: Many times in her book, *Going Within*, MacLaine stated that contacting God within was very difficult.

Word of Faith

> I cannot teach you how to walk in the spirit in seven easy steps. I can only point you the way and share with you truths that I have learned and that are working in my life. I am still learning myself.[82]

Gnosticism and Special Knowledge:

New Age: Shirley MacLaine says:

> To me, the miracle of all is that the alignment is always there whether we are aware of it or not; but only through conscious acknowledgement, only through deliberate recognition of our natural harmony, do we derive its strength. We are what we're conscious of.[83]

Word of Faith Charles Capps says,

> Notice, it's not *just* the truth that sets you free. Everyone who has the Bible has the truth. But you must have *the knowledge of the truth*. You can't believe any further that [sic] you have knowledge.

---

[76]Ibid., p. 108.

[77]Ibid., p. 115.

[78]E. W. Kenyon, *The Father and His Family: A Restatement of the Plan of Redemption* (Seattle: E. W. Kenyon, 1937), p. 129.

[79]Ibid., p. 44.

[80]Ibid., pp. 127, 235.

[81]Mary Baker Eddy, *Science and Health*, p. 115.

[82]Gloria Copeland, *Walk in the Spirit*, p. 55.

[83]MacLaine, *Going Within*, p. 144.

You have to *know the truth* before it can set you free.[84]

Kenneth Copeland is even stronger, seeming to say that knowledge itself brings results: "Knowledge of His will brings results. Once you know for sure that something is God's will, you should not be without it any longer."[85] Hagin agrees,

> All believers should thoroughly understand that their healing was consummated in Christ. When they come to know that in their spirits — just as they know it in their heads — that will be the end of sickness and disease in their bodies.[86]

Conclusion

Could it be that the "Jesus" Hagin and others have talked to are spirit guides, demons who are teaching another gospel? It would seem this way. Ms. MacLaine claims that she sees her spirit guide who "has a human form (a very tall, androgynous being) but sometimes it is only a voice."[87] This is exceedingly dangerous, and no doubt she is greatly deceived.

The New Age leaders place themselves between "God" and their followers, forcing their followers to go to "God" through them. They are mediators between "God" and man, maintaining a tight grip on their followers. The same is true of the Word of Faith leaders. With Sai Baba and the New Age, there "was the impermeable blind-faith closed system of belief fundamental to the whole path."[88] One is not allowed to question the truth of the guru or the system that is handed down. The same is true in Word of Faith; followers are told (brain-washed) not to read anything contrary to what the leader is telling them, as this would be of the devil. In fact though, God's people should be the most objective people in the world, being able and willing to evaluate anything in light of the objective, written Word of God. When Jehovah's Witnesses come to my door, I always want to exchange literature with them, but they refuse. What do they fear if they have the truth? Satan does not like his slaves investigating anything but what he gives them.

Reader, if you are caught up in Word of Faith, please read the chapters on Scripture (9), the person and work of Christ (12), and the Gospel (last chapter). Confess that Jesus is Lord, has always been God Almighty before, during, and after His incarnation, that He died as a substitute for His people, bearing their sins and punishment, that He raised Himself from the dead and ever lives to make intercession for His people. Confess that Jesus *alone* is

---

[84] Charles Capps, *Kicking Over Sacred Cows* (England, AR: Charles Capps, 1983), p. 2.

[85] Kenneth Copeland, *The Laws of Prosperity* (Ft. Worth: KCP Publications, 1989), p. 45.

[86] Kenneth Hagin, *Seven Things You Should Know About Divine Healing*, p. 54.

[87] MacLaine, *Going Within*, p. 84.

[88] Brooke, *Lord of the Air*, p. 317.

necessary for forgiveness of sins and the free gift of righteousness and for all other gifts. Confess that Scripture *alone* is sufficient for guidance. Confess that faith *alone* is what God honors in our relationship with Him. Confess that God's glory *alone* is our primary concern, not ours *and* His.

We have heard that Christians who were formerly in the New Age movement are saying that their leaders told them to go hear Kenneth Copeland because his teaching is what the New Age leaders wanted their people to believe. These converted Christians are saying that they loved Copeland's teaching before they were converted, but now they realize that it was thoroughly New Age.[89]

---

[89]West Coast Believers Convention as quoted in *Word Faith: The Cancer Within* (Adonai Productions, 1991), a video.

Appendix Two

"Baptism in the Holy Spirit"

This appendix is not meant to be exhaustive, but a few observations are in order. They will be divided into exegetical considerations and theological considerations. Pentecostalism in general and the new charismatics in particular promote a second work of grace in receiving the Holy Spirit sometime after conversion. In Pentecostalism one must speak in tongues or he has not had the "baptism" while in other circles it is enough just to receive Him.

Exegetical Considerations

Here are given all the references to the baptism in the Holy Spirit in Scripture, and quoted in the Greek and rendered into literal English.

Matt. 3:11: αυτος υμας βαπτισει εν πνευματι αγιω [και πυρι].
"He will baptize you [plural] in [with, by] the Holy Spirit [and fire]."
(Words in brackets are not found in the majority text.)

Mark 1:8: αυτος δε βαπτισει υμας εν πνευματι αγιω.
"And He will baptize you [plural] in [with, by] the Holy Spirit."

Luke 3:16: αυτος υμας βαπτισει εν πνευματι αγιω και πυρι.
"He will baptize you [plural] in [with, by] the Holy Spirit and fire."

John 1:33: ουτος εστιν ο βαπτιζων εν πνευματι αγιω.
"He is the One who baptizes in [with, by] the Holy Spirit."

Acts 1:5: υμεις δε βαπτισθησεσθε εν πνευματι αγιω.
"And you [plural] will be baptized in [with, by] the Holy Spirit."

Acts 11:16: υμεις δε βαπτισθησεσθε εν πνευματι αγιω.
"And you will be baptized in [with, by] the Holy Spirit."

1 Cor. 12:13: γαρ εν ενι πνευματι ημεις παντες εις εν σωμα εβαπτισθημεν.
"For in [with, by] one Spirit we were all baptized into one body."

(1) Observe that there are only seven times that the "baptism in the Holy Spirit" is mentioned in Scripture: once in each Gospel, twice in Acts, and once in 1 Cor. The verb for *baptize* is active voice in the Gospels and passive elsewhere. The subject of the active voice is always Jesus, disclosing that He does the baptizing. The passive voice indicates that this is not the receiver's

activity, but something done to him. He is not active in the reception nor commanded to do anything.

Secondly, the mood of the verb is indicative, indicating that this is something that will happen, not a command that they are to seek something. There is no command anywhere to seek the "baptism." Christ promised that this would come (Acts 1:8), but He did not tell them to seek it. The mood shows that it is certain. Christ has also promised that the end of the world will come, but we do not need to seek it. They are to wait for the promise of the Father, but no conditions are given for its fulfillment. Indeed, a promise needs no conditions.

Thirdly, the verbs in the Gospels and in Acts 1:5 are all future tense, indicating that the "baptism" is in the future.[1] There are no conditions attached to the "baptism" coming. It is simply asserted as a future event. The tense in Acts 11:16 is also future as Peter rehearses what had happened and places himself before the Pentecostal event. The tense in 1 Corinthians 12:13 is aorist or past, indicating an event that had already happened. *Therefore, since all the tenses before Pentecost are future and the one after Pentecost past, we conclude that the "baptism" occurred in Acts 2.* Thus began the New Testament body of believers, which, like the blood of Christ, was no doubt retroactive to include the Old Testament saints. Why look for another Pentecost and another "baptism" since this has fulfilled what the Gospels foretold. How many times does something need to be fulfilled?

(2) Grammatically speaking, there is no such thing as the baptism *of* the Holy Spirit. However we translate the Greek preposition (*en*), it cannot mean *of*. We would think that we would translate the preposition consistently throughout the seven occurrences. The rendering I favor is *with*. The church was baptized *with* the Holy Spirit, not *in*, for we are *in* Christ, not in the Holy Spirit. The Holy Spirit is in us. Furthermore, the subject Who does the baptizing is the same in all occurrences. In the Gospels the Subject is specifically stated to be Jesus, the verb being the active voice in each case. In the Acts and 1 Corinthians, the verb is passive voice, but the fulfillment is what was spoken in the Gospels, making Jesus the implied Subject Who baptizes. For some to take the 1 Corinthians passage and think that this is not the same Spirit baptism as the other six occurrences is to strain the meaning greatly. *When such a technical expression is used only seven times in the whole Bible, we would naturally think that they all point to the same event.*

(3) That the disciples spoke in tongues is co-incidental to the baptism of the Holy Spirit. It appears to have been a special occurrence; it was languages. I doubt that women ever spoke in tongues.

That it was a special occurrence seems clear from its occurrence on the Day of Pentecost, which only came once a year. This was the birthday of the new body of believers. One's literal birthday only comes once, the other

---

[1] The present participle is used in John 1:33 with a future meaning.

"birthdays" being a celebration of the one day. "Tongues were a sign not because they were expected, required, or usual, but precisely because they were unexpected, unrequired, and unusual. . . ."[2]

That it was languages is clear from what Luke says: "And when this sound occurred, the multitude came together, and were confused, because everyone heard them speak in his own *language*" (Acts 2:6, 8). The Greek word used in verses six and eight always means language (*dialektos*) as does normally the word for "tongues." Then Luke lists the languages represented in verses 9-11. Some have doubted that these were languages because some who heard accused the disciples of being drunk, which allegedly infers that the sounds were ecstatic, not lingual, but Luke specifically says they were languages. Furthermore, perhaps those who accused them of being drunk were the local Jews who did not understand the foreign languages, whereas those who did understand were from outside Jerusalem, having come for the feast.

That women did not speak in tongues may be a possible if not the probable interpretation since Paul stated that he did not allow a woman to speak in tongues in the church (1 Cor. 14:34). One may object that this is not what 1 Corinthians 14:23 means, but if one reads the context before and after he will see that the context is tongues. In any case, Paul said it is not lawful for women to speak or teach in church (see also 1 Tim. 2:11-15), and tongues would definitely be both.

The context in Acts 2 also implies that women did not speak in tongues. Though women had been in the Upper Room (Acts 1:14, 15), when the Day of Pentecost came some days had passed (Acts 2:1). The last people mentioned in chapter one were "the eleven apostles" and Matthias. Then in Acts 2:1, Luke states that "when the Day of Pentecost had fully come, they [the twelve in 1:26] were all with one accord in one place." "Fully come" is the time that passed, and "in one place" is not the Upper Room. The "they" of 2:1 refers to the "eleven" of the last verse of chapter one. The solid proof is that in 2:14 Luke says: "But Peter, *standing up with the eleven*, raised his voice and said to them, 'Men of Judea and all who dwell in Jerusalem, let this be known to you, and heed my words.'" Peter spoke for the twelve apostles, not for the one hundred and twenty. Indeed, there is no instance of a woman speaking in tongues in the New Testament, and yet they have a prominent part in tongues-speaking today.

Another objection is from 2:17 where Peter, quoting Joel, says: "your daughters will prophesy." There were New Testament prophetesses (Acts 21:9; Luke 2:36; 1 Cor. 14:34) and Old Testament ones (Ex. 15:20; Judges 4:4; 2 Kings 22:14; 2 Chron. 34:22; Neh. 6:14; Isa. 8:3). There is no indication that tongues went with the gift of prophecy. We know that tongues were not given in the Old Testament, and yet the gift of prophecy was given.

Someone may object that there are more nationalities listed (vv. 9-11)

---

[2]Frederick Dale Bruner, *A Theology of the Holy Spirit* (Grand Rapids: Wm. B. Eerdman's Pub. Co., 1974), p. 192.

than there are apostles so that there must have been more speaking in tongues than the twelve men. Of course, one apostle could have spoken in several languages, but this is not needed. The listings include groups of people from common areas, grouped according to their languages.[3] The first group is "Parthians and Medes and Elamites, those dwelling in Mesopotamia" whose common language was Aramaic.[4] Judea is also listed though theirs was not a foreign language. Cappadocia, Pontus and Asia, Phrygia and Pamphylia were all districts of Asia Minor and had different dialects of the same language. Egypt and the parts of Libya adjoining Cyrene, visitors from Rome, both Jews and proselytes, probably spoke the universal language of the day, Greek, and to some extent perhaps Latin. Of course, some probably had a local language, too, and others probably knew several languages. Luke does not say precisely which languages the apostles used, though with this listing and the Greek word for languages he makes it quite clear that the "tongues" were known languages, not ecstatic nonsense.

Another strong point against universal tongue speaking is that Jesus was "baptized" in the Holy Spirit, or at least the Holy Spirit came on Him at His baptism, and He never spoke in tongues. The perfect Man who never sinned, Whom we are to imitate in our lives, never spoke in tongues! Surely at best this indicates that tongues are not necessary to live the Christ-like life.

That Pentecost was unique is also seen in that the apostles were to receive power to be "witnesses." I have already shown that the Greek word for "witness" is a technical term in Acts for one who was an eye witness of the resurrection of Jesus. (See the paragraph beginning with "Often the 'miracle workers'" on page 96.) Therefore, the receiving of power and the "baptism in the Holy Spirit" that Jesus told them would come shortly was for the twelve who would bear this special witness. We have no one today who is an eye witness of His resurrection; thus the "baptism" is not repeatable.

We have on this Day of Pentecost a reversal of the tower of Babel with its curse of many languages. In the Gospel the curse is lifted, national boundaries are lowered, and racial tensions melt away. This is a miniature view of the restored world under His sovereign majesty, King Jesus. Furthermore, we have Word and sacrament instituted in this first apostolic sermon. With the preaching of the Gospel (Word), Peter institutes the sacrament of baptism, closely associating baptism with the receiving of the Holy Spirit. Even the Lord's Supper is here (v. 42).

It is very significant that occult practicers,[5] New Age people and the metaphysical cults all promote speaking in tongues. It is possible that Satan

---

[3] The Greek structure makes this obvious, especially with the particle τε.

[4] F. F. Bruce, *The Acts of the Apostles: The Greek Text with Introduction and Commentary* (Grand Rapids: Wm. B. Eerdmans Pub. Co., 1973), p. 84.

[5] See Dave Hunt & T. A. McMahon, *The Seduction of Christianity* (Eugene, OR: Harvest House Publishers, 1985), p. 129ff.

could counterfeit the genuine, but it is more probable that he would want to create a diversion from the true Gospel. Metaphysical writer Agnes Sanford states: "Now in speaking in tongues, this latent power in the unconscious mind of all people is . . . quickened. . . ."[6] Ms. Sanford goes on to describe how through tongues one can minister to someone else below the conscious level or who may have lived before or in the future! The point is that we see these same kinds of statements in the writings of the Word of Faith leaders. Ms. Sanford even speaks of her "baptism of the Holy Spirit" that came "through the sun and the waters in the lake and wind in the pine trees."[7]

(4) The association of the Holy Spirit with baptism is a major point in Acts. Jesus gave the *baptism* of the Holy Spirit on this day, which is to say that water baptism infers Spirit baptism and the reverse also. The reception of the Spirit is usually associated with water baptism, and every one who receives the Gospel also partakes of that one baptism of the Holy Spirit on the Day of Pentecost (1 Cor. 12:13). That the reception of the Spirit, forgiveness of sins, and water baptism go together, see 2:38; 8:12ff, 36ff; 9:18; 10:37ff; 16:15, 31ff; 18:8; 19:1ff; 22:16. Likewise in Rom. 6 water baptism infers Spirit baptism, and if one has Spirit baptism, in other words if he is converted, then sin does not have dominion over him (Rom. 6:1, 7, 14).

(5) The filling of the Spirit is not the same as the baptism with the Holy Spirit. There is nothing in the Acts that would indicate that the two are identical. Yet Pentecostals often speak as if the two are the same. The baptism with the Holy Spirit occurred only once in founding the new body, while the filling of the Spirit may occur many times. The "filling" in Acts 2:4 must be defined from the rest of the Acts, which does not indicate that it is synonymous with the "baptism." In fact the other occurrences seem to indicate that it was something that God simply did without their asking (Acts 4:8, 31; 9:17; 13:9, 52). Nor is there anywhere in Acts that anyone is commanded to be filled with the Holy Spirit or to seek the filling. The single time the command to be filled occurs in Scripture is Eph. 5:18, and the parallel passage (Scripture interpreting Scripture) makes it clear that to be filled in the sense Paul uses the term is to be obedient to Christ's Word (Col. 3:16). One who obeys Scripture is filled or controlled by Him for sanctification. Thus the manner of being filled, according to Paul, is not to plead and beg the Holy Spirit to come on one but to be obedient to the Bible.

Theological Considerations

(1) The Holy Spirit is a Person, not a substance or an "it." I often hear Pentecostals speak of receiving "it," which makes my skin crawl. This is an implicit denial of the Trinity though I'm sure that they do not intend to commit

---

[6]Ibid., p. 128.

[7]Ibid., p. 129.

this error. Since He is a Person, one either has *Him* or he does not; and to speak as they often do of receiving more of the Holy Spirit after conversion in the "baptism of the Holy Spirit" is to speak nonsense. It is as though one had a little of a person and could get more of him.

(2) One cannot believe without the working of the Holy Spirit; therefore, to speak of receiving the Holy Spirit after conversion is to commit a grave theological error: thinking that a sinner can believe the Gospel out of the "goodness" of his heart apart from His sovereign grace. Acts 13:48; 16:14; 18:27; Rom. 9:14-22, etc. deny this. In fact one must be born again to be able to believe the Gospel (see Appendix Three), which means he has the Spirit.

Someone will object, using the passage in Luke 11:13 where the Lord says the Father will give the Holy Spirit to those who ask Him. We make a false assumption that the one who asks does not have, which is not always the case. We ask for grace because we cannot be Christians without constantly having grace. Yet we rightly ask for more. For a Christian to ask for the Holy Spirit is to ask for more grace, for more power in the Christian life, for more of His control over our lives. He is not asking for that which he does not have nor for more of the Person of God the Holy Spirit. That the person in Luke 11:13 is a Christian is obvious because the Lord says the person asks his heavenly Father, and one cannot call Him Father without the Holy Spirit: "And because you are sons, God has sent forth the Spirit of His Son into your hearts, crying out, 'Abba, Father!'" (Gal. 4:6). Furthermore, one cannot be a Christian without having the Holy Spirit: "But you are not in the flesh but in the Spirit, if indeed the Spirit of God dwells in you. Now if anyone does not have the Spirit of Christ, he is not His" (Rom. 8:9).

(3) One of the worst errors of Pentecostalism is legalism; that is, they think that they can clean themselves up enough to merit the "baptism of the Holy Spirit." They imagine all manner of conditions to receive this new experience, such as removing all sin from one's life, persevering in prayer, being still, quiet, in a constant state of meditation, and so on. If one could remove all sin from his life apart from the Holy Spirit's sanctifying work, then why would he need the Spirit? The main purpose of the Holy Spirit is to enable the Christian to overcome the works of the flesh and to put to death the deeds of the body (Rom. 7:14-8:17; Gal. 5:16-25).

They reverse the biblical order of "enabling to obey" and make the order "obey to get enabling." This is precisely the Galatian error that Paul staunchly opposed as a breach of the Gospel: "Are you so foolish? Having begun in the Spirit, are you now being made perfect by the flesh?" (Gal. 3:3). The Galatians wanted to add something to receiving the Holy Spirit besides the pure Gospel, to which the Apostle responds in utter horror: "Therefore He who supplies the Spirit to you and works miracles among you, does He do it by the works of the law, or by the hearing of faith?" (Gal. 3:5). In other words, "the Spirit is the *source*, not the *goal* of the moral life [emphasis his]."[8] Does not Paul

---

[8]Bruner, *A Theology of the Holy Spirit*, p. 231. This is the best book available on the

assume in the verse that the Holy Spirit is continually supplied apart from human effort? Does not Paul state that we cannot merit Him or His working by our efforts? We do not seek Him, He seeks us. He does not lead us to Himself but to Christ. Any extra conditions to the *really* "victorious" Christian life are man's works. As Bruner rightly observes: "There is, in fact, no great distance between magic and conditions. Both seek beyond faith to get hold of supernatural powers."[9] Indeed, "*only* sinners receive the Holy Spirit" [emphasis his].[10] Again Bruner is to the point:

> Grace itself, or the forgiveness of sins, appears in Pentecostalism to play a role only in the Christian's conversion, rarely appears in other discussions, and thus ceases for all practical purposes to be the center, accompaniment, and determinant of the whole Christian life. The reversal of the apostolic sequence of grace-then-obedience lies at the bottom of the Pentecostal error.[11]

The person who thinks that he must obtain something apart from the Gospel, apart from the Lord's free gifts, must do so by human effort alone. And in seeking the "baptism" they commit the sin of the devil, being lifted up in pride, for they "made it" while others have not arrived at this super-plane of spirituality. They are like the Pharisee who thanked God that he was not like others. The difference between themselves and the mundane Christian is that they did enough to merit the "baptism" while the "average" Christian did not. According to them, there is the Gospel, but then there is the *full* Gospel, and only the few who perform properly will attain to this higher level of spirituality. This is the epitome of pride and self-righteousness. Paul again reveals: "These things indeed have an appearance of wisdom *in self-imposed religion, [false] humility*, and neglect of the body, but are of *no value against the indulgence of the flesh*" (Col. 2:23). The Word of Faith leaders do not deny faith's *necessity*, but they deny its *exclusiveness*. In other words, it is not faith *alone* that is sufficient for the Christian life but faith plus works. They need to study Galatians, where Paul maintains, as we have seen, that all conditions for the "Spirit filled life" were fulfilled by Jesus in the Gospel.

All statements such as we must "appropriate" Him, "lay hold on Him," "yield" to Him, are nothing more than subtle ways of making faith a work, for our very "appropriating" is dependent on His constant supply of grace. How can we fulfill anything in Scripture apart from His indwelling presence? How can we "yield" — whatever that means — without His enabling? One of the most characteristic features of cults in general, without exception, and of Pentecostalism in particular (though they are not a cult), is the reversal of

---

Pentecostal experience.

[9] Ibid., p. 183.

[10] Ibid., p. 232.

[11] Ibid., p. 233.

the way of grace in Scripture: They promote the idea that the divine activity is activated by human activity.[12] Notice how Paul confirms this of Judaism in Rom. 10:2-4:

> For I bear them witness that they have a zeal for God, but not according to knowledge. For they being ignorant of God's righteousness, and seeking to establish their own righteousness, have not submitted to the righteousness of God. For Christ is the end of the law for righteousness to everyone who believes (Rom. 10:2-4).

There is nothing more after Christ. We receive everything by receiving Him. We shall have new bodies that cannot get sick, we shall inherit the wealth of the world, walk and talk with Jesus, and have complete victory over our and His enemies — all from His Gospel! "It is not flattering to faith in Christ when it is identified only with a semi-initiation and is allowed only a trickle of nearly powerless life,"[13] which has to be supplemented with human "appropriation" or whatever. Pentecostalism leaves the simple believer like the man on the Jericho road, half-dead, and even worse, he must go it alone without the Good Samaritan to help him! The teaching that only the "absolutely" surrendered, tongues speaking, baptized in the Holy Ghost with fire and constantly yielded person can expect God's best is to turn the Gospel on its head. Indeed, it is actually an implicit denial of the Gospel that they claim to embrace. Anytime a condition is attached in order to receive a grace, the "grace" is earned — period. "Self-emptying" is a condition in Pentecostalism in order to receive the "fulness" of the Gospel whereas in Paul it is the result of the Gospel. We are on a see-saw, whenever human effort is exalted, God's grace is lowered; whenever God's grace is lifted, man's effort is lowered.

There are four Greek words used in Acts to guard the doctrine that the Holy Spirit is given freely, without conditions: "promise" (*epaggelia*: 1:4; 2:33, 39), "gift" (*dorea*: 2:38; 8:20; 10:45; 11:17), "given" (*didonai*: 5:32; 11:17, 18), and "receive" (*lambano*: 1:8; 2:38; 8:17; 10:47; 19:2). These words are decidedly against conditions and emphatically emphasize that He is a gift, unmerited by anything we do, freely given in the Gospel.[14] Paul's argument is crystal clear that human effort and the Gospel are opposites (Eph. 2:8, 9; Rom. 4:1-8; Gal. 2:16). If it takes more than the Gospel to *really* please God, then we are cast back on a works salvation, which means we are all doomed to hell.

In Scripture the Spirit is received precisely because one needs to be cleansed from sins (Jer. 31:31-34; Ez. 36:24-27). God cleanses our hearts by faith through the reception of the Spirit: "So God, who knows the heart, acknowledged them, by giving them the Holy Spirit just as [He did] to us, and

---

[12] Ibid., p. 249.

[13] Ibid., p. 254.

[14] Ibid., p. 184.

made no distinction between us and them, purifying their hearts by faith" (Acts 15:8, 9). The Holy Spirit enables us to love God: "Now hope does not disappoint, because the love of God has been poured out in our hearts by the Holy Spirit who was given to us" (Rom. 5:5). The Holy Spirit is given as the "down payment"[15] or guarantee of more to come (2 Cor. 1:22; Eph. 1:13, 14); He Himself is not the "more to come" but the guarantee of more to come. One washes away his sins by calling on the Name of the Lord (Acts 22:16), not by doing so himself so the Holy Spirit can come in. "The forgiveness covers our major problem; the gift [of the Spirit] brings our major provision."[16]

The way we know we have the Spirit is that we are overcoming the deeds of the body, putting to death the works of the flesh. "This very fight [against the flesh] is the sign of the Spirit's presence in our lives. The Spirit is absent when we stop fighting, not when we lose."[17] Read Rom. 6:1-8:18 to see that this is true. *His evidence in our lives is not physical nor ecstatic but ethical.* "Generally speaking, in the New Testament the demand to see a special evidence of the divine presence is not praised (see John 7:3-5; Matt. 12:38-42; 16:4)."[18] The Gospel gives us ethical power, not physical power nor metaphysical power to control our own circumstances. (See the heading "Man Is Sovereign" on page 19.) The true Gospel gives us grace to give to our neighbor, not to get riches for ourselves. This search for more than the Gospel has led to many schisms in the experience movements, for since experience does not satisfy, one must have more and more. If the group one is in does not have the ultimate experience, then the tendency is to invent new ones, which gives birth to another denomination. The entire sanctification taught by Wesley became the second work of grace, which became the baptism in the Holy Spirit, which became the tongues movement as desirable and then as necessary, which became the baptism in fire movement, which now has become the health and wealth gospel. Norvel Hayes speaks of this latter movement this way:

> How do you get baptized in the fire? By praying in tongues. Just get flat on your face before God and start praying in tongues. Pray for several hours. Ask the Holy Ghost to burn the chaff out of you. It'll hurt. I can promise you that. It'll feel like a burning sensation on the inside of you. But it will get rid of the chaff that's in you.[19]

Of course he does not give any Scripture for this as there isn't any. Who knows

---

[15] So the Greek means.

[16] Ibid., p. 69.

[17] Ibid., p. 274.

[18] Ibid., p. 278.

[19] Norvel Hayes, *Visions: The Window to the Supernatural* (Tulsa: Harrison House, 1992), p. 122.

what will emerge next? "A movement which begins by dividing the reception of deity culminates in the dividing the fellowship of Christians."[20] They divide the reception of God by saying that we receive Jesus at conversion and the Spirit of God later, whereas Jesus said we receive all Three (John 14:15, 17, 20, 23).

These distinctions among Christians are another part of gnosticism with its "average" Christian and the "elite" who have arrived. There are the common Christians who grope, and the super-Christians who have attained. "The Gnostic's spirituality lifted him *over* rather than *to* his brother" [emphasis his].[21] It is interesting that we seldom if ever find love for the brethren on the Pentecostal's list of conditions to receive the fulness of the Spirit. Everything is turned inward to self.

(4) That one receives the Holy Spirit in believing the Gospel is clear from Galatians 3:3 and from Romans 8:9. It is also clear from Acts. Peter tells his hearers that they will receive the Holy Spirit when they repent (Acts 2:38). In Acts 10:44-48 the Holy Spirit was received when they believed the Gospel Peter preached. The Holy Spirit comes as a result of the Gospel and is never to be pursued separately; He is permanently a part of what one receives in the Gospel. He is inseparable from the Gospel. One cannot believe the Gospel and not receive the Holy Spirit, as Paul says in Rom. 8:9. Paul characterizes the Gentiles in receiving the Holy Spirit: "In Him you also [trusted], after you heard the word of truth, the gospel of your salvation; in whom also, *having believed, you were sealed with the Holy Spirit of promise*, who is the guarantee of our inheritance until the redemption of the purchased possession, to the praise of His glory" (Eph. 1:13, 14). In Greek the "being sealed" is the main verb (aorist) and the believing is an aorist participle which takes place simultaneously with sealing. This means one is "sealed" with the Holy Spirit at the moment of belief.

The apparent exceptions to this are only two. In Acts 8 Peter was used to give the Holy Spirit to Samaritans after they had been baptized in order to preserve the unity of the church. In other words, there could not be a Jerusalem and a Samaritan church, especially since there was so much prejudice between the two, so an apostle was used to keep the church united under the apostles. There is no mention of either a baptism in the Holy Spirit or speaking in tongues, and this is the Bible's *only* reference to one being baptized with water without immediately receiving the Holy Spirit.

In Acts 19 Paul asks some disciples of John if they had received "the Holy Spirit *when*" they believed (v. 2).[22] Again these disciples of John had to be

---

[20] Bruner, p. 293.

[21] Ibid., p. 276.

[22] The King James said *since* they believed, which some have mistakenly understood to mean some time after they had believed. But the Greek and the King James meant this: "in light of the fact that you believed" did you receive Him. In other words the "since" was logical, not temporal.

united under the Jerusalem church by an apostle, in this case Paul. Though they spoke in tongues, there is no mention of a baptism in the Holy Spirit. In Acts 8 and 19, hands were laid on the believers, but in Acts 10 it was not done. It is also very important to notice that when Paul learned of their ignorance concerning the Holy Spirit, he did not tell them of the Holy Spirit but of Jesus. The reason should be obvious, namely, the Holy Spirit is a free gift included in the Gospel.

One must not rely too heavily on these transitional phases in Acts in taking the Gospel to the Samaritans (Acts 8) and to John the Baptist's disciples (Acts 19). The norm for Gentiles is in Acts 10 and Rom. 8 where the Holy Spirit is received when one believes the Gospel. Once the church was unified under the apostles, there was no more need for these special circumstances of the Holy Spirit being given through an apostle. Never again do we see the Holy Spirit being given through an apostle. The only occasions that appear to be exceptions were with the various groups that the Lord said they should take the Gospel to: Jerusalem, Samaria, and the rest of the world (Acts 1:8). Jerusalem received the Gospel under Peter's preaching and received the Holy Spirit simply by repenting. The Samaritans received the Holy Spirit through the laying on of hands by Peter; the Gentiles simply by believing the Gospel. Finally, John's disciples received Him from Paul. This covered all the various groups possible.

Someone may object that we receive the Holy Spirit in the Gospel but that we must still have a completion or another work to complete His initial residency. This is not so. "There is . . . no record in Acts or in the rest of the New Testament of a first, partial infilling of the Holy Spirit completed, perfected, or filled later by a second personal reception of the Spirit."[23] Not one example or one passage says that we do not receive all of Him in the Gospel, nor is there any passage that demonstrates by example or states that there was only a partial receiving of Him to be completed later — not one.

In none of the cases, even the so-called exceptions, are we to assume that people were able to believe the Gospel without the Holy Spirit regenerating them, which means that He was already within them. The *visible* manifestation of the Spirit, though, was certainly by the presence of an apostle. After these examples, there is never again any mention of such manifestations.

(5) Virtually every book or booklet I've read presenting the baptism in the Holy Spirit has been an argument from experience. Fred Price has a booklet entitled *The Holy Spirit: The Missing Ingredient*[24] in which he argues that we should have this *experience*. He typically alludes to Acts 1:8 and Acts 2, and then quickly moves on to the experience of others and himself. I would trade a thousand experiences for one Bible verse! If it cannot be supported by the Word, then I don't want it. How God's church managed for two thousand

---

[23]Ibid., p. 214.

[24]Published by Harrison House in Tulsa, 1978, now in the 16th printing.

years without this "necessary" experience is a mystery — unless it is not necessary!

Conclusion

Pentecost was unique in the history of the church and will never be repeated. The resurrection of Christ was unique as were the Ascension and His birth. "The believer must not have separate crisis experiences of first Christmas, then Good Friday, then Easter, then Ascension, and finally Pentecost before he is a full Christian."[25] When one believes the Gospel, he receives God's best, and all the lesser things are thrown in as extra blessings, all as a consequence of the one glorious Gospel:

> He who did not spare His own Son, but delivered Him up for us all, how shall He not with Him also freely give us all things? (Rom. 8:32).

---

[25] Bruner, *A Theology of the Holy Spirit*, p. 179.

Appendix Three

The Sovereignty of God in the New Birth

Who were born, not of blood, nor of the will of the flesh, nor of the will of man, but of God (John 1:13).

How is regeneration or the new birth accomplished? Or to rephrase the question, how is one born again? Where in the Bible are instructions presented on how we can be born again? If it is a sovereign work of God, then man is not the determiner of his salvation, does not set the date of his regeneration, and therefore is not in control of God. The problem is this: If man sets the date of his conversion, then any time he professes salvation we must say it is genuine because God is always willing. And what are we to say if he produces no fruit in his life? Some have invented a theory to camouflage these easy decisions, namely, the idea that man can know Christ as Savior and optionally as Lord. So the first question is this: How is one born again? By faith? By God? By works? No evangelical would say by works, and all evangelicals would say by God.

When I was in seminary, I used to ask my brethren where the New Testament said we are born again by faith in Christ. This was an assumption taken for granted. Usually they would point to John 3:1-8. Then I would ask where in the passage did the Lord tell Nicodemus *how* to be born again. They would usually say that it was necessary or one could not enter the kingdom, an observation I was eager to agree with. The word for "must" in John 3 (Greek *dei*) means "it is necessary" but it is not a command to do so. Even if it were, a command does not mean the person in question would have the ability to do the thing commanded. God commands us to be perfect even as the Father is perfect, and who can do this? How could a command to have the new life of regeneration make the person able to give himself that new life? The Lord commanded the paralytic to get up, but he could not do so with "free will."

But still the question remained, How was one born again? They could not answer, and for good reason. There are no instructions given. Consider these observations. Jesus never told Nicodemus how. In fact Nicodemus asked how, even wondering if it would entail re-entering his mother's womb. But the Lord gives His answer in v. 8 when He compares the working of the Spirit to the working of the wind. Just as the wind blows when and where it wills, so the Spirit "blows" or regenerates whom He wills, and just as we see the effect of the wind, so we see the effect of the new birth by the results in the lives of new Christians.

The verb "born" in John 3 is in the passive voice in all cases, indicating that it is done by someone other than and outside of the sinner. The word "again" in "born again" usually means "from above," again disclosing that it is not a work of man.

Usually frustration would lead them to another passage: John 1:12. They would say that we become God's children by faith, to which I would agree. They would say that if we become God's children by faith, then we must be born again by faith, because both are necessary if we are to see Him in glory. Again I would agree that both are necessary, but then I would point to the next verse: "who were born, not of blood, nor of the will of the flesh, *nor of the will of man*, but of God." We see here the reason the faith in v. 12 exists, that is, they were born of God. No instructions are given as to how, only it is given as the supporting reason for v. 12![1]

Once I was studying the syntactical relationship of tenses in 1 John, and to my great surprise I discovered something I thought was original.[2] In each of the following passages there is a cause-effect relationship between the perfect and present tenses in Greek. In 2:29 the effect (present tense) of the new birth (perfect tense) is "practicing righteousness." Who would ever say we are born again by practicing righteousness? No one but the worst of heretics would say we are born again by our works. In 3:9 the effect (present tense) of the new birth (perfect tense) is "not practicing sin." Again, are we born again by not practicing sin? No. In 4:7 the effect (present tense) of the new birth (perfect tense) is love for the brethren. In 5:4 the effect (present tense) of regeneration (perfect tense) is overcoming the world. Now here is the clincher: in 5:1 the effect (present tense) of the new birth (perfect tense) is *faith in Christ*! The effect, I say again, of the new birth is faith in Christ — we are not born again by faith in Christ but we have faith because we are born again! The syntax is exactly the same.

James 1:18 echoes the same thing: "In the exercise *of His will* He brought us forth by the word of truth." But what is "the word of truth?" The verse emphasizes that it was *He* who brought us forth, by an act of *His* will (see Rom. 9:16) so that the word is His sovereign power, such as Jesus calling Lazarus to life by His word. First Peter 1:3 also supports my thesis as the NASB brings out the causative force of the verb: "Blessed be the God and Father of our Lord Jesus Christ, who according to His great mercy *has caused* us to be born again."

One day a fellow student objected with a passage that I had just worked through, 1 Peter 1:23: "For you have been born again not of seed which is perishable but imperishable, through the word of God which lives and abides forever." He said that the "word" in this verse was the same as the Gospel in v. 25. He was correct. And even though there are two words for "word" used in these verses, Peter is only quoting the Septuagint and interpreting "word"

---

[1] The "translation" of the NIV here in rendering "the will of man" as the "will of the husband" is inexcusable. But then this is typical of the NIV.

[2] I should have known better! I later discovered the same observation by John Murray in *Redemption Accomplished and Applied* (Wm. B. Eerdmans Pub. Co., 1973), pp. 100ff.

(*logos*) in v. 23 as the "word" (*rhema*) which is the Gospel in v. 25. A fact I could not deny. However, Peter is very careful in his use of prepositions in these verses: v. 23 says we are born *from* the source (*ek*) of the seed and *through* (dia) the means of the word. In other words, the seed gives us life which is manifested through our belief in the Gospel, the exact thing John had maintained in 1 John! The seed is the Holy Spirit (1 John 3:9) and the word is the Gospel. To say we are given life through faith is a denial of the passage, for life is manifested through faith. We are given life immediately by the Holy Spirit, which life is necessarily manifested by believing the Gospel. And just in case we should become hyper-Calvinists, believing that some are born again who have not yet believed, 1 John makes it clear that there is no temporal gap between regeneration and belief, for it can be said of every one who has been regenerated that he does not practice sin as a habit, that he does practice righteousness, that he overcomes the world, and that he believes that Jesus is the Christ.

I have virtually never seen it fail that when one is presented with the truth of God's sovereign, yes, irresistible, grace, the person becomes irrational and retreats to some compromise between God's sovereignty and man's supposed "free will." Very often this solution is what they call an "antinomy," an apparent contradiction to man but not to God. Now there is no question there are many things about God we do not know (Deut. 29:29), but this idea of regeneration is not in that class! People use the antinomy excuse so they can maintain their antinomian license, legalistic merit, or human sovereignty. We have to face facts: God regenerates whom He wills, when He wills, and there is not a thing you or I can do about it. Of course we preach the Gospel, because 1 Peter 1:23-25 and 1 John indicate that the person believes the Gospel at the point of regeneration, leading us to believe that regeneration takes place in the context of the preaching of the Gospel. But it is still sovereign. John the Baptist was regenerated in his mother's womb, and Lazarus was called out of death by the regenerating power of the Son of God in fulfillment of John 5:21, 25.

Maybe other biblical examples will help to illustrate what I am saying. In Acts 16:14 we see that "the Lord *opened* her [Lydia] heart to respond to the things spoken by Paul." Did you catch the logical — not temporal — order? The Lord opened her heart (regenerated her) and then she responded (faith) to the things Paul was preaching. The same thing can be seen in Acts 13:48: "as many as were ordained to eternal life believed." Likewise Peter says the source of the new birth is the seed or Holy Spirit and the means of manifesting this life is belief in the Gospel (1 Peter 1:23).

Or take the clear example of Lazarus. We have seen in other chapters that the miracles in the Gospel of John were done to point to some saving grace in the Lord Jesus (bread of life in feeding five thousand, light of the world in healing the blind man, etc). The Lord had stated that He was calling sinners to life in John 5:25, and in John 11 Jesus claims to be the resurrection and the life. Martha thought He was speaking of the Last Day resurrection, but Jesus meant this for *now* as well as the Last Day. As is so often the case in Scripture, the physical infers the spiritual meaning. To demonstrate His sovereign grace in calling men to life, He raises Lazarus from the dead! Did Lazarus call out to Jesus to raise him? Did Lazarus set the date of his resurrection? Did Lazarus even have the ability to blink his eyes? In all the cases, the answer is a resounding No! Did this hinder Jesus? Not in the least. By name and with creative power, He called Lazarus to physical life, forever illustrating His ability to call dead sinners (Eph. 2:1ff) to life. Did Lazarus believe first and gain life or was it the reverse? Obviously, Lazarus was given life (regeneration), the grave clothes removed, and then he followed Jesus (belief). Do you think Lazarus ever considered going back to the grave? No, and neither does the regenerate sinner. Once one is thoroughly changed, he perseveres to the end (1 John 2:19).

Nature of the New Birth

Take special note of 1 John 3:9 where John says those born of God *cannot* live a life style of sin anymore. I might add that John is not presenting sinless perfectionism because he mentions sinning Christians in 1:6-2:2. John Calvin's commentary on this cannot be improved:

> Here the Apostle ascends higher, for he plainly declares that the hearts of the godly are so effectually governed by the Spirit of God, that through an inflexible disposition they follow his guidance.[3] This is indeed far removed from the doctrine of the Papists [Roman Catholic Church]. The Sorbons, it is true, confess that the will of man, unless assisted by God's Spirit, cannot desire what is right; but they imagine such a motion of the Spirit as leaves to us the free choice of good and evil. Hence they draw forth merits, because we willingly obey the influence of the Spirit, which it is in our power to resist. In short they desire the grace of God to be only this, that we are thereby enabled to choose right if we will. John speaks here far otherwise; for he not only shows that we cannot sin, but also that the power of the Spirit is so effectual, that it necessarily retains us in continual obedience to righteousness. Nor is this the only passage of Scripture which teaches us that the will is so formed that it cannot be otherwise than right. For God testifies that he gives a new heart to his children, and promises to do this, that they may walk in his commandments. Besides, John not only shows how efficaciously God works once in man, but plainly declares that the Spirit continues his grace in us to the last, **so that inflexible perseverance is added to newness of life**. Let us not, then, imagine with the Sophists that it is some neutral movement, which leaves men free to follow or to reject;

---

[3] By "guidance" Calvin does not mean a subjective leadership but sanctification.

but let us know that our own hearts are so ruled by God's Spirit, that they constantly cleave to righteousness.[4]

Calvin does not mean that Christians do not sin, but that God's grace rules our hearts, causing us to persevere in faith and holiness. Notice also that Calvin understands regeneration as not only new life but also a change of the heart or the governing disposition of the soul.

Nor is it true that the regenerate person has two natures, a new nature and an old one. In regeneration the person himself is changed, not simply something being added to the person leaving *him* unchanged. We know this because of what John has said in 1 John and because it is the *regenerate* who are being changed into the image of Christ (2 Cor. 4:15-18), not some abstract new nature.

To say the regenerate only have one nature is not to say that we do not have indwelling sin. We struggle every day of our lives with indwelling sin, even as Paul did in Rom. 7:14ff. The one who ceases struggling indicates that he loves his sin, that he does not love God, that he has not truly been born again (1 John 2:29). God reaches behind the intellect, will, and affections and cleans up the source so that now the sinner does what John says in 1 John.

The problem with the sinner before regeneration was a wicked soul, a bad heart. He did not want God (will), did not think of God (mind), and hated Him and His people (affections). All these things — and more — came from within, out of the heart (Mark 7:21ff). Man could not morally change himself anymore than a leopard could change his spots (Jer. 13:23) nor even reach out to Jesus. Everything that comes out of him without exception is sin ("Then the Lord saw that the wickedness of man was great in the earth, and that *every* intent of the thoughts of his heart was *only* evil *continually*" Gen. 6:5). So in the new birth God cleans up the mouth of the stream (heart) so that it will be clean downstream (mind, will, affections).

And why did God use the illustration of new birth except to show that *He* does it and that the person born is *new*? Just as we did not choose to be born, so He chose to give us new life; and just as our birth produced a new person, so does the second birth.

---

[4] John Calvin, *Commentaries on the Epistles of John*, translated by the Rev. John Owen, reprinted by Baker Book House, 1979, pp. 213-14.

Appendix Four

Who Is Sovereign in Salvation?

This is where most people abandon ship. Virtually no one considers God to be sovereign in salvation; man is considered the sovereign one who sets the date and place of his conversion. God is presented as always waiting to save and man as the one who *lets* Him. (We are not going to delve into this in great detail, but for those who want to read more I highly recommend the unabridged version of *The Sovereignty of God* by A. W. Pink published by Baker Book House.)

Richard Eby sees God's salvation this way:

> First He offered them [human creatures] a righteous Law. They rebelled. He offered them adoption as His chosen people. They fled to idol worship. In *desperation* He sent His only Son to reveal His long-suffering love. They slayed Him on a cross. [emphasis added].[1]

God kept trying until He found the right solution: in *desperation* He sent Jesus. I supposed Jesus died in great anxiety wondering if anyone would ever believe in Him. Maybe everything He did was for nothing. Incredible. From Genesis 3:15 God promised the Messiah, and "in the volume of the Book it is written of" of Him (Heb. 10:7). Jesus was not one way of many, but He was the only way and the way in which God had planned from all eternity, the Lamb slain before the foundation of the world (Rev. 13:8). (See heading "Old Testament Justification: Works Without Faith" on page 351 and following.)

Many Christians do not understand the sovereignty of God in this area. They would rightly oppose the godhood of man presented in the Word of Faith movement but then promote "free will." They despise the magic involved in the new charismatics but promote it when it comes to salvation. They do not want man to be sovereign over God in making Him, through manipulation of spiritual forces, do what man desires. Yet this is precisely what they present man doing in salvation when they say that God responds to man's initiations. God has done all He can; now it is up to man to will his way into a right relationship with God, they maintain. Virtually any act of the will that man makes toward God is taken as conversion. The disastrous fruit of this is that many are not truly converted, but to cover these easy "decisions" the doctrine of the carnal Christian was invented which states that one can know Christ as Savior and optionally as Lord. In other words, they make statements that most Christians are carnal, not living for Christ, producing only the works of the flesh (contrary to Gal. 5:21 which says that all those who do so will not inherit

---

[1] Richard E. Eby, *Didn't You Read My Book?* (Shippensburg, PA: Companion Press, 1991), p. 136.

the kingdom of God). They accept the sovereignty of God in some areas but not in all areas. As Hunt so accurately says of the Word of Faith leaders in their view of God's sovereignty: "If everything works according to the 'laws of success,' then God is irrelevant and grace obsolete."[2] It is too bad that many cannot see the same in God's grace in salvation.

The Protestant Reformers knew that "free will" was really the key issue in the Reformation. If man's will was determinative in his salvation, then the implication was that man was not totally sinful but only partially so. If man could do the good work of willing his own salvation, then why stop there? Why not include other human works? The Reformers correctly understood that this would open the door to the whole works system of Roman Catholicism. Therefore, all the Reformers wrote against "free will," and by denying "free will" they meant that man was so enslaved to sin that his every thought, word, and action was sinful: "Then the Lord saw that the wickedness of man was great in the earth, and that *every* intent of the thoughts of his heart was *only* evil *continually*" (Gen. 6:5). Man's heart was wicked without exception ("*every* intent"), without mixture ("*only* evil"), and without intermission ("*continually*"). If this were so, even man's salvation was dependent on the grace of God, and even his "decision" to trust in the death and resurrection of Christ alone was done by the irresistible grace of God.

Consequently, Martin Luther wrote *On The Bondage of the Will*, which was a reply to the humanist and Roman Catholic scholar Erasmus. John Calvin wrote *The Eternal Predestination of God*. Zwingli and John Knox wrote treatises against human sovereignty as expressed in "free will." Most of the Puritans wrote against this. Jonathan Edwards, the last of the Puritans, wrote a treatise against "free will."

Theologically, the concept of "free will" has become a modern fetish. Everyone believes in it and defends it with a passionate vengeance, but no one knows what it means. It means that man determines whether he becomes a Christian or not, the assumption being that God wants everyone saved, having done all He can. In other words, man is not so enslaved to sin that he cannot will himself out of it at anytime.

The question, of course, is where in the "goodness" of man's totally sinful heart did this capacity arise to will correctly and believe the Gospel? If man has no goodness, then where did this good act arise? The Roman Catholics to this day say that man is able to will good things since he is not totally but only partially depraved. The Arminians maintain "free will" for believing but then deny that other works merit anything. Thus the Catholics allow all manner of good works to merit salvation and the Arminians only the good work of willing to come to Christ. Calvinists, however, following the Reformation, Augustine, the Synod of Dort, and the Puritans — and all the great confessions, as well as the Bible — state that man *cannot* and *does not want* to come to Christ.

---

[2] Dave Hunt & T. A. McMahon, *The Seduction of Christianity* (Eugene, OR: Harvest House, 1985), p. 25.

Most people are not aware that all Protestants in 1608-09 at the Synod of Dort declared that both the Roman Catholics and the Arminians were heretics for believing that man can will his own salvation, pulling himself up by his boot straps.

Biblically, there is much the Bible says against "free will." Scripture is so replete with examples that sometimes when I speak on this I ask the audience from the pulpit for their favorite New Testament books, and then I read passage after passage from their chosen books to show that God irresistibly enables us to believe the Gospel. Here are a few:

> But you do not believe, **because you are not of My sheep**, as I said to you. My sheep hear My voice, and I know them, and they follow Me (John 10:26, 27).

> Therefore **they could not believe**, because Isaiah said again: "He has blinded their eyes and hardened their heart, lest they should see with their eyes and understand with their heart, lest they should turn, so that I should heal them" (John 12:39, 40).

> At that time Jesus answered and said, "I thank You, Father, Lord of heaven and earth, because **You have hidden these things from the wise and prudent and have revealed them to babes.** Even so, Father, for so it seemed good in Your sight. All things have been delivered to Me by My Father, and no one knows the Son except the Father. **Nor does anyone know the Father except the Son, and he to whom the Son wills to reveal Him**" (Matt. 11:25-27).

> Now when the Gentiles heard this, they were glad and glorified the word of the Lord. And **as many as had been appointed to eternal life believed** (Acts 13:48).

> Now a certain woman named Lydia heard us. She was a seller of purple from the city of Thyatira, who worshiped God. **The Lord opened her heart** to heed the things spoken by Paul (Acts 16:14).

> And when he desired to cross to Achaia, the brethren wrote, exhorting the disciples to receive him; and when he arrived, he greatly helped those **who had believed through grace** (Acts 18:27).

> He chose us in Him **before the foundation of the world**, that we should be holy and without blame before Him in love (Eph. 1:4).

> For to you **it has been granted** on behalf of Christ, not only **to believe in Him**, but also to suffer for His sake (Phil. 1:29).

> Who has saved us and called us with a holy calling, not according to our works, but according to His own purpose and grace **which was given to us in Christ Jesus before time began** (2 Tim. 1:9).

> They stumble, being disobedient to the word, **to which they also**

were appointed (1 Peter 2:8).

There are several objections that those who love human sovereignty always raise, and they are answered in Romans 9. First, they say that God only *foreknew* who would accept Him and thus chose those who had first chosen Him (see John 15:16: "You did *not* choose Me"), but Paul says of Esau and Jacob: "For the children not yet being born, nor having done any good or evil, that the purpose of God according to election might stand, not of works but of Him who calls, it was said to her, 'The older shall serve the younger'" (vv. 11, 12). Notice that neither one had done anything, which includes choosing Him; it was God's purpose according to election that made the discriminating difference.

Secondly, we hear people say "That's not fair! This would make God unjust." Paul knows that his teaching leads to this objection so he responds:

> What shall we say then? Is there unrighteousness with God? Certainly not! For He says to Moses, 'I will have mercy on whomever I will have mercy, and I will have compassion on whomever I will have compassion.' So then it is *not of him who wills*, nor of him who runs, but of God who shows mercy and on whom He does not. Therefore *He has mercy on whom He wills, and whom He wills He hardens* (vv. 14-16, 18).

Why is this not unfair? Because God said it was not. He chooses those on whom He grants mercy. Paul does not really answer the question but proclaims that the choice is His. With this we must be satisfied (Deut. 29:29).

Thirdly, they object, "If this is so, then God cannot find fault with anyone because they are only doing His will. If they sin, it is His fault for making them do it." Paul responds,

> You will say to me then, "Why does He *still* find fault? For who has resisted His will?" But indeed, O man, who are you to reply against God? Will the thing formed say to him who formed it, 'Why have you made me like this?' Does not the potter have power over the clay, from the same lump to make one vessel for honor and another for dishonor? (vv. 19-21).

Again Paul knows that what he is teaching leads to this objection, and his answer is that *we do not have the right to judge God!*

Another objection is this: "What about all the *whosoever will* passages?" The answer is simple. All these passages tell us who *will* be saved *if* they believe, not who *can* believe. If we promised a million dollars to anyone who will keep the Ten Commandments perfectly for one year, does the offer confer on the listener the ability to keep the commandments? No. It is a promise to anyone *if* he can do it. Strictly speaking, God does not "offer" salvation in the sense of pleading with sinners, but He *commands* sinners to repent (Acts 17:30; 20:21).

The whole Arminian/humanist scheme is based on an assumption that Scripture specifically denies. The assumption is that *ought* means *can*. In other words, if God says you *ought* to do something this means you *can*.[3] But God specifically denies that the lost can believe or do anything pleasing to Him. Consider these verses:

> But the natural man does not receive the things of the Spirit of God, for they are foolishness to him; **nor can he know them,** because they are spiritually discerned (1 Cor. 2:14).

> Because the carnal mind is enmity against God; for it is not subject to the law of God, **nor indeed can be** (Rom. 8:7).

> No one **can** come to Me unless the Father who sent Me draws him; and I will raise him up at the last day. It is written in the prophets, "And they shall all be taught by God." Therefore everyone who has heard and learned from the Father comes to Me (John 6:44, 45).

> But we are all like an unclean thing, and all our righteousnesses are like filthy rags; we all fade as a leaf, and our iniquities, like the wind, have taken us away. ***And there is no one who calls on Your name, who stirs himself up to take hold of You***; for You have hidden Your face from us, and have consumed us because of our iniquities (Isa. 64:6, 7).

> Then the Lord saw that the wickedness of man was great in the earth, and that **every** intent of the thoughts of his heart was **only** evil **continually** (Gen. 6:5).

It is true that the lost do not *want* to believe, but it is also true that they *cannot*. There will never be a person in hell who did not want to be there. Likewise anyone who wants to go to heaven can and will because it was God who gave him the desire and the ability: "Therefore, my beloved, as you have always obeyed, not as in my presence only, but now much more in my absence, work out your own salvation with fear and trembling; *for it is God who works in you both to will and to do* for His good pleasure" (Phil. 2:12, 13). God produces the desire ("to will") and the ability ("to do"). Salvation is *all* of grace.

It is also true that sometimes God turns man over for judgment. In Genesis 6:3 God says that His Spirit shall not always strive with man (see also Deut. 20:10ff). We see occasions in the prophets that God gave His people over and refused to answer their prayers (Isa. 50:2; 59:1, 2; Jer. 7:13ff; 23:55; 35:17; Ez. 14:4ff, etc.). His grace had temporarily left them so that none could believe.

Another objection is that if God decreed sin to come to pass then we have

---

[3]E. W. Kenyon, *Two Kinds of Righteousness*, p. 56; E. W. Kenyon, *What Happened from the Cross to the Throne*, p. 124.

two contradictory wills in God: One will desires all sinners to believe in Christ and the other will decrees that only some will believe in Him. We agree with the objector that there appear to be two wills in God, but we disagree that they are contradictory. Perhaps they seem that way to us, but we know this cannot be. God commands all men everywhere to repent (Acts 17:30), but He hardened Pharoah's heart (Rom. 9:18). We do not invent Scripture; we seek only to explain it. We believe both while the objector only wants to believe one set of passages.

By contrast we read repeatedly in the health and wealth writings that man is sovereign in his salvation. Gloria Copeland says, "The Holy Spirit is not a dictator. He will only move you to yield to Him."[4] If one does not need grace to "yield" — whatever that means — why would he need the Holy Spirit at all? Again she says that "God wants" or we must "allow" Him to do something about seven times in three pages.[5] Mrs. Copeland exudes: "All the power and wisdom you need to overcome every obstacle and solve every problem is available *right now* in the spirit [no capital] realm in God. All you have to do is tap into it. . ." [emphasis hers].[6] Of course one must have power to be able to "tap into it." Repeatedly she presents God as impotent to do anything or save anyone unless we *allow* Him.[7]

Hagin is worse. When Jesus allegedly appeared to him, an evil spirit that looked like a monkey (!) also appeared and made so much chatter that he (Hagin) could not hear what Jesus was saying.[8] Finally in desperation Hagin commanded the spirit to shut up in Jesus' Name, and it did, immediately. Jesus' alleged response was: "If you hadn't done something about that, I *couldn't* have" [emphasis added]. Hagin responded that what Jesus meant was that He *wouldn't*. Again Jesus is reported to have said very emphatically, "No! I didn't say I *wouldn't*; I said I *couldn't*" [emphasis his]. We see from this alleged dialogue that they know the difference between *will* not and *could* not. Furthermore, we observe that Jesus' hands are tied in all circumstances until man does something because He has delegated all authority to His church.[9]

And why did Christ allegedly delegate His authority? It is because no one, not even God, can have authority on the earth unless he has a physical body. This would be hilarious if they were not so serious. When Jesus ascended, "He lost His right to minister anymore on earth as a man."[10] This authority

---

[4]Gloria Copeland, *Walk in the Spirit* (Ft. Worth: KCP Publications, 1984), p. 67.

[5]Ibid., pp. 73-75.

[6]Ibid., Introduction.

[7]Ibid., pp. 4, 40, 42, etc.

[8]Kenneth Hagin, *ZOE: The God-Kind of Life* (Tulsa: Faith Library Publications, 1981), p. 47ff.

[9]Ibid., p. 50. Of course Jesus has done no such thing.

[10]Charles Capps, *Authority in Three Worlds* (Tulsa: Harrison House, 1982), p. 226.

has supposedly been given to the church.

Of course, the forty days that Jesus remained on the earth after the resurrection are conveniently overlooked. As a man He is not omnipresent and thus not on the earth at the present time, but as God He has always been on the earth and always will. As man He can certainly intercede for us and do many mighty things for us that affect us on earth.

The transferring of sovereignty from God to man is very convenient for the Word of Faith people, for it allows them to be the boss rather than God. They are the ones who command things to be and not to be; they seduce their followers with all sorts of supposed visions; and they command God. By contrast the Bible presents grace as God giving and us responding, never that we engage Him. Buchanan sums up the views well:

> The [biblical view] begins with God, the other with man. The one has for its object the vindication of the divine supremacy and sovereignty in the salvation of men; the other has for its characteristic aim the assertion of the rights of human nature.[11]

---

[11] James Buchanan, *The Doctrine of Justification* (Grand Rapids: Baker Book House, 1867, 1977), p. 410.

Appendix 5

Did Jesus Go to Hell?

Did Jesus go to hell? Historically, while the Apostles Creed says, "He descended into hell," apparently someone added the expression in the late fourth century.[1] It was probably done simply to counter the hypothesis that Jesus had been in a trance and had not died. It was added to emphasize that He had died; He had been placed in the grave. This addition was not to add a new doctrine but to explain an old one.[2]

The Episcopal Church, however, has not regarded the "descent into hell" as a necessary part of the Christian faith. One plausible explanation is this:

> The scripture doth assure us that the soul of the holy Jesus, being separated from his body, went to Paradise (Luke 23:43), and from thence it must descend into the grave or sepulchre to be united to his body that this might be revived. And thus it may be truly said: "He was dead and buried; his soul descended afterwards into Hades (the grave), to be united to his body; and his body being thus revived, he rose again the third day."[3]

There are good exegetical reasons to reject the idea that He literally went to hell. First, in Luke 23:42, 43 we read: "Then he said to Jesus, 'Lord, remember me when You come into Your kingdom.' And Jesus said to him, 'Assuredly, I say to you, *today* you will be with Me in Paradise.'" The Lord said that the thief would be with Him that very day in heaven, not in hell. That *Paradise* means heaven is seen from Paul's statement where he speaks of the "third heaven" and "Paradise" as synonymous (2 Cor. 12:2-4). Kenyon and the Jehovah's Witnesses try to punctuate the sentence differently: "Assuredly,

---

[1] William G. T. Shedd, *Dogmatic Theology* (Grand Rapids: Zondervan Publishing House, 1888, rpt. 1969), 2:603-04.

[2] Ibid.

[3] Ibid., 2:607. Another interesting historical explanation is that the Nicene Creed only used "was buried" and the Athanasian Creed only used "descended into hell," both expressions being used interchangeably for some centuries. It was only after the false doctrine of purgatory was developed that the expression "descended into hell" was taken to mean that the Lord had delivered all those from Hades, from a temporary place of torment (Shedd, 2:608). Even today some churches say the phrase in the Apostles Creed and others do not, and those who do say it do not mean that He literally went to hell but that He was dead. Furthermore, even those who mean He went to hell certainly do not teach that He paid off Satan nor that He suffered but only that He preached to them. In other words He confirmed those in hell; or if one holds to the theory that there were two compartments to Hades (*sheol*), upper and lower, He took the upper compartment to heaven. (Read Shedd above for a refutation of these theories.)

I say to you *today*, you will be with Me in Paradise." No serious Bible scholar, to my knowledge, has ever taken such a view. It is a redundancy to tell the thief He was speaking to him that day (today) — that was obvious. Furthermore, the Greek adverb *today* is put forward in its clause for emphasis: "*Today* you will be with Me," and so cannot be applied to a foreign part of the sentence.

Furthermore, in Luke 23:46 the Lord said: "And when Jesus had cried out with a loud voice, He said, 'Father, into Your hands I commend My spirit.' And having said this, He breathed His last." He did not commit His spirit to Hades or to the devil. "The hands of the Father . . . are in heaven above, not in *sheol* [or *Hades*] below."[4]

A correct understanding of Peter's use of David's words, "You will not leave my soul in Hades, nor will You allow Your Holy One to see corruption" (Acts 2:27), is necessary. *Hades* here does not mean the fire but the grave. The early church understood it to be the grave.[5] Also, "Hades" sometimes means the grave (1 Cor. 15:55). Peter used the word to speak of the bodily resurrection of Christ, proving from the Old Testament that Messiah would rise from the *dead* (see v. 30), the dead being those who are in graves, not in hell. Finally, the latter part of the verse clarifies it as the grave: "will not allow Your Holy One to see *corruption*." Only the body can see corruption or decay, and is in the grave.

When Paul speaks of Christ descending to "the lower parts of the earth" (Eph. 4:9), he uses a construction (genitive of apposition) that means "the lower parts, the earth" (see Isa. 44:23). This is a very common usage in Greek. Such usage is strengthened by Paul's contrast between ascending and descending. If "descended" means His going to Hades, then His "ascension" would be His resurrection. Similarly, if "ascending" is going to heaven, then "descending" would be coming to earth. The problem, though, is that the Greek word for "ascended"[6] is never used in the New Testament of the bodily resurrection, but it is used of ascending to heaven (John 1:51; 3:13; 6:62; 20:17; Acts 2:34; Rom. 10:6, etc.). Therefore, the "descending" is coming to the earth and "ascending" is returning to heaven, which is consistent with the Greek words and with the parallelism. The forces He led captive were the Satanic hosts (see Col. 2:15).

The "spirits in prison" to whom Christ preached (1 Peter 3:18) are defined by Peter as those "who formerly were disobedient" "in the days of Noah." Christ preached to them through Noah by His Spirit, the same as He preaches to enslaved souls today by His Spirit through us (Rom. 10:14; [see paragraph beginning with "Romans 10:17 says" on page 185]; Eph. 2:17: Christ

---

[4]Ibid., 2:603.

[5]Ibid., 2:604.

[6]In the LXX the word for "lower" can refer to the underworld or to the earth so this gives us no clue. The Greek word for "ascended" is αναβαινω.

"preached peace to you who were far off"). Why look for something bizarre and complicated when a simple explanation fits the context? Likewise, preaching to "those who are dead" (1 Peter 4:6) cannot mean those in Hades, for Peter says these dead ones can live by God in the Spirit, whereas we know that those in Hades do not have another opportunity to hear the Gospel and live (Heb. 9:27). Also, Paul stated that we were all once dead in our sins but now have been made alive spiritually (Eph. 2:1), words that almost exactly parallel Peter's.

In fact, in Romans 10:7 Paul tells us what he is speaking of when he says "Who will descend into the abyss?" by stating "that is, to bring Christ up *from the dead.*" The Greek word for "to bring up" means to raise one physically from the dead.[7]

---

[7] When the Lord said, "No one has ascended to heaven but He who came down from heaven, that is, the Son of Man who is in heaven (John 3:13), He did not mean that no sinner was in heaven as He spoke but that no one had gone to heaven to bring down special knowledge about God — except Himself. See William Hendriksen's excellent discussion in his commentary on John.

Bibliography

Evangelical Works

Augustine, "Ten Homilies on the First Epistle of John," Vol. VII, *The Nicene and Post-Nicene Fathers*.

Berkhof, Louis, *Systematic Theology* (Grand Rapids: Wm. B. Eerdmans Publishing Co., 10th ed., February 1968).

_____, *The History of Christian Doctrines* (Carlisle, PA: Banner of Truth, 1937).

Berkouwer, G. C., *The Person of Christ* (Grand Rapids: Wm. B. Eerdmans Pub. Co., 1954, 1977).

Bridges, Jerry, *Trusting God* (Navpress: Colorado Springs, 1988).

Brooke, Tal, *Lord of the Air* (Eugene, OR: Harvest House Publishers, 1990).

Brown, Colin, *Miracles and The Critical Mind* (Grand Rapids: Wm. B. Eerdmans Pub. Co., 1984).

Bruner, Frederick Dale, *A Theology of the Holy Spirit* (Grand Rapids: Wm. B. Eerdmans Pub. Co., 1974).

Buchanan, James, *The Doctrine of Justification* (Grand Rapids: Baker Book House, 1867, 1977).

Calvin, John, *A Reformation Debate* (Grand Rapids: Baker Book House, 1966, translated by John C. Olin).

_____, *Institutes of the Christian Religion*, editor John T. McNeill (Philadelphia: Westminster Press, 1975).

_____, *Treatises Against the Anabaptists and Against the Libertines*, translated by Benjamin Wirt Farley (Grand Rapids: Baker Book House, 1982).

Chemnitz, Martin, translated by J. A. O. Preus, *The Two Natures in Christ* (Saint Louis: Concordia Publishing House, 1578, 1971).

Chilton, David, *Paradise Restored* (Tyler, TX: Reconstruction Press, 1985).

Chrysostom, John, *Homilies on First Corinthians*, Vol. XII of *The Nicene and Post-Nicene Fathers*, Hom.

Clark, Gordon, *Faith and Saving Faith* (Jefferson, MD: The Trinity Foundation, 1983).

Dabney, R. L., *Christ Our Penal Substitute* (Harrisonburg, VA: Sprinkle Publications, 1978).

Dallimore, Arnold, *Forerunner of the Charismatic Movement, The Life of Edward Irving* (Chicago: Moody Press, 1983).

Delitzsch, Franz, *A System of Biblical Psychology* (Grand Rapids: Baker Book House, 1899, 1977).

Friesen, Gary, *Decision Making and the Will of God* (Multnomah Press,

1980).

Girardeau, John L., *Discussions of Theological Questions* (Sprinkle Publications, 1905, 1986).

Gromacki, Robert Glenn, *The Modern Tongues Movement* (Philadelphia: Presbyterian and Reformed Pub. Co., 1967).

Hengstenberg, E. W., *Christology of the Old Testament* (MacDill, FL: MacDonald Pub. Co.).

Hodge, A. A., *The Atonement* (Memphis, TN: Footstool Publications, republished in 1987, first published in 1907).

Hodge, Charles, *Systematic Theology* (Wm. B. Eerdmans Pub. Co., 1964), 3 vols.

_____, *The Constitutional History of the Presbyterian Church in the United States of America* (Philadelphia: Presbyterian Board of Publication, 1851).

Horton, Michael Scott, *Made in America* (Grand Rapids: Baker Book House, 1991).

_____, *The Agony of Deceit* (Chicago: Moody Press, 1990).

Lee, Philip J., *Against the Protestant Gnostics* (New York: Oxford University Press, 1987).

MacArthur, John F., *Charismatic Chaos* (Grand Rapids: Zondervan Pub. House, 1992).

_____, *The Charismatics* (Grand Rapids: Zondervan, 1979).

Marshall, Jr., Peter, *The Light and the Glory* (Old Tappan, NJ: Fleming H. Revell Co., 1977).

Mather, Cotton, *The Great Works of Christ in America*, reprinted from the 1702 edition, (Banner of Truth).

McLeod, Alexander, *Messiah: Governor of the Nations of the Earth* (Elwood Park, NJ: Reformed Presbyterian Press, 1803, 1992).

Murray, John, *Collected Writings of John Murray, 1: The Claims of Truth* (Edinburgh: Banner of Truth Trust, 1976), 3 vols.

_____, *Redemption Accomplished and Applied* (Wm. B. Eerdmans Pub. Co., 1973).

North, Gary, *Unholy Spirits* (Ft. Worth: Dominion Press, 1986).

Philpot, J. C., *The Eternal Sonship of the Lord Jesus Christ* (Harpendon, England: Gospel Standard Baptist Trust, 1861).

Rushdoony, R. J., *Infallibility: An Inescapable Concept* (Vallecito, CA: Ross House Books, 1978).

_____, *The Foundations of Social Order* (Fairfax, VA: Thoburn Press, 1968).

Shedd, William G. T., *Dogmatic Theology* (Grand Rapids: Zondervan Publishing House, 1888, rpt. 1969), 3 vols.

Singer, C. Gregg, *A Theological Interpretation of American History* (Phillipsburg, NJ: Presby. & Reformed Pub. Co., second edition, 1981).

_____, *From Rationality to Irrationality* (Phillipsburg, NJ: Presbyterian and Reformed Pub. Co., 1979).

Smeaton, George, *The Doctrine of the Atonement According to Christ* (Winona Lake, IN: Alpha Publications, 1979, from the 1871 edition).

Sproul, R. C., *Lifeviews* (Old Tappan, New Jersey: Fleming H. Revell Co., 1986).

Storms, C. Samuel, *Healing and Holiness* (Phillipsburg, NJ: Presbyterian and Reformed, 1990).

Stott, John R. W., *The Cross of Christ* (Downers Grove, IL: InterVarsity Press, 1986).

Turretin, Francis (1623-1687), *The Doctrine of Scripture* (Grand Rapids: Baker Book House, 1981).

Walvoord, John, *Jesus Christ Our Lord* (Moody Press).

Warfield, B. B., *Biblical and Theological Writings* (Philadelphia: The Presbyterian and Reformed Pub. Co., 1952).

_____, *Christology and Criticism* (reprinted by Baker Book House).

_____, *Counterfeit Miracles* (London: Banner of Truth Trust, 1918, 1972).

_____, *Perfectionism* (Philadelphia, PA: Presbyterian and Reformed Pub. Co., 1959).

Word of Faith Works[1]

Buess, Bob, *The Laws of the Spirit* (Van, TX: Bob Buess, 1968).

Capps, Charles & Annette, *Angels* (Tulsa, OK: Harrison House, 1984).

Capps, Charles, *Authority in Three Worlds* (Tulsa: Harrison House, 1964).

_____, *Believers Voice of Victory* magazine, September, 1992.

_____, *Dynamics of Faith & Confession* (Tulsa: Harrison House, 1987).

_____, *God's Image of You* (Tulsa: Harrison House, 1985).

_____, *How You Can Avoid Tragedy* (Tulsa: Harrison House, 1980).

_____, *Kicking Over Sacred Cows* (England, AR: Capps, 1983).

_____, *The Substance of Things* (Tulsa: Harrison House, 1990).

Cho, Paul Yonggi, *The Fourth Dimension* (South Plainfield, NJ: 1979).

Copeland, Gloria, *Walk in the Spirit* (Forth Worth: KCP Publications, 1984).

Copeland, Kenneth, *The Force of Faith* (Fort Worth: KCP Publications, 1989).

_____, *The Force of Righteousness* (Forth Worth: KCP Publications, 1990).

---

[1]Those with a "?" indicate that they *may* be Word of Faith promoters.

_____, *The Laws of Prosperity* (Ft. Worth: KCP Publications, 1989).

_____, *The Mercy of God* (Ft. Worth: KCP Pub., 1986).

Eby, Richard E., *Didn't You Read My Book?* (Shippensburg, PA: Companion Press, 1991).

Hagin, Kenneth E., *Faith Edition Bible* (Tulsa: Kenneth Hagin Ministries, 1972).

_____, *Having Faith in Your Faith* (Tulsa: Faith Library, 1980).

_____, *Hear and Be Healed* (Tulsa: Faith Library Pub., 1987).

_____, *How God Taught Me About Prosperity* (Tulsa: Faith Library Publications, 1988).

_____, *How To Write Your Own Ticket With God* (Tulsa: Kenneth Hagin Ministries, 1979).

_____, *How You Can Be Led by the Spirit of God* (Tulsa: Faith Library Publications, 1989).

_____, *How You Can Know the Will of God* (Tulsa: Faith Library Publications, 1983).

_____, *Man on Three Dimensions* (Tulsa: Faith Library Publications, 1991).

_____, *Prevailing Prayer to Peace* (Tulsa: Faith Library Publications, 1992).

_____, *Redeemed from Poverty, Sickness, and Spiritual Death* (Tulsa: Faith Library Publications, 1983).

_____, *Right and Wrong Thinking* (Tulsa: Kenneth Hagin Ministries, 1989).

_____, *Seven Things You Should Know About Divine Healing* (Tulsa: Faith Library Publications, 1987).

_____, *The Believer's Authority* (Tulsa: Faith Library Publications, 1992).

_____, *The Human Spirit* (Tulsa: Faith Library Publications, 1985).

_____, *The Interceding Christian* (Tulsa: Faith Publication Library, 1991).

_____, *The Present Day Ministry of Jesus Christ* (Tulsa: Faith Library Publications, 1983).

_____, *The Real Faith* (Tulsa: Faith Library Pub., 1985).

_____, *ZOE: The God-Kind of Life* (Tulsa: Faith Library, 1989).

Hagin, Jr. Kenneth, *Because of Jesus* (Tulsa: Faith Library Pub., 1989)

_____, *God's Irresistible Word* (Tulsa: Kenneth Hagin Ministries, 1989).

_____, *How To Be a Success in Life* (Tulsa: Faith Library

Pub., 1983).

Hamon, Bill, *Prophets and Personal Prophecy* (Shippensburg, PA: Destiny Image, 1987).

Hayes, Norvel, *God's Power Through the Laying on of Hands* (Tulsa, OK: Harrison House, 1982).

_____, *Visions: The Window to the Supernatural* (Tulsa: Harrison House, 1992).

Kenyon, Essek William, *The Blood Covenant* (Lynnwood, WA: Kenyon's Gospel Pub. Co., 1969).

_____, *The Father and His Family: A Restatement of the Plan of Redemption* (Seattle: E. W. Kenyon, 1937).

_____, *The Wonderful Name of Jesus* (Kenyon's Gospel Publishing Society).

_____, *Two Kinds of Righteousness* (Lynnwood, WA: Kenyon's Gospel Pub. Society, no date).

_____, *What Happened from the Cross to the Throne* (Kenyon's Gospel Publishing Society, 1969, fourth edition).

Kuhlman, Kathryn, *I Believe in Miracles* (New York: Pyramid Books, 1970).

_____, *Never Too Late* (Minneapolis: Bethany Fellowship, 1975).

McCrossan, T. J., *Bodily Healing and the Atonement* (Tulsa: Faith Library Pub., 1989) (?).

Osborn, T. L., *Healing the Sick* (Tulsa: OSFO International, 1959).

Osteen, John, *Four Principles in Receiving from God* (Houston: John Osteen Publications, no date given).

_____, *Receive the Holy Spirit* (Houston: John Osteen Ministries, 1980).

Price, Frederick K. C., *Living in the Realm of the Spirit* (Tulsa: Harrison House, 1989).

_____, *The Holy Spirit: The Missing Ingredient* (Harrison House in Tulsa, 1978).

Prince, Derek, *Faith To Live By* (Ann Arbor: Servant Books, 1977).

Roberts, Oral, *11 Major Prophecies* (Tulsa: Oral Roberts, 1992).

_____, *A Daily Guide to Miracles* (Tulsa: Pinoak Publications, 1975).

_____, *If You Need Healing, Do These Things* (Tulsa: Healing Waters, Inc., 1950).

_____, *Miracle of Seed-Faith* (Tulsa: Oral Roberts, 1970).

_____, *Prayers for Seed-Faith Living* (Tulsa: Oral Roberts, 1970).

_____, *Seed-Faith Scriptures with Personal Commentary* (Tulsa: Oral Roberts, 1972).

_____, *The New Testament with Personal Commentary* by Oral Roberts (Tulsa: Oral Roberts Evangelistic Association, Inc., 1969).

Robertson, Pat, *The Secret Kingdom* (New York: Walker and Company, 1982) (?).

Tilton, Robert, *God's Miracle Plan for Man* (Dallas: Robert Tilton Ministries, 1989).

Wigglesworth, Smith, *Faith That Prevails* (Springfield, MO: Radiant Books, 1938, 1989).

Works about the Word of Faith Movement

Barron, Bruce, *The Health and Wealth Gospel* (Downers Grove: InterVarsity Press, 1987).

Frodsham, Stanley Howard, *Smith Wigglesworth: Apostle of Faith* (Springfield, MO: Gospel Publishing House, 1948).

Hunt, Dave & McMahon, T. A., *The Seduction of Christianity* (Eugene, OR: Harvest House, 1985).

McConnell, D. R., *A Different Gospel* (Peabody, MA: Hendrikson, 1988).

Moriarty, Michael G., *The New Charismatics* (Grand Rapids: Zondervan Publishing House, 1992).

Roberts, Patti, *Ashes to Gold* (New York: Jove Books, 1987).

Robinson, Wayne A., *Oral* (Los Angeles: Acton House, 1976).

West Coast Believers Convention as quoted in *Word Faith: The Cancer Within* (Adonai Productions, 1991), a video.

Metaphysical Works

Cady, H. Emilie, *Lessons in Truth* (Unity Village, MO: Unity Books, no date).

Eddy, Mary Baker, *Science & Health*.

Fox, Emmet, *The Mental Equivalent* (Unity Village, MO: Unity School of Christianity, no date).

_____, *The Seven Main Aspects of God* (Marina del Rey, CA: DeVross & Co., 1942).

MacLaine, Shirley, *Going Within* (New York: Bantam, 1990).

Ponder, Catherine, *Dare to Prosper* (Marina del Rey, CA: DeVross & Co., 1983).

_____, *The Millionaires of Genesis, The Millionaire Moses, The Millionaire Joshua, The Millionaire from Nazareth*.

Russell, Robert, *God Works Through Faith* (Marina del Rey, CA: DeVross & Co., 1957).

Sanford, Agnes, *The Healing Power of the Bible* (San Francisco Publishers, 1984).

Shinn, Florence Scovel, *The Power of the Spoken Word* (Marina del Rey, CA: DeVorss & Co., 1945).

Weinman, Ric A., *Your Hands Can Heal* (New York: E. P. Dutton, 1988).

Woodward, Mary Ann, *That Ye May Heal* (Virginia Beach: Edgar Cayce

Foundation, 1970).

Commentaries

Alexander, J. A., *The Prophecies of Isaiah* (Grand Rapids: Zondervan Pub. House, 1974).

Bridges, Charles, *Proverbs* (Carlisle, PA: The Banner of Truth Trust, 1846, 1979).

Bruce, F. F., *The Acts of the Apostles: The Greek Text with Introduction and Commentary* (Grand Rapids: Wm. B. Eerdmans Pub. Co., 1973).

_____, *The New International Commentary on the New Testament: The Epistle to the Hebrews* (Grand Rapids: Wm. B. Eerdmans Pub. Co., 1964).

Calvin, John, *Commentaries on the Epistles of John*, (translated by the Rev. John Owen, reprinted by Baker Book House, 1979).

Cranfield, C. E. B., *The International and Exegetical Commentary, The Epistle to the Romans* (Edinburgh: T. & T. Clark, 1977).

Davids, Peter, *New International Greek Commentary: James* (Grand Rapids: William B. Eerdmans Pub. Co., 1982).

Eadie, John, *Colossians* (Minneapolis: James and Klock Pub. Co., 1856, 1977).

Geldenhuys, Norval, *Commentary of the Gospel of Luke* (Grand Rapids: Wm. B. Eerdmans Pub. Co., p. 1975).

Godet, Frederick Louis, *Commentary on the Gospel of Luke* (Grand Rapids: Zondervan Pub. House, 1887).

Hendriksen, William, *New Testament Commentary: 1 and 2 Thessalonians* (Grand Rapids: Baker Book House, 1974).

_____, *New Testament Commentary: 1-2 Timothy, Titus* (Grand Rapids: Baker Book House, 6th ed., 1974).

_____, *New Testament Commentary: Luke* (Grand Rapids: Baker Book House, 1978).

Hughes, Philip Edgcumbe, *A Commentary on the Epistle to the Hebrews* (Grand Rapids: Wm. B. Eerdmans Pub. Co., 1977).

Keil and Delitzsch, *Old Testament Commentary* (Grand Rapids: Associated Authors and Publishers), 6 vols.

Lightfoot, J. B., *Saint Paul's Epistles to the Colossians and to Philemon* (Grand Rapids: Zondervan Pub. House, 1879, 1974).

Marshall, I. Howard, *The Gospel of Luke: A Commentary of the Greek Text* (Grand Rapids: Wm. B. Eerdmans Pub. Co., 1978).

Murray, John, *The New International Commentary on the New Testament: Epistle to the Romans* (Grand Rapids: Wm. B. Eerdmans Pub. Co., 1957, 1975), 2 vols.

Robertson, A. T., *Word Pictures in the New Testament* (Nashville: Broadman Press, 1933), 6 vols.

Shedd, William G. T., *A Critical and Doctrinal Commentary . . . on Romans* (1879; rpt. 1978 Klock and Klock).

Sweet, Henry, *Commentary on Mark* (Grand Rapids: Kregel, 1977).
Young, Edward J., *The Book of Isaiah* (Grand Rapids: Wm. B. Eerdmans Co., 1972), 3 vols.

Reference Works

Arndt and Gingrich, *A Greek English Lexicon of the New Testament and Other Early Christian Literature*, first and second editions.

Blass, F. & DeBrunner, A., *A Greek Grammar of the New Testament* (Chicago: The University of Chicago Press, 1970).

Brown, Driver, Briggs, *Hebrew & English Lexicon of the Old Testament*.

Brown, Colin, *The New International Dictionary of New Testament Theology* (Grand Rapids: Zondervan Publishing House, 1975), 3 vols.

Bullinger, E. W., *Figures of Speech Used in the Bible* (Grand Rapids: Baker Book House, 1968, originally printed in 1898).

Douglas, J. D., *The New International Dictionary of the Christian Church* (Grand Rapids: Zondervan, 1974).

Edersheim, Alfred, *Sketches of Jewish Social Life* (Grand Rapids: William B. Eerdmans Pub. Co., 1974).

Elwell, Walter A., editor, *Evangelical Dictionary of Theology*, (Grand Rapids: Baker Book House, 1984).

Eusebius' Ecclesiastical History, translated by Christian Frederick Cruse (Grand Rapids: Baker Book House, reprinted from the 1850 edition).

Harris, Archer, Waltke, *Theological Wordbook of the Old Testament* (Chicago: Moody Press, 1980), 3 vols.

Gibbons, Edward, *The Decline and Fall of the Roman Empire* (New York: Harcourt, Brace and Co., 1960).

Koehler & Baumgartner, *Lexicon in Veteris Testamenti Libros* (Leiden: E. J. Brill, 1958).

Jackson, Samuel MacAuley, *The New Schaff-Herzog Encyclopedia of Religious Knowledge* (Grand Rapids: Baker Book House, 1910).

Kittel, Gerhard, *Theological Dictionary of the New Testament* (Grand Rapids: Wm. B. Eerdmans Pub. Co., 1964), 10 vols.

Latourette, Kenneth Scott, *A History of Christianity*, (New York: Harper & Row, 1953).

Moulton and Milligan, *The Vocabulary of the Greek New Testament* (Grand Rapids: Wm. B. Eerdmans Pub. Co., 1972).

Pagels, Elaind, *Adam, Eve, and the Serpent* (New York: Vintage Books, 1989).

Percival, Henry R., *The Seven Ecumenical Councils of the Undivided Church* (Grand Rapids: Wm. B. Eerdmans Pub. Co., 1979).

Schaff, Philip, *History of the Christian Church* (Grand Rapids: Wm. B. Eerdmans Pub. Co., 1910, 1979).

_____, *Creeds of Christendom,* Vol. III (Grand Rapids: Baker Book House, originally published 1877, reprinted 1977), 3 vols.

Turner, Nigel, *A Grammar of New Testament Greek* (Edinburgh: T. & T. Clark, 1963).

_____, *Grammatical Insights Into the New Testament* (Edinburgh: T. & T. Clark, 1965).

Trench's *Synonyms of the New Testament*.

Webster's New Twentieth Century Dictionary, Unabridged, Second Edition.

Zerwick, Maximillan, *Biblical Greek* (Rome: Biblical Institute Press, 1963).

Other

Cogan, Rev. William J., *A Catechism for Adults* (Chicago: ACTA Publications, 1958).

Eck, John, *Enchiridion of Commonplaces: Against Luther and Other Enemies of the Church* (Grand Rapids: Baker Book House, 1979).

Nietzsche, Friedrich, *Joyful Wisdom* (New York: Frederick Ungar Pub. Co., 1975).

Schroeder, Rev. H. J., *The Canons and Decrees of the Council of Trent* (Rockford, IL: Tan Books and Publishers, 1978).

Stevenson, Burton Egbert, *The Home Book of Verse* (New York: Holt, Rinehart & Winston, 1965).

Index to Subjects & Persons

Adam, God on earth?	255, 272
____, lost the earth to Satan?	270
Alexander, J. A.	145
Anabaptists	39ff
Arminianism	413ff
Athanasius	88
Atonement	129ff
____, benefits	132ff
Augustine	84, 374
Barron, Bruce	156, 208
Bible, becomes word of God	217
____, clear to all	219
____, Council of Trent	220
____, God tells Capps what it means	219
____, God tells Hagin what it means	219
____, Holy Spirit inseparably bound to	235ff
____, human experience	27
____, infallibility inescapable	214
____, intuition	238
____, new revelation today	232
____, not enough?	19
____, not the word until you speak it?	216
____, only elite can interpret?	220
____, personal experience	217
____, revelation knowledge also God's Word	216ff
____, *rhema* and *logos*	217
____, Roman Catholic leaders interpret	220
____, sufficient	222ff
____, the only revelation knowledge	222ff
____, true interpretation	221
____, vagueness in modern prophecy	239ff
____, visions also for today?	218
Brooke, Tal	381
____, intuition is New Age	238
Brown, David	50
Bruner, Frederick	63
Buess, Bob	72, 180
____, Jesus not use deity on earth	324
Call to ministry	37, 247, 295ff
Calvin, John, Bible & Spirit inseparable	237ff
____, on 1 John 3:9	410
____, on miracles	99
Capps, Annette	34
____, infallible interpretation	234

Capps, Charles, Bible not word unless confessed 216
—————————, doctors for weak in faith 108
—————————, faith in faith 149
—————————, healing, Old Testament wrong 117, 11
—————————, Hebrews 11 men not subject to trials 284
—————————, Jesus born again 318
—————————, Jesus not use deity on earth 323ff
—————————, magic and positive confession 179
—————————, man is God 257
—————————, not Trinitarian 326
—————————, on Hebrew language 118
—————————, on Hebrews 12:5-16 288
—————————, on Romans 8:28 287
—————————, only Satan causes disasters 280
—————————, positive confession, and angels 196
—————————, positive confession, twists Scripture 193ff
—————————, prosperity 163
—————————, purpose of miracles 97
—————————, redemption not finished on Cross 340
—————————, unity versus doctrine 251
—————————, virgin birth by man's mind 312ff
—————————, two deaths 134
Chalmers, Thomas 46, 47
Chemnitz, Martin 307
Chilton, Rev. David 226
Cho, Paul Yonngi....................74, 74-77, 178
—————————, 4 dimensions 78
—————————, Bible only potential truth 217
—————————, we control Jesus with words 204
Christian Science 11, 32
Chrysostom, John 84, 238
Church versus individualism 301ff
——————, accountability 300ff
——————, call to ministry 295
——————, no salvation outside? 295
——————, not important? 294
Coleridge, Samuel Taylor 46
—————————, influenced Irving 3 ways 48, 316
—————————, on the Spirit 49
Copeland, Gloria, Jesus sinful 316ff
—————————, full of pride 258ff
—————————, Hagin a prophet 232
—————————, not need Bible 233
—————————, Second Coming hysteria 37, 250
Copeland, Kenneth, Adam was God 255
—————————, Jesus born again 318
—————————, man is one with God 327
—————————, plagiarizing Kenyon 203

Index to Subjects & Persons 437

_____, poverty is of the devil ...170
_____, prosperity ...164
_____, Second Coming hysteria ...250
_____, trials not help Christians ...281
Cotton, John ...40
Council of Constantinople II ...309
_____ Ephesus ...309
Creator/creature distinction ...12
Crouch, Paul ...86, 202
Dabney, R. L., on atonement ...130
Dallimore, Arnold ...316
Deaths, two ...133f
Dowie, John Alexander ...51ff
Eby, Richard, man is sovereign in salvation ...413
_____, writes God's Word ...235
Eck, John ...220
Eddy, Mary Baker ...69
_____, healing is of God ...103
_____, man one with God ...327
_____, positive confession ...185
_____, virgin birth by mind ...312
Eusebius ...83
Faith alone or faith plus? ...359
_____ in faith ...149
_____, a force? ...391
_____, how does it work for them ...71
_____, its object ...372ff
_____, seed-faith ...77
_____, true ...258, 351
_____, word of faith versus Bible ...73ff
_____, works without faith ...351
Finney, Charles ...56ff, 294
Freeman, Hobart E. ...57
Frye, Pete ...125, 126, 157, 260
Gibbon, Edward ...85
Gnosticism ...11ff
_____, 3 kinds of people ...18, 25
_____, dualism ...13, 68, 332
_____, elitism ...24, 404
_____, "faith" determines all ...23
_____, individualism ...25
_____, knowledge ...14, 392
_____, man is sovereign ...19
_____, narcissism ...26
_____, no Old Testament ...28
_____, pragmatism ...27
_____, pursuit of power ...19
_____, revelation knowledge ...18

———, salvation 26
———, spiritual law 21
———, syncretism 26
God, accountable to man? 278
___, & evil 265ff
___, believes in us? 208
___, controls our trials 282ff
___, created by faith? 204
___, dominion 260
___, enslaved to man & Satan? 279
___, has things in a mess? 274
___, just to the devil? 278
___, legally can't do anything? 274ff
___, limited in knowledge? 277
___, limited in power? 277
___, lonely? 276
___, Lord of natural disasters 280
___, not manipulated 258
___, offered kingdoms to Jesus 275
___, sovereign 255ff
___, under spiritual law? 204ff
Gordon, A. J. 87, 88
Gospel, divine nature 348
———, examples of theirs 370ff
———, justification & sanctification 347
———, new birth, biblical view 350ff
———, not enough? 24
———, not work of the Holy Spirit 368
———, obey for grace or reverse? 400
———, Old Testament saints believed Gospel 352ff
———, overcoming flesh 403
———, restored by them? 32
———, righteousness 346
———, what is it? 367ff, 373
Grace, deny common grace 104
Gregory of Nyssa 88
Gromacki, Robert Glenn 227
Guidance, how to have 245
————, must use mind 239ff, 245ff
————, New Age say not use mind 243
————, not use mind? 238ff
————, obey inner voice? 243
————, providence 248
Hagin, Kenneth, Adam was God 272
—————, Bible not enough 229
—————, Bible Word of God only when confessed 217
—————, Cross was a defeat 340
—————, deny symptoms 103

Index to Subjects & Persons

_____, faith in faith 149
_____, God has things in a mess 274
_____, God speaks directly to us 213
_____, in new birth we receive God's essence 349
_____, intuition is God's voice 238
_____, James 5 for the weak........................ 110
_____, Jesus cannot shut up Satan 418
_____, Jesus not use deity on earth 323
_____, Jesus says Satan is lord 272ff
_____, Jesus sinful 316
_____, obey inner voice 243
_____, on healing 124ff
_____, plagiarized 55
_____, point of contact 148
_____, positive confession 77
_____, prosperity 165
_____, redemption not finished on Cross ... 340
Hagin, Jr., Kenneth, heir to his father's ministry 230
_____, Jesus not unique 327
_____, Jesus not use deity on earth 323
Hamon, Bill 62
_____, Bible not enough 227, 22
_____, collects new prophecies 234
_____, peace in heart for guidance 241
_____, receives prophecies in KJV 235
Hayes, Norvel 105
_____, 17 yr. old girl called to ministry....... 296
_____, get mind out of way 239
_____, healing in hands 153
_____, man's words bind God 281
_____, visions 218
Healing and magic 107
_____ in hands, Norvel Hayes 153
_____, a substance 385
_____, atonement 129ff
_____, by Holy Spirit to our spirits 387
_____, Charles Capps, doctors for the weak 108
_____, death 157
_____, deny symptoms 103
_____, doctors only for weak in faith 108
_____, fear, Unity School of Christianity 113
_____, Fred Price 150
_____, Fred Price, being sick stupid 156
_____, gradual 151
_____, is faith necessary? 146
_____, Kenneth Hagin on 124ff
_____, lack of, who blamed 155
_____, Lord healed all 156

_____, New Age, Shirley MacLaine 106
_____, objections to orthodox view 142ff
_____, Old Testament wrong 117
_____, Oral Roberts, God heals only Christians 105
_____, physical, 3 cults 21, 54
_____, physical, proof one is of God? 103
_____, point of contact 148, 153
_____, prayer cloths 152ff
_____, rules for 154
_____, through spirit 384
_____, T. J. McCrossah 140ff
_____, Warfield on superstition 106
Hell, only one sin send to? 369ff
Hengstenberg, E. W. 145
Henley, W. E. 259
Hinduism 75
Hinn, Benny 202
_____, what is God like? 255
History, how to explain their newness 65
_____, learn from the past 31ff
Hodge, A. A. 145
Holy Spirit (see Mysticism also)
_____, baptism in 395ff
_____, filling of 399
_____, received when one believes 404
_____, speaks in the heart? 211
_____, "yielding" 418
Horton, Michael 201, 208
Hughes, Philip 121, 200
Hunt, Dave, doing God's will 291
Hutchinson, Ann 41ff
Interpretation, directly from God 194
_____, get mind out of way 239
_____, method 184
_____, must use mind 240
Irenaeus 63
Irving, Edward 45ff
_____, converted? 46
_____, healing means one is of God 103
_____, his imagination 49
_____, Jesus was sinful 314ff
_____, loved transcendentalism 46ff
_____, Second Coming near 231
Jefferson, Thomas 289
Jehovah's Witnesses 32
Jesus, ancient heresies 308
____, born again & justified? 317ff
____, born again? 317

Index to Subjects & Persons 441

____, claimed to be God 304
____, confesses Satan as lord? 272ff
____, created? 323
____, emptiedHimself of His deity? 328
____, finished redemption on Cross 341
____, firstborn 319
____, God again after the resurrection? 324
____, God while on earth 309
____, has no right to minister on earth? 418
____, how many mediators? 357ff
____, "It is finished" 340
____, Lord of earth 268ff
____, not functioned as God on earth? 323
____, not unique? 323
____, "only begotten" 320
____, orthodox teaching 303ff
____, redemption to Satan? 336ff
____, sinful? 314ff
____, subject to our authority? 418
____, substitute 334ff
____, "Today I have begotten Thee" 321
____, took curse of poverty? 332
____, upholds all things 263
____, virgin birth by man's mind? 312ff
____, went to hell? 421ff
Kayser, Rev. Phil 226
Kenyon, E. W. 157
_____, attended metaphysical college 54
_____, father of movement 32, 53ff
_____, God is accountable to man 278
_____, God limited in knowledge 277
_____, God limited in power 277
_____, God was lonely 276
_____, in new birth we receive God's essence 348-49
_____, Jesus born again & justified 317ff
_____, Jesus did not claim to be God 304
_____, Jesus not use deity on earth 323
_____, Jesus paid off Satan 336ff
_____, Jesus sinful 316
_____, Jesus taken out of Godhead 329
_____, learned from Quimby 53
_____, magic 179
_____, man is one with God 327
_____, man ruled the universe 280
_____, positive confession key to grace 216
_____, pride 17
_____, prophet? 33
_____, redemption not finished on Cross 340

_____, salvation 32
Keswick 57
Kuhlman, Kathryn 61
_____, healed without faith 147
_____, her beliefs 62
_____, no miracles done 100
Lacunza 50
Laws, spiritual, how work 69ff
Luther, Martin 220
MacArthur, John F. 95, 202
_____, God not manipulated 258
MacLaine, Shirley, "going within" 44
_____, mysticism 12
_____, New Age healers 106
_____, "we are gods" 45
Man, 3 parts? 18, 360ff
___, as God (see pantheism)
___, as gods? 199, 257, 391
___, has authority over Jesus? 418
___, his words bind God? 281
___, ruled the universe? 280
Martyr, Justin 84
Mather, Cotton 39
McConnell, D. R. 54ff
McCrossan, T. J., on healing 127, 140ff
_____, rules for healing 154
_____, unbelief & healing 148
McLeod, Alexander 271
Mills, Rev. Douglas 23, 52, 98,
..... 110, 160, 178
..... 180, 185
Minister, must be male 296
Ministry, 17 yr. old girl called to? 296
_____, call to (see Call to ministry)
Miracles, 3 time periods 89ff
_____, ceased in early church 82
_____, in John's Gospel 88
_____, John Calvin on 99
_____, Kathryn Kuhlman, none done 100
_____, no proof one is of God 101
_____, Pat Robertson 100
_____, permanent? 37
_____, Roman Catholic Church 98
_____, Sai Baba of India 381
_____, search for power 85
_____, validate 92
_____, versus ethics 87
_____, Warfield 88

Index to Subjects & Persons

Montanism 34ff
Morecraft, Joseph..222
Moriarty, Michael G. 333
Murray, John, guidance 242ff, 249
Mysticism 212
_____, against traditional doctrines 215
_____, brain washing 214
_____, by-passing the mind 213
_____, God speaks to us directly 213
_____, intuition 213
_____, Unity School of Christianity 212
Nee, Watchman 361
Neo-evangelicals 211
New Age 75
New Age & Word of Faith 381ff
New Birth, sovereignly done 407ff
_____, what is it? 410ff
_____, we receive God's essence? 345ff, 349
Nietzsche, Friedrich 259
Occultism, heart of 22
Osborn, T. L., on Paul's thorn 122
Osteen, John 166ff, 180
_____, against church doctrines 215
_____, visions 233
Packer, J. I. 158
Pantheism 12, 199ff
_____, in the new birth 349ff
_____, is man one with the Father? 327ff
Pink, A. W. 413
Ponder, Catherine 159
Positive confession 77
_____, angels 196
_____, Capps twists Scripture 184ff
_____, Capps, "What you say is what you get" ...177
_____, creating our own realities 179, 187ff
_____, Fred Price 178
_____, how it works 182ff
_____, Karma 389
_____, Kenyon 179
_____, magic 179
_____, man as God 199
_____, mantra 257
_____, Mary Baker Eddy 185
_____, metaphysical writers agree ...178
_____, negative ones 206ff
_____, passages used 191ff
_____, Pat Robertson 181
_____, Paul Cho 178

_____, personal relationship God	187
_____, tell God what His obligation is	179
_____, Unity School of Christianity	181, 183
_____, visualization	180, 181
_____, we control God and Jesus	204
_____, where does prayer come in?	188
Prayer of agreement	190
Prayer, does God always answer?	188ff
Price, Fred	156
_____, God can't trespass on earth	335
_____, God legally can't do anything on earth	274ff
_____, healing versus miracles	150
_____, Holy Spirit	405
_____, Jesus took curse of poverty	332
_____, positive confession	178
_____, Satan is lord of world	273
Prince, Derek, virgin birth by man's mind	312
Prosperity, Capps, results guaranteed	163
_____, Capps, twists Scripture	169ff
_____, covetousness	168
_____, each promoter has different scheme	161
_____, get greedy	167
_____, give to get	160
_____, in metaphysical cults first	159
_____, indulgences	162
_____, John Osteen	166ff
_____, Kenneth Copeland	164
_____, Kenneth Hagin	165
_____, "make a vow" (Tilton)	165
_____, seed-faith	163, 166
_____, Unity School of Christianity	167
_____, used credit cards	166
_____, what God says	168
Providence	248
_____, denied	22
_____, versus spiritual laws	289ff
Quakers	42ff
Rev. Ike	160
Revelation, must use mind	240
Roberts, Oral, Bible not only revelation	216
_____, God heals only Christians	105
_____, Gospel	371
_____, his life	58ff
_____, his techniques	60ff
_____, his theology	60
_____, miracles	88
_____, not heal people	58, 61
_____, only Satan brings disaster	281

Index to Subjects & Persons

_____, orator 46
_____, point of contact 148
_____, positive confession 77, 178
_____, prayer cloths 152ff
_____, preach the Gospel? 58
_____, prophet? 35, 229
_____, prosperity 162
_____, *rhema & logos* 217
_____, Second Coming hysteria 36, 250
_____, seed-faith 163, 166
_____, writes God's Word himself 234
Roberts, Patti 61
_____, left the movement 59
_____, lived it up 161
_____, seed-faith 163
Roberts, Richard, credit cards 166
_____, heir to his father's ministry 59ff, 230
_____, lived it up 161
Robertson, Pat 181
_____, healing by spirit 387
_____, Jesus not function as God 326
_____, miracles 100
_____, positive confession 199
Robinson, Wayne A. 58
Sacraments 297ff
Sadoleto, Jacopo 236
Salvation, "free will" 414
_____, God is sovereign 413ff
_____, "whosoever will" 416
Satan, cast people into hell? 271ff
_____, god of this world 273
_____, lord of world? 273ff
_____, offered kingdoms to Jesus? 275
_____, only he causes disasters 280ff
_____, owns planet earth 335
Schuller, Robert 75
Second Coming, Gloria Copeland 37
_____, hysteria 180
_____, near? 36, 231
_____, nearness excuss for excess 250
_____, Oral Roberts 36
Shedd, William G. T. on Romans 8:3 315
Sickness, from Satan? 385
Smeaton 341
Spiritual law, above God 78ff
Star Wars 68
Storms, Sam 95, 143
Tetzel 162

Tilton, Robert, "make a vow" 165
————————, positive confession 179
————————, prayer cloths 152
————————, pride 38
————————, prophet? 35, 229
————————, prosperity 161ff
————————, women 34
————————, word miracle used repeatedly 82
Tongues, common to New Age & occult 398
————————, no woman ever spoke in 396ff
Transcendentalists 46
Trials, fear 285ff
———, Hebrews 12:5-16 288
———, Job 284ff
———, not for Christians? 281ff
———, not to be gloried in? 282
———, Romans 8:28 287
———, spiritual growth 290
Trinity, deny 38
Unity School of Christianity 77
————————————————, doctors 108
————————————————, healing & fear 113
————————————————, healing means of God 103
————————————————, prosperity 167
————————————————, we are one with God 327
Unity versus doctrine 251
Visualization 74ff
Warfield, B. B. 16
————————, Christ is all 225
————————, definition of miracle 88
————————, on leading of Spirit **244ff**
Wiersbe, Warren 333
Wigglesworth, Smith 52ff
————————, demon of Christian Science 107
Women leaders 12
———, Irving 49ff
———, Montanism, prominent 35, 36
———, prominent 34, 43
Worship 297ff
Young, E. J. 145

Index to Scripture

Genesis
1:26, 28 281
1:28 260
2:7 143
3:5 20
3:15 .... 313, 314
.... 413
6:3 417
6:5 .... 73, 411, 417,
.... **414**[1]
12:17 136
20:6 265
20:17 .... 140, 141
25:23 138
31:28 118
32:22-32 126
49:1 227
50:22 141

Exodus
3:14 98
4:6ff 126
4:11 .... **206**, 304
4:21 265
4:22 320
4:29 90
7:3 265
7:9-11 381
11:1 136
12:22 342
14:4 265
15:20 397
15:26 .... 108, 115,
.... 140, 141
21:12-14 280
22:9, 28 306

Leviticus
5:1, 17 135
5:21 146
7:18 135
13-14 114
14:3, 48 140
15 115
16:22 .... 135, 146
17:16 135
17:17 135
19:8 135
19:8, 17 146
20:17,19,20 . 135

22:9 146
24:15 .... 135, 146
26:14-16 115

Numbers
5:31 146
9:13 146
11 63
12:9-15 116
12:10ff 126
12:13 141
14:13 140
14:19 135
14:41 171
16:46-49 116
19:6, 18 342
24:14 227

Deuteronomy
3:26 336
4:2 223
6:5 364
7:12, 15 116
7:15 .... 135 (2)
8 .... 76, 300
8:1 245
8:2 127
8:2-3 282
8:18 .... **173**
13:1-4 230
17:6 243
18:21-22 ...... 36, 231
19:15 243
20:10ff 417
24:8 193
28 .... 76, 107,
.... 300
28:1 .... **193**, 194 (2)
28:27, 35 140
28:58-61 116
28:59, 61 135
29:29 .... 409, 416
30:3 140
31:29 227
32:39 140

Joshua
1:8 .... **191**
4:1-7 31
11:20 265

Judges
4:4 397
14:6, 19 171
15:14 171

1 Samuel
1:13 192
1:15 363
10 63
15:23 178
16:10-11 320
18:10 265

2 Samuel
7:14 136
12:13-16 119
12:22-24 119
24:1 .... 123 (2)

1 Kings
3:6-14 190
6:3 140
8:37-38 136
15:1-5 126
17:17 135
17:24 90
18:39 90
19:11-12 ...... **240**
22 266
22:20-23 265

2 Kings
1:2 135
6:15-17 198
8:1 263
8:8-9 135
13:14 .... 119, 135
15:5 126
20:1 120
20:5, 8 ...... 140, 141
22:14 397

1 Chronicles
21:1 123

2 Chronicles
5:14 98
6:28ff 136
6:30 139
7:14 .... 139 (2)
16:12 .... 103, 135
21:12-15,18 . 117
21:15,18,19 . 135

---

[1] Bold numbers are pages where biblical text has extended treatment.

34:22 397
Nehemiah
4:2 139
6:14 397
8:7-8 221
Job
1-2 113
1:6-8 .... **285**
1:16 286
1:21 285
1:22 285
2:3 286
3:5 286
5:18 140
7:11 363
12:21 140
13:4 114
13:15 286
16:19 355
19:25 355
20:27 .... **387**
23:13 261
40:1-2 279
42:7 287
42:11 286
Psalms
2 .... **275, 321**
2:7 321
2:8-9 .... **270**
6:2 139
8:5 .... **200**
18:2 138
22:28 .... 260, 265
29:2 139
30:2 136
32:2 363
33:10-11 262
34:18 363
36:3 172
41:3 115
41:3-4 .... 136 (2)
41:4 .... 135, 139
41:5 142
42:1-6 363
51:10,12,17 . 363
60:2 139
63:5 363
64:9 172
66:18 189
73 206
75:7 279

82:1, 6 200
88 335
89:26-28 320
90:2 329
91:11 198
97:7 200
102:3 139
103:1-2 363
103:3 140
103:20ff 198
105:4-5 31
106:14-15 191
106:20 140
110:5-6 271
115:3 261
115:16 270
118:25 .... **174**
119:71 281
119:89 254
130:6 363
135:6 261
138:1 200
145:13 260
146:3 139
147:3 142
Proverbs
1:3 172
1:7 272
2:1ff 248
6:2 .... **198**
10:22 159
11:13 363
11:14 .... 229, 248
16:4 261
16:9 249
16:19 363
16:32 20
16:33 258
18:1 300
18:14 150
20:27 .... **240**
21:1 261
21:16 172
22:7 100
23:4-5 168
28:9 189
28:20 159
29:18 75
30:5-6 254
30:7-9 168
31:6 114

Ecclesiastes
3:3 140
5:17 135
6:2 135
Isaiah
1:5 135
1:6 111
4:23 338
8:3 397
8:14-15 226
8:16 227
8:19-20 .... **226**, 248
9:6-7 .... **269**
14:26-27 261
19:22 .... 136 (2), 140,
 141
25:1 261
26:9 .... 363 (2)
28:16 354
29:13 228
37:16 67
37:26 262
38:21 114
42:1 363
44:18 172
44:23 422
44:28 261
45:1 265
45:7 118
45:9 279
46:10 261
50:2 417
52:13 172
53 .... 135 (2)
53:3 331
53:3-5 .... 136 (2)
53:4 .... 129, 136, 137 (3),
 .... **144, 145**
53:5 .... 141, 142
53:5-6 132
53:8 137
53:9 .... **133**, 134,
 219
53:10 171
53:12 135
54:17 171
55:11 .... 199 (2)
57:15 363
57:18 136
57:18-19 136
59:1-2 417
61:3 142

Biblical Index

64:6 371
64:6-7 417

Jeremiah
2:20 275
3:15 172
3:21-22 139
4:13ff 417
5:5 275
6:7 135
6:14-15 139
7:14 142
8:22 111
10:19 135
10:21 172
13:23 411
15:18 139
16:4 134
17:9 73
17:14 139
19:11 .... 139, 142
20:11 172
23 231
23:13 231
23:55 417
30:13 114
30:17 141
31:31-34 402
31:33 350
33:6 141
35:17 417
51:8-9 141
51:9 142

Lamentations
3:23 290
3:31-33 283

Ezekiel
11:19 363
13 231
14:4-9 232
14:4ff 417
18:31 363
28:8, 10 134
36:24-27 402
36:26 363
36:26-27 350
38:14-16 227
47:12 114

Daniel
2:21 264
2:28 227
2:36 264

3:17 .... **91**
3:18 91
4:3 261
4:17 264
4:35 255
7:14 .... 261, 269, ... 276
8:27 120
9:3 91
9:24 .... **224**

Hosea
4:6 .... **15**
5:13 135
6:1 141
11:3 141

Micah
5:2 310
6:13 117

Habakkuk
3:17-18 168

Zechariah
4:7 192
14:4 192

Matthew
1:18-23 313
1:23 .... 311, 334
2:5 137
2:15 137
2:17 137
2:23 137
3:11 395
4:1 .... 127, 245, ... 282
4:6 106
4:7 106
4:10-11 273
4:11 198
5:5 172
5:17-18 214
5:43-48 189
5:45 104
6:9 276
6:10b 189
6:11 190
6:13 .... 127, 283
6:25 362
6:33 .... 169, 190
7:15 82
7:16 58
7:22 218
7:22-23 81

8:3 307
8:8, 13 140
8:17 .... 110, 122, ... **135**, 136(2) .... 137 (2), **144**, ... **145**, 146 (2)
8:20 169
9:1ff 304
9:2, 22, 28 ... 147
9:5-7 112
9:6 91
9:12 113
9:27 313
9:35-38 274
9:38 .... **276**
10:28 .... 271, 272, ... 362
10:32 199
10:32-33 371
11:15 186
11:23-24 370
11:25-27 415
11:27 .... 273, 305
11:28 371
11:29 362
12:13 147
12:18 363
12:23 313
12:25-26 366
12:28, 39 362
12:38ff 81
12:38-42 403
12:39 148
13 184
13:9, 43 186
13:14 140
13:15 .... 140, 141
13:49 366
13:58 148
14:13ff 147
15:3ff 28
15:9 228
15:22 313
15:28 140
15:32 147
16:3 95
16:4 .... 81, 82, ... 403
16:14 377
16:18 293
16:19 198
16:24-25 169

17:1ff............331	9:24 ....147, 206	10:34............111
18:16 243	9:27 112	11:13............400 (2)
18:18 ....**198**	10:30 165	12:4-5 271
18:19 ....164, 190	10:45 ....82, 132 (2),	12:13............366
20:30 313	...............303, 342, 347	12:15............286
21:9, 15 313	11:22 ....**205**	12:20............362
21:28-31 207	11:22-24 ......**191**	12:48............370
22:30 295	11:23-24 ......164, 196	13:10ff..........147
22:37 ....244, 364	11:24 ....**388**	14:4...............140, 307
22:42 313	11:29-33 219	14:35............186
23 ....9, 206	12:30 ....364, 365	16...................219
24:3, 30 95	12:30, 33 364	16:11............168
24:24 ....99, 251	12:31 189	17:10............259, 374
24:36 250	12:40 189	17:11-14 ......**151**
25:31-46 272	12:42-43 161	17:12-19 ......**146**
25:32 366	14:7 170	17:14............151
26:2, 17-20..111	14:65 123	17:15............140
26:11 170	15:38 342	18:1-8 189
26:38 ....177, 207,	15:42-47 219	18:11-12 259
...............363	16:20 99	22:3................124
26:39 189	**Luke**	22:22............124
26:67 123	1:32-33 225	22:42............189
27:50 362	1:38 313	23:42-43 421
27:51 342	1:46-47 363	23:43............421
27:57-60 219	1:50 272	23:45............342
28:18 ....269, 276	2:7 320	23:46............422
28:18-20 271	2:25-26 355	23:50-56 219
Mark	2:34 226	22:51............140
1:8 395	2:36 397	24:25-27 354
1:31 ....112, 147	2:38 355	24:38-39 340
1:41 147	2:49 329	24:44-45 238
2:9-12 112	2:52 329	24:44-47 354
2:17 113	3:16 395	**John**
3:24-26 366	4:1-8 ....**274**	1:1.................82, 310
4 184	4:6 274	1:1, 14..........331
4:9, 23 186	4:11 ....**127**	1:12............371, **408**
4:13 147	4:18 ....140 (2), 141	1:13..............407
4:39 147	4:40 156	1:14..............82, 331
5:29 ....140, 147	5:17 140	1:29..............137
5:41 147	5:31 113	1:33..............395
6:5 148	6:17, 19 140	1:41..............354
6:13 111	6:38 ....166, **173**	1:46..............355
6:41 366	6:47-48 164	1:47-51 305
7:20-22 370	7:7 140	1:48..............304
7:21ff.............411	7:12 320	1:49..............225 (2)
7:33 307	7:14 307	1:51..............422
7:35 147	8:8 186	2:9.................147
8:12 363	8:42 320	2:11..............93
8:22 ....**152**	8:47 140	2:19..............306
8:22ff.............147	9:2 140	2:19ff............4
8:22-26 151	9:11, 42 140	2:21-22 82
8:26ff.............147	10:27 364	2:23..............93

Biblical Index

2:24 304	10:27-28 305	**Acts**
3 319	10:30 .... 82, 305	1:4 402
3:1ff 323	10:31ff 306	1:5 395
3:1-8 .... **407**	10:33-39 ..... **305**	1:8 .... 96, 396 (2),
3:2 93	10:35 .... 28, 214	.... 402, 405 (2)
3:3-4, 10 352	11 409	1:14-15 397
3:8 362	11:4 .... 113, 146	1:26 397
3:13 .... 304, 338,	11:25ff 94	2 .... 396, 405
.... 422	11:36ff 147	2:1 397
3:16 131	11:43 307	2:4 399
3:16-17 333	12:8 170	2:6, 8 397
3:20 86	12:10 86	2:9-1 398
3:27 374	12:17-18 94	2:14 397
3:36 369	12:27 363	2:14-21 227
4:24 363	12:31 .... 273 (2)	2:16-17 227
4:25 355	12:39-40 415	2:17 .... 227, 397
4:46ff 147	12:40 .... 140 (2), 141	2:23 .... 262, 370
4:47 140	12:49 238	2:27 .... 362, 422
4:48 93	12:50 238	2:30-31 225
4:52 .... **151**	13:21 363	2:32 96
5:13 140	14:6 .... 48, 189,	2:33, 39 402
5:18 .... 4, 82,	 357	2:34 422
.... 304,	14:9 225	2:36 269
.... 306	14:10 238	2:38 .... 399, 402 (2),
5:21, 25 409	14:11 97	 404
5:25 .... 305, 409	14:12 88	2:42 398
5:26 264	14:13 .... **188**	3 146
5:36 97	14:15,17,20 . 404	3:7 112
5:39 .... 237, 354	14:30 .... 273 (2)	3:11 140
6 94	15:16 .... 189, 416	3:11-26 91
6:2 93	15:24 97	3:13 370
6:44-45 417	16:8-11 .... 237, 369	3:15 96
6:62 422	16:11 273	4:8, 31 399
6:63 .... 183, 184	16:13-15 237	4:12 377
7:3-5 403	16:23 189	4:16 .... 86, 150
7:31 93	16:30 304	4:25 270
8:22ff 306	17:1-2 .... 271 (2)	4:27-28 .... 124, 262
8:24 .... 304, 372	17:5 331	4:33 96
8:24, 58 82	17:15 292	5:30 370
8:24,28,58 ... 304	18:6 .... 98, 303	5:31-32 96
8:44 274	18:36 269	5:32 402
8:56 354	19:7 306	5:41 283
8:58 98	19:30 .... 341, **342** (2),	6:2-4 246
9 .... 89, 92, 94	.... 342, **339**	7:59 364
9:1-3 126	19:38-42 219	8 .... 404, 495
9:1ff 113, 147	20:17 .... 340, 341,	8:6 86
9:3 144	 422	8:12ff,36ff ... 399
9:6 307	20:22 307	8:17 402
9:17-21 150	20:27ff 4	8:20 402
10:18 342	20:28 .... 82 (2), 132,	8:33 270
10:25-42 97	 333	9:16 283
10:26-27 415	20:30-31 ...... 94, 372	9:17 399

9:18 399	26:22-23 354	7:18 14
9:34 140	28:8 140	8:1-16 347
10 405	28:27 .... 140 (2), 141	8:3 .... 282, **315**
10:35 272	28:23-24 354	8:7 .... 279, 417
10:37ff 399	**Romans**	8:9 .... 400, 404 (2)
10:38 140	1:1-3 .... 354 (2)	8:11 347
10:39-41 96	1:3-4 311	8:14 .... **244**
10:43 .... 82, 353	1:4 .... 317, 322	8:16 .... **242**
10:44-48 404	1:9 364	8:18-23 129
10:45 402	1:18, 32 339	8:18-39 287
10:47 402	1:18-32 367	8:20-22 339
11:16 .... 395, 396	1:18ff 86, 370	8:22ff 170
11:17 402	1:25 291	8:23 133
11:17-18 402	2:1-3:8 367	8:26ff 276
12:15 207	2:3 339	8:28 .... 22, 23, 257,
12:23 .... 120, 265	2:15 242	.... **287**, 358
13:9, 52 399	3:5-6 375	8:29 319
13:33 .... **321ff**	3:9-20 .... 367, 375	8:32 .... 208, 358,
13:48 .... 73, 273,	3:21-26 .... 132, 367	.... 360, 406
.... 400, 409, 415	3:26 339	8:32-34 347
14:3 99	3:27-5:21 367	9 .... **416**
14:22 364	4:1-4 353	9:1 242
15:8-9 403	4:1-5 368	9:5 311
15:28-29 247	4:1-8 402	9:11-12 416
16:14 .... 73, 273,	4:1-9 357	9:11-23 257
.... 400, 409, 415	4:1-13 347	9:14-16, 18 .. 416
16:15,31ff 399	4:4-5 166	9:14-22 400
16:18 219	4:11 .... 95, 298	9:16 408
17:2, 17 221	4:14 331	9:18 418
17:11 221	4:17 .... 167, **196**	9:19-21 .... 279, 416
17:24-26 264	4:25 343	9:22 375
17:27-28 264	5:1 347	9:32-33 226
17:30 .... 416, 418	5:3 282	9:33 354
18:4, 19 221	5:5 403	10:2-4 .... 375, 402
18:8 399	5:8 347	10:4 238
18:21 290	5:9 375	10:6 422
18:27 .... 73, 400, 415	5:9-11 132	10:7 423
19 .... **404**, 405 (2)	5:10 279	10:9-10 371
19:1ff 399	5:12ff 157	10:14 422
19:2 402	5:21-6:2 347	10:14-15 186
19:8-9 221	6 .... 298, 399	10:17 .... **185**
19:11-12 154	6:1 .... 267, 368	12:3 366
19:12 .... **152**, 154	6:1, 7, 14 399	13:8 100
19:13-16 179	6:1-14 347	14:23 286
19:19 370	6:1-8:18 403	15:32 290
20:21 416	6:12 13	**1 Corinthians**
20:28 .... 132, 311,	6:23 .... 76, 339, 347	1:13 366
.... 333	6-8 367	1:18ff 87, 101
21:9 397	7:5 268	1:19, 31 222
22:14-15 96	7:7-25 357	1:22 81
22:16 .... 399, 403	7:14ff 411	1:30 311
23:8 362	7:14-8:17 400	2:7-8 124

Biblical Index

2:9 222
2:10 387
2:11 .... **241**, 364
2:11-12 .... **387**
2:12-16 237
2:14 417
3:19 222
4:6 .... 211, **222**
4:7 113
4:9-13 169
4:19 290
4:21 362
5:5 364
5:7 .... 111, 342
6:3-5 247
6:9-10 370
6:17 364
6:17, 20 364
6:19 268
6:20 364
7:9 248
7:17 366
7:34 .... 362 (2),
.... 364, 366
7:39 248
9:1 96
9:9-10 222
9:15 331
10:2-4 354
10:7, 11 222
10:13 .... 121, 127,
.... 283, 291
11:-14 297
11:30-32 113
12-14 63
12:8 239
12:13 .... 395, 396,
.... 399
13:8 227
13:8-13 .... **227**
13:11 243
14:5 92
14:21 222
14:23-25 299
14:23ff 244, 297
14:34 .... 297, 397 (2)
15:17 343
15:24 269
15:25 269
15:26 157
15:45, 54 222
15:55 422
16:3-4 246
16:7 290

2 Corinthians
1:22 403
2:16 199
4:4 273
4:15-18 411
4:16-18 .... 101, 133,
.... 157
5:17 350
5:18-21 279
5:21 .... 129, 332
6:14 218
7:1 .... 362 (2)
7:10 371
8:9 332
9:3 331
9:6 .... **173**
10:13 366
11:3-4 344
11:13-15 11
11:14-15 4
12 121
12:1ff 113
12:2-4 421
12:5 282
12:7-10 .... 120, **122**,
.... 128
12:12 95
13:5 243

Galatians
1:8 .... 223, 327
1:8-9 .... 9, 252,
.... 344, 345
2:16 .... 347, 357,
.... 402
2:18-19 357
2:21 374
3:2, 5 186
3:3 .... 400, 404
3:5 400
3:6-8 332
3:8-10, 26 353
3:10 339
3:13 .... 129, 332 (2),
.... 341
3:16,19,29 ... 313
3:19 357
3:26 332
3:29 332
4:6 400
4:13ff 121

4:13-15 121
5:16-25 400
5:16-26 245
5:21 413
6:18 364

Ephesians
1:4 415
1:11 .... 249, 255,
.... 262, 290
1:13-14 .... 403, 404
1:19-21 271
2:1 423
2:1ff 410
2:2 273
2:3 375
2:8-9 .... 357, 402
2:8-10 356
2:12 354
2:17 422
2:21-22 301
3:20 206
4:9 422
4:11ff 64
4:11-16 .... 31 (2), 301
4:14 32
4:20 347
4:23 364
5:5 370
5:6 376
5:18 399
5:24 296
5:25ff 295
6:1ff 229
6:4 288

Philippians
1:6 347
1:27 364
1:29 .... 73, 146,
.... 273, 415
1:29-30 .... 120, 207
2 328
2:6-7 .... 324, 325,
.... **330ff**
2:6-8 323
2:7 .... **328**, 327 (2)
2:9-11 271
2:12-13 .... 347 (2), 417
2:25-26 .... 120, 246
3:9 347
3:20-21 172
3:21 .... 133, 347
4:11-12 169

453

4:18 120
4:19 .... **174**
Colossians
1:15 319
1:15-16 263
1:17 329
1:18 319
1:19-20 129
1:20-21 279
2:5 362
2:9 .... 82, 309, 310
2:11-12 .... 111, 298
2:14 137
2:15 .... 338, 339,
.... 422
2:18-19 359
2:23 401
3:10 347
3:15 .... **241**
3:16 399
4:14 113
1 Thessalonians
1:9-10 376
2:13 186
3:1-3 246
3:3-4 283
3:4 207
5:23 .... **364**, 365 (3)
2 Thessalonians
1:4-5 207
2:9 .... 82, 99
2:9-12 266
2:13 347
3:3 292
1 Timothy
1:5 155
1:10 172
1:20 9
2:5 .... 189, **357**
2:11-15 397
2:11-3:5 35
2:12 296
2:12-14 43
3:1 247
3:1ff 110
3:2 296
3:2-7 247
3:4-5 229
3:5 296
3:5, 15 296
3:6 296

3:16 .... **316** (2)
.... 342
4 207
4:1-2 227
4:1-3 82
4:14 .... 38, 296
5:18 223
5:22 .... 38, 296
5:23 114
6:3 172
6:3-6 162
6:10 160
6:17-19 160
2 Timothy
1:5 155
1:9 415
1:13 172
2:2 .... 31, 64
2:8 313
2:16-17 .... 228, 232
3 207
3:1 227
3:12 207
3:14-15 354
3:16-17 .... 28, **223**,
.... 231
4:3 172
4:6 177
4:6-16 207
4:22 364
Titus
1 110
1:9, 13 172
1:16 356
2:1, 2, 8 172
Philemon
25 364
Hebrews
1:1 227
1:1-2 225
1:3 .... **195**, 263,
.... 329, 331
1:5 .... 270, **321ff**
1:5-8 323
1:8 322
1:11, 12 329
1:14 .... 164, **196**,
.... 197
2:2-4 225
2:4 366
2:7 200

2:7-9 269
2:9-10 363
2:14 157
2:14-15 334
2:14-17 313
2:14-18 .... 132, 325
2:17 225
4:2 186
4:12 .... **365**, 366
4:14 225
4:15 325
5:5 .... 270, **321ff**
5:7-8 363
5:8 331
6:1-3 290
7:2 366
7:25-28 225
8:10 350
9:7-8,24-27 .. 342
9:14 .... 132, 317,
.... 333
9:27 423
10:7 413
10:10 .... 224 (2)
10:10,12,14 . 333, 341
10:12-14 225
11 284
11:1 206
11:24-26 353
11:30-12:11 . 126
11:32-34 283
11:38-40 283
11:39 284
12 232
12:2 282
12:5-16 .... **288**
12:6 288
12:12-13 ...... 140, 141
12:13 .... 140 (2)
12:14 347
12:23 364
13:5 170
13:7 296
13:8 .... 118, **142**,
.... 310 (2), 329
13:12 317
James
1:2-3 283
1:5 248
1:12 282
1:13 .... 127, 266,
.... 325

1:18 ....**408**	4:6 423	5:1-3 21
1:21 364	**2 Peter**	5:4................351, 408
2 373	1:4 348	5:14.............189
2:8-12 221	1:10-11 243	5:16-17 113
2:17 356	2..................40	5:18.............347
2:26 362	2:2 382	5:19.............273
4:2 ....189, **190**	2:8, 14 364	**2 John**
4:3 ....**190**	3:3 227	2:5, 11..........113
4:11-12 248	3:15-16 223	**3 John**
4:12 ....211, 272	**1 John**	2....................**170**, 172
5 146	1:1-3 96	**Jude**
5:3 227	1:6-10 347	1....................40
5:14-16ff **109**	1:6-2:2 410	3....................**224**
5:16 140	2:3-4 ....243, 356	24.................292
5:19-20 113	2:19 410	**Revelation**
5:20 364	2:29 ....351, 408,	1:5................271, 319
1 Peter	411	2:7,11,17......186
1:3 408	3:2 ....133, 154,	2:27.............271
1:6-9 284	368	3:6,13,22......186
1:9, 22 364	3:2-3 347	6:9................364
1:11 354	3:3 347	11:15............270
1:23 ....**408**, 409	3:4 ....248, 347	13:8..............124, 262,
1:23-25 409	3:5 137	413
1:25 408	3:8 339	13:9..............186
2:8 ....226, 416	3:9 ....347 (2),	20.................270
2:11, 25 364	.....................351, 408,	20:4..............364
2:17 272	.....................**410**	20:14............157
2:20 ....123, 227	3:22 189	21:8..............370
2:24 ....140 (3),	4:1-3 82	22:15............370
.....................**139**, 141,	4:1-6 ....230, 231	22:18............211
.....................142, 347	4:7 ....351, 408	22:18-19 223
3:18 ....132, 317,	4:10 131	
.....................**422**	4:20 301	
3:20 364	5:1 ....351, 408